Benjamin Franklin Burnham

Records of Jesus Reviewed

And Fifty Questions Answered through Five Hundred Reverent Reasoners

Benjamin Franklin Burnham

Records of Jesus Reviewed
And Fifty Questions Answered through Five Hundred Reverent Reasoners

ISBN/EAN: 9783337211073

Printed in Europe, USA, Canada, Australia, Japan

Cover: Foto ©Lupo / pixelio.de

More available books at **www.hansebooks.com**

RECORDS OF JESUS REVIEWED,

AND

FIFTY QUESTIONS ANSWERED

THROUGH

FIVE HUNDRED REVERENT REASONERS.

BY

BENJAMIN F. BURNHAM.

They were dulling their teeth at the shell while I was enjoying the kernel. — *Goethe.*

BOSTON:
THE UNION COMPANY.
1883.

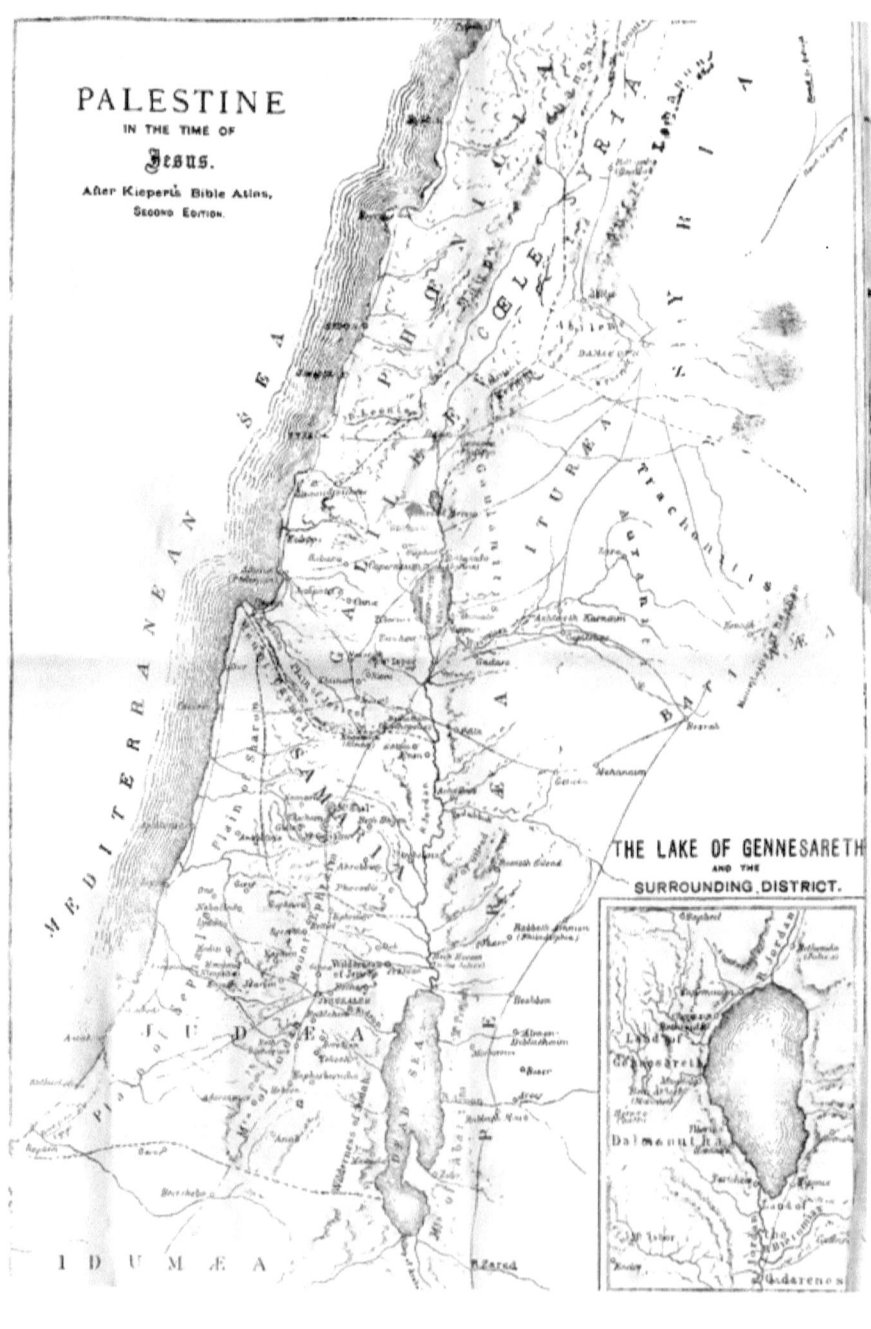

INTRODUCTION.

ONE can hardly have too many aids to be "ready always to give an answer to every man that asketh you a reason of the hope that is in you with meekness and fear, having a good conscience," and at the same time heed Shakspere's hint that "your reasons" be "sharp and sententious, pleasant without scurrility, witty without affectation, audacious without impudency, learned without opinion, and strange without heresy."

Of books whose theme is the birth, the life, the death, and the character of Jesus Christ, the name is legion. None of them, except one or two of limited scope, seem to present impartially the most advanced thought extant on the fifty principal topics of that theme. Most of the authors evince that "self-interest, the long habit of looking mainly at one side, and steady training in opposition to the other side, are influences for casuistry too powerful to be matched by the best intentions. They have each," adds Moncure D. Conway, "brought his little block of stone, under impression that it was the whole temple, to a point where comparative study may take it up and fit it to every other block, that the sacred edifice of humanity may arise."

The success of the writer or reader who has in hand this fitting will depend much on how little he strains to avoid mal-adjustment of his spiritual stature to the proportions of any Procrustean creed-bed; on how impartially he selects his appliances; on how readily he draws his weapons for Truth from the whole religious armory of Christendom. Nay, even heathendom will be brought under tribute, and Seneca shall testify that "he who determines anything without

INTRODUCTION

hearing both parties, though he may have determined justly, has not himself been just."

Indeed, the old Hebrew admonition against so answering a matter has cumulative corroboration in the codes of legislatures and the decrees of judiciaries; in the insight of the philosopher testifying, with John Stuart Mill, that "he who knows only his own side of the case knows little of that"; and, in the reflection of the divine, observing with the Anglican that "no man who knows nothing else knows even his Bible." To form an opinion is not always to form a judgment. Many people treat their beliefs as Don Quixote treated his armor. He first tried it by a heavy blow of his sword against his helmet, cutting off the visor, and undoing in a moment the work of a week. So he mended it, and made it stronger, but concluded not to try it again; to let it pass for a good, strong helmet, without further experiment. And thus the adage: "That man does not believe his creed who is afraid of hearing it attacked."

In studying the life of any historic personage,—that of Jesus not excepted,—the proper selection, arrangement, and treatment of the subjects have been well suggested by a premise in President Garfield's Memorial Address on General George H. Thomas: "Given the character of a man, and the conditions of life around him, what will be his career? Or, given his career and surroundings, what was his character? Or, given his character and career, of what kind were his surroundings? The relation of these three factors to each other is severely logical. From them is deduced all genuine history."

The word "severely" was here well chosen. Imagination is so much easier than reasoning that, even when we revert to the scenes of Galilee and Judea, it requires effort to divest ourselves of indolent habits of assuming. Few of us can sincerely disclaim appreciation of the surprise voiced by the society woman at the first exhibition of Holman Hunt's picture of "The Finding of Jesus in the Temple," when she exclaimed, "Well, I declare, if Mr. Hunt hasn't made Jesus look just like a little Jew boy." Few of us there be who do not need to substitute thinking for day-dreaming.

And if, incidental to the study of Jesus' character and teachings, we desire to trace the identity of his doctrine of "the kingdom of heaven" with that of "religious evolution," it certainly is best to avail ourselves of the matured thoughts of sages thereon, which, crystallized in terse, aphoristic form, have outlasted the centuries;

INTRODUCTION

verdicts on which judgment has been entered up and affirmed on appeal to humanity at large.*

The proportion of such aphoristic matter can hardly be too great in a book whose function is principally for meditative and leisurely reference. Or, as George William Curtis felicitously expressed it,† to "break the fetter, not with the might of the trip-hammer that shatters, but with the touch of the *sunbeam* that melts. . . . Channing once declared that 'God has not intrusted the reform of the world to passion.' The calm statement is the permanent one, the argument that our children's children will read and feel to be invincible. It may not have the glow, the fervor, the palpitation of speeches, and appeals wherein the trumpet mingles above the flute; but it will shine always with the calm light of the stars in heaven." A "sunbeam" reminding us of John Milton's "Truth is as impossible to be soiled by any outward touch as the sunbeam." Or, as Dr. James McCosh puts it, "In the end, thought rules the world, though at times impulses and passions are more powerful." Or Merle d'Aubigné, "Ideas make their way in silence, like the waters that, filtering behind the rocks of the Alps, loosen them from the mountain on which they stand."

And this, too, without diffuse transitional matter, if any. Robert Southey testifies that "it is with words as with sunbeams: the more they are condensed, the deeper they burn." And George Herbert,—

`A verse may find him who a sermon flies.

---

* For such store of pertinent aphorisms, both in prose and poetry, the surviving author would here acknowledge his indebtedness to his deceased coadjutor, his wife, Celeste, daughter of Rev. Henry Shute, born at Columbia, N.Y., 1830; died at Boston, 1880. Her rare spiritual intuition had rendered her — what James T. Fields calls Leigh Hunt, in comparing him to the African bird that befriends the bee-hunter — "a honey-indicator" in religious literature. The longer quotations (wherein book and page are cited) are made with consent of the respective authors or publishers. In these, later authors, writing under superior advantages for reviewing and comparing, are preferred to earlier; for instance, Dr. Geikie, to any one in the list of nearly two hundred authors consulted by him in the preparation of his *Life and Words of Christ*. So, also, as to Drs. I. Hooykaas, J. F. Clarke, James Strong, etc., and recent encyclopædists. (Compare the Analytical and the Quotation Indexes.) For some unquoted matter in chapters upon the Sermon on the Mount, Prayer, and Immortality, acknowledgment is due to skeleton notes of sermons delivered forty years ago at North Yarmouth, Me., and Groton, Vt., by Rev. Benjamin Burnham, born at Rumney, N.H., 1791; died at Groton, Vt., 1875.

† In his response at the Brooklyn Channing Centennial.

INTRODUCTION

And Alexander Pope, "Half our knowledge we must snatch, not take." And Francis de Voltaire, "The multiplicity of facts and writings has become so great that everything must be reduced to extracts." And William Wirt: "The age of ornament is over, that of utility has succeeded: the *pugnæ quam pompæ aptius* is the order of the day; and men fight now with clenched fist, not with open hand, — with logic, and not with rhetoric." Dr. Samuel Johnson's remark, "Classical quotation is the parole of literary men all over the world," applies to other quotation and to the "community of mind" among all thinkers.

In some chapters herein, especially those upon the "Sermon on the Mount" and the "Immortality of the Soul," it seems best to let certain trite abstract matter yield place to concretions, and not to ignore the fact that an age of thought has succeeded to an age of sentiment, and prescribes to theology new conditions, unlike researches under systems "framed," as lately remarked Dr. Frederic H. Hedge, "when this earth was supposed to be the centre and the only rational body of the sidereal universe, and sun, moon, and stars were believed to be movable lanterns circulating around it,— the heavens a solid frame fitted to it like a cap,— the whole created at one stroke a few thousand years back, and destined to last a very few years longer; framed when men believed in dragons and griffins and devils with bats' wings, and a jail underneath the earth for the damned, and a palace above the sky for the blest."

Both writer and reader must recognize the tendency of modern philanthropists to throw mere unpractical, controversial matter into the background, nor longer animadvert upon the famous "Item xxi." of Stephen Girard's will, enjoining that no ecclesiastic hold any station in his orphans' college; he would "keep their tender minds free from controversy, until the purest principles of morality be planted therein." He believed with Milton that to know that which before us lies in daily life is the prime wisdom. A young girl was lately asking a very common question as to the ethics of horse-car tickets, and, on being asked in return if such questions were not taken up in her Sunday-school class, answered that they were learning only about the kings of Judah. It recalls a line or two in Mr. Chadwick's Ode on Channing:—

> . . . Sects
> Still making with their war of texts
> The pleasant earth a kind of hell. . . .

INTRODUCTION

> Our Father, God; our brother, Man:
> On these commandments twain be hung
> The law and prophets all; and rung
> For all the churches' eager ban,
> A hundred changes deep and strong.

Now o' days, the common sense discountenances the logic dilemma of the Mohammedan that burned the Alexandrian library: namely, if the books accorded with the Koran, they were superfluous; if not, they were pernicious. Rather pleasanter to contemplate is the humor of the late Hebrew Lord Mayor of London, who, in making the customary contributions, cheerfully included the one to the Society for the Conversion of the Jews. No doubt, he parted with the jewel consistency; but, in his reciprocity,— his recognition of the good which Christianity does for "sheep on the other side of the fence,"— he kept the Koh-i-noor of the crown of his heart-treasure. Fishers of men may properly "fling a sprat to catch a herring." Bishop William Warburton lost nothing by his playfully whispered concession to Lord Sandwich, puzzled for a definition in the debate on the Test Law: "Orthodoxy is my doxy; heterodoxy is another man's doxy." Nor President Hayes, by saying in the face of partisans, "He serves his party best who serves his country best." It is becoming a popular sentiment that nothing is gained to religion by branding Justin Martyr "heterodox," though he declared the Logos was manifested before it appeared in Jesus. Not in secular politics alone do whole congregations "wander and apply" Goldsmith's animadversion on Burke,—

> Who born for the universe narrowed his mind,
> And to party gave up what was meant for mankind.

W. H. H. Murray's remark, "To abuse another man's piety is a sorry way to prove your own," was also a seed dropped in good soil: it outgrows hostile sowings of tares, and finds welcome garners. More and more is getting appreciated the generous exclamation of O. B. Frothingham: "How cheering the summons to render full justice to the aspirations of mankind; to bring harmony out of the discordant utterances of faith; to demonstrate the fraternity of earnest thinkers and deep feelers in all time!" And clear and sunny above dispersing fogs of olden dark days — above both *odium theologicum* and *odium scepticum* — stand forth wise words of Jefferson: "Error of opinion may be tolerated where reason is left free to combat it." And of Lincoln: "With charity for all, with malice toward none, with firmness in the right as God gives us to see the right." And of Judge Thomas Russell, at the recent Plymouth celebration: "And we, honoring where we cannot always follow, admiring where we cannot all agree, reverence the belief of our fathers. And to all attacks and to all ridicule we reply,— and we love to repeat it,— The excesses of faith are better than the best thoughts of unbelief, and even the errors of faith may be imputed to the founders of a nation for righteousness and power." And, finally, the accordant harmony of Tennyson: —

> O thou that after toil and storm
> Mayst seem to have reached a purer air,
> Whose faith has centre everywhere,
> Nor cares to fix itself in form,
> Leave thou thy sister, when she prays,
> Her early heaven, her happy views . . .
> Her faith through form is pure as thine,
> Her hands are quicker unto good;
> Oh, sacred be the flesh and blood
> To which she links a truth divine !
> See thou that countest reason ripe
> In holding by the law within
> Thou fail not in a world of sin,
> And e'en for want of such a type.

Thus much as to toleration and reason. But, at the threshold of our study of the subject, we are met by another preliminary inquiry; namely, as to the relation of reason and faith. This, then, shall constitute the topic of the first chapter.

B. F. B.

SOUTH BOSTON, Feb 22, 1883

CONTENTS.

CHAPTER I. INTERPRETATION. 9–20.
In studying the Bible, what is the function of Faith, and what that of Reason?

CHAPTER II. CONSECUTION. 21–25.
What is the chronological order of the early records of the life and teachings of Jesus?

CHAPTER III. INSPIRATION. 26–31.
What two views concerning inspiration of the Bible writers?

CHAPTER IV. COMPOSITION. 32–37.
What two diverse opinions as to the circumstances of the writing and of the writers of the four canonical Gospels?

CHAPTER V. NARRATION. 38, 39.
What is the order of the principal events narrated in the four canonical Gospels?

CHAPTER VI. ACCRETION. 40–43.
What two views as to the exemption of narrations concerning Jesus from the ordinary liability to accretion; (and herein) what may safely be considered the uses of the Oriental imageries?

CHAPTER VII. GENERATIONS. 44, 45.
What two different views of the genealogical records of Jesus?

CHAPTER VIII. ANNUNCIATION. 46–48.
What two views concerning the annunciation to Mary, the star-heralding, and the angel-chorus?

CONTENTS

CHAPTER IX. LOCATION. 49, 50.

What diverse views of the date and place of the birth of Jesus?

CHAPTER X. CONCEPTION. 51–57.

What three views concerning the paternity of Jesus?

CHAPTER XI. DEIFICATION. 58–64.

What threefold classification of men's views of God and the expression of Jesus, "Our Father"?

CHAPTER XII. PREMONITION. 65–67.

How does John the Baptist rank in the order of prophets and of martyrs?

CHAPTER XIII. RENUNCIATION. 68–70.

Did John the Baptist belong to any secret order whose rites would suggest to him the ordinance of Baptism, and what the possible relation of Jesus thereto?

CHAPTER XIV. INITIATION. 71, 72.

What two views as to the phenomena at the baptism of Jesus?

CHAPTER XV. TEMPTATION. 73–82.

What are the eight principal views concerning the temptation of Jesus, and in what two convenient categories? (And herein) what is the effect of success and of defeat in the formation of individual character?

CHAPTER XVI. INTROSPECTION. 83–86.

What three forms of temptation would be likely to arise and to return "for a season" in the mind of a young man, if he were placed in the then circumstances of Jesus?

CHAPTER XVII. HARMONIZATION. 87–92.

Wherein are Introspection and Self-renunciation, as exemplified by Jesus, effective toward harmonizing the lower human tendencies with the higher and resisting temptation to sin?

CHAPTER XVIII. DEMONIZATION. 93–95.

What are the three principal views concerning the existence of a personal devil, and the teachings of Jesus in general thereon?

CONTENTS

CHAPTER XIX. TRANSGRESSION. 96–101.

What are the different Orthodox and other leading **metaphysical views** concerning the "mystery of the Fall" and Christ's teachings thereon?

CHAPTER XX. INCEPTION. 102, 103.

Why did Jesus choose Capernaum for the beginning of his public ministry, and how did the associations of the place affect his discourses

CHAPTER XXI. INAUGURATION. 104, 105.

In opening the gospel work, what were the personal habits of Jesus; and what the order of incidents, including the choice of disciples?

CHAPTER XXII. EXPANSION. 106–109.

What two views concerning the development of Christ's character and mission?

CHAPTER XXIII. ADAPTATION. 110–112.

What other explanation of the fact of Christ's use of approximative language?

CHAPTER XXIV. ALLOCUTION. 113–117.

Where, when, and how were the principal discourses of Jesus delivered?

CHAPTER XXV. VENERATION. 118–124.

Wherein and what the regenerating tendencies of the indoctrination of faith in Christ and in the mutuality or "solidarity" of the human race?

CHAPTER XXVI. EVOLUTION. 125–129.

What is meant in the Beatitudes by the "kingdom of heaven," **and** what the progress of its development?

CHAPTER XXVII. INDOCTRINATION. 130–137.

What is the most important characteristic of the Sermon on the Mount, and what the first four precepts against selfishness?

CHAPTER XXVIII. REALIZATION. 138–147.

What three leading experiential precepts in **the** Sermon on the Mount?

CONTENTS

CHAPTER XXIX. SUPPLICATION. 148–155.

What three views of Christ's precepts on prayer?

CHAPTER XXX. ASPIRATION. 156–165.

What generally indorsed sentiments of experienced thinkers upon best promoting the aspirational element of prayer?

CHAPTER XXXI. ALLEVIATION. 166–171.

What two views of the curative ministrations of Jesus to minds and bodies diseased?

CHAPTER XXXII. TRANSFIGURATION. 172–174.

What three views concerning the Transfiguration?

CHAPTER XXXIII. AGGRESSION. 175–178.

What three views concerning Christ's ejecting traders from the temple; and what generally as to his self-assertion or aggression?

CHAPTER XXXIV. MINISTRATION. 179–188.

What is the common enumeration of the miracles alleged in the four Gospels to have been performed by Christ; and what the present different leading views of the accounts thereof?

CHAPTER XXXV. VERIFICATION. 189–192.

What is the present tendency of the age in applying the rule of Paul, "Make the doctrine prove the miracle," and the converse rule of Trench and Mill that "No miracle proves a doctrine"?

CHAPTER XXXVI. RESURRECTION. 193–200.

What two views concerning a resurrection of the body of Jesus?

CHAPTER XXXVII. ELECTION. 201–203.

What two views as to "divine election and foreordination," and the teachings of Christ and Paul thereon?

CHAPTER XXXVIII. REDEMPTION. 204–206.

What two views of redemption of the soul from consequences of sin?

CONTENTS

CHAPTER XXXIX. TRANSITION. 207–211.

What transitional condition is implied in the "Free-will" explanation of Paul's words " all be made alive," etc.?

CHAPTER XL. REGENERATION. 212–217.

What is the evolutional view of regeneration, and what concerning emotion, subordination, and profession, as factors or as results?

CHAPTER XLI. SALVATION. 218–221.

What is the evolutional view concerning the later as compared with the earlier teachings of Paul upon the scope of the life and death of Christ with reference to our salvation?

CHAPTER XLII. DAMNATION. 222–232.

What three views concerning Christ's intendment in the use of the words "Gehenna," "Condemnation," etc.?

CHAPTER XLIII. PERPETUATION. 233–247.

What are the five principal arguments in behalf of the immortality of the soul?

CHAPTER XLIV. EXALTATION. 248–254.

What two views as to Christ's intendment concerning heaven?

CHAPTER XLV. INTELLECTION, EMOTION, VOLITION. 255–263.

Supplementary to the teachings of Socrates, Plato, Christ, and Paul, what are the four principal philosophical theories of the mind's knowledge of God?

APPENDIX. 265.

        Two angels guide
The path of man, both aged and yet young,
As angels are, ripening through endless years.
On one he leans: some call her Memory,
And some Tradition; and her voice is sweet
With deep mysterious accords. The other,
Floating above, holds down a lamp, which streams
A light divine and searching on the earth,
Compelling eyes and footsteps. Memory yields,
Yet clings with loving cheek, and shines anew,
Reflecting all the rays of that bright lamp
Our angel Reason holds. We had not walked
But for Tradition. We walk evermore
To higher paths by brightening Reason's lamp.

George Eliot.

Chapter I.

INTERPRETATION.

In studying the Bible, what is the Function of Faith, and what that of Reason?

THE Bible is a book of books. Some were written many centuries before the others. The writers wrote under different circumstances. Some of the records are more fragmentary than others. Some are more poetical or legendary than others. To view the collection as a unit, a theocratic ukase, a fetich or idol, is to look with the eyes half shut. Even assuming that there are three aspects of human existence,—the life practical, the life intellectual, and the life religious or mystical,—and that each has its own requirements in point of understanding, still our obligation to revere must be at one with our necessity to analyze. With *mysteries*, with whatever *surpasses* reason, ratiocination meddles in vain. But as to *absurdities*, as to whatever *contradicts* reason, it is our duty to guard and exercise the function of a faculty quite as heaven-bequeathed as imagination, emotion, or intuition. Hereon concur certain pretty generally accepted aphorisms of some fifty most eminent thinkers. Incidentally, in many of them, "wisdom" will be found to be distinguished from "knowledge."

First of all, Jesus and Paul:—

> And where, then, is the final judge of truth
> But in the reason of the heart of man?
> "Why, of yourselves, judge ye not what is right?"
> Said Jesus; and Paul after him, "I speak
> As unto wise men, judge ye what I say. . . .
> Prove all things, and hold fast to what is good!"

Shakspere next:—

Sure he that made us with such large discourse, looking before and after, gave us not that capability and godlike reason to rust in us unused.

Reason is the only faculty we have wherewith to judge concerning anything, even Revelation itself. Its duty in relation to the Scriptures is to judge not whether they contain things different from what we should have expected from a wise, just, and good Being, but whether they contain things plainly contradictory to wisdom, justice, and goodness, as elsewhere taught us of God.— *Bishop Joseph Butler.*

If reason justly contradicts an article, it is not of the household of faith.— *Jeremy Taylor.*

He that takes away reason to make way for Revelation puts out the light of both, and does much the same as if he would persuade a man to put out his eyes, the better to receive the remote light of an invisible star by telescope. ... Every sect, as far as reason will help them, gladly use it: when it fails them, they cry out, It is a matter of faith and above reason.— *John Locke.*

It may be said, almost without qualification, that true wisdom consists in the ready and accurate perception of analogies. Without the former quality, knowledge of the past is uninstructive; without the latter, it is deceptive.— *Archbishop Richard Whately.*

Faith affirms many things respecting which the senses are silent, but nothing that they deny.— *Charles Pascal.*

In religion, which is the science of life in its relations Godward, we want facts first, and imagination, with all its treasures of worship, idealism, sentiment, and mysticism, afterwards.— *Vicar Thomas W. Fowle (Reconciliation of Religion and Science,* p. 153).

Faith evermore looks upward, and descries objects that are remote; but reason can discover things only near,— sees nothing that's above. — *Francis Quarles.*

Reason cannot show itself more reasonable than to cease reasoning on things that are above reason.— *Sir Philip Sidney.*

The only right contrast to set up between faith and reason is not that faith grasps what is too hard for reason, but that reason does not, like faith, attend to what is at once so great and so simple. The *difficulty* about faith is to *attend* to what is very simple and very important, but liable to be pushed by more showy or tempting matters out of sight. The *marvel* about faith is that what is so simple should be so all-sufficing, so necessary, and so often neglected. And faith is neither the submission of the reason, nor is it the acceptance simply absolutely upon testimony of what reason cannot reach. ... Faith is the being able to cleave to a power of goodness appealing to our higher and real self, not to our lower or apparent self.— *Dr. Matthew Arnold.*

Reason is but analyzed faith.—*Schumann.*

When my reason is afloat, my faith cannot long remain in suspense, and I believe in God as firmly as in any other truth whatever; in short, a thousand motives draw me to the consolatory side, and add the weight of hope to the equilibrium of reason.—*Jean J. Rousseau.*

Accurate and just reasoning is the only catholic remedy fitted for all persons and all dispositions, and is alone able to subvert that abstruse philosophy and metaphysical jargon, which being mixed up with popular superstition renders it in a manner impenetrable to careless reasoners and gives it the air of science and wisdom.—*David Hume.*

In religious concerns, reason without faith tends to casuistry. Not in jurisprudence alone applies the ancient maxim: [*Apices juris non sunt jura*] Subtleties of law are not law.*—*Judge John McLean.*

Extremely reverential and extremely analytical tendencies of mind both have their dangers.—*L. Maria Child.*

Conscience is not law; no, God and reason made the law, and have placed conscience within you to determine.—*Laurence Sterne.*

Christian faith is a grand cathedral with divinely pictured windows. Standing without, you see no glory nor can possibly imagine any; standing within, every ray of light reveals a harmony of unspeakable splendors.—*Nathaniel Hawthorne.*

The common lights of reason and conscience and love are of more worth and dignity than the rare endowments which give celebrity to a few.—*Dr. William E. Channing.*

Love reasons without reason.—*Shakspere.*

The heart has reasons that reason does not understand.—*Bishop Jacques B. Bossuet.*

A loving heart is the truest wisdom.—*Charles Dickens.*

> The heart o'erwhelms, with whisper clear,
> The cavil, "Who awoke to see?"
> And balms, for Sorrow's yearning ear,
> The wail of lone Gethsemane.
> *George Whitfield Burnham (New England Puritan,* 1845).

---

* See *post*, chap. xxxiv., Tyndall's reply to Mozley, as to two distinct courts of appeal, etc.

Reason is, so to speak, the police of the kingdom of art, seeking only to preserve order. In life itself, a cold arithmetician who adds up our follies. Sometimes, alas! only the accountant in bankruptcy of a broken heart.— *Heinrich Heine.*

Man is a reasoning rather than a reasonable being.— *Sir **William Hamilton**.*

It is useless to attempt to reason a man out of anything he was never reasoned into. . . . Reason is a very light rider and easily shook off.— *Dean Jonathan Swift.*

Virtue is an angel; but she is a blind one, and must ask of Knowledge to show her the pathway that leads to her goal. Mere knowledge, on the other hand, like a Swiss mercenary, is ready to combat either in the ranks of sin or under the banners of righteousness,— ready to forge cannon-balls or to print New Testaments, to navigate a corsair's vessel or a missionary ship.— *Horace Mann.*

> A few strong instincts and a few plain rules
> Among the herdsmen of the Alps have wrought
> More for mankind at this unhappy day
> Than all the pride of intellect and thought.
> *William Wordsworth.*

Revelation may be conceived of as a divine education of the race.— *Gotthold E. Lessing.*

The wildest theories of the human reason were reduced to practice by a community so humble that no statesman condescended to notice it, and a legislation without precedent was produced off-hand by the instincts of the people.— *George Bancroft.*

Almost all the great truths relating to society were not the result of scholarly meditation, "hiving up wisdom with each curious year," but have been first heard in the solemn protests of martyred patriotism and the loud cries of crushed and starving labor. . . . New England learned more of the principles of toleration from a lyceum committee doubting the dicta of editors and bishops when they forbade it to put Theodore Parker on its platform; more from a debate whether the anti-slavery cause should be so far countenanced as to invite one of its advocates to lecture; from Sumner and Emerson, George William Curtis and Edwin P. Whipple refusing to speak unless a negro could buy his way into their halls as freely as any other,— New England has learned more from these lessons than she has or could have done from all the treatises on free printing from Milton and Roger Williams, through Locke down to Stuart Mill.— *Wendell Phillips (The Scholar in a Republic,* p. 12).

The tree of knowledge is not that of life.— (*Geo. **G.** Byron?*)

Knowledge dwells in heads replete with thoughts of other men; wisdom, in minds attentive to their own.— *William Cowper.*

To be wiser than other men is to be honester than they; and strength of mind is only courage to see and speak the truth.— *William Hazlitt.*

He that will not reason is a bigot; he that cannot reason is a fool; and he that dares not reason is a slave.— *Sir William Drummond.*

> Where men have several faiths to find the true,
> We only can the aid of reason use;
> 'Tis reason shows us which we should eschew,
> When by comparison we learn to choose.
> *Sir William Davenant.*

Knowledge comes, but Wisdom lingers.—*Alfred Tennyson.*

Reason lies between the spur and the bridle.— *George Herbert.*

Truly a thinking man is the worst enemy the Prince of Darkness can have.— *Thomas Carlyle.*

The mind is the atmosphere of the soul.— *Francis Joubert.*

> Seize wisdom ere 'tis torment to be wise;
> That is, seize wisdom ere she seizes thee.
> *Dr. Edward Young.*

Experience, the shroud of illusions.—*J. De Finod.*

No man is wiser for his learning.* —*John Selden.*

We cannot live on probabilities. The faith in which we can live bravely and die in peace must be a certainty, so far as it professes to be a faith at all, or it is nothing.—*Anthony Froude.*

Intuition, instinct, experiment, syllogism,—vast quadrants of research! Gigantic reflectors of a light not their own! At the focal point of the four, religious science, strictly so called, lights its immortal torch.—*Joseph Cook.*

Syllogism is of necessary use, even to the lovers of truth, to show them the fallacies that are often concealed in florid, witty, or involved discourses.—*John Locke.*

> Reason the root, fair Faith is but the flower;
> The fading flower may die, but Reason lives,
> Immortal like our Father in the skies.
> *Dr. Edward Young.*

---

* An echo of the Saxon proverb: "No fool is a perfect fool until he has learned Latin." Selden was the profoundest scholar of his day; died 1654.

> He that is of reason's skill bereft,
>   And wants the staff of wisdom him to stay,
> Is like a ship in midst of tempest left,
>   Without an helm or pilot her to sway:
> Full sad and dreadful is that ship's event,
> So is the man that wants intendiment.
>
> *Edmund Spenser.*

> Reason, my guide, . . . should be my counsellor,
> But not my tyrant. For the spirit needs
> Impulses from a deeper source than hers,
> And there are motions in the mind of man
> That she must look upon with awe.
>
> *William C. Bryant.*

> The steps of Faith
> Fall on the seeming void, and find
> The rock beneath.
>
> *John G. Whittier.*

More light! — *Goethe.* (His last words.)

In general, his faithfulness is a safe confession of faith. A framework of thought, or doctrine, forms itself in his mind, like the bones in his body. With fair feeding and exercise, life builds its own bones. But men never seek the companionship of a naked skeleton. Dry bones tell of a church-yard rather than of a church. The public nostril is quick to detect the odor of death in those theological circles where

> "Our meddling intellect
> Misshapes the beauteous forms of things
> We murder to dissect."

. . . Alas for him who thinks it necessary to settle the authorship of the Fourth Gospel, or the primacy of Peter, or the possibility of miracles, or the genesis of life, before he can begin to live like a glad-hearted child of God! — *Charles G. Ames (Saratoga Sermon,* 1882).

There are no negations so sweeping and dangerous as the affirmations of superstition. The most powerful plea against all faith is made by a church which imposes an elaborate system of oracular dogmas, which ring hollow to the knock of rational inquiry. Catholic Europe to-day is illustrating the value of such positive doctrines. The only true positiveness in doctrine is reasonableness. Carry down the roots of faith below all secondary soils, external authorities of councils or of books, into "the constitution and nature of things," and you have struck hold in a soil sure to feed the future with beneficent and beautiful beliefs. . . . There is a faith in Jesus as much harder than the lofty formulas of the Nicene Creed as a life is harder than a philosophy.— *Dr. R. Heber Newton.*

See Dr. J. F. Clarke's *Essentials and Non-essentials in Religion, passim* ; also *Unitarian Affirmations, passim.*

The first and the last fact of human experience is intelligence and will. Matter, pressed to the utmost, declares itself to be Force. Force, pressed to the utmost, declares itself to be Thought and Will. And Thought, pressed to the utmost, declare that they are the breath of the Spirit of God. The Alpha and the Omega of human experience is Spirit. Our science, when it has held up the world to the most searching scrutiny, must drop it back again into the hand of the Almighty, from whence it came. Reason, following motion from star to star, and into the infinite past, cannot escape the necessity of looking beyond the bounds of the visible universe for the First Cause, which it always seeks, but never finds within the limits of the seen.— *Dr. Newman Smyth (Old Faiths in New Light,* p. 164).

In the argument from prophecy, we have to do with a forest, not with a single bough or a basket of leaves; with the whole trend of a coast, not with single headlands or inlets of the sea; with a zone of constellations, not with scattered stars. We have to do with the whole tenor of Scripture, with the prolonged course of centuries of history, with the multitudinous testimonies of the human soul in many generations, with the arrangements and combinations of many events in one continuous and resplendent revelation of the glory of the Lord.— *Idem,* 248.

If we analyze faith to see what it is, we shall find that it is, first, faith in persons. This is the faith of the child. Next, it is faith in ideas, in laws, in principles. And, lastly, it is the union of both, faith in God, in whom law and love are one,—the Divine Being whose nature is truth, who is the sum of all the laws of the universe. By this faith we live, by this faith we grow, by this faith we accomplish everything, by this faith we are saved. We cease to be animals as we arise out of sensation and sight into belief and trust in ideas. All great men, all the souls who govern the world and lead on society, are great in proportion to their strength of conviction. They act not by what they see, but by their strong confidence in what they do not see. . . .

Salvation by faith is a universal law of the moral universe. It is no arbitrary enactment of Christianity alone, but it is based in the very nature of man. All moral and spiritual life comes from faith in things unseen. All real knowledge has its roots in faith. He who doubts is a lost soul; that is, he has lost his way. Jesus came to seek and save these lost souls by giving them some clear, strong convictions by which to live and die. Inspired by him, "all who are in their graves" hear his voice and come forth. The poor, suffering, lonely man, bereft of all, sick, in prison, condemned to die, is safe and happy if he has faith in God, truth, immortality. What can man do to him? He may have trials of cruel mockings and scourgings, yea, moreover, of bonds and imprisonment. But his hope sustains him; for he believes that neither life nor death, nor things present nor things to come, can ever separate him from the love of God. What we need most of all and always is some great belief, some strong conviction, some realizing sense of spiritual things. Then, we are young, though years and cares have marked wrinkles on our brow. We are full of life, though on the verge of the tomb. We are happy, hopeful, contented, and have an inward peace which is better than all the treasures of this world.—*Dr. J. F. Clarke* (*Common Sense in Religion*, pp. 333, 349).

All moral teaching, then, whether within the Bible or without, addresses itself to the *consciousness* of the disciple. Neither Reason nor Faith is to be flouted at. Reasoning is not to be subordinate, but co-ordinate with the function of Faith; Faith being defined as fidelity to religious conviction, and not merely as a synonyme of credulity. Thus, the prayer that the Holy Spirit may guide us into all truth imports the aspiration,— May Reason, combined with the good-will essential to fair-mindedness, be the verifying faculty whereby we shall sift and appropriate the good-inspired in everything we read, the Bible not excepted.

> Truth and Beauty but impart
> Gleams to whom they can allure;
> Only are the pure in heart
> Blest with insight of the pure.
>
> *Celeste Shute Burnham.*

Defining Reason as the faculty by which the mind distinguishes truth from falsehood and good from evil, and which enables the possessor to deduce inferences from facts or from propositions, there must be, in its application to the study of the Bible, not only isolated analysis, but also critical comparison of scriptures. Thus, in the unimportant inquiry, What did David pay for Araunah's threshing-floor? or, What was the footing of Joab's enumeration of Israel and Judah? one who had consulted only the last chapter of Second Samuel would give a more unsatisfactory answer than one who had also studied the twenty-first chapter of First Chronicles. Illustrations in more important questions will be adduced hereafter. Other instances will be suggested in comparing the new English version with the King James. Especially is the compositional ground for discrimination apparent in the Old Testament and Apocrypha.

Minor narratives were fused together one after the other; and at length, in exile, a final redactor completed the great work, on the first part of which Ezra based his reformation, while the latter part was thrown into the second canon. The curious combination of the functions of copyist and author, which is here presupposed, did not wholly disappear till a pretty late date; and whereas, in the Books of Samuel, we have two recensions of the text, one in Hebrew and one in the Septuagint translation, the discrepancies are of such a kind that criticism of the text and analysis are separated by a scarcely perceptible line.* — *Dr S. Davidson.*

And not only must the circumstances of the writers, but also those of the personages, be considered.

At first, they knew him only as a village enthusiast, a Galilean teacher, at best a rabbi like other interpreters of the law, one of the school, perhaps, of Rabbi Hillel or Rabbi Simeon, like them setting the weightier matters of justice and mercy above the mint, anise, and cumin of current exposition. For a background to the understanding of his discourses, we should know something of the wonderful, well-meaning pedantry of the rabbinical interpreters, and something, too, of the genuine and wholesome ethics which the better sort, Hillel at their head, had tried to engraft upon it.... Only as an after-result came his strong conviction that he was the chosen deliverer of his people, though by a way they could not understand or follow.— *Joseph H. Allen.*

The duty of reasoning is inculcated in the Westminster Confession: "The whole counsel of God concerning all things necessary for his own glory, man's salvation, faith, and life, is either expressly set down in Scripture, or by good and necessary consequence *may be deduced* from Scripture."

Often has the undue consideration of one passage to the exclusion of others been apparent in discussing ethical or political questions; as, for instance, the citing of alleged declarations of Noah in support of slavery or of capital punishment, similarly polygamy and intemperance. Indeed, almost every discovery in science has had to run a gauntlet of missiles moulded from such distorted materials. There be those who

> Would torture pages of the Bible
> To sanction whim or blood,
> And in Oppression's service libel
> Both man and God.

---

* See *Alleged Discrepancies*, etc., by Dr. J. W. Haley.

Hereto come two voices from Scotland: —

I look into the Scriptures with humble hope of extracting a rule of conduct and a law of salvation. But I expect to find this by an examination of their general tenor and of the spirit which they uniformly breathe, and not by wresting particular passages from their context or by the application of Scriptural phrases to circumstances with which they have often very slender relation.— *Sir Walter Scott* (*Old Mortality*, chap. 21).

When a few more years are past, Buckland and Sedgwick, Lyell, Jameson, and the group of brave men who accompanied and followed them, will be looked back to as moral benefactors to their race, and almost as martyrs also, when it is remembered how much misunderstanding, obloquy, and plausible folly they had to endure from well-meaning fanatics, like Fairholme or Granville Penn and the respectable mob at their heels, who tried, as is the fashion in such cases, to make a hollow compromise between fact and the Bible by twisting facts just enough to make them fit the fancied meaning of the Bible, and the Bible just enough to make it fit the fancied meaning of the facts.— *Hugh Miller.*

The Church of Rome fought long and desperately against the Copernican system of astronomy, which seemed to conflict with a scrap of poetry in the Book of Joshua. It issued bulls to make the earth stand still, a significant symbol of what theology has often attempted. It was a vain contest: Rome might imprison Galileo, but "the stars in their courses" fought against Ptolemy, and Rome was finally forced to yield. The poetry of Joshua was allowed to be poetry, and the facts of astronomy were allowed to be facts. In our own time, a similar battle has been waged by theology against geology, in the interest of another scrap of poetry in the Book of Genesis. Geology discovers that it took a good while to make the world, more than a week, more than a year, more than a hundred thousand years; but theology insists on making a week's work of it, and fancies the credit of the Bible involved in that despatch.— *Dr. F. H. Hedge.*

Dr. N. Smyth and others detect upon the surface of the Genesis narrative signs of a mnemonic purpose,— a first lesson made easy before the days of printing-presses.

That the volume outlasts misuse and outrage by both friend and foe is proof that there is in it somewhere and somehow a mighty preservative leaven. The Sermon on the Mount will survive as long as human conduct needs guidance or human sorrows beatitude.

> Dwelt there no divineness in us,
> How should God's divineness win us?

But no one can habitually utilize reason in seeking

> How to o'errule the hard divorce
> Which parts things natural and divine,

without being constantly reminded of Dr. H. Ballou's aphorism: — .

Nothing is more easy than simple religious sensibility, nothing more difficult than sound religious principle.

Or of the two not wholly dissimilar definitions : —

Religion is living all the truths we possess.—*Augusta Cooper Bristol.*

Religion is the practical recognition of God: Christianity is the practical recognition of God in Christ.—*Rev. Henry Shute.*

More recently has this co-operation of the intellect, the sensibilities, and the will, in Biblical interpretation, found further pithy expression : —

One must have what I can only describe as the *faith-temper*, a delicate and disciplined sensitiveness and loyalty to the spiritual aspects of life. This temper will express itself in one man in a very definite belief in a personal God and a personal immortality. Another man, in whom the faith-temper is no less fine and deep, will hesitate to define God as "personal," or to affirm how much of its present elements the soul carries into its future life. But in both of these men there will be a spirit of reverence, humility, passive trust, and active loyalty toward some transcendent and divine reality. It is a spirit hard to analyze or define; but, whenever a man has it, it is *felt* by those he meets, felt more quickly, more powerfully, more beneficently, than almost any other personal trait. If a preacher has this, the reality of faith, of which a theological creed is but a shadow or simulacrum, it will pervade his sermons, his prayers, his words and tones and gestures, as subtly as the perfume of a flower, as vitally as the air that feeds the life of man. Whatever ideas, whatever methods he may employ, his people will be helped and uplifted by him; they will get the "enlarged horizon," the "transfiguring view," and in their own lives and characters some transfigurations will be wrought.—*Geo. S. Merriam* (*Christian Register*, March 2, 1882).

Now let five "woman-wise" witnesses conclude the chapter:

Reason, guided by humility and reverence, is *never* "unassisted." "*Every* good gift cometh from above."—*Lydia M. Child.*

> O thou of little faith, lift up thine eyes!
> Are the ten thousand glowing stars of night
> But a vain dream, because thy feeble sight
> May not behold them in the noonday skies? *Mary Howitt.*

However deep be the mysterious word,
  However dark, she disbelieves it not :
Where Reason would examine, Faith obeys,
  And "It is written" answers every doubt.

Caroline Fay.

Two travellers started on a tour
  With trust and knowledge laden :
One was a man with mighty brain,
  And one a gentle maiden.
They joined their hands, and vowed to be
  Companions for a season.
The gentle maiden's name was Faith,
  The mighty man's was Reason.

He sought for truth above, below,
  All hidden things revealing ;
She only sought it woman-wise,
  And found it in her feeling.
He said, "This earth's a rolling ball,
  And so doth science prove it" :
He but discovered that it moves,
  She found the springs that move *it*.

All things in beauty, science, art,
  In common they inherit ;
But *he* has only clasped the form,
  While *she* has clasped the spirit.
God's wall infinite now looms up
  Before Faith and her lover ;
But, while *he* tries to scale its heights,
  She has gone safely over.

He tries from *earth* to forge a key
  To ope the gate of heaven :
That key is in *the maiden's heart*,
  And back its bolts are driven.
They part. Without her, all is dark,
  His knowledge vain and hollow ;
For Faith has entered in with God,
  Where Reason may not follow.

Lizzie York Case.

Perhaps, however, in a future chapter, we shall conclude that Reason will eternally keep company with Faith ; and this, without denying the testimony of Dr. Edward Young, that

Swift Instinct leaps, slow Reason feebly climbs ;

although John Dryden's inquiry, "How can finite grasp infinity?" may have to go unanswered.

Life grows dark as we go on, till only one clear light is left shining on it ; and that is faith.—*Anna S. Soymonof Swetchin.*

Chapter II.

CONSECUTION.

What is the Chronological Order of the Early Records of the Life and Teachings of Jesus?

THE data necessary for precisely determining this are not available. The first New Testament was compiled by Marcion, A.D. 145. It contained ten Epistles of Paul. He knew of no Epistles to Timothy, to Titus, or to the Hebrews; or, if he did know of them, he did not consider them genuine. It had but one Gospel. This closely resembled Luke, but was much shorter. Canon Westcott, Baring-Gould, Griesbach, and Schleiermacher acquit Marcion of the charge of using — or at least of corrupting — the Luke Gospel. The three most ancient Gospels now extant are, according to Judge Waite,* the Protevangelion, *circa* 125 A.D.; an Aramaic Gospel, called by Origen the "Book of James"; the Gospel of the Infancy, *c.* 130 A.D.; and the Acts of Pilate, *c.* 130 A.D. One copy of the last, containing many patristic interpolations, is known as the "Gospel of Nicodemus." The two first-named Gospels have also many interpolations. They are, however, supposed by recent collators, named by the last-cited author, to afford evidence of interpolations in the four canonical Gospels in the final redactions thereof. But earlier Biblical students have been of the opinion that those three uncanonical Gospels are wholly fabrications gotten up to "fill the bill" as to certain references made by Justin Martyr, *c.* 150 A.D., to Gospels of those names respectively. Partial exceptions may be mentioned. Thus, Bishop Ellicott,† while rejecting the rest, accepts the Acts of Pilate. Some have thought that portions of Luke were taken from the Protevangelion.‡

---

* *History of the Christian Religion to the Year* 200. By Charles B. Waite. Chicago, 1881.

† Cambridge Essay, 1856.

‡ See *Schleiermacher on Luke*, p. 24.

As to the chronological order of the canonical New Testament records, students differ.* After citing Prof. G. P. Fisher † in support of a view that the Fourth Gospel could not have appeared later than "a few years after the beginning of the second century," Rev. Joseph Cook says that "the upper date of A.D. 34 and the lower date of A.D. 60, as established by exact research, are the two merciless blades of shears between which the latest and most deftly woven web of doubt is cut in two. [Applause.]" ‡

The following table presents the conclusions of three very careful and industrious investigators; namely, Dr. Samuel Davidson,§ Dr. Abraham Kuenen, Professor of Theology at Leiden,∥ and Judge Waite, above cited.

	Davidson	Kuenen	Waite
II. Thessalonians,	A.D. 52	After 70 (?)	52
I. Thessalonians,	53	54 (?)	53
Galatians,	56	56 (?)	52
I. Corinthians,	57	58 (?)	57
II. Corinthians,	57	58 (?)	57
Romans,	58	59 (?)	58
Philemon,	62	64	62
Colossians,	62	After 70 (?)	62
Philippians,	62	64	63
Hebrews,	66	**After** 70 (?)	160
James,	68	90 (?)	80
Revelation,	69	68	130
Ephesians,	75	After 100	63
I. Peter,	77	After 100	80
Jude,	80	After 130 (?)	80
Matthew,	70 and 100	90 (?)	180
Luke,	115	After 100	170
Mark,	120	90 (?)	175
Titus,	(?)	After 130 (?)	130
II. Timothy,	(?)	After 130 (?)	130
I. Timothy,	(?)	After 130 (?)	130
Acts,	125	After 100	180
I. John,	130	Before 150 (?)	130

* See Prof. J. H. Scholten's answer to Tischendorf's *Wann mare our Gospels written?*

† *Essays on the Supernatural Origin of Christianity*, 1870. Preface, p. xxxvii.

‡ *Transcendentalism*, p. 30. (Published Lectures.)

§ *Introduction to the Study of the New Testament*. London, 1868.

∥ See *The Bible for Learners*, by Drs. Kuenen, Oort, and Hooykaas, vol. iii., p. 696.

CONSECUTION

	Davidson.	Kuenen.	Waite.
II. John,	A.D. 131	Before 150 (?)	130
III. John,	131	Before 150 (?)	130
John,	150	Before 150 (?)	178
II. Peter,	170	After 150 (?)	170

It is not within the scope of this Manual to set forth the grounds of different writers' conclusions as to what is the actual order of these records.* It may, however, be for occasional convenience here to note Dr. Kuenen's order of portions of the older Jewish literature.

Before the Assyrian Period: the "Decalogue"; Song of Deborah (Judges v.); David's Poems (II. Samuel i., 19-27 and iii., 33, 34); Genesis xlix.; "Book of the Covenant" (Exodus xxi., 1-xxiii., 19).

In the Assyrian period, *circiter* 800-700 B.C.: Psalm xlv.; Deuteronomy xxxiii.; Numbers xxii.-xxiv.; Amos; Hosea; Zechariah ix.-xi.; certain narratives in the Pentateuch, in Judges, and in Samuel; Song of Solomon; Micah; part of Isaiah, of the Proverbs, and of Deuteronomy.

In the Chaldean Period, *c.* 700-500 B.C.: Nahum; Zephaniah; Zechariah xii.-xiv.; Habakkuk; Jeremiah; many of the Psalms; earliest edition of Joshua; Judges; Samuel; Kings; Lamentations; Isaiah xl.-lxvi.; xiv., 4-21; xxxv., etc., Jeremiah li., lii.

In the Persian Period, *c.* 500-300 B.C.: Haggai; Zechariah i.-ix.; Joel, Book of Origins; many of the priestly laws in Leviticus and Numbers; Ruth; Jonah; Malachi; Job; many of the Psalms and Proverbs.

In the Greek Period, 300-50 B.C: final edition of the Pentateuch and Joshua; Chronicles; Ezra; Nehemiah; Esther; many of the Psalms; Proverbs of Jesus ben Sirach; Ecclesiastes; Daniel; Psalms xliv., lxxiv., cxviii.; Baruch; Epistle of Jeremiah; oldest portions of the Book of Enoch; I. and II. Maccabees; additions to Esther; Tobit; Prayer of Manasseh.

In the Roman Period: (B.C.) Psalms of Solomon; Ascension of Moses; (A.D.) Susanna; Bel and the Dragon; III. Maccabees; Wisdom; Philemon; IV. Maccabees; Book of Jubilees; Judith; Apocalypse of Baruch; IV. Esdras; Josephus; The Talmudic Mishna.— *The Bible for Learners*, vol. iii., p. 697. (For other tabulations, see Rev. G. F. Piper's *Sunday-school Lessons*, etc., Part II.,pp. 55, 71, and 83. Also Rev. J. W. Chadwick's *The Bible of To-day*, pp. xv.-xviii.)

A single illustration of the mode of determining relative dates must suffice. Take Daniel: Jesus ben Sirach, *c.* 200 B.C., makes no mention of Daniel or of his three friends, although a place might have been given them with such per-

---

*See II. Kings xxi., 13; xxii., xxiii.; II. Chronicles xxxiv., 14-32; II. Maccabees ii., 13, 14; iii., 3; Ecclesiasticus.

fect appropriateness in his "Song of Praise of the Fathers" (chap. xliv.). In the Hebrew Bible, Daniel is not placed among the prophets, but in the third division containing the Hagiographa, and among them the very latest. In chapters vii.-xii., Daniel always speaks in the first person, but in i.-vi. in the third person, in a strain of admiration.

For ordinary purposes, we shall more conveniently speak of Malachi as the last of the Old Testament canonical writers, though it be with but approximate correctness. In transition to the New Testament, the following suggestions, respectively from three recent writers, will be of good service:—

When the curtain rises on the scenes of the New Testament, Judea is the province of an empire of which even the pseudo-Daniel did not dream, and which lay far, far beneath the horizon of Malachi and his contemporaries. Moreover, scribes, Pharisees, Sadducees, and Essenes, sects of which Malachi was entirely ignorant, jostle each other on the narrow stage. The synagogue, an institution of which the Old Testament is wholly innocent, in the New Testament is of more importance than the temple. Again, the language of the speakers in the New Testament is entirely strange, not merely that it is Greek or Aramaic instead of Hebrew, but that it is concerning angels and devils, concerning immortality and the resurrection of the body, and paradise and hell, of all which Malachi and his contemporaries had only learned the alphabet.—*Rev. John W. Chadwick (The Bible of To-day, p. 155).*

The writings of the prophets and apostles were read and pondered for long periods,—indeed, ages, I should conjecture. They lay like seed at first alone; and as the influences of reflection, conscience, and piety, were brought to bear upon them, their inner meaning developed and grew, until at length the people—the plain, uncritical, devout, unprofessional portion of the people—treasured them for the spiritual help they afforded, without considering the literary defects or historical mistakes they contained, without imputing any specially sacred character to them nor to their authors; reading them very much as vast numbers of Episcopalians read the Prayer-Book or the *Imitation of Jesus*, and as Protestants generally read the *Pilgrim's Progress*, because they speak what is helpful and interesting, not because their favorite authors are impeccable or infallible. Then, the priests, ever mindful of the authority of prevailing opinion, yielded assent to the popular verdict, and officially announced what before had been informally but generally expressed, and so far compromised themselves in their eagerness to sail with the wind as to garnish the tombs of the prophets they had slain.—*Richard A. Griffin (From Traditional to Rational Faith, p. 134).*

There follows an age when the voice of the prophet ceases. The drill of the schoolmaster has its appointed time. The hedge is built around the law. The heroic warrior recovers the sacred rolls which the "Madman of Syria" had left unburned. The scribe sits in Moses' seat. Already, the soil is prepared by the Roman ploughshares for the seeds of a better faith. But the life of the true religion must first, it would seem, return into itself, become dry in the hard kernel of Judaism, be buried in the ground, and die, before it can rise again in the new vigor of Christianit , and bear the ripe fruit of the gospel for the world.— *Dr. Newman Smyth* (*Old Faiths in New Light*, p. 80).

The Bible is not like a chain, the whole of which is no stronger than its weakest link, than some casual, uncritical remark in its history, chronology, astronomy, or geology. . . . It is various because life is various. It touches somewhere all parts of human life. It often seems inconsistent with itself, just as life is inconsistent. One passage appears to contradict another, just as some of our earthly experiences seem opposed to others. The Bible aims at no logical consistency, at no metaphysical or systematic coherence. It is too large, too full, too wide in its sweep and scope, to fit itself to any of our creeds. It sometimes speaks of divine providence, as if God did everything and man nothing. We are the clay, and he is the potter. And, then, it speaks of man's ability, as if he had power to convert himself by the mere force of his own will. Sometimes, it cries, "Create in me a new heart, and renew a right spirit within me." And, in other places, it says, "Repent, and be converted"; "Make to yourselves a new heart and a new spirit." The breadth of the Bible is perhaps one of its most wonderful qualities. Every creed finds support in it: every Church has its proof-texts in it. This, which has been brought as an objection, is one of its chief glories.—*Dr. J. F. Clarke* (*Sermon of Nov.* 26, 1882).

Chapter III.

INSPIRATION.

What Two Views concerning Inspiration of the Bible Writers?

(1) THE supernatural: that there was a certain supernatural impression of the divine will upon their minds, whereby they set forth truth with no admixture of error; or, as Sir Walter Scott makes the White Lady of Avenel enunciate it,—

> Within this awful volume lies
> The mystery of mysteries...
> And better had he ne'er been born
> Who reads to doubt or reads to scorn.

(2) The natural: that in most instances they wrote under extraordinarily elevating influences, but were not entirely exempt from liability to mistakes. The latter view has been well set forth as follows:—

There are two methods of getting truth; one is perception or looking out; the other, inspiration or looking in. Perception without inspiration makes the pedant, the dry man of details, the collector of facts who can do nothing with them after he has them. Inspiration without perception makes the mystic, the visionary, the mere theorist. Perception joined with inspiration makes the man of genius, the man of science, the discoverer, the statesman, the poet, the prophet. No great thing was ever accomplished in this world without inspiration. But inspiration is of different kinds and different degrees. There is the inspiration of the artist and poet, or of the thinker and philosopher. There is the inspiration of the lawgiver and statesman, of the prophet and saint. There is artistic inspiration, poetic inspiration, religious inspiration. The common quality in all is the reception of influence from a higher sphere, an opening of the mind for higher influence, a light from within and from above....

The common-sense view of the Bible is that it is our guide and our teacher, because it is full of truth. It is because it is so compact with divine things that we say it is from God. We do not say it is true because it is inspired, but we say it is inspired because it is true. It is a book, we may safely say, that will never be superseded, any more than Homer, Dante, Shakspere, will be superseded. It will grow in interest immensely, in proportion as we study it intelligently and freely. When we make no extravagant claims for it, but let it rest on its own merits, infidelity will cease to attack it. If there is anything in it you do not understand, wait until you do. If there is anything you cannot believe, pass it by. There is enough left which you can believe.

The Bible is profitable for doctrine, for reproof, for correction, for instruction in righteousness. It has guided men to God through all these long centuries; it has civilized humanity, sustained mourners, comforted sorrow, created happy homes, made family life peaceful, awakened an interest in truth, quickened the intellect, opened heaven to the dying, and given hope in the midst of despair. A book that does this does not need to be propped up by theological theories: it can stand and walk alone, and take care of itself. It does not need to be protected by laws against blasphemy: the love and gratitude of men are a sufficient protection. It does not need to be made a master, to enslave the intellect: the more free our thought is to inquire and examine, the more we shall come to honor it, to love it, and to believe in it. Why is not this enough? Why manufacture a theory of inspiration to strengthen that which is already strong enough without it? It is as though you should erect a wooden scaffold round the Great Pyramid to hold it up.

Inspiration is insight, and insight is immediate knowledge. The inspired poet sees beauty, the inspired prophet sees truth. Knowledge carries its own evidence. He who knows anything thoroughly becomes an authority to us. That is enough. . . . You go to the Mammoth Cave in Kentucky. You take a guide, perhaps the guide Stephen, a colored man, formerly a slave,—an ignorant man. You know nothing of him but this, that he has guided hundreds of travellers before you, and has guided them safely. You enter the mysterious chambers. Passages diverge in all directions. Still, you follow through the great darkness his feeble lamp. You descend precipices, you climb ladders, you come to a river and cross it in a boat beneath an overhanging roof of rock. You go on and on, mile after mile, until you seem to have left forever the day and upper air. Immense darkness, perpetual night, undisturbed silence, broods around. You are many miles from the entrance. If your guide has made any mistake, you are lost. But you follow him with entire confidence. Why? Do you believe him to be plenarily inspired? Do you think him infallible? Not at all. But you trust in his long experience. He has guided travellers safely for years, and that is enough. So the Bible has guided the footsteps of travellers seeking truth and God. It has brought generation after generation out of darkness into light. It leads us through the mysterious depths of our own experience. It goes sounding on along the dim and perilous way of human life.

It points out on either side the false paths which would lead you to death. It speaks with authority, a far higher than that of a theological infallibility. It is full of the spirit of God, which is the spirit of truth; and its power is not dependent on the theories of inspiration which the Church may devise, but on its own immortal life, its sublime elevation, its power of bringing the soul to God and to peace.— *Dr. J. F. Clarke (Common Sense in Religion*, pp. 88, 93, 98).

Other eloquent adherents of the natural theory have not been always equally so careful to distinguish inspiration from perception: —

Inspiration is a perpetual fact. Prophets and apostles are not monopolists of the Father. He inspires men to-day as much as heretofore. In nature, also, God speaks forever. Are not these flowers new works of God? Are not the fossils under feet, hundreds of miles thick, old words of God, spoken millions of years before Moses?— *Theodore Parker.*

The importance of the inquiry, as applied to prophecy, justifies a second quotation from the former discriminating writer, this, also, impossible to abridge without marring: —

The old view of prophecy assumed that it was a miraculous violation of the laws of the human mind, by which a sudden knowledge of earthly events was communicated. Prophecy was regarded as so foreign from natural human experience that the prediction shows that God must have directly interposed to put this foreign knowledge into the mind, as a gardener may put the scion of a pear-tree on the stock of a quince, or a plum on an apricot. But the new view of prophecy assumes that it is no violation of the laws of the intellect, but an intense activity of powers usually latent or imperfectly developed. It is insight of the present which gives foresight of the future. He who sees deeply into principles can foresee their unfolding into that which is to be. Jesus sometimes used the phrase, "The hour cometh, and now is." This is the key to prophecy. The future is in the present, as the oak is in the acorn: therefore, he who really knows the "hour which now is" can predict "the hour which cometh." Thus, Columbus, being familiar with the geography of the Eastern Hemisphere, foresaw that by going west he would come to that continent again. So Dr. Channing, before the Civil War and before the emancipation of the slaves, foresaw the dangers which would follow emancipation. He said, "I do not believe that the emancipated slaves will assassinate their masters, as many predict, for they are by nature too affectionate and too submissive a race for this; but I foresee that the masters will refuse to give them equal rights as fellow-citizens, which will be an evil to both races." Thus, the seer, a man who looks into the present, becomes a prophet, and is able to look into the future.

Is prophecy, then, only the exercise of common sagacity? No, but of uncommon sagacity. It is a human sagacity made divine by a heavenly influence. Inspiration does not create the faculty of foresight, but develops it in a high degree. The prophet, under the influence of this divine power, foresees what to others is unseen. Therefore, the prophet is often disliked and hated, stoned and persecuted, because he announces coming woes and punishments. He is called a fanatic and a madman; he "troubles Israel"; he disturbs the slumbers and the comforts of those who only care for the present. When he speaks of the judgment to come, Felix trembles, and says, "At a more convenient season, I will listen to thee."

Inspiration gives knowledge of the substance of truth, but leaves the prophet fallible in regard to the circumstances. Thus, the prophetic soul of Columbus saw truly that by sailing west he would arrive at a continent; but he supposed it would be Asia, when in fact it was America. Theodore Parker wrote a letter to John P. Hale, in 1856, in which he said: "If Buchanan is president, I think the Union does not hold out his four years. It must end in civil war." Buchanan *was* chosen president; the Union did *not* hold out to the end of his term; civil war *did* come. So far, Parker foresaw what hardly any one else did at that time. But he was mistaken as to the circumstances; for he predicted the "worst fighting at the North, between the friends of freedom and the Hunkers," which never came, since nine-tenths of the so-called Hunkers ceased to be Hunkers, turned around and defended the Union, and the other tenth was silenced.

Paul's inspiration led him to foresee the coming of Jesus as the Christ, to make a new heaven and a new earth. In that, he foresaw the truth; for Christ has come, is coming, and will come more and more. Paul was right in foreseeing the coming manifestation (*parousia*) of Jesus as the Christ. But, in his earliest letters written to the Thessalonians, he seems to have looked for an outward, visible coming in the air, with audible sounds and accompanying marvels. Afterward, he appears to have dismissed these expectations, and speaks of sitting in heavenly places *now* with Christ Jesus; speaks of being already risen with him; speaks of Christ *within*, the hope of glory. His inspiration, which gave to him to foresee the essential truth, did not prevent him, for a time, from unessential error.—*Dr. J. F. Clarke* (*The Ideas of Paul, Boston Saturday Evening Gazette, May* 7, 1881).

Similarly, in answer to the question as to Paul, has an eminent "Free-Religious Anglican" written:—

Where, then, is the force of that argument of despair, as we called it, that, if St. Paul vouches for the bodily resurrection of Jesus and for his appearance after it, and is mistaken in so vouching, then he must be an imbecile and credulous enthusiast, untruthful, unprofitable? We see that for a man to believe in preternatural incidents, of a kind admitted by the common belief of his time, proves nothing at all against his general truthfulness and sagacity. Nay, we see that, even while affirming such preternatural incidents, he may with profound insight seize the true and natural aspect of them, the aspect which will survive and profit when the miraculous aspect has faded. He may give us, in the very same work, current error and also fruitful and profound new truth, the error's future corrective.— *Matthew Arnold* (*St. Paul and Protestantism*).

Many of our traditional constructions of Scripture are Japhetic interpretations of Semitic texts.— *Dr. Daniel D. Whedon.*

Every error is a truth abused.— *Bishop J. B. Bossuet.*

Aristotle says: "No great genius was ever without some admixture of madness; nor can anything grand or superior to the voice of common mortals be spoken, except by the agitated soul." And Mr. Emerson adds: "We might say of these memorable moments of life that we were in them, not they in us. We found ourselves by happy fortune in an illuminated portion of meteorous zone, and passed out of it again, so aloof was it from any will of ours."[*] "'Tis a principle of war," said Napoleon, "that, when you can use the lightning, 'tis better than cannon. Earnestness is the thunder-bolt."

In studying inspiration, Ewald's view of revelation is in point,[†]—namely, that God stands alike over against all man's powers and capacities, though at times drawing nearer to one side of us than to another; and, therefore, man must turn his spirit, with all its powers and capacities, perfectly unto God in order not to be estranged from him. Thus, when we consider the manifoldness of God's relations to us, and the variety of our possible impressions of the Being who besets us behind and before and on every side, we should expect that a revelation from God would be a divine manifestation "at sundry times and in divers manners";[‡] we should expect to find it as a great diversified fact and manifold influence in human history, pressing in upon man from different sides of his complex being, moulding society, shaping events, forming history.

Similarly, Max Müller has remarked §that a revelation ready made and given to men, like a language formed in heaven, would have been a foreign religion that men could not understand. And Prof. W. Beyschlag,—"So long as the majority of

---

[*] *Letters and Social Aims*, p. 225.
[†] *Lehre der Bibel von Gott*, vol. ii., p. 101.
[‡] Hebrews i., 1.
[§] *Contemporary Review*, November, 1878, p. 709.

theologians treat the word of God as a book of oracles, so long will it appear as a book of fables to the majority of the educated laity." And Dr. Newman Smyth: —

We fall into hopeless contradictions, if we begin by regarding the Bible as a text-book of divinity. *It is rather a book of life; and we must discover its meanings as we would study the mysteries of nature or interpret the changeful drama of life. Jesus regarded the truth of revelation as a word to be done.* Revelation is pre-eminently truth which has been done in history. The Bible certainly presents a spectacle of the contests of embodied truths with falsehoods clothed in human forms; a spectacle in which we behold right and wrong coming and going in a prophet's mantle or the armor of a king; where we see truth succeeding, and error dying, in the issues of human lives and the rise and fall of kingdoms. The great doctrines of the Bible are vividly revealed through its characters and their work, and in the progress of the whole history. In this book for all peoples and ages, the most abstract and impalpable truths seem taken, as it were, from the very air, from distant realms of the spirit, and clothed with flesh and blood; they are revealed walking with men, dwelling in their homes, made concrete and visible in the person of patriarch, prophet, or apostle; and they are summed up and declared in the vernacular of every man's heart, in the Word made flesh — *Old Faiths in New Light*, p. 37.

There is no other entrance to the kingdom of man, which is founded in the sciences, than to the kingdom of heaven into which no one can enter but in the character of a little child.— *Francis Bacon.*

> The word by seers or sibyls told,
> In groves of oak, or fanes of gold,
> Still floats upon the morning wind,
> Still whispers to the willing mind.
> One accent of the Holy Ghost
> The heedless world hath never lost.
>
> *Ralph W. Emerson.*

---

* John iii., 21.

CHAPTER IV.

COMPOSITION.

What Two Diverse Opinions as to the Circumstances of the Writing and of the Writers of the Four Canonical Gospels?

(1) THE evangelical that the first, second, and fourth were penned respectively by three disciples of Christ, and the third by a personal acquaintance.

(2) The traditional: that the three Synoptic ("together-view") Gospels, Matthew, Mark, and Luke, are simple, un-apostolic digests of earlier traditions.

Matthew consists of (1) the Triple Tradition; (2) extracts from a book or tradition of the words of the Lord, from which Luke also borrowed; and (3) an introduction, framework, and appendix, all added by one hand; though possibly the introduction and appendix, being borrowed; the former from an Aramaic source, may show differences of idiom not wholly concealed by the overlying style of the author who works up the materials.—*Dr. Edwin A. Abbott* (*Encyclopædia Britannica*, vol. x., p. 805, article "Gospels," note).

Convenience dictates that we designate the four as Matthew's, Mark's, Luke's, and John's, respectively, whatever may have been their authorship. As to that of the Fourth Gospel, very elaborate arguments have lately been published both for and against its genuineness; each side finding it not very easy, in procuring data for their premises, to resist a tendency "to draw," as Lightfoot somewhere expresses it, "unlimited checks on the bank of the unknown." As to its date, industrious investigators differ all along between 100 and 178 A.D. Theodor Keim says 130 A.D.:[*] Daniel Schenkel, 115-120 A.D.[†]

Dr. Matthew Arnold argues very ingeniously, both "from without" and "from within," that the Fourth Gospel had a "redactor," who was a Gnostic disciple of St. John.[‡] So, too, M. D. Conway, mentioning the original of the wrongly translated passage, John viii., 44, "He is a liar, and so is his father,"

---

[*] *Geschichte Jesu*, etc., 1875, p. 40.
[†] *Das Charakterbild Jesu*, 1873, p. 370.
[‡] *God and the Bible*, chaps. v. and vi.

as indicating the Gnostic Demiurge; mentioning also the style of John xi., 42.*

And as to the omission of the Sermon on the Mount, Mr. Conway thinks "the homely, every-day virtues of that sermon were too human, too commonplace, to arrest the attention of a speculative enthusiast, absorbed in the tremendous work of remodelling the theosophic schools of Egypt and Greece, harmonizing their divisions, and solving the problems of ages." The words "Salvation is of the Jews" he deems a Jewish interpolation, in the noble utterance to the Samaritan woman upon worship: "This bit of bigotry remains there like an insect in translucent amber." He also cautions us to make allowance for "Luke's polemical attitude toward the Jews, and slightly speculative tendency toward Greek superstition."

From thirty to forty years after the death of Jesus, the tradition of his life and ministry and death had shaped itself into the basis of our present Gospels of Matthew, Mark, and Luke. The contents of this fundamental tradition — fundamental to our Gospels, but in its turn, no doubt, the result of various accretions — are as flattering to the anti-supernaturalist as he could reasonably expect. Accounts of miracles are here, even some of the most startling; but there is not a hint of the miraculous birth of Jesus nor of the legends of his infancy, and the tradition ends with the discovery that his tomb is empty, without a word to signalize that he was seen again by any woman or disciple. In this tradition, the personality of Jesus is revealed in lines so firm and strong that the accretions of a later time add little to their force. The man behind the myth is there, no thin abstraction, but an individual with blood in his veins, and in his heart the love of human kind.—*J. W. Chadwick (The Man Jesus, p. 34).*

The traditional view of the composition of the four Gospels may be better understood by considering also that of some of the other books. Dr. Newman Smyth, who regards the Bible as "a growth slowly matured under the influence of both natural and supernatural forces," refers to the composite structure of Genesis, and contrasts Ezra, the editor, with the royal shepherd-poet:—

Very much as the wood-cutter can judge, from the successive layers of wood laid bare by his axe, how many seasons the tree has been growing, so a close scrutiny of the Bible shows unmistakable signs of the different ages and conditions of its growth. ... However the spirit of God may have used for his higher purposes the minds of men, we can be assured that he did not overpower their natural

---

* *Idols and Ideals*, App. Essay, p. 8.

habits of expression, or hold individual genius, as one might catch a song-bird, passive and palpitating, in the grasp of his Almighty hand.... The successive sparks of divine illumination were struck, all of them, out of the necessities of the times.— *Old Faiths in New Light*, pp. 39, 43.

Similarly another, as to the **Acts and the** Epistles:—

Little did St. Paul pause to consider how his confidential utterances, born of the pressing exigencies of the moment, might be turned into the formulæ of a literal creed. He was writing for the needs of the hour, and thus gives us, unwittingly, a chapter from the history of his own times.... The value of his letters for religious inspiration is indeed very great. But, we should bear in mind that they were designed to meet special questions and special difficulties.

By about A.D. 64, all Paul's Epistles had probably been written. They constituted, so far as is known, the entire Christian literature of that period. Soon after his death appeared the Epistle to the Hebrews, written by some unknown person who sympathized with Paul in believing that the old covenant was virtually superseded by the new. But he differed from Paul in putting an allegorical interpretation upon the Old Testament. Everything there contained was but a type of something to be fulfilled in the Church of Christ. But other writers took other views.... The Epistle of James was written to counteract the tendency of Paul's doctrine as to the efficacy of faith. Avoiding all metaphysical discussion, he addresses himself with great beauty and force of language to the purely practical side of Christian duty, and, like many a preacher of reconciliation to-day, urges the followers of Christ to forget their wordy disputations and devote themselves to good works. Peculiar in style, though Jewish in sentiment, the Apocalypse appeared before the fall of Jerusalem, and predicted the coming of the Messiah.

But the Messiah did not come, and the little band of Christians **must** address themselves to the necessities of the present. They **must** organize, and collect for immediate use the teachings and memories of their Master. No memoranda of word or act had been kept, and the companions and witnesses of his ministry had been dropping away year by year. Certain local traditions survived, and many personal reminiscences had been orally transmitted. But these **were** vague and contradictory. They did not agree, for instance, **whether** the family of Christ sprang from Bethlehem or from Nazareth, whether his ministry lasted one year or three years, whether he taught chiefly in Jerusalem or almost entirely in Galilee. But, such as they were, these traditions were collected, freed from their more palpable legendary accretions, and woven into the form of biographical sketches or collections of the Master's "sayings." Just when this **was** first done, we cannot tell. But we know (Luke i., 1) that many had taken in hand to set forth in order a declaration of those things which were most surely believed; and that, of these numerous collections, three, to which in the second century the names of Matthew, Mark, and Luke were attached, have survived, and give us the best knowledge we have of the beginnings of Christianity.

Soon after these three Gospels were written, the author of the third undertook to collect all the traditions still existing as to the lives of the apostles and the fortunes of the early Church. The materials for this compilation were also fragmentary and vague; but the book, as it stands, is our first ecclesiastical history. This is the Book of the Acts, which, like all historical narratives written in an uncritical age, betrays clearly enough the writer's own feelings and opinions. Consciously or unconsciously, it is written in a harmonizing spirit, to reconcile the conflicting tendencies of the Church.

But there was another school of theology besides that of the rabbis, whose influence, after Paul's time, imposed itself more and more upon Christianity. At Alexandria, in Egypt, had long existed a school of thinkers of Greek descent, inheriting the methods and traditions of Platonic philosophy; and with this school the Jewish Christians in Egypt had been brought for several generations into close contact. Prominent among these Hellenistic Jews was one Philo, who sought by means of allegorical interpretation to make the Mosaic scriptures the vehicle of philosophic mysticism. In the same spirit, another follower of the same school sought to interpret the new phenomena of Christianity; and in the Fourth Gospel we have Christianity pervaded by the spirit of the Alexandrian philosophy. Here, the incidents of the earlier Gospels are given with their interior significance; their kingdom of heaven is a spiritual realm; their Messiah is the pre-existent world. A tradition of the second century ascribes this Gospel to the Apostle John. There are many difficulties in the way of this supposition, and not least among them is the difficulty of supposing that a disciple who had the training of a Galilean fisherman, and who during his Master's lifetime begged a place at his Master's side in the Messianic kingdom, should, in his old age, prove the most spiritually-minded of Christ's followers, and deeply versed in mystic philosophy.—*E. H. Hall* (*Saratoga Essay*, 1880).

Prof. Ezra Abbot exhaustively considers four points of historical evidence of the genuineness of the Fourth Gospel, namely: (1) The general reception of the Four Gospels as genuine among Christians in the last quarter of the second century; (2) The question respecting the inclusion of the Fourth Gospel in the Apostolical Memoirs of Christ appealed to by Justin Martyr; (3) Its use by the various Gnostic sects; (4) The attestation to this Gospel which has come down to us appended to the book itself. The few statements made by Justin, in his two "Apologies" written to the Roman emperor and senate, *c.* 147 A.D., that are not authorized by the Four Gospels,—*e.g.*, that Jesus was born in a cave, that the Magi came from Arabia, and that Jesus made ploughs and yokes,— Prof. Abbot would explain as "founded on oral tradition, or as examples of that substitution of *inferences* from facts for the facts themselves, which we find in so many ancient and modern writers, and observe in every-day life."*

Several of Justin's additions of detail seem to have proceeded from his assumptions of the fulfilment of what he regarded as Old Testament prophecy.

It has been observed that each of the four evangelists aims not merely to give a biography, but also to maintain his own particular thesis: Matthew, that Jesus was the Jewish Messiah; Mark, that he was the son of God; Luke, that a Catholic Christianity is possible, inclusive of Petrine and Pauline elements; John, that Jesus was the incarnate Word of God.†

Between the Synoptics and the Fourth Gospel, Mr. Chadwick has drawn a well-contrasted parallel, substantially as follows: —

In the Synoptics, Judaism, the temple, the law, the Messianic kingdom, are omnipresent. In John, they are remote and vague. In Matthew, Jesus is always yearning over his own nation. In John, he often has for it a sentiment of scorn. In Matthew, the sanction of the prophets is his great credential. In John, his dignity can tolerate no previous approximation: all that came before him were "thieves and robbers." . . . The Synoptics represent him as dying on the 15th Nisan, and as eating the paschal supper on the 14th. John represents him as dying on the 14th, and as not partaking of the passover at all. His cleansing of the temple is, in the Synoptics, the climax of his opposition to the prevailing orthodoxy, and the immediate precursor of his arrest and crucifixion. John puts it at the beginning of his ministry. The Synoptics confine his ministry principally to Galilee, and bring him up to Jerusalem at the end. In John, his ministry is mainly in Judea. In the Synoptics, his ministry is only one year long; in John, from two to three. In the Synoptics, we have a natural and human representation of the Jews, some stiffly orthodox, others liberal. In John, they are the chief priests and Pharisees; the Sadducees, the Herodians, the scribes, so prominent in the Synoptics, do not appear at all. In the Synoptics, the emphasis is upon conduct; in John, upon belief. In the Synoptics, miracles are acts of mercy. In John, they are manifestations of the divine glory. The Synoptics narrate. John demonstrates.— See *The Bible of To-day*, pp. 291–294.

In view of these distinct characteristics, some writers have sought to set forth the early schools of Christian doctrine as four: (1) the Jewish, of James and Peter; (2) the Gentile, of Paul; (3) the Alexandrian, of [Apollos?] the writer of the

---

* *The Authorship of the Fourth Gospel*, 1880. p. 24.
† See Mr. Conway's *Idols and Ideals*, App. Essay, p. 10.

Epistle to the Hebrews; and (4) the intuitional of John. This may be adverted to in a future chapter.

The idea of the Logos or Word came into Jewish thought from two sides,—from Persia by way of Babylon, from Greece by way of Alexandria. The Persian-Zoroastrian religion taught that God created all things by his Word. The cosmology in Genesis is of Persian origin. "God *said*, Let there be light; and there was light." His word is the creative power. Before the time of Jesus, this Word of God had become personified in Jewish thought, most frequently under the name of Wisdom. "Wisdom hath been created before all things," we read in Proverbs, also in Ecclesiasticus; and in the Wisdom of Solomon, "She is a reflection of the everlasting light, the unspotted mirror of the power of God, and the image of his goodness." The Greek influence contributed to the same tendency of thought. The later followers of Plato, the Neo-Platonists, had personified his doctrine of the divine idea or reason. They called it the first-born Son of God, born before the creation of the world, itself the agent of creation. It was the image of God's perfection, the mediator between God and man. Philo-Judæus, who was born about twenty years before Jesus, was possessed with these ideas, and endeavored to connect them with the Old Testament teachings. He quoted, "Let *us* make man in our own image," to prove that God had an assistant who did all the work, thus saving God from any contact with matter,—a necessity of the Persian system imported into Jewish thought. He calls the Logos the "first-born Son of God," "Second God," and even "God," but this always in a qualitative, never in a quantitative sense.

On the one hand, then, the writer of the Fourth Gospel found this doctrine of the Logos; and, on the other hand, he found a conception of Jesus expressed in terms the most exalted, and bearing a very strong resemblance to the terms of the Logos doctrine of Philo. True, Philo had never dreamed of a human incarnation of the Logos; and Paul had never identified his exalted Christ with the Alexandrian Word. The first to do this was pretty certainly not the writer of the Fourth Gospel. It occurred to many writers at about the same time. To effect an alliance between Christianity and Alexandrian Platonism was the one passionate enthusiasm midway of the second century. Of this enthusiasm, the Fourth Gospel is the grandest monument. The opening verses might have been written by Philo-Judæus,—"In the beginning was the Word, ... and the life was the light of men." But Philo never could have written, "And the Word was made flesh, and dwelt among us," etc. To Philo, this incarnation of the Logos in a human personality would have seemed a blasphemous proceeding; and, even in John, the union of the Logos with the human personality of Jesus is purely verbal.... "He that hath seen me hath seen the Father." ... "As the Father hath life in himself, so hath he given to the Son to have life in himself."—*J. W. Chadwick* (*The Man Jesus*, p. 240).

Chapter V.

NARRATION.

What is the Order of the Principal Events narrated in the Four Gospels?

This it is impossible to determine. Dr. James Strong, the indefatigable harmonist (Methodist), believes Luke probably intended to observe the chronological order; but the evangelists do not generally.* In the Synoptics, he thinks "the facts themselves in the respective accounts agree too well in time and circumstances, and the narrators confine themselves too evidently to the position of writers of memoirs, to allow the supposition of a (conscious) transformation of the events or any such developments from Old Testament prophecy. Moreover, if truth and pious poetry had already become mingled in the verbal traditionary reports, the eye-witnesses, Matthew and John, would have known well in a fresh narration how to distinguish between each of these elements, with regard to scenes which they had themselves passed through." He, however, concedes that "the four Gospels were all written down a long time after the occurrences." †

Another writer thinks we can only rely upon "the triple tradition,"—the element in common of the Synoptics, except where the text indicates that the disciples misinterpreted Jesus. For instance, had they known that Jesus had commanded them to "disciple all nations," the early and bitter dispute as to the admission of the Gentiles to the Church would never have arisen.‡

In the Matthew report of the Sermon on the Mount, Mr. Chadwick and others perceive that we have fragments of a **great many** different discourses arbitrarily joined together. "**Some famous** hillside talk became a nucleus around which

---

* Harper's *Cyclopedia of Biblical, Theological, and Ecclesiastical Literature*, article "Harmony."
† *Idem*, article "Jesus Christ." ‡ Minot J. Savage, *Talks about Jesus*, p. 4.

various sentences spoken by Jesus at other times gradually clustered. In Mark and Luke, the sentences which are here joined together into a tolerably consistent whole are assigned to various occasions. But there is internal evidence not only of spontaneous growth, but of conscious manipulation." Several of the joints are easily apparent. In Matthew x., the instructions to the disciples savor strongly of a later time. "Actual experience of persecution is here reflected back upon the time of thought of Jesus." Chapter xiii. "groups into arbitrary unity a number of striking parables, which certainly, when originally spoken, did not come galloping upon each other's heels in any such fashion. Equally arbitrary is the grouping of events in chapters xiv. and xvii. And yet a certain progress is discernib e. The period of conflict becomes more clearly marked, and it hardly needs a prophet to foretell the ultimate catastrophe."*

As to time for the incidents, etc., the same writer elsewhere deems "the one year of the Synoptists fully adequate to all the conditions of the problem, while the three years of John land us amid a host of incongruities. The Jesus of John is always appearing and vanishing and flitting back and forth between Jerusalem and Galilee in a vague and purposeless manner, entirely suitable to the Logos phantom of this Gospel, but entirely at variance with the human personality of Jesus."†

Edmund H. Sears thinks Christ made five visits to Jerusalem.‡

In harmonizing the records and determining the preponderant portions, it will be found useful to consider the six rules laid down by Dr. Simon Greenleaf in his *Testimony of the Evangelists examined by the Rules of Evidence administered in Courts of Justice*, pp. 7-28.

---

* *The Bible of To-day*, p. 268.
† *The Man Jesus*, p. 116.
‡ *The Fourth Gospel the Heart of Christ*, p. 370.

Chapter VI.

ACCRETION.

What Two Views as to the Exemption of Narrations concerning Jesus from the Ordinary Liability to Accretion; (and herein) what may safely be considered the Uses of the Oriental Imageries?

(1) THE conservative: **that** either the oral statements and written records of fact were by special providence preserved from perversion, or else (as was quoted by Dr. Strong in the last chapter) there was, owing to presence of eye-witnesses, etc., **no** opportunity for misrepresentation originally, and hence the four Gospels essentially import absolute historical verity.

(2) The radical: that there does not appear to be intrinsic evidence that, during the interval between the death of Jesus and the recording, all the narratives of the events of his life entirely escaped the usual fate of tradition and history as to amplifications **and** glosses, but that the pith is, however, preserved. The main and fundamental features of the information, however distorted in the stream of time, is essentially unperverted and reliable,

> As sunshine, broken by the rill,
> Though turned aside is sunshine still.

Like the bon-mots that circulate in society, a legend is tossed from believer to poet, from poet to believer, everybody adding a grace, dropping a fault, rounding the form, until it gets an ideal truth. Religious literature, the psalms and liturgies of churches, are of course of this slow growth,—a fagot of selections gathered through ages, leaving the worse and saving the better, until it is at last the work of the whole communion of worshippers. The Bible itself is like an old Cremona: it has been played upon by the devotion of thousands of years, until every word and particle is public and tunable. And whatever undue reverence may have been claimed for it by the prestige of Philonic inspiration, the stronger tendency we are describing is likely to undo. What divines had assumed as the distinctive revelations of Christianity, theologic criticism has matched by exact parallelisms from the Stoics and poets of Greece and Rome. Later, when Confucius and the Indian scriptures were made known, no claim to monopoly of ethical wisdom could be thought of; and the surprising results of the new researches into the history of Egypt have opened to us the deep debt of the churches of Rome and England to the Egyptian hierology.— *Ralph W. Emerson (Letters and Social Aims*, p. 147).

And here may properly be considered the utility of the similes, parables, etc. Without either affirming or denying the correctness of any of the views of the Tübingen school as to myths, the words of a reviewer of Dr. D. F. Strauss' last publication may not prove entirely unenlightening in the premises:

> The use of allegory as an educational agent is so familiar that, in examining the structure of a matured mythology, especially that which has gathered round a creed, we may assume a large portion to be made up of distorted symbolism. How the premeditated emblems of poet-priests became misconceived by their disciples may be illustrated by the kindred instance of idolatry, which is nothing but an ignorant worship of the sign for the thing signified. It is often, however, a matter of no little difficulty to ascertain, under the corrupted mask of age, whether the features of a legend be truly allegorical or not. The criterion must be mainly negative. Where an elaborate basis of knowledge supports the imaginative structure, the mythist may be reasonably credited with design rather than delusion. The application of this theory is indefinitely extensive and fatally provocative of unintentional mythology on the part of those who employ it.— *Anonymous Reviewer (Home Journal)*.

It has been well observed that from end to end the Bible supposes and states that the Idea creates the Fact, that Spirit rules Matter, that the Word makes and controls the Thing. God spoke by Moses' lips, or ruled by Joshua's leadership. "This statement of what is the real substance, namely, the soul or life, with the corresponding statement that things, bodily and visible, are but transitory forms, gives dignity and character to what would else be petty in these histories. True, you can find the same lesson in all history; but you do not find it everywhere written in this Eastern naïveté or simplicity. This is, indeed, the distinction of Eastern thought, habit, and expression. Those Eastern nations were never startled by the idea of spiritual power, unseen, incalculable, but always present.... It is the story of the Master's life, it is his stories of the good Samaritan, of the Prodigal Son, and the rest, which have taught men what life is, what divine life is, and have made them seek to be sons of God. Paul's letters have helped them, when they came to the detail of character. His epigrams have been texts for action and memory. But it is not a letter of

Paul that sends John Augustus into the prison: it is that he follows his Leader. It is no discussion in the Epistle to the Romans which turns round tearful and repentant woman with the struggling hope of a new life, to leave a house of shame: it is the story of Mary Magdalene." Thus remarks Dr. Hale, adverting to an actual result wrought by Sarah D. Greenough's poem, "Mary Magdalene." And he adds that Bibles are not made by forethought or to order: —

This **book made** itself. Gospels there were, which are lost, alas! These four were so divine that men would not let them die. Hundreds of letters Paul wrote, and James, the secretary at headquarters. These letters here had in them that which men must have. The law of selection worked, and they kept these in being. Nay, you know yourselves how some parts of the Bible are strange to you, because they do you no good, while what you need is a household word and a blessed memory. It is by such compulsion, which no scholarship can overthrow or undermine, that a book like the Bible makes its own way into the affections of the world. And, whenever the world adds to its canon new treasures of wisdom or of imagination, it will repeat its old history. It will read not the digest of a law-book, not the abstractions of a philosopher, but the intense visions of a poet, or the tale throbbing with pathos, which makes visible the struggles of a life.

I have chosen to say this to-day, because, in a few weeks now, the new version of the New Testament will be awaking a new external interest in the shape of the Gospels and Epistles, the Book of Acts and the Revelation. Happily, we shall not handle the book as an idol. Happily, we shall come to it for fruit, for medicine, as we need fruit or medicine; and, where we find neither, we shall not force the words for what they do not give. In the common-sense notion of the Bible to which the youngest child in this church is trained, it has a power far surpassing what it had in any of the days of superstition. That power is the power which, narrative, dramatic, or historical,— when it is the story of God with man, man with God, man's life hid in God,—commands of its very nature. Men must remember; and, if they remember, one day they will comply.

"Therefore speak I to them in parables, that hearing they may hear, even if they do not yet understand; and seeing they may see, even if they do not yet perceive." "Happy are your eyes, for they do see; and your ears, for they do hear"

> What kings and prophets waited for,
> And died without the sight.
> *Dr. Edward Everett Hale*
> (*Parable and Bible: Sermon of March* 13, 1881).

Dr. Newman Smyth, however, insists that there was a forethought, an "ante-historic power in Israel and the Bible," some inner principle of development of religious life and truth, struggling against the outward historical environment, "while other people, though taught by many wise men and seers, and not without their truths, still can show no one connected and progressive revelation like this"; and he notes two special characteristics of such educational plan:—

There is a plain progress of doctrine in the Bible from without inward, from external restraints to inward principles, from law to love. The object lesson is given first, the truth of the spirit afterward. The discipline of conduct precedes the renewal of the heart. The sign and symbol prepare for the essential and the real. God's method in the Bible is like the mother's method with her child. The best truths of the home are the last learned. . . . The educational progress or pedagogical intent of the Bible may also be characterized as an advance from the general to the specific, from the indefinite to the more definite. . . . This may easily be traced in the succession of the names of God which occur in the Old Testament, . . . further by certain results,—. . . the worth of the family, . . . the abolition of human sacrifice and the abolition of slavery, . . . personal immortality. . . . The Bible is its own commentary and corrective. When that which is perfect is come, that which is in part of itself falls away from the divine law.— *Old Faiths in New Light*, p. 82, ff.

And still the world is "adding to its canon new treasures of wisdom or of imagination."

Slowly the Bible of the race is writ,
And not on paper leaves nor leaves of stone;
Each age, each kindred, adds a verse to it,
Texts of despair or hope, of joy or moan.
While swings the sea, while mists the mountain shroud,
While thunder's surges burst on cliffs of cloud,
Still at the prophet's feet the nations sit.
James R. Lowell.

And this, too, the wisdom of the heart rather than of the head alone:—

Not from a vain or shallow thought
His awful Jove young Phidias brought,
Never from lips of cunning fell
The thrilling Delphic oracle;
Out from the heart of nature rolled
The burdens of the Bible old;
The litanies of nations came,
Like the volcano's tongue of flame,
Up from the burning core below,—
The canticles of love and woe;
The hand that rounded Peter's dome,
And groined the aisles of Christian Rome,
Wrought in a sad sincerity:
Himself from God he could not free;
He builded better than he knew:—
The conscious stone to beauty grew.
Ralph Waldo Emerson (*The Problem,— Poems*, p. 14).

Chapter VII.

GENERATIONS.

What *Two Different Views of the Genealogical Records of Jesus?*

ONE affirming, and one denying the historical reliability of the accounts thereof in the First and Third Gospels. According to the latter view, the division in Matthew into three sets of fourteen generations, six times the sacred number seven, savors of artifice. Luke has eleven times seven generations. The first list, mounting up to Abraham and representing Jesus distinctly as Israel's Messiah, is thought to have originated in Jewish Christian circles. The other, going up to "Adam, the son of God," and attaching Jesus to the whole human race, would seem to have been revised in a Gentile Christian spirit. It is now generally conceded by students on either side that the ancestral names in the two accounts are irreconcilable.* From the circumstance that Jesus wore a seamless coat, Dr. Ewald argues that Mary was of the priestly tribe. St. John, her nephew, was known to the high priest, etc.†

It has been remarked that the effort to trace the line of Jesus to David is characteristic of the deference which writers in all monarchical countries pay to "blood"; that, before the oral traditions had crystallized into biography, the recorded yearnings for a coming prince would naturally give shape to a popular belief that one who so well filled the ideal for the Messiah must certainly have descended from that royal soul, David; that little can be inferred from the meagrely reported disclaimer: "If David then called him Lord, how is he his son?"

From the whole record, it would seem that one inference is unavoidable; **namely,** that the genealogical writers themselves entertained **no doubt** that Joseph was the father of Jesus.

---
* See Schleiermacher's *Essay on Luke*, p. 45. See also Harper's *Cyclopedia of Biblical, Theological and Ecclesiastical Literature*.
† Ewald's *Life of Jesus Christ* (Glover's translation), pp. 54, 353.

Otherwise, the descent of Joseph would not have been in the least to the point.

There may be some grounds for supposing that Joseph and Mary were not in poor circumstances.*

But it will not be denied that facts in the after-life of Jesus are symbolized in the accessories — whether legendary or historical — of the nativity alleged. He is cradled in a manger : he will never find so much as a place to lay his head, until, persecuted on every side, he drops it weary and thorn-pierced on the cross. The event that earth passes by unnoticed is celebrated with intensest joy and brightest radiance in heaven. The tidings are brought to humble shepherds : it will be the ambition of Jesus to befriend the poor and simple.

It may here be remarked that, independently of either the canonical or uncanonical Gospels, Christ stands an historical person. The testimony therefor is (1) that of Paul; (2) that of Josephus, who in his *Antiquities*† speaks of James as the brother of Jesus, who was called Christ; and (3) Tacitus, who in his *Annals*‡ mentions Christus, who in the reign of Tiberius was put to death as a criminal by the procurator, Pontius Pilate. Some, however, have considered the two latter to be interpolations. But, considering the whole context of Tacitus, while it is improbable (but not impossible) that so candid and philosophical an observer, narrating as early as in the first century, would, in adverting to Nero's accusing the Christians of setting fire to Rome, accept the current slanders of popular heathen prejudice against the character of the Christians, it seems more improbable that any "monk on pious fraud intent" would so overdo the job as to write down Christianity a "baneful superstition."

---

* See Mr. Conway's *Idols and Ideals*, App. Essay, p. 17.
† Book xx., chap. 9.
‡ Book xv., chap. 44.

Chapter VIII.

ANNUNCIATION.

What Two Views concerning the Annunciation to Mary, the Star-heralding, and the Angel-chorus?

(1) That these were veritable historical and supernatural occurrences.

(2) That they are the poetic legendary outgrowth of the loving imagination of the friends and followers of Jesus, when he became famous. The adherents of this view have argued that no prediction that Mary would bear a son who would sit on "the throne of his father David," as a temporal ruler, has ever been fulfilled; that Mary's song * is a reproduction of Hannah's; † that Gabriel — from the ranks ‡ "that stand in the presence of God," § arranged like the royal court of an Oriental monarch, and whom the tongue of Zacharias or of any other mortal must, on peril of being struck dumb, beware of interrupting with bothersome requests for proofs — is borrowed from some apocryphal writer ‖ (so, also, as to the "Gabriel" that came to Mary,¶ and the angel in Joseph's first dream **); that Mary, if unequivocally told by an angel from heaven that her son was going to be a leader worthy of following, would not be very like most mothers, if she did not "ponder" the message to sufficient purpose thenceforth invariably to heed it, — to recognize the lofty significance of his personality instead of afterward aiding and abetting his unbelieving and protesting brothers; that, if she made the journey to the hills of Judea and had an interview with her aged cousin Elizabeth under such circumstances as Luke mentions, the relations of the two and of their two sons would have been such that Jesus would not have been received by

---
* Luke i., 46–55.   † I. Sam. ii., 1–10.
‡ Perhaps of the supposed seven chiefs, Michael, Raphael, Uriel, etc.
§ Luke i., 19.   ‖ Daniel ix., 21; x., 15.
¶ Luke i., 26.   ** Matt. i., 24.

John at Jordan as a stranger; that perhaps the "star" got into an Ebionite document in the hands of the Matthew evangelist from the words in the Balaam legend,—"a star that rises out of Jacob"; that, had the moving star and the shining choir been literal entities when the Messianic expectation was at a feverish height, the news would have spread like fire, and history would never have shown the general public to have been ignorant of such remarkable phenomena;* that such prodigies had in centuries of Oriental tradition been associated with the birth of many a greatly adored personage (as, for instance, the star of Æneas and the thirty-two signs of the conception of the Buddha); that not merely in the case of Moses, Romulus, and Cyrus, had impending danger been one of the afterthought properties in the stage-setting of an infant whose future life-drama had proved sensational; that the fact that Luke, Josephus, and other historians ignore the Matthew episode of the slaughter of the innocents (which, if occurring, could not escape being a horridly renowned political event) confirms the suspicion of artifice † of Jeremiah's Rachel refraining from weeping for children that should "come again from the land of the enemy"; ‡ that it is strange the star left the "wise" men in uncertainty at Jerusalem, inquiring whereabouts, etc.; that it is absurd that the crafty Herod, if afraid the Magi would not return, aroused their suspicions by a secret summons, and sent no scout to observe them, or that in so small a place as Bethlehem he could not easily have discovered the particular house and child that had been honored by so distinguished a visit, and thus avoided a senseless wholesale massacre, or that so notorious a crime would have escaped the pen of Josephus, who gives a minute account of the atrocities perpetrated up to the very last moment of Herod's life; in fine, that the details of the Matthew narrative in this regard show the narrator to be too intensely Jewish partisan to be safely credited thereon without corroboration. Concerning the possibility of making the Luke framework fit the Matthew incidents of the nativity, or conversely, there has been much discussion.§

Did Mary so ponder as immovably to believe that the Messiah should see the light of life through her? The Gospels leave us too

---

* As to the stars, arising from a conjunction of Jupiter and Saturn, 747 U.C., see Glover's note in Ewald's *Life of Jesus Christ*, p. 350.
† Matt. ii., 17.   ‡ Jer. xxxi., 15, 16.
§ See Harper's *Cyclopedia of Biblical, Theological, and Ecclesiastical Literature*

clearly to think the opposite. There was a time long after this, when Christ was already a teacher, when she wavered between him and his brethren, who did not believe in him; when she went out with them to draw him away from his course, and bring him back to her narrower circle of home life, as one who was hardly in his right mind. Firm, unwavering trust, that knows no passing cloud, is a work of time with all who have an inner personal nearness to the Saviour; and it was so with Mary. She reached it only, like us all, through manifold doubts and struggles of heart, by that grace from above which roused her, ever anew, and led her on from step to step.—*Dr. Cunningham Geikie* (*Life and Words of Christ*, chap. ix.).

The angel's salutation is given by Luke in almost the very words of the seer Tiresias to the mother of Hercules: "Be of good cheer, thou mother of a noble offspring. Blessed art thou among Argive women!"

What are the miracles of law's imagined violation to the miracles of inviolate law? The miraculous birth of Jesus! As if every birth into this world were not a wonder past enough to stir

> Thoughts that do often lie too deep for tears.

His immaculate conception! Thank God, that century-living slur upon the purity of all the mothers in the world but one is hastening to its doom!—*John White Chadwick* (*The Man Jesus*, p. 42).

CHAPTER IX.

LOCATION.

*What Diverse Views of the Date and Place of the Birth of
Jesus?*

THE date was in A.D. 525, arbitrarily set at the year of
Rome 753. But Herod the Great had died early in 750 U.C.
Perhaps most Biblical students now place the birth in the
spring of 4 B.C.* The putting of the day at December 25 was
perhaps an adaptation to the Roman festival of "the Uncon-
querable Sun," just after the winter solstice. The same day
had been similarly observed among the Greeks, Persians, and
Egyptians; and pre-eminently so might be the rise of "the
light of the world" on the long night of sin, the warmth and
life of good-will shed into hearts of men the world around.

As to the place of the birth, two theories have been adduced:
(1) Bethlehem; (2) Nazareth. The latter theorists urge that
the words of Jesus himself indicate that he was a native of
Nazareth; that local names were given to men from the place
of their birth, but their residence was changeable; that the
presumability of the alleged journey to Jerusalem depends
chiefly on the probability of the alleged occasion therefor, and,
had there been a simultaneous coming up of everybody in the
land,—a census of Syria, as parenthetically averred by Luke,
or of the whole Roman world,—it would have been mentioned
in profane history, whereas, although Publius Sulpicius Quirinus (Cyrenius), pro-consul, when governor of Syria, made a
registration in Judea and Samaria when they became a Roman
province, this was not until nearly ten years after the death of
Herod the Great, and did not extend to Galilee nor concern
Joseph's family:† that, at the probable time of the birth, the

---

* In Harper's *Cyclopedia of Biblical, Theological, and Ecclesiastical Literature*, and in Canon F. W. Farrar's *Life of Christ* (App. of the Cassel ed.), the conflicting theories are fully considered.
† See Dr. Davidson's *Introduction*, ii., p. 68.

governor of Syria was not Cyrenius, but Saturninus; that Mark and John, while not directly mentioning the place of the birth, confirm the primitive tradition of early residence at Nazareth; that Matthew virtually confesses that, to make out his case that Jesus is the Messiah, he adapts his location to Micah v., 2,— out of Bethlehem Ephratah shall come a ruler, etc.; that this suspicious bias is also disclosed in Matthew's misapplication of Hosea xi., 1, "When Israel was a child, then I loved him, and called my son out of Egypt"; and that there are some discrepancies in Matthew's minor details,— " the revolving-light behavior of the star at Jerusalem," etc.

The Gospel of the Infancy * says Jesus was born on the road before his parents reached Bethlehem,— according to the Protevangelion, three miles distant,— and adds that, when he was born, "wise men came from the East to Jerusalem, as Zorodascht † (Zoroaster), had predicted; and there were with them gifts," etc. The account adds that Mary gave them a swaddling cloth instead of a blessing, and on their return they cast it into a fire, and it remained unharmed: also that they were guided by an angel in the form of a star. Another account stated that Jesus was born in a cave.‡

---

* See *ante*, chap. ii.
† In the ante-Nicene copy, "Zeruduscht." See (in Du Perron's translation of the Zend-Avesta) the Life of Zoroaster, vol. i., Part II., p. 45.
‡ See Judge Waite's *History*, etc., *to the year* 200, *passim*.

CHAPTER X.

CONCEPTION

What Three Views concerning the Paternity of Jesus?

(1) THAT he was supernaturally "conceived by the Holy Ghost," and had no natural human father.

(2) That all the natural conditions necessary to an ordinary human birth were present, but to these there was added "an absolutely creative act which did away with the traducian sinful influence."*

(3) That Joseph was the father, in the most natural sense; that before the conception he had been lawfully married to Mary. For this view, some have argued that the thesis inducing the attempt of the Ebionite redactor† to adapt the paternity to a record of words addressed to Ahaz‡ is absurd, and contrary to the preponderance of evidential data of the four canonical Gospels. It has also been argued that the Hebrew word for "spirit," being of the feminine gender, the saying that the Holy Spirit was the father of Jesus must have arisen among the Greeks, and not among the first believers, who were Jews; that, even if the story did not so arise, it would be very natural for the figurative tendency of Oriental expression to have so pure a character as Jesus created of a holy spirit, and for tradition, along down the years following the crucifixion, to enhance this appropriate simile to the present metaphor or hyperbole.§

---

* Schleiermacher.
† Matt. i., 22, 23.
‡ A Virgin shall conceive, and bear a son, and shall call his name Immanuel. Butter and honey shall he eat, that he may know to refuse the evil and choose the good, for before the child shall know to refuse the evil and choose the good, the land that thou abhorrest shall be forsaken of both her kings. . . . A man shall nourish a young cow and two sheep. . . . For the abundance of milk that they shall give, he shall eat butter."—*Isaiah* vii., 14, 22.
§ For a rather incisive review of the patristic ideas of the paternity, see Mr. Savage's *Talks about Jesus*, pp. 57-59.

It is also argued that the thesis of the author (or of the redactor) of the Fourth Gospel is unquestionably Gnostic ; * that, from the doctrine of Pythagoras and Plato,— that all natures, intelligible, intellectual, and material, are derived by successive emanations (æones) from the infinite fountain of Deity,— the transition was easy, by a little revision of the traditions of the Jewish Christians, to that of the Neo-platonic Christians, concerning the pre-existence of the soul of Jesus: "The Word was made flesh." †

In support of this view, it is asserted that the New Testament, and especially the Fourth Gospel, is covered with finger-marks of the Gnostic belief,— namely, that the original and supreme God dwelt apart and afar from the operations of the material universe, and had nothing whatever to do with matter; and the world was created by a sub-deity, Demiurgus ; and that a corresponding allowance must be made for the stand-point of a writer saying Christ created the world. Pope's lines have pretty general indorsement : —

> All are but parts of one stupendous whole,
> Whose body Nature is, and God the soul ,
> Who changed in all, and yet in all the same,
> Great in the earth as in the starry frame ;
> Warms in the sun, refreshes in the breeze,
> Glows in the stars, and blossoms in the trees ;
> Lives through all life, extends through all extent ;
> Spreads undivided, operates unspent,—
> To Him no high, no low, no great, no small,
> He fills, He bounds, connects and blesses all.

In this connection, after adverting to the Trinitarian view and certain technical distinctions essential thereto, Dr. J. F. Clarke says : —

We find more of God in Christ, not less, because we do not embarrass ourselves by these technical and theological distinctions, but accept him as he appears everywhere to be, a simple man; a man who, by the divine gift and help and inspiration, was able to rise till he came so near to God that, when we see him, we catch something of the reflected light of the Deity shining in his face. An old English religious poet has said : —

> A man who looks on glass,
> On it may stay his eye,
> Or if he pleases through it pass,
> And then the heavens espy.

---

* See Dr. M. Arnold's *God and the Bible*, chap. v., "The Fourth Gospel from Within."
† John i., 14; after a personification of the idea in Prov. viii., 22-30,— "The Lord possessed me in the beginning," etc. ; also Wisdom vii., 25-27.

Christ as a man is the glass. If we please, we can look on the glass, stay our eyes on that. Then, we see his human character. Or we can look through the glass, and see that he is a mediator of God who shines through his mind and heart, and so fills us with a sense of the great Deity.—*Discourse on Acts* xxiv., 14, *American Unitarian Association Tracts*, Series 4, No. 28, 1878.*

Egyptian paganism still insisted on three gods; philosophy demanded unity: the compromise was a triune godhead.—*M. D. Conway* (*Idols and Ideals*, App. Essay, p. 54).

According to the three synoptics, Jesus made no allusion to any miraculous circumstances connected with his birth. He looked upon himself as belonging to Nazareth, not as the child of Bethlehem; he reproved the scribes for teaching that the Messiah must necessarily be a descendant of David, and did not himself make any express claim to such descent.—*Albert Réville* (*History of the Doctrine of the Deity of Christ*).

Arius, of Alexandria, excommunicated by Bishop Alexander, but recalled by Constantine, taught that the Son was created out of nothing by the will of the Father, and hence was inferior to the Father in nature and dignity; and that the Holy Spirit is created by the power of Christ. Sabellius, of Libya, in the third century taught that the Son and Holy Spirit are only different powers, operations, or offices of the Father. Socinus of Sienna, in the sixteenth century, taught that Christ was an inspired man.

The animating motive of Arius was apparently to steer the ship of dogma clear of the rock of ditheism, the notion of two Gods. Two beings, one unbegotten, the other eternally begotten, seemed to him no better than two Gods. As for himself, he would not say that "*there was a time* when Christ was not," but "*there was* when Christ was not." He was before time, but God was before him. How clear this is; how palpable; how wholesome; how nutritious! Then, too, Arius stuck at the word "begotten." If Christ was begotten, then, as begotten from the unbegotten, he must inherit the unbegottenness of his begetter!—*John White Chadwick*.

Joseph Cook, in his Boston lecture of March 26, 1877, adduced four theses: (*a*) The Father, Son, and Holy Ghost are one God; (*b*) Each has a peculiarity incommunicable to the others; (*c*) Neither is God without the others; (*d*) Each with

---

*See also discussions between Messrs. Clarke and Joseph Cook on the "Triunity," the "At-one-ment," etc., 1877. Also a pamphlet, *The Doctrine of the Trinity defended against the Attacks of "I. F. C.,"* by John H. Eager, B.D. Also Channing's *Works*, vol. iii., p. 70. Also Swedenborg's *Brief Exposition*, n. 35.

the others is God. He would not say that there are literally three wills, three sets of affections, three intellects. Whereupon "E. A. H.," in the *Inquirer* of April 12, 1877, commented: —

Here is the old, futile attempt renewed to make the sent equal with the sender; that which proceeds equal with the source. Compare this trinity with George W. F. Hegel's. The divine nature (or idea) unfolds itself in three forms: (1) Being eternally, in and with itself, the kingdom of the Father; (2) The form of manifestation in physical nature and in the finite spirit, the kingdom of the Son; (3) The Deity in the sphere of the religious community, the kingdom of the spirit. In such a definition there are no quibbles, no self-contradictions. It is philosophic: we recognize lucidity and mental integrity in the premises, though our acceptance may not be given any more to Hegel's trinity than to Mr. Cook's.

"It is not a definition that I wish to give, but a life," says the lecturer. Which expression, when probed, means this: I wish to make evident that Christ must be worshipped as God, or else our way is dark. It is the same ground Mr. Beecher has long taken. He says: I cannot know God as he is, but Christ has been revealed that I may have something personal to worship. He *is* God in that sense, our best idea of Deity; an object for finite grasp to seize. The Unitarian finds no such necessity in his nature: he desires to worship the one living God, and finds it possible. His Scriptures do not direct him to address prayers to Jesus; his idea of the "nature of things" conflicts with any such assignment of rank to him. As a Way, as a Life, as a Guide, he leads to the Father. The Son is but the servant of the Most High, whose will he came to do.

Another modified form of the creed was recently criticised: —

Dr. Smyth believes "in one God, existing in three eternal distinctions of being, of absolute moral perfection." God then exists as three eternal beings who are eternally distinct, which is an unthinkable absurdity. There is not room in the universe for three eternals. —*James K. Applebee* (*The Commonwealth*, Oct. 14, 1882).

In the theological controversy at the council of Nicæa, A.D. 325, the only argument recorded is that of Nicholas of Myra, which was literally "a knock-down argument"; for he gave Arius of Alexandria such a blow in the jaw that this offending member must have been incapacitated for its legitimate functions for a time. His creed, however, was produced and read to the assembly. A storm of disapprobation greeted it, and it was torn in fragments by the opposing party. Another creed, that of Eusebius of Cæsarea, was read, disapproved, and torn in pieces. To read this creed, though Eusebius was himself an Arian, any one would suppose that it might give satisfaction to the most orthodox. It had given satisfaction to the emperor Constantine, who, before the meeting of the council, had leaned undisguisedly to the Arian side; but the very fact that this creed was satisfactory to the Arians insured its condemnation by the opposite party. What this party wanted was a creed that Arius could not accept; and it was furnished them, or, at least, its crucial word, by one of the Arian party, Eusebius of Nicomedia, who declared that "to assert the Son to be uncreated would be to say that he was *homoöusian*,— that is, *of one substance* with the Father." Great was the excitement caused by this letter. It was torn in pieces, as the obnoxious creeds had been before it; and then a creed was fashioned by the Athanasian party, in which the word "homoöusian" was embodied. So hateful to the Arians, it was just the word the Athanasians wanted. The creed, so far as it concerned the nature of Christ, affirmed belief in "one Lord, Jesus Christ, the Son of God, begotten of the Father; only begotten, that is to say, of the substance of the Father; God of God, Light of Light, very God of very God, begotten, not made, being *of one substance* with the Father, by whom all things were made," etc.

At once, the emperor threw himself with his whole weight on the side of this statement. What he wanted was unanimity, and he cared little how it was gained. To Eusebius, he privately confessed that he understood homoöusian to mean homoiöusian, "of the same substance" to mean "of like substance," and advised Eusebius to sign, with this private understanding! All of the Arian bishops, except some five or six, proved their subserviency and duplicity by following his example. Constantine, determined to do nothing by halves, issued a decree of banishment against all who refused to sign the creed, denounced Arius and his disciples as impious, and ordered that he and his disciples should be called Porphyrians, and his books burned, under penalty of death to any one who perused them.— *J. W. Chadwick* (*The Man Jesus*, p. 252).

Some of the principal "technical and theological distinctions" to which Dr. Clarke above referred are thus presented by Bishop Hans Lassen Martensen: —

When we say that God knows himself as a Father, we say that he knows himself as the ground of the heavenly universe which proceeds eternally forth from him, solely because he knows himself as the ground of his own outgoing into this universe, in which he hypostatizes himself as Logos. When we say that God knows himself as Son, we say, God knows himself as the one who from eternity proceeded forth from his own fatherly ground, he knows himself as the *deuteros theos*, who objectively reveals the fulness wrapped up in the Father. Without the Son, the Father could not say to himself *I;* for the form of the Ego, without an objective something different from the Ego (a non-Ego, a Thou) in relation to which it can grasp itself as Ego, is inconceivable. What the outward world, what nature, what other persons are for us, to wit, the condition of our own self-consciousness, the Son and the objective world which arises before the Father in and through (*dia*) the Son are for the Father,—to wit, the condition of his own identity.

But, if the **inner** revelation were terminated in the Son, God would be manifest to himself merely according to the necessity of his nature and thought, **not** according to the *freedom* of his will. It would be merely in intellectual contemplation that God would stand related to the heavenly world, which, by a necessity of nature, proceeds forth from him in the birth of the Son; but he would not stand to it in the relation of a free formative cause. It is only because the relation of God to his world is that of a freely *working*, moulding, creating agent, as well as that of a natural logical necessity, that he constitutes himself its *Lord*. If, then, the "birth" of the Son out of the essence of the Father denotes the momentum of necessity, the "procession" of the Holy Spirit from the Father and the Son denotes the momentum of freedom in the inner revelation. The Spirit proceeds from the Father and the Son, as the *third* hypostasis, whose work it is to transform and glorify the necessary subject of thought into the free act of the will, and to 'mould the eternal kingdom of ideas into a kingdom of inner creations of free conceptions. The fatherly *plērōma* which is revealed in the Son as a kingdom of ideas, of a necessity proceeding out of the depths of his being, is glorified by the free artistic action of the Spirit into an inner kingdom of glory (*doxa*), in which the eternal possibilities are present before the face of God as magical realities, as a heavenly host of **visions, of** plastic architypes, for a revelation *ad extra*, to which they desire, as it were, to be sent forth. Only on the basis of such a free procession of the Spirit, which is at the same time a free retrocession, can the relation between the Father and the Son be one of love. In the Spirit alone is the relation of God to himself and his inner world, not merely a metaphysical relation, a relation of natural necessity, but a free, an ethical relation. But, notwithstanding that the Spirit is a distinct hypostasis, perfecting, completing momentum in the Godhead, the entire Trinity must also be designated Spirit. "God is a Spirit," says Christ; and this is the comprehensive designation of the Trinitarian God.

There are, therefore, three eternal acts of consciousness; and the entire divine Ego is in each of these three acts. Each hypostasis has being solely through the other two. Here there is no temporal first or **last.** The entire Trinity stands in one present Now, three eternal flames in the one light.— *Christian Dogmatics*, § 56 (*Urwick's Translation*).[*]

Many, **however, who** are apprehensive of " wading in pursuit of abstractions **too** far out from *terra-firma* concretions for

---

[*] But see Dr. Matthew Arnold's *God and the Bible*, chap. ii., "The God of Metaphysics." Also *Letters to a Trinitarian*, by George Bush. Also *Letters of B. F. Barrett to Rev. H. W. Beecher on the Divine Trinity*. Also *Discussion of the Doctrine of the Trinity*, by Luther Lee and Samuel J. May.

logical safety," fain content themselves with the reflection of H. B. Thoreau: —

> I had but few companions on the shore;
> They scorn the strand who sail upon the sea;
> Yet oft I think the ocean they've sailed o'er
> Is deeper known upon the strand to me.
>
> The middle sea contains no crimson dulse,
> Its deeper waves cast up no pearls to view;
> Along the shore my hand is on its pulse,
> And I converse with many a shipwrecked crew.

All of which suggests the utterance of Thoreau's friend, who also would "see the natural before the supernatural": —

Above all men do I bow myself before that august personage, Jesus of Nazareth, who seems to have had the strength of man and the softness of woman,— man's mighty, wide, grasping, reasoning, calculating, and poetic mind; and woman's conscience, woman's heart, and woman's faith in God. He is my best historic ideal of human greatness; not without errors nor.... — *Theodore Parker.*

And also that of another "Concord philosopher": —

Always put the best interpretation on a tenet. Why not on Christianity, wholesome, sweet, and poetic? It is the record of a pure and holy soul, humble, absolutely disinterested, a truth-speaker, and bent on serving, teaching, and uplifting men. Christianity taught the capacity, the element, to love the All-perfect without a stingy bargain for personal happiness. It taught that to love him was happiness,— to love him in others' virtues. An era in human history is the life of Jesus; and the immense influence for g od leaves all the perversion and superstition almost harmless. Mankind have been subdued to the acceptance of his doctrine, and cannot spare the benefit of so pure a servant of truth and love. Of course, a hero so attractive to the hearts of millions drew the hypocrite and the ambitious into his train, and they used his name to falsify his history and undo his work.— *Ralph Waldo Emerson*, (*Unitarian Review* January, 1880).

After all such conflict of opinion, how sweetly soothing are Emerson's wise words! Not always is the yearning vain: —

> How might her reconciling notes
> Have symphonized earth's din,
> And turned life's outward dissonance
> To harmony within.
>
> *Luella Clark.*

Chapter XI.

DEIFICATION.

What Threefold Classification of Men's Views of God and the Expression of Jesus, "Our Father"?

(1) THE anthropomorphic, or extreme personal; (2) the atheistic, or extreme impersonal; (3) the empiric or ideal. Dr. Hedge, in his chapter on "The Natural History of Theism," after tracing the idea of God in the way of natural religion through the several stages of fetichism, astrolatry, impersonation of physical forces, and theanthropism,— God as terrestrial creature, God as celestial radiance, God as personified elemental power, and God as man,— adds:—

God reveals himself not by sensible apparition, **but** by his witness in the soul. That testimony first heard by elect individuals,— meditative men, like Abraham, Zoroaster, Moses, Jesus,— and declared by them, becomes what we call a "revelation." or divine dispensation of religion. Monotheism comes not by the way of natural religion, seeking God without and fusing its many gods into one, but by reflection, seeking God within; and the difference between natural and revealed religion consists in this, that in the former the religious sentiment is turned outward, in the latter inward. . . . It finds in **the** dictates of the moral sense, in imperative warnings and obligations, in the consciousness of spiritual wants and aspirations, a God unknown to natural religion,— a God who is not mere power and intelligence and commanding will, but goodness, holiness, truth, love. These constitute the God of moral intuition,— a God self-evident and one in the double sense of onliness and unity. The very idea of such a God excludes multitude. There can be but one absolute Good. Hence, revealed religion is necessarily monotheistic. . . . Inward and ever inward is the way to God.— *Dr. F. H. Hedge* (*Ways of the Spirit*, p. 140).

Dr. Matthew Arnold traces the **word** "God" back to a root signifying "brilliance." His favorite designation is "the power not ourselves that works for righteousness." * M. D. Conway

---

* *God and the Bible, passim.*

would call the power "God, as best expressing that sacred influence which is the main fact of our inward life." Every experience must seek its expression. As a term for the ideal elements within and without us which denote their reality, the word "God" appears to him the least daring, the least descriptive, while popularly it suggests the Good. It must become an increasingly impersonal expression by the very necessity of being detached from the several personified patron deities of the various races, "Vishnu," "Jehovah," "Jupiter," "Allah," etc.

When the great Religion of Man has come, this term will necessarily stand — as it stands now in the pages of Goethe, Carlyle, Emerson, and many poets — for the indefinable but majestic supremacy of perfect and eternal principles; for their unity, universality, and harmony; for their superlative glory in all things fair and grand, and the passionate love and longing they awaken in the breast of man....

It is anthropomorphic to say, "God loves," for to love is the act of man: not so to say, "God is Love," for we can have no idea of a man who is love. To say, "God knows" is anthropomorphic: not so to say, "God is Wisdom." When Jesus said, "God is a Spirit,"— in his own sense of a viewless influence, whose effect we feel as we do the breath of the wind, while we cannot tell whence it cometh or whither it goeth,— he raised the mind above every anthropomorphic conception to the pure elemental realm of ideal and moral existence.... Nor do I worship the Unknown. What I do worship is my ideal as perfect as I can make it. Love, reason, right, beauty, are blended and consummate in it. In what mode or modes these subsist in the universe none can know, but it is not my ignorance that I worship: it is the ideal which I do know, though knowing not the metaphysics of it....

But is all this real? Is there in the universe any reason apart from the brain of man, or any principle of love beyond that manifested in the human heart? For myself, I cannot doubt that there are in nature these supreme elements which make and mould us rather than we them. There is in nature an evolutional order, a geometry, a mathematical uniformity, by which are built the worlds and the cells of bees, and which make possible the sciences of man. Upon man, the universal laws are compulsory.... Reason is a principle in nature which reaches consciousness in man, but it does not grow into existence through man; for man's growth is an ascension to an inward harmony with it, in place of that coercion by it which, in his lower condition, he shares with plant and animal.

Love exists in nature. It is the principle of progress, and to believe in progress is to believe in God. Recognizing as highest within us the attraction of the best, and individual growth as its expression, we look forth upon the world, and discern a like law operative there. Life has journeyed from the zoöphyte to Shakspere. Art has journeyed from a naked savage swimming across his river on a log to a civilized man crossing the ocean in a floating palace; from the scrawled picture letter to the cartoon of Raphael. Humanity has journeyed from the normal war of nomadic savages to courts of law, arbitration, and social comity. Honesty has become the best policy. The peaceful more and more inherit the earth: animal and human ferocities pass away, gentleness and benefit survive and increase. Evermore a progress toward the better! Why is this movement not backward? Why has there not been a steady survival of the morally unfittest? Why should there not have gone on a steady growth of the slave-trade, a multiplication of slaves, an advance in Russia to double the extent of that serfdom which has been abolished? Why has not dishonesty become the best policy? Why this phenomenon of a totality ever moving onward, not backward, even the decays of this or that fragmentary and partial civilization followed invariably by a finer combination, and so contributing to swell the general impulse upward?

Some theological theists appear to smile at Mr. Matthew Arnold's reverential homage to a "stream of tendency": nevertheless, it is in that ark that Faith is to float past the deluge of scepticism and denial. For that stream of tendency is a stream of love; and it must needs pass through mysteries of iniquity, pain, seeming chaos. As we stand on its banks, we look forth and see the cyclone in India, with its two hundred thousand mortals cut down in a moment, as it were, mere weeds under a scythe. What recourse has Faith but to believe the Ages against the Hour, as they attest the power that makes for righteousness, abandoning the whole problem of the *Why* which a discredited metaphysic has foisted upon the religious sentiment? . . . We cannot comprehend the mystery of love and thought in our own nature. No Franklin has yet snatched from the air that finer flame which spiritually awakens and renews the universe. To try to analyze ourselves, to find a soul, is like digging into a stone to discover its electricity. We feel — and why should feeling be denied its weight? — that these onward-drawing forces, these longings for a completer life, are the profoundest realities of our existence, and correspond to their like reality in the universe.

There is an influence beneath which mankind must bend, as trees beneath the invisible wind. Sacred ideals arise and overawe our lower nature. We cannot, we will not, endure the thought that the intimations of our immortality mean nothing, because they mean not the egotism of the vulgar, and that the promise of our heart is false. While we muse, the fire burns. Emotions ascend, and life struggles to ascend with them. From the fair Kosmos whence we have derived a life — how strange, undreamable! — that is real, equally have we derived ideals and cravings that seek their satisfaction in things invisible, — in moral beauty, self-forgetting love, the harmony of the inward and outer worlds; and even as a seed in its sod may feel the warm, quickening touch of the sun it has never seen, so amid the darkness of the earth the heart may feel stirring within the mystical attraction whose nature it cannot dream, whose sweetness seems to promise a far-off flowering into joy.—*Moncure D. Conway* (*Idols and Ideals*, p. 135, ff.).

This well-enunciated recognition of the existence yet indefinability of God, especially the reference to Goethe, will recall the familiar passage in *Faust*:—

> Who dare express Him?
> And who profess him,
> Saying: I believe in him!
> Who, feeling, seeing,
> Deny his being,
> Saying: I believe him not!
> The All-enfolding,
> The All-upholding,
> Folds and upholds he not
> Thee, me, himself?
> Arches not there the sky above us?
> Lies not beneath us firm the earth?
> And rise not on us shining
> Friendly the everlasting stars?
>
> Look I not eye to eye on thee,
> And feel'st not, thronging
> To head and heart, the force,
> Still weaving its eternal secret,
> Invisible, visible, round thy life?
> Vast as it is, fill with that force thy heart,
> And when thou in the feeling wholly blessed art,
> Call it then what thou wilt,—
> Call it Bliss! Heart! Love! God!
> I have no name to give it!
> Feeling is all in all:
> The name is sound and smoke,
> Obscuring Heaven's clear glow.
>
> *Goethe* (*Faust*, J. Bayard Taylor's translation, p. 221).

Also his Proem to "Gott und Welt":—

> To Him who from eternity, self-stirred,
> Himself hath made by his creative word;
> To him, supreme, who causeth faith to be,
> Trust, hope, love, power, and endless energy;
> To him, who, seek to name him as we will,
> Unknown, within himself abideth still!
>
> Strain eye and ear, till sight of sense be dim,
> Thou'lt find but faint similitudes of him:
> Yea, and thy spirit in her flight of flame
> Still strives to gauge the symbol and the name:
> Charmed and compelled, thou climb'st from height to height,
> And round thy path the world shines wondrous bright,
> Time, space, and size, and distance cease to be,
> And every step is fresh infinity.
>
> What were the God who sat outside to scan
> The sphere that 'neath his finger circling ran?
> God dwells within, and moves the world, and moulds,
> Himself and nature in one form enfolds;
> Thus, all that lives in him, and breathes, and is,
> Shall ne'er his puissance, ne'er his spirit miss.

> The soul of man, too, is a universe:
> Whence follows it that race with race **concurs**
> In framing all it knows of good and true,
> God,— yea, its *own* God,— and with homage due:
> Surrenders to his sway both earth and heaven,
> Fears him, and loves where place for love is given.
> *Translated by J. A. S., in the Spectator*, Sept. 24, 1870.

And the like thought has lately found other good expression:

Absolute fulness and perfection of being, including of course and especially moral perfection, as the ground of the existence of this universe of which we are a part, is a postulate of our whole nature, intellectual, moral, emotional, affectional. That or nothing. Imperfection utterly fails of satisfying our thought. And, moreover, as we dwell on that thought, it is revealed to our deepest contemplation that the absolute perfection of being is love. Love, free from every element of human weakness,— wise, holy, righteous, ever expressing itself in the promotion of the highest good that spiritual beings can receive, that is, moral good, ever strictly holding all moral beings to that highest end of their existence, and never withholding from them any discipline necessary to lead them into it,— such love, inhabiting eternity and immensity, and wielding all the forces of nature, fills our conception of absolute being. In the realm of spirit, it is as impossible to set aside that idea as in the physical realm to get rid of the infinity of space and duration. That intense reality is God.— *Cazneau Palfrey (Christian Register*, Dec. 29, 1881).

The same idea has manifold expression in all hymnology. Some illustrations hereof, with views concerning God as parent, etc., will be presented in the chapters on "Christ's Precepts on Piety, Devotion, and Prayer." For the present suffice the never out-worn quotation from Pope's "Universal Prayer":—

> Father of all, in every age,
>   In every clime adored,
> By saint, by savage, or by sage,
>   Jehovah, Jove, or Lord!
> Thou great First Cause, least understood,
>   Who all my sense confined,
> To know but this,— that thou art **good**,
>   And that myself am blind. . . .
> To thee, whose temple is all space,
>   Whose altar earth, sea, skies,
> One chorus let all beings raise,
>   All nature's incense rise!

As to what proof of the existence of God is most relied upon by modern metaphysicians, perhaps J. D. Morell has given the most concisely comprehensive answer, including the argument from design, which some, considering the existence of pain, etc., think would prove two deities rather than one:—

Of all the evidences, man is himself a living embodiment If you want the argument from *design*, then you see in the human form the most perfect of all known organization. If you want the argument from *being*, then man in his conscious dependence has the clearest conviction of that independent and absolute *One* on which his own being reposes. If you want the argument from *reason* and *morals*, then the human mind is the only known repository of both. Man is, in fact, a microcosm,— a universe in himself; and whatever proof the whole universe affords is involved in principle in man himself. With the *image* of God before us, who can doubt of the divine type? — *Hist. and Crit. View Spec. Philos. of Europe Nineteenth Cent.*, p. 740.

Victor Cousin's reference to God as a Trinity, being at the same time God, Nature, and Humanity, is, if not a "mixed metaphor," an allegorical view from which many dissent, lest familiarity breed contempt; preferring, while Thomas Campbell's line is true,—

'Tis distance lends enchantment to the view,

not to think that

God is the green in every blade,
The health in every boy and maid;
In yonder sunrise flag he blooms
Above a nation's well-earned tombs;
That empty sleeve his arm contains;
That blushing scar his anger drains;
That flaunting cheek beneath the lamp
  He hoists for succor from a heart
Where love maintains a wasted camp
  Till love arrives to take its part;
That bloodless face against the pane
  Goes whitening all the murky street
With God's own dread, lest hunger gain
  Upon his love's woe-burdened feet.   *John Weiss.*

I myself am an irradiated manifestation of the Supreme Being. There is only one Deity: he is the Great Soul. He is called the Sun, for he is the Soul of all Beings.— *Oldest of the Vedas* (1500 B.C.).

God appears in the best thought, in the truest speech, in the sincerest action. Through his pure Spirit, he giveth health, prosperity, devotion, and eternity to the universe. He is the Father of all Truth.— *Zoroaster* (*Zend-Avesta*).

He is the Primeval Father, the Immortal Virgin, the Life, the Cause, the Energy of all things.— *Orpheus* (perhaps contemporary with Abraham).

Heaven and earth take refuge with thee, as a child with its mother. — *The Vedas* (800 B.C.).

The reason which can be reasoned is not the Eternal Reason. ... Man takes his law from the earth; earth takes its law from heaven; heaven takes its law from reason; reason takes its law from within itself. Use the light to guide you home to its own brightness.— *Lao-tze* (604 B.C.).

I appeared unto Abraham, Isaac, and Jacob, by the name God Almighty; but by my name Jehovah* was I not known to them.— *Exodus* vi., 3.

There is One Universal Soul diffused through all things; eternal, invisible, unchangeable; in essence like truth, in substance resembling light; not to be represented by any image, to be comprehended only by the mind; not as some conjecture, exterior to the world, but in himself entire, pervading the universal sphere.— *Pythagoras.*

Learn from the things which are produced to infer the existence of an Invisible Power and to reverence the Divinity.— *Socrates.*

As nothing is like the sun except through solar influences, so nothing can resemble the First Good except by an emanation of his divine light into the soul.— *Plato.*

There is One Supreme Intelligence, who acts with order, proportion, and design, the Source of all that is good and just.— *Aristotle.*

Heaven penetrates to the depths of all hearts as daybreak illumines the darkest room.— *Confucius.*

I do not blame the variety of representations: only let men understand there is but one Divine Nature.— *Maximus Tyrius*

I am pervaded by Thee. Thou containest me. Thou art scriptures and laws, planets and suns, the formed and the formless. Those who possess knowledge and whose minds are pure see the whole world as the form of thy wisdom.— *The Purana.*

There is but one religion, under many forms, whose essential creed is the Fatherhood of God and the Brotherhood of Man; disguised by corruptions, symbolized by mythologies, ennobled by virtues, degraded by vices, but still the same. To say that different races worship different gods is like saying that they are warmed by different suns.— *Thomas W. Higginson.*

There remains one question: Is the anthropomorphic tendency predicable of Jesus?

I am obliged to think that in the fatherly tenderness of the God of Jesus we have simply a reflection of the tenderness of his own heart. He was not a student. He was not a reasoner. With him, feeling was all in all. He was not such an egotist as to suppose that his own love would outstrip the love of Heaven. Less from observation of the fact than because the sunshine of his own affection fell equally upon the evil and the good, the rain of his own pitying tears equally upon the just and the unjust, he made bold to predicate these attributes of the Eternal.— *John White Chadwick (The Man Jesus,* p. 124).

---

*The Am, Was, and Shall-be.

Chapter XII.

PREMONITION.

How does John the Baptist rank in the Order of Prophets and of Martyrs?

AT intervals along down the centuries from Samuel to Malachi there had appeared individuals of a distinctively marked order. Generally, each would suddenly come, a mature man, nobody knew from whence. Each by his holy mien, his austere life, his pure patriotism, his inspired zeal, his inspiring rhapsodies in behalf of righteousness, reverence, and mercy, and especially by his audacious forecasting of the sure consequences of injustice, arrogance, cruelty, sensualism, and idolatry, would at once arrest, attract, and irresistibly overawe the multitude. John the Baptist revived the function of the prophet. It had been recorded* that a prophet like Moses should be raised up. No one had come after Moses that had made so deep an impression as Elijah. Malachi had distinctly announced a reappearance of this prophet. The three or four centuries following Malachi were clouded with calamities to the nation; and, when John appeared, everybody was straining in expectance of a deliverer.

John came. He gazed with surprise and loathing on the selfishness, corruption, and narrowness of the Jewish leaders; retired aloof to

A lodge in some vast wilderness;

meditated long and intensely; "grew" physically, mentally, and religiously; "waxed strong in spirit"; † resolutely dedicated himself to the desperate, single-handed struggle of reform; had the courage to wait no longer for a prophet who had been dead a thousand years to come to earth again, to seize the work from Elijah's hand, with the fiat to his own soul, "*I* will do it!" And, anon, he walked forth with the battle-cry, "Repent! The

---

* Deut. xviii., 15.   † Luke i., 80.

Messianic kingdom *must* come now and here! Repent, ye proud and wicked, or be consumed like stubble, when 'the day cometh that shall burn as an oven'!"*

If we ascribe the later Jewish tinge in John's conception of God to the influence of his age, and set aside the purely menacing character of his language as due to his special conception of his mission, then the burden of his preaching perfectly agrees with that of all the other prophets. It is a new variation upon the old theme familiar to every one of them without exception: "Amend your ways, for Yahveh's justice sends all these disasters to chastise you, nor will it suffer him to do to you according to his covenant; but, if you repent, he will comfort you with such bliss and glory as has never yet entered into the heart of man to conceive.". . . In that which constituted the very essence of the prophetic character, the irresistible impulse to stand up before the people, the hallowed inspiration to speak to them in the name of God, and, above all, the unshaken hope that a glorious morrow would with infallible certainty dissipate the gloom and darkness of to-day,—in all this John might bear comparison with Jeremiah and Micah themselves.— *Dr. I. Hooykaas (The Bible for Learners*, vol. iii., p. 103).

John feared nothing, and spared no impenitent. To one who among wild beasts of the desert had laid down his head under no canopy but the sky, and with no defence but the to him assured providence of the Most High, a scowling Pharisee, a mocking Sadducee, a fawning publican, a rough soldier, or even a riotous mob, was only a jolly sight. Around a man who can despise accommodations, deal with nature in ancient simplicity and independence, and move among social and religious institutions like a traveller from another world, free to judge, to censure or approve, as having himself nothing at stake,—around such a man (as an English preacher long ago remarked †) "there is a moral grandeur and authority, to which none but the narrowest and most bigoted minds will refuse a certain awe and reverence. And when such a personage assumes to himself divine commission, and publishes new truth with divine authority, and rebukes all wickedness and scorns all consequences, he takes, by the natural right of the wiser, the bolder, and the better man, a high place above those who feel themselves enslaved and enshackled by customs which they despise." Three centuries before John came had Aristotle remarked that "there is no distinguished genius altogether exempt from some infusion of madness."

That such was the character of John, the testimony of Josephus

---
* Mal. iv., 1.   † Edward Irving.

and the four Gospels is most explicit. To the more arrogant and self-orthodox Pharisees that came to him, no doubt he thundered forth: "What are *you* here for? You! of a set that has not germinated a decent square new idea for centuries! You! who hope to escape damnation because you are a coterie descended from Abraham! Why, I tell you children of Abraham could be made out of the multitudinous pebbles of this river-bank! Slimy vipers! before you ask baptism of me, overcome your stony-heartedness, your sneaking, wolfish ravenousness! Be generous and merciful! When you shall have shown by your lives that your application for this emblem means business, means work,— the work of purification therein symbolized,— come, and welcome! Until then, begone!"

Not even the royal purple could overawe him. His denunciation of the corruption of the court of Herod Antipas, the tetrarch, resulted as might be expected. The prophet was imprisoned in the castle of Machærus, on the east side of the Dead Sea, and finally assassinated. Well did he win the title,— not in its vulgar acceptation of supernatural foreteller, but in the lofty and more philosophical sense of prophet-martyr!

But there has been a further suggestion in the premises: —

Herodias's first husband was her uncle Herod, a son of Mariamne, whom his father, Herod the Great, had disinherited. Desiring a royal husband, she forsook Herod for her uncle Antipas, who had wearied of his Arabian wife. It is not likely, however, that this dramatic situation, sure to attract an evangelist, had anything to do with John's imprisonment. But Antipas felt the waves of popular enthusiasm beating against the bases of his throne; his recollection was still vivid of the insurrection of Judas the Gaulonite, and he could not be expected to distinguish between the spirit of Judas and that of John. Nor is it unlikely that the movement of John was rapidly assuming a political character. Such was the tendency of every Messianic movement.— *John W. Chadwick* (*The Man Jesus*, p. 115).

Chapter XIII.

RENUNCIATION.

Did John the Baptist belong to any Secret Order whose Rites would suggest to him the Ordinance of Baptism, and What the Possible Relation of Jesus thereto?

PROBABLY each was at least acquainted with the Essenes, a sect of Jewish monks who were very scrupulous in the observance of whatever ceremonies the law prescribed in type of personal purity. To avoid contamination and turmoil, these communists had withdrawn to the neighborhood of the Dead Sea, where at that time their colonies or hamlets were quite numerous,— perhaps they numbered four thousand souls. Bee-tending was their favorite occupation. They exacted a novitiate of three years, a solemn oath, and an iron discipline. They had eight degrees. They were unmarried, abstained from the use of meat and wine, partook of a common meal, and devoted themselves to pious reflections and speculations as to the future, prominent in which, no doubt, was the Messianic expectation. Just how far the intercourse of either John or Jesus with this sect extended cannot now be determined: if never novices thereof, they certainly, as to the "pith of the principles" relating to personal purity of life, were very good "outside-insiders."

And that, when the predicted Jahveh [*] should come, he might find a band set apart to him, what better initiative step, what more appropriately impressive rite, than baptism? Would not the ordinance at once commend itself to the favor of the visitor from Nazareth, who, no less than John, was casting about for every available help toward effecting the moral and religious redemption of his people? He might not approve of some of John's ways,—some proceedings better calculated incipiently to arouse reform than to render it permanent; but his own deep and holy inspiration, welling from the same source as that of the puritan prophet of the desert, would tend to flow in a

---

[*] Mal. iii., 1.

common channel therewith, and prompt the visitor to second whatever instrumentality might make for the establishment and maintenance of peace and brotherhood in the human family.

The evidence is conflicting whether the two reformers were cousins. Between kindred spirits, no previous acquaintance is necessary for each to recognize each. Whenever Jesus first approached the prophet — whether on the occasion of the baptism or previously — there was *

> A glance, a soul revealed by eye to eye,
> A thrill, a voiceless challenge and reply.

There was no hesitation: both were about their Father's business, and, as Milton says,

> Zeal and duty are not slow,
> But on occasion's forelock watchful wait.

"Enthusiasts," says Washington Irving, "soon understand each other." There were no doubt subsequent interviews,† and other Hebrew patriots than themselves ‡ felt to exclaim:—

> A world of blessings on my soul,
> If sympathy of love unite our thoughts.

And so also "Gentiles."

To be influenced by a passion for the same pursuits, and to have similar dislikes, is the rational groundwork of lasting friendship.— *Sallust.*

> No social care the gracious lord disdains;
> Love prompts to love, and reverence reverence gains. *Lucan.*

Even if there was no kinship of blood, would it be anything strange if, ere the lapse of half a century, fond legend should link together the family circles of the two soul kinsmen, and glorify the births of both by angel ushers? Or strange if the same tender afterthought should fuse — or confuse — the metaphors of the Mightier One than John, the Winnowing Husbandman, the Stern Judge, the Coming Baptizer, the Wielder of the Axe, into signifying another than Jahveh himself,§ focus them upon the grand individuality of Jesus? Or should even go to the length of such "a violent exegetical proceeding " ‖ as to concentrate in one personage Daniel's Son of Man coming with the clouds of heaven,¶ the first Isaiah's Branch out of the root of Jesse, who should smite the earth with the rod of his

---

* Varying Willis' "The world is full of meetings such as this."
† John i., 29, 35.   ‡ John i., 37.
§ See *The Bible for Learners*, vol. iii., p. 110.
‖ Dr. Matthew Arnold.   ¶ Dan. vii., 13.

mouth, slay the wicked with his breath, and reign in glory, peace, and righteousness,* the second Isaiah's meek and afflicted Servant of God, charged with a precious message of a golden future,† the Lamb of the passover and temple service,‡ and the Holy One of Israel, the Redeemer,§ who for these prophets was the Eternal himself, and then to call the resulting combination the Messiah,—and Jesus this Messiah? Or, in fine, that the lofty rapture of one Oriental mind should kindle that of a second, and this that of a third, until the rhapsodies of the whole procession would, when viewed from any other stand-point than their own, constantly incur peril of being utterly misunderstood?

Yet while it was natural that John the prophesier had an intuition of Jesus, the prophesied comer, and while they were both young men of pre-eminently moral and religious motives, a radical difference remains to be noted. The spirit of John was fed from the past by the ancient sages of Israel, that of Jesus from his own pure consciousness of the Highest within him. Consequently, while John was austere and narrow, the insight of Jesus was unfathomably deeper, his outlook a world more extensive, and his aim infinitely more lofty. Each of the two, in the then existing condition of things, clearly saw a coming judgment,—a kingdom of God,—and proclaimed it. But it was not in the temperament of John to go far enough to see any other salvation from the impending national catastrophe than a renewed and thorough conformity, on the part of the people, to the old Hebrew standard of righteousness. To the clearer discernment of Jesus, "the approaching revolution was to result in the establishment, upon the old order, of a new and grander order of things." ‖

---

*Isaiah xi., 1, 4.
† Isaiah liii., 4. Ewald denotes the author of Isaiah ... as the "Great Unnamed One" (*Life of Jesus Christ*, Glover's translation, p. 28).
‡ Exodus xii., 3.
§ Isaiah xliii., 14; lix., 19, 20; Jer. l., 4.
‖ Dr. W. H. Furness.

CHAPTER XIV.

INITIATION.

What Two Views as to the Phenomena at the Baptism of Jesus?

(1) THAT there was a supernatural opening of the heavens, a literal "Dove" and "Voice." (2) That, as to the alleged prodigies, the accounts are mere accretions of oral tradition upon some casual incident of a flying dove or of light on the water; possibly some suggestion to the Ebionite mind from Isaiah's words, "The melting fire burneth, and causeth the waters to boil."

The Gospel of the Hebrews has it: "He saw the spirit in the form of a dove come down and enter into him.... And immediately the place about them was lightened by a great fire. And when John (who had not seen the dove or heard the voice, which were for Jesus alone) perceived the fire he said to Jesus, Who art thou, Lord? And again a voice from heaven said to him, This is my beloved Son, in whom I am well pleased. Then John fell down on his face before him, and said, I pray thee, Lord, do thou baptize me! But Jesus restrained him, saying, Let it be, for thus must all that has been prophesied of me be fulfilled."*

In this connection, Prof. Drummond remarks † that Justin quotes the voice from heaven at the baptism in this form: "Thou art my Son: this day have I begotten thee." "This day have I begotten thee" is also in the Ebionite Gospel; but there it is awkwardly appended to a second saying, thus: "Thou art my beloved Son. In thee was I well pleased; and again this day have I begotten thee." So that the passage is quite different from Justin's, and has the appearance of being

---

* As to the threefold voice from heaven, and the date of the Greek and Aramaic fragments of the Gospel of the Hebrews, see a summary of the views of Lipsius, Holtzmann, Kirchofer, and other Biblical scholars, in Prof. Ezra Abbot's *Authorship of the Fourth Gospel*, p. 98,—incidental to the discussion of Justin Martyr's use, etc., already referred to (*ante*, chap. iv.).

† *Theological Review*, October, 1875.

a later patchwork. Justin's form of quotation is still the reading of the Codex Bezae in Luke, and according to Augustine was found in good manuscripts, though it is said not to be in the older ones. Justin also says that, when Jesus *went down upon* the water, a fire was kindled in the Jordan. The Ebionite Gospel relates that, when Jesus *came up from* the water, immediately a great light shone round the place. The author of the anonymous *Liber de Rebaptismate* says that this event was related in an heretical work entitled *Pauli Prædicatio*, and that it was not found in any Gospel. This, of course, may refer only to the canonical Gospels.

As to the remaining phenomenon alleged, it has been remarked that the dove, as the first voice of spring, symbolized renovation, whether sent out from the ark to hover over a baptized world, or descending on a baptized Christ, or appearing still to the Hindu devotee emerging from the stream of immortality which the god Siva created at Amlah-Naut, where the pilgrim meets that deity in the form of a dove, in whose flight an omen is discovered.

Chapter XV.

TEMPTATION.

What are the Eight Principal Views concerning the Temptation of Jesus, and in What Two Convenient Categories? (And herein) What is the Effect of Success and of Defeat in the Formation of Individual Character?

THOSE assuming and those not assuming the existence of a person, visible or invisible, who, though not having an attribute supplanting God's omnipresence, is so ubiquitous as to pass or send messengers from one human being to another to incite to misdoing, the most consequential of which incitements occurs on the occasion of a young man's determining his life career.

In the first category are two theories: (1) That the tempting agency was a visible, supernatural person, and that the narrative is literally true in every respect. (2) That it is a description in Oriental dramatic language of an actual temptation through evil thoughts which did not voluntarily arise in the mind of Jesus, but were suggested by an invisible devil.

In the second category are six theories: (1) That the event was not a supernatural one, the transportation to the temple being simply in a figurative sense; namely, that the tempter was a wicked man by whom Jesus was led to Mount Zion, where the glory of a temporal ruler was described to him and plots against the Romans suggested. (2) That it is a dream or vision, or other abnormal mental operation. Prof. J. R. Seeley says, "What is called Christ's temptation is the excitement of his mind which was caused by the nascent consciousness of supernatural power."* (3) That it is a myth. (4) That it is a parable, wherein Jesus, to get one of the characters, utilized the mental furniture bequeathed to his people from Babylon, and, to get the other, made himself the central figure, and whereby he taught his disciples how it is temptations assail us all, and how we are to resist them. (5) That it was an in-

---

* *Ecce Homo*, p. 12 [18].

ward experience of Jesus, in which the different forms of temptation mentioned came to his mind unsuggested by any one, and that it was related by him to his disciples in the dramatic form in which we have it in the First and Third Gospels. (6) That it is such experience account, expanded by the accretions of oral tradition into the proportions of the "Matthew" and "Luke" records thereof. In the last case, the account has been compared to the Buddhist account of Gautama's conflict under the bow-tree. Neander and Ewald treat the temptation of Jesus as threefold: (1) to work miracles for his own comfort or advantage; (2) to work them to prove himself the Christ; (3) to establish his Messianic kingdom by human means and devices of human expediency.*

Before more directly considering temptation and — what has been termed "the Method and Means of Jesus" — introspection and self-renunciation, it will be well here to note certain generally accepted aphorisms of eminent and more or less inspired thinkers concerning the wisdom of choosing a life of discipline, hardship, discomfort, beneficence, and possible obscurity, as against one of license, ease, luxury, selfishness, and possible renown.† As to the effect of desire and defeat on fortitude, expertness, and courage, abundant will be found the confirmation of Paul's declaration that tribulation works patience, experience, hope. The dubiousness, deviousness, demoralization of yesterday may bring determination, directness, and discipline to to-day; the paradox may hold that a step backward is a step forward.

> What I aspired to be,
> And was not, comforts me,

sings Robert Browning, in "Rabbi Ben Ezra." Life's promise is in life's failure. The soul's wealth is in its want. The very saddest thing the eye can see on earth,—a high and noble spirit swept back from the harbor of ease by the tumult of life's sea, driven from the chosen course by tides and storms that heed no supplication and stay for no prayers, and wrecked at last with all its vast freightage of hopes far from the peaceful port,—this turns to grandest eloquence of prophecy in the large musing of the same philosophic poet:—

> For thence — a paradox
> Which comforts while it mocks —
> Shall life succeed in that it seems to fail?

It was a wise resolution of the Hebrew singer, "I will lift up mine

---

* *Life of Jesus Christ* (Glover's translation), p. 158.
† The trite lesson of indulgence in alcoholic or narcotic stimulants impairing the will is said to have recently had conspicuous illustration in the death of an esteemed Southern statesman from "smoker's cancer."

eyes unto the hills, from whence cometh **my** help." Man's help must be sought from a contemplation of the unattained. He must refuse to believe himself beaten when he is cast down. He must refuse to despair in any abyss of evil or folly. **He** must cultivate a noble shame and a noble discontent. . . .

The Faust of the great drama, given into the hands **of the** mocking fiend, seemed lost beyond hope in the entanglements and illusions of sense. Guilty and heart-broken, he wandered through a world of weariness and shams. But he was too clear-sighted to be deceived into thinking the **sham** a reality, and too noble in aspiration **to** be satisfied with what was base. His soul, that never ceased to desire the good, outlived its trial; and when he stumbled, old and blind, through the gate of death, there was heard the chanting of angels, **who** said in their song : —

> The noble spirit now is free,
> And saved from evil scheming:
> Whoe'er aspires unweariedly
> Is not beyond redeeming.
> And, if he feels the grace of Love
> That from on High is given.
> The Blessed Hosts, that wait above,
> Shall welcome him to heaven.
>
> *W. H. Savage (Christian Register).*

Only he that *overcometh* can truly gain and advance. The impulses to a higher life come with renewed force as they are cherished and acted on. As we advance, the cords of a divine love draw us more steadily and firmly upward, and the ties which bind us to earthly objects and desires become weaker. As Dr. Holland truly says : —

> Heaven is not reached at a single bound;
> But we build the ladder by which we rise
> From the lowly earth to the vaulted skies,
> And we mount to its summit round by round.
>
> *Joseph H. Mansfield.*

The old theology regards man as being sent into this world as a place of probation: the new theology looks on life as a place of education. According to one, it is a court-house; according to the other, a school.— *Dr. J. F. Clarke (Sermon on the Installation Council's Examination of Dr. N. Smyth, Saturday Evening Gazette,* Oct. 28, 1882).

Nature fashions **no** creature without implanting in it the strength needful for its action and duration; least of all does she so neglect her masterpiece and darling, the poetic soul. Neither can we believe that it is in the power of *any* external circumstances utterly to ruin the mind of a man; nay, if proper wisdom be given, even so much as to affect its essential health and beauty. The sternest sum total of all worldly misfortunes is Death: nothing more *can* lie in the cup of human woe; yet many men, in all ages, have triumphed over Death, and led it captive; converting its physical victory for themselves into **a** seal and immortal consecration for all that their past life had achieved. What has been done may be done again; nay, it is but the degree and not the kind of such heroism that differs in different seasons; for without some portion of this spirit, not of boisterous daring, but of silent fearlessness, of self-denial in all its forms, no good man, in any scene or time, has ever attained to be good.—*Thomas Carlyle (Essay on Burns).*

Possession pampers the mind, privation trains and strengthens it.—*William Hazlitt.*

Calamity is man's true touchstone.—*Richard Fletcher.*

Afflictions clarify the soul.—*Francis Quarles.*

Experience is the extract of suffering.—*Arthur Helps.*

Sanctified afflictions are spiritual promotions.—*Matthew Henry.*

Afflictions are the medicine of the mind. If they are not toothsome, let it suffice that they are wholesome.—*Bp. J. P. K. Henshaw.*

All the clouds are angel faces, and their voices speak harmoniously of the everlasting chime.—*Lydia M. Child.*

When God makes the world too hot for his people to hold, they will let it go.—*William S. Powell.*

Let us learn upon earth those things which call us to heaven.—*St. Jerome.*

A good man fixes the root, and all else flows out of it. The root is filial piety, the fruit brotherly love.—*Confucius.*

Through danger safety comes; through trouble, rest.—*J. Marston.*

Adversity is the trial of principle. Without it, a man hardly knows whether he is honest or not.—*Fielding.*

We may measure our road to wisdom by the sorrows we have undergone.—*Earle Bulwer-Lytton.*

The more solitary, the more friendless, the more unsustained I am, the more I will respect and rely upon myself.—*Charlotte Brontë.*

Who hath not known ill-fortune never knew himself or his own virtue.—*David Mallet.*

Christianity is hard, but gainful and happy. The greatest labors that have answerable requitals are less than the least that have no regard.—*Bishop Joseph Hall.*

The life of a mere worldly man is like an African river that wastes itself by soaking into the desert sands.—*H. W. Beecher.*

Character is a perfectly educated will.—*Novalis.*

A vigorous mind is as necessarily accompanied with violent passions as a great fire with great heat.—*Edmund Burke.*

Shallow seas have no whirlpools: superficial men have no absorbing passion.—*Samuel Maunder.*

A wide, rich heaven hangs above you, but it hangs high; a wide, rough world is around you, and it lies very low.— *Donald G. Mitchell.*

Strength of character is not mere strength of feeling; it is the resolute restraint of strong feeling. It is unyielding resistance to whatever would disconcert us from without or unsettle us from within.— *Charles Dickens.*

Tie down a hero, and he feels the puncture of a pin: throw him into battle, and he is almost insensible to pain.—*John C. Calhoun.*

The frivolous work of polished idleness.—*Sir James Mackintosh.*

I cannot praise a fugitive and cloistered virtue unexercised and unbreathed, that never sallies out and sees her adversary, but slinks out of the race where that immortal garland is to be run for, not without dust and heat.—*John Milton.*

Massena was not himself until the battle began to go against him.— *Napoleon Bonaparte.*

The setting of a great hope is like the setting of the sun, the brightness of our life is gone: shadows of the evening fall behind us, and the world seems but a dim reflection itself, a broader shadow. We look forward into the coming lonely night, the soul withdraws itself, then the stars arise and the night is holy.—*Henry W. Longfellow.*

The passions act as winds to propel our vessel, our reason is the pilot that steers her. Without the winds she would not move, without the pilot she would be lost.— *Anon. (from the French).*

They asked Lucman, the fabulist, "From whom did you learn manners?" He answered, "From the unmannerly."— *Moslih-Eddin Saadi.*

The only equitable manner of judging the character of a man is to examine if there are personal calculations in his conduct: if there are not, we may blame his manner of judging, but we are not the less bound to esteem him.— *Baronne de Staël-Holstein.*

Surely, surely, the only true knowledge of our fellow-man is that which enables us to feel with him, which gives us a fine ear for the heart pulses that are beating under the mere clothes of circumstance and opinion.—*George Eliot.*

Our follies and errors are the soiled steps to the Grecian temple of our perfection.—*J. P. F. Richter.*

When we embark in the dangerous ship called Life, we must not, like Ulysses, be tied to the mast: we must know how to listen to the sirens and to brave their blandishments.— *Arsène Houssaye.*

That virtue which requires to be ever guarded is scarce worth the sentinel.— *Oliver Goldsmith.*

Even in evil, that dark cloud which hangs over the creation, we discern rays of light and hope, and gradually come to see in suffering and temptation proofs and instruments of the sublimest purposes of wisdom and love.— *Dr. W. E. Channing.*

What pains and tears the slightest steps of man's progress have cost! Every hair-breadth forward has been in the agony of some soul, and humanity has reached blessing after blessing of all its vast achievement of good with bleeding feet.— *Dr. C. A. Bartol.*

If we rightly estimate what we call good and evil, we shall find it lies much in comparison.— *John Locke.*

The great desiring heart of man, surging with one strong, sympathetic swell, even though it be to break on the beach of life and fall backward, leaving the sands as barren as before, has yet a meaning and a power in its restlessness with which I must deeply sympathize. — *Harriet B. Stowe.*

A liberal education is that which frees a man from himself. "Ye shall know the truth, and the truth shall make you free." No one is so much a slave as the man who is tied by his own appetites, ambitions, vanities, conceit.— *Dr. J. F. Clarke.*

> Stone walls do not a prison make,
> Nor iron bars a cage;
> Minds innocent and quiet take
> That for an hermitage;
> If I have freedom in my love,
> And in my soul am free,
> Angels alone that soar above
> Enjoy such liberty.
> — *Richard Lovelace.*

> Let but the sympathizing heart be spared,
> What sorrow seems not light, what peril is not dared?
> — *Mary Tighe.*

> A deep distress has humanized my soul.
> — *William Wordsworth.*

> As night to stars, woe lustre gives to man.
> — *Dr. Edward Young.*

> Alas! by some degree of woe
> We every bliss must gain;
> The heart can ne'er a transport know
> That never feels a pain.
> — *George, Lord Lyttleton.*

> The path of sorrow, and that path alone,
> Leads to the land where sorrow is unknown.
> — *William Cowper.*

Hold the hand that is hapless, and whisper, "They only the victory won Who have fought the good fight, and have vanquished the demon that tempts us within;
Who have held to their faith unseduced by the prize that the world holds on high;
Who have dared for a high cause to suffer, resist, fight,— if need be, to die."

Speak, history! who are life's victors? Unroll thy long annals, and say,—
Are they those whom the world called the victors, who won the success of a day?
The Martyrs, or Nero? The Spartans who fell at Thermopylæ's tryst,
Or the Persians and Xerxes? His judges, or Socrates? Pilate, or Christ?
William W. Story ("*Io Victis*," *Blackwood's Magazine*).

The best of men
That e'er wore earth about him was a sufferer;
A soft, meek, patient, humble, tranquil spirit,
The first true gentleman that ever breathed.
Thomas Dekker.

The good are better made by ill,
As odors crushed are sweeter still.
Samuel Rogers.

Love took up the harp of Life, and smote on all the chords with might;
Smote the chord of Self, that trembling, passed in music out of sight.
Alfred Tennyson.

The thousands that, uncheered by praise,
Have made one offering of their days;
For truth, for heaven, for freedom's sake,
Resigned the bitter cup to take;
And silently, in fearless faith,
Have bowed their noble souls to death.
Felicia D. Hemans.

The pious man,
In this bad world, when mists and couchant storms
Hide heaven's fine circlet, springs aloft in *faith*
Above the clouds that threat him, to the fields
Of ether, where the day is never veiled
With intervening vapors, and looks down
Serene upon the troublous sea, which hides
The earth's fair breast; that sea whose nether face
To grovelling mortals frowns and darkens all,
But on whose billowy back, from man concealed,
The glowing sunbeams play.
Henry Kirke White.

But all through life I see a cross,
Where sons of God yield up their breath;
There is no gain except by loss,
There is no life except by death.
There is no vision but by faith,
No glory but by bearing shame,
Nor justice but by taking blame;
And that Eternal Passion saith,
Be emptied of glory and right and name.
Olrig Grange.

So many great
Illustrious spirits have conversed with woe,
Have in her school been taught, as are enough
To consecrate distress, and make us
E'en wish the frown beyond the smile
Of fortune.
James Thomson.

Ah! languid hand, safe in some scented glove,
Drop that bright prayer-book; catch at rock and thorn;
Give alms of bread — give truer alms of love —
To other hands whose stains and scars you scorn!
Sarah M. Bryan Piatt.

There is a grandeur in the soul that dares
To live out all the life God lit within;
That battles with the passions hand to hand,
And wears no mail, and hides behind no shield; . .
And that with fearless foot and heaven-turned eyes
May stand upon a dizzy precipice,
High over the abyss of ruin and not fall.
Sara J. Clarke Lippincott.

I know the hand that is guiding me
  Through the shadow to the light,
And I know that all betiding me
  Is meted out aright;
I know that the thorny path I tread
  Is ruled by a golden line;
And I know that the darker life's tangled thread,
  The richer the deep design.
Anon. (British Evangelist).

I've found some wisdom in my quest
  That's richly worth retailing:
I've learned that, when one does his best,
  There's little harm in failing.
I may not reach what I pursue,
  Yet will I keep pursuing;
Nothing is vain that I can do,
  Since soul-growth comes of doing.
Charles G. Ames.

Ah! let us hope that to our praise
  Good God not only reckons
The moments when we tread his ways,
  But when the spirit beckons;
That some slight good is also wrought
  Beyond self-satisfaction,
When we are simply good in thought,
  Howe'er we fail in action.
James R. Lowell.

Who never ate his bread in sorrow,
  Who never spent the darksome hours
Weeping and watching for the morrow,
  He knows you not, ye unseen Powers.
Thomas Carlyle.

[A paraphrase of
  Wer nie sein Brod mit Thränen ass,
    Wer nicht die kummervollen Nächte
  Auf seinem Bette weinend sass
    Der kennt euch nicht, ihr himmlischen Mächte.
Goethe (Wilhelm Meister, Book II., chap. xiii.).]

How happy is he born or taught,
  Who serveth not another's will;
Whose armour is his honest thought,
  And simple truth his highest skill:
Whose passions not his masters are;
  Whose soul is still prepared for death;
Not tied unto the world with care
  Of prince's ear or vulgar breath:
Who God doth late and early pray
  More of his grace than goods to lend,
And walks with man from day to day,
  As with a brother and a friend.

TEMPTATION

> This man is freed from servile bands
> Of hope to rise, or fear to fall.
> Lord of himself, though not of lands,
> And having nothing, yet hath all.
>   *Sir Henry Wotton.* 1568–1639.

[A paraphrase of

> Non possidentem multa vocaveris
>   Recte beatum; rectius occupat
> Nomen beati, qui deorum
>   Muneribus sapienter uti,
> Duramque callet pauperium pati,
>   Pejusque leto flagitium timet;
> Non ille pro caris amicis
>   Aut patri perire.   *Horace* (*Odes IV.* 9). *Died* 9 *B.C.*]

> No specious, transient boon I bring:
>   Stern Truth alone thy faith can speed.
> The source whence all pure blessings spring
>   Is thy Creator. He decreed
> To sluggards no immortal deed.
> There's many a maze that goes amiss.
>   One straight and narrow path doth lead
> To heights of Glory and of Peace;
>   And Toil and Vigil guard the gates of Bliss.

Socrates ("*Arete,*" *in the Choice of Hercules in Xenophon's Memorabilia*). 470–400 B.C. *Paraphrase by B. F. B.*

It is better by a noble boldness to run the risk of being subject to the evils that we anticipate than to remain in cowardly listlessness for fear of what may happen.— *Herodotus.*

The heroic, disciplinary, probationary, testing phase of human experience thus particularly emphasized by Socrates and Herodotus has been recently well considered in a discourse by Dr. J. F. Clarke,— text, James i., 2: " Count it all joy when ye fall into divers temptations ":—

All that man does needs to be tested. "He that is first in his own cause seemeth just, but his neighbor cometh and searcheth him." Critics may be an evil, but they are a necessary evil. Even critics themselves need to be criticised. Who shall judge the judges? There comes after them all a much more awful critic, a judge whose decisions are infallible, subject to reversal in no higher court of appeal,— time, the avenger, the great critic of all human works. Time applies to all the deeds of man the test of God's laws and the nature of things. These condemn and acquit, punish and reward, strictly according to truth. In the long run, the good and the bad are both found out. This fire tries every man's work, burns the wood, hay, and stubble, and when its flame has ceased leaves the gold, silver, and marble standing in their permanent beauty, a joy forever. All the critics in the world cannot put down a good book, and all the puffs in all the magazines and newspapers cannot give to a poor one a permanent success. You may call a bad general a Napoleon a thousand times, but the terrible day of battle comes, and the fire tries his work.

The machine which will not work may be ever so ingenious, but it is a failure. The doctor who cannot cure his patients may have graduated with the highest honors and be covered over with decorations; the lawyer who cannot gain his cases, the minister who cannot interest his hearers, the architect whose houses are cold, damp, ill-arranged, the painter whose pictures do not give pleasure,— all popularity, all mutual admiration, cannot save them. This is the fire which tries every man's work. Does it do what it was made to do? that is the question. I have listened to old men talking together. They were successful men,— great lawyers, mighty merchants, world-renowned statesmen. Of what did they speak with the most satisfaction? They loved to talk of their boyhood and youth, of their days of poverty and hard struggle. The rich man described the time when he found it hard to get a half-dollar. Daniel Webster used to tell with delight how he went out as a boy in the early, chilly morning to drive in the cows, went barefoot through the frosty grass, and warmed his poor little bare feet in the places where the cows had been lying. These men felt they then got their strength of character. At the time, these things seemed hard; but, as they look back on them, they enjoy them better than all their subsequent successes.

Perhaps, in some other world, we shall, in a like manner, look back on our hours of anguish, our long days of bereavement, loneliness, and sorrow, and feel that in those moments the seeds were planted of the greatest and noblest development of our souls. Then we learned generosity, loyalty, truth, manliness. Then we were becoming fittest to do some work for God and man. It seems hard and unintelligible now: perhaps hereafter it will be all plain.— *Boston Saturday Evening Gazette*, July 2, 1881.

> The mighty pyramids of Stone
>   That wedge-like cleave the desert airs,
> When nearer seen and better known,
>   Are but gigantic flights of stairs.
> The distant mountains that uprear
>   Their solid bastions to the skies
> Are crossed by pathways that appear
>   As we to higher levels rise.
> The heights by great men reached and kept
>   Were not attained by sudden flight;
> But they, while their companions slept,
>   Were toiling upward in the night.
> Standing on what too long we bore
>   With shoulders bent and downcast eyes,
> We may discern — unseen before —
>   A path to higher destinies.
> Nor deem the irrevocable Past,
>   As wholly wasted, wholly vain,
> If, rising on its wrecks, at last,
>   To something nobler we attain.
>   *Henry W. Longfellow* (*The Ladder of St. Augustine*).

Chapter XVI.

INTROSPECTION.

What Three Forms of Temptation would be likely to arise and to recur "for a Season" in the Mind of a Young Man, if he were placed in the then Circumstances of Jesus?

To GET body gratification, to get fame, to get power. Jesus may be imagined to have come to the baptism with the problem considerably well solved, that had long been depressing his tender nature: How shall the misfortunes that through human selfishness befall the Jewish people — nay, even the whole world — be remedied? Evidently, the entire community will be righted, if all the individuals thereof be righted. Next, then, how is the individual soul to be harmonized with its environment? Evidently, by making the will at one with the design of its Author. Next, then, how is attainable this at-one-ment, this faith that works by love, this fidelity to the unseen Force and Source of goodness, this holding on to the Power not ourselves that makes for righteousness? Jesus had verified Micah's answer: let one do justly, love mercy, and walk humbly, and to him that ordereth his life conduct aright shall be shown salvation from selfishness. His Ideal shall save and be saved.

In a word, objectively all depends on conduct, and subjectively all depends on spiritual condition. His observation, his experience, and his recent prolonged meditations in solitude had resulted in his hitting upon the two essentials of such spiritual condition: (1) The Method, Introspection; (2) The Secret or Means, Self-renunciation. To this condition he had attained, until there was in his person, his presence, his manner, his accents, a something full of grace and truth, a something which can best — but, then, only approximately — be translated * sweet reasonableness. It needed no proclamation from the Baptist, no voice from the sky, to convince Jesus that there was

---

* From "*epieikeia*" (II. Cor. x., 1), "gentleness of Christ."

in himself that rare and remarkable combination of sweetness and light, of all that goes to make divinity of character, which soothes, attracts, subdues, overawes, and uplifts the wayward, the fretful, the disheartened, the distracted, the passion-torn, the guilt-tortured. He knew the wants of the times. He saw that, however effectively the impetuous John might awaken the masses, there must be something further. John's exhortations excited a deep yearning which they left unsatisfied. New impulses, however grand, must have guidance, training into habit, before they bloom into character and fructify into reliable conduct.

What a gigantic work! His thoughtful spirit has taken him into desert solitude. He surveys the whole ground. The audacious John must fall a victim of the profligate, foxy, rapacious Herod. What can one man do then toward revolutionizing permanently the currupt theocracy or lifting the iron yoke of Rome? He must stand alone against the world, must pass sentence on all its religious wisdom, must create a new world of spiritual thought. Long he ponders. He becomes worn out with hunger. "If," questions he, "the Eternal wants this work done, will he keep his chosen agent spending all his time and energies earning bread at the carpenter's bench? There is a sacred legend that he miraculously supplied Israel with manna. If victuals cost the Almighty no more than stones, why should not the task of reform be compensated by at least the reformer's board and keeping? Conscious of possessing extraordinary powers, why not experiment upon the Creator's peculiar favor, why not verify whether those powers be not miraculous? But, then, why conceive the Almighty to be restricted to a single means of sustenance? No: I will wait until my heavenly Father gives me what he chooses and in whatever way pleases him." Many a person in Jesus' place would not have been so free from morbid fancies as not to have, moreover, a momentary temptation to test his own immunity from the consequence of some natural law, as, for instance, of gravitation. But that this was the fact in the case of Jesus seems to many reverential reasoners extremely improbable.

Otherwise as to the whisper of ambition. How magnificent the splendor of the Roman Empire! How can he utilize the grand power within him in obtaining preferment, and perhaps finally becoming an emancipating prince? But Rome worships idols. This had always been the line of sharp demarcation that separated the self-reputed chosen people from heathendom. Shall he turn traitor to the law of his ancestors? "No!" resolves he, "Jahveh alone shall be my God! Jahveh stripped of the monstrosities of prodigy-loving chroniclers, shall be my ideal of the True, the Beautiful, and the Good, forevermore. I will be his son. He shall be my father. My allegiance, as between the two opposite masteries, is chosen. Henceforth, the redemption of the world from infernal tumult and woe by the salvation of single souls from selfishness shall be my life-work. Come hunger, come privation, come toil, come torture, come death! To the very last in myself will I exemplify the sole method, self-renunciation,— dying to live,— the subordination of the lower self to the higher, of the ephemeral to the eternal. To John's watchword, Repentance, here, and now do I add Regeneration.

"But how that Sanhedrim? How those priests, frozen and fossil-bound between two tables of stone? How if their desperate bigotry, jealousy, and rage shall have soon compassed my death? Stalwart successors I must have,— sturdy Simon first and foremost, and his good brother, Andrew. Noble Nathanael and other docile ones must be joined, and all be indoctrinated. I must move circumspectly at first,— away from impatient, precipitate John, and away from Jerusalem and the stung hierarchy. Busy Capernaum, seated in the world's highway, will have to be the starting-point whence the light and warmth shall radiate. Thence around shall circulate the leaven. Thus must begin the domain of good-will, and thus only I be the Messiah to a kingdom of heaven on earth."

And with this resolve of Jesus came peace,— came sweet thoughts, and ministered unto him like welcome, consoling messengers from some never failing Friend. In that travail — that conjuncture of inspiration and exaltation — was born the Sermon erelong to be uttered on the Mount that overlooked the budding blooms of Genesareth. And so with Milton define we the Temptation: —

> Victorious deeds
> Flamed in thy heart, heroic acts,— one while
> To rescue Israel from the Roman yoke;
> Men to subdue, and quell, o'er all the earth,
> Brute violence and proud tyrannic power,
> Till Truth were freed and equity restored;
> Yet held it more humane, more heavenly just
> By winning words to conquer willing hearts,
> And make persuasion do the work of fear.

Not substantially differing from the foregoing is another view of the workings of the mind of Jesus at another period: —

In the second part of Isaiah (chap. xl. to lxvi.), which we know to have been written by some prophet of the captivity, about 536 B.C., but which Jesus, like all his contemporaries, ascribed to the true Isaiah of the eighth century B.C., in this wonderful fragment, the cap-sheaf of Old Testament prophecy, there figures prominently "the servant of God," who is represented as a teacher or prophet, thus: "Behold my servant, whom I uphold; mine elect, in whom my soul delighteth. I have put my spirit upon him: he shall declare judgment to the Gentiles. He shall not strive nor cry. He shall declare judgment with truth. He shall not fail nor be discouraged till he set judgment in the earth: far lands wait for his law." We may be sure, I think, that, so far as the Messianic self-consciousness of Jesus nourished itself upon Scriptural food, it found it in these and other similar passages of the Deutero-Isaiah. Jesus was here less critical than the rabbis of his time, for they understood the "servant of God" in these passages to mean the Jewish people, or the body of faithful Jews; and modern criticism has almost unanimously corroborated their opinion. Now, in the same fragment (chap. liii.), the Servant of Jehovah is represented as debased and suffering, while at the same time his ultimate triumph is portended. "He was despised and rejected of men, a man of sorrows, and acquainted with grief." In the oratorio of "The Messiah," the tenderest passage in the music is that which corresponds to these words. This is as it should be, for we may well believe that no other passage in the Old Testament was so central to the thought of Jesus. I do not mean that his anticipation of a catastrophe ending to his ministry was entirely derived from this text and its context. His observation of the spirit of the Pharisees, as he saw them in Galilee, led him to expect the worst when he should meet them in Jerusalem, as he meant to meet them with a gesture of defiance; but what was predicated in Isaiah liii. of the Servant of Jehovah tallied almost exactly with his natural anticipation. "Surely," the prophet says, "he hath borne our griefs; . . . yet it pleased the Lord to bruise him." The contemporaries of Jesus did not apply these words to the Messiah; but Jesus did, and therefore to himself. Even before the announcement at Cæsarea-Philippi, he must often have brooded over them. The future which they pictured for him was very different from that which his own hopeful and loving heart had pictured at the beginning of his ministry, only ten months ago; but there had been no break in the development of his ideas. Now, the conviction of impending shame and death would haunt him more and more. Meantime, the idea of a suffering Messiah would shock the zealots and the Pharisees, and excite their animosity. Nor was it strange that it should do so. For one man to set up his idea of the Messiah in opposition to the entire community, an idea diametrically opposed to the popular idea, was certainly audacious, and could hardly meet with anything but fierce resentment. . . . We have recently been told that, to appreciate the sufferings of Jesus, we must apprehend him as a suffering God. What an absurdity is this! Who could not suffer anything with the resources of an infinite nature to fall back upon? The glory of Jesus is that as a man, and so considering himself,—for being the Messiah did not unman him,—he went to meet a miserable doom with an unquestioning submission to the logic of events.—*J. W. Chadwick (The Man Jesus, pp. 147, 154).*

Chapter XVII.

HARMONIZATION.

Wherein are Introspection and Self-renunciation, as exemplified by Jesus, effective toward harmonizing the Lower Human Tendencies with the Higher and resisting Temptation to Sin?

"AN ounce of prevention is worth a pound of cure." The question involves a definition of "sin." Sin is the voluntary violation of the law of one's being. This law demands such harmonious exercise of the function of any one faculty of the human organization that the proper function — the being — of another faculty shall not be overborne. Moralists and legislators declare that conduct resulting from intellectual and emotional inaction, causing passivity or absence of volition, is often as ruinous and wrong as actively wilful misdoing. In the plain, terse parlance of the prayer-meeting, "a realizing sense of the exceeding sinfulness of sin" must include "sins of omission as well as of commission."

So the categories of sin interact in a circle. Misuse of the intellect, or of the sensibilities, or of the will, or of the body, is abuse of the whole. When a man fails to comply with the corporal command for food, inadequacy of replenishment of blood, sinew, nerve, and brain, enfeebles intellectual forecast. "No man," says George Eliot, "can be wise on an empty stomach." Conversely, want of forecast imports want of provision: by popular synecdoche, subject and object are one. So also as to the other correlations. Want of clear thinking imports want of resolution; and, conversely, irresolution imports uncertainty of determination. Want of attention to the *pros* and *contras* of the exercise of the motive, the executive, the procreative, or any other power,— instinctive, emotional, or semi-intellectual,— reacts in paralysis and disorder of the entire circuit. "Modesty," says Mirabeau, "has its sins, and a kiss its innocence." In phrenological nomenclature, there are possible both uses and abuses of every talent,— of combativeness, destructiveness, amativeness, firmness, nay, even of conscientiousness, veneration, and self-respect. Indeed, the liability extends to the action of the ratiocinative and æsthetic faculties. Even in the perception of incongruities and the exposure of errors is there opportunity to operate the choosing of "the middle extreme."

More and more, all along down the centuries, do sages confirm Izaak Walton's prefatory observation, disallowing a "severe, sour-complexioned man" to be a competent judge in discerning the value of genial pabulum to the soul.

Give me an honest laugher.— *Sir Walter Scott.*

God smiled when he put humor into the human disposition, and said, "That is good."— *Henry Ward Beecher.*

Mildly commingled, mimicry and mirthfulness make good medicine for many minds' maladies.— *Thomas Jefferson Burnham.*

> Alas for him who never sees
> The sun shine through his cypress trees!
>
> *John G. Whittier.*

> How charming is divine philosophy!
> Not harsh and crabbed, as dull fools suppose.
>
> *John Milton.*

> For other things, mild heaven a time ordains,
> And disapproves that care, though wise in show,
> That with superfluous burden loads the day,
> And, when God sends a cheerful hour, refrains.
>
> *John Milton.*

> And ever against eating cares
> Lap me in soft Lydian airs,
> Married to immortal verse,
> Such as the melting soul may pierce,
> In notes, with many a winding bout
> Of linked sweetness long drawn out, . .
> Untwisting all the chains that tie
> The hidden soul of harmony.
>
> *John Milton.*

Asceticism,— "that way madness lies." Of this fault of John the Baptist, Jesus might be said to have taken warning,— if need of warning were at all predicable in the premises,— and to have been convivial whenever duty so demanded. And, as to the methods of truth against sham and show, satire is often considered a legitimate pulpit weapon. But he who holds the mirror up to the foibles and idiosyncrasies of some public speakers must have a care against the sin of "scoffing." And so on through Paul's entire list of "things which are not convenient." To shun sin is to avoid everything abnormal,— symmetrically to develop a sound mind in a sound body.*

---

* See Swedenborg's N. J. D., n. 196.

But, in defining symmetry, the criticism once made on Pope's line,

An honest man's the noblest work of God,

may be considered; namely, "the reputation of men is to be prized not from their exemption from fault, but from the size of those virtues they are possessed of."

A true mental philosophy accepts all the facts of human experience. It sees the mechanism of mind, but it also observes the nobler powers which make man a living soul and a child of God.... We grow broader not by seeing error, but by seeing more and more of truth.— *Dr. James Freeman Clarke.*

Character is not cut in marble,— is not something solid and unalterable. It is something living and changing, and may become diseased as our bodies do.— *George Eliot.*

Insanity is not a distinct and separate empire: our ordinary life borders upon it, and we cross the frontier in some part of our nature. — *Hippolyte Adolphe Taine.*

The higher feelings, when acting in harmonious combination, and directed by enlightened intellect, have a boundless scope for gratification: their least indulgence is delightful, and their highest activity bliss.— *George Combe.*

When we speak against one capital vice, we ought to speak against its opposite: the middle betwixt both is the point for virtue. — *Alexander Pope.*

A character that is all piety is as much a perversion as one that is all business. The complete man is "not slothful in business," while, at the same time, he is "fervent in spirit."— *Dr. W. H. Ryder (Open Letter to Dwight L. Moody).*

A taste of every sort of knowledge is necessary to form the mind, and is the only way to give the understanding its due improvement to the full extent of its capacity.— *John Locke.*

It is the glorious prerogative of the empire of knowledge that what it gains it never loses. On the contrary, it increases by the multiple of its own power: all its ends become means; all its attainments help to new conquests.— *Daniel Webster.*

In order to be greatly good, one must imagine intensely and comprehensively; he must put himself in the place of another and of many others; the pains and pleasures of his species must become his own. The great instrument of moral good is imagination, and poetry administers to the effect by acting upon the cause.— *Percy B. Shelley.*

The seeds of knowledge may be planted in solitude, but must be cultivated in public.— *Dr. Samuel Johnson.*

Knowledge has in our time triumphed, and is still triumphing, over prejudice and over bigotry. The civilized and Christian world is fast learning the great lesson that difference of nation does not imply necessary hostility, and that all contact need not be war. The whole world is becoming a common field for intellect to act in. Energy of mind, genius, power, wheresoever it exists, may speak out in any tongue, and the world will hear it.—*Daniel Webster.*

Even genius itself is but fine observation strengthened by fixity of purpose.—*Earle Bulwer-Lytton.*

Principle is a passion for truth.—*William Hazlitt.*

There is no music in a "rest" that I know of, but there's the making of music in it. . . . Patience is the finest and worthiest part of fortitude, and the rarest too.— *John Ruskin.*

I was never less alone than when by myself.—*Edward Gibbon.*

For solitude sometimes is best society,
And short retirement urges sweet return.
John Milton.

By all means use sometimes to be alone.
Salute thyself. See what thy soul doth **wear.**
Dare to look in thy chest,— for 'tis thine own,—
And tumble up and down what thou find'st there.
George Herbert.

Self-reverence, self-knowledge, self-control,
These three alone lead life to sovereign power,
Yet not for power (power of herself
Would come uncalled for), but to live by **law,**
Acting the law we live by without fear,
And because right is right to follow right
Were wisdom in the scorn of consequence.
Alfred Tennyson.

He was a-weary; but he fought his fight,
And stood for simple Manhood: and was joyed
To see the august broadening of the light,
And new worlds heaving heavenward from the void.
He loved his fellows, and their love was sweet
Plant daisies at his head and at his feet.
Richard Realf.

There is no ending to thy road,
No limit to thy fleeting goal,
But speeds the ever greatening soul
From truth to truth, from God to God.
John W. Chadwick.

Yet I doubt not through the ages one increasing purpose runs,
And the thoughts of men are widened by the process of the suns.
Alfred Tennyson.

Build thee more stately mansions, O my **soul,**
As the swift seasons roll.
Leave thy low-vaulted past;
Let each new temple, nobler than the last,
Shut thee from heaven with a dome more **vast;**
Till thou at length art free,
Leaving thine out-grown shell by life's unresting sea.
Dr. Oliver W. Holmes.

> The flower horizons open, the blossom vaster shows;
> We hear the wide world's echo,— "See how the lily grows!"

Sin has sometimes been defined a violation of conscience; * conscience, "a sympathetic recognition of social equity passing into appropriate action"; and virtue, the acquired strength of will to transmute such recognition into such action. This, like facility of recognition of duty, or like any other power, comes through trial and by exercise of the faculty itself. Accordingly, each temptation overcome renders every succeeding recurrence less and less formidable. †

Perfection — as culture, from a thorough, disinterested study of human nature and human experience, learns to conceive it — is an harmonious expansion of all the powers that make the beauty and worth of human nature, and is not consistent with the over-development of any one power at the expense of the rest. But this idea of perfection is at variance with our want of flexibility, with our inaptitude for seeing more than one side of a thing, with our intense energetic absorption in the pursuit we happen to be following.— *Dr. Matthew Arnold (Culture and Anarchy,* p. 14).

To be ignorant of one's ignorance is the malady of ignorance.— *A. Bronson Alcott.*

In judging of others, a man often erreth; but, in examining himself, always laboreth fruitfully.— *Thomas à Kempis.*

One power rules another, none can cultivate another; in each endowment, and not elsewhere, lies the force which must complete it. There are few who at once have Thought and the capacity for Action. Thought expands, but lames; Action animates, but narrows. A man is never happy till his vague striving has itself marked out its proper limitation.— *Goethe (Wilhelm Meister's Apprenticeship).*

Action is generally defective, and proves an abortion without previous contemplation. Contemplation generates, action propagates.— *Owen Feltham.*

Reading seeks, meditation finds, prayer asks, contemplation tastes.— *St. Augustine.*

A man's collective dispositions constitute his character.— *Dr. L. H. Atwater.*

This self-confident, this hurrying, unripe, aspiring character which makes nothing of meditation; this boldness without strength and ardor without depth,— let us bring it to the touchstone of our perfect

---

* Sin is choosing and acting in opposition to our sense of right.— *Dr. W. E. Channing (Works,* iv., 151).
† See Aphorisms, chap. xv., pp. 74, ff., *ante.*

Lord, and see how his character rebukes it.— *Dr. Theodore D. Woolsey.*

Mark this well, ye proud men of action! Ye are, after all, nothing but unconscious instruments of the men of thought.— *Heinrich Heine.*

A man is the prisoner of his power. A topical memory makes him an almanac; a talent for debate, a disputant; skill to get money makes him a miser,— that is, a beggar. Culture reduces these inflammations by invoking the aid of other powers against the dominant talent, and by appealing to the rank of powers. It watches success. For performance, Nature has no mercy, and sacrifices the performer to get it done; makes a dropsy or a tympany of him. If she wants a thumb, she makes one at the cost of arms and legs, and any excess of power in one part is usually paid for at once by some defect in a contiguous part.— *Ralph Waldo Emerson (Conduct of Life).*

> All are architects of Fate,
>   Working in these walls of Time;
> Some with massive deeds and great,
>   Some with ornaments of rhyme.
>
> Build to-day, then, strong and sure,
>   With a firm and ample base;
> And ascending and secure
>   Shall to-morrow find its place.
> Thus alone can we attain
>   To those turrets, where the eye
> Sees the world as one vast plain,
>   And one boundless reach of sky.
>
> *Henry W. Longfellow.*

Another phase of this topic will be considered in discussing the precepts of the Sermon on the Mount, chap. xxvii.

Chapter XVIII.

DEMONIZATION.

What are the Principal Different Views concerning the Existence of a Personal Devil, and the Teachings of Jesus in General thereon?

(1) **That** of Schleiermacher, who is positive that the expressions of the New Testament concerning the devil cannot be harmonized in one conception, but have been blended together from various constituent parts; that the doctrine of such an entity subverts itself; and that Jesus and his apostles must have availed themselves incidentally of the popular belief without intending to develop or to ratify any doctrine upon the subject. Thus, one element was disclosed by the **remark to Simon that Satan had desired to have him and to sift him,** indicating the tendency of the unstable in faith **and life to be** taken by surprise in evil machinations. The other element was derived from the Persian Dualism, so far as the essential existence of evil could be adopted by a monotheistic people.

(2) That the fasting produced an ecstatic state of mind, which was interpreted as opening communication with the unseen world. The old Oriental idea, still **common** among the Arabs, is adduced, **that the soul of an** insane person is possessed by some higher power. Luther's mental condition is instanced, wherein he had a vision of the devil in his room in the castle of the Wartburg, and flung his inkhorn at him. The legend of angels coming and ministering unto Jesus reminds R. v. M. J. **Savage** of Gautama, the last Buddha: —

> He, too, was tempted by all the evil spirits in all the heavens and in all the hells. And, when at last he had conquered, the waiting and ministering spirits filled the air with perfumes and scattered flowers all around him, and came and lifted him up and helped him. Stories like these belong to more than one of the world's religions. We cannot believe their literal truth, for the reason that Macaulay said he could not believe in ghosts, — he had "seen too many of them." — *Talks about Jesus*, p. 72.

(3) The "Orthodox" view has been most ably set forth by Bishop Martensen. He thinks the "cosmical" principle, the tempting principle, becomes the actual devil, the personal devil, for the first time when man has allowed him entrance into the sphere of consciousness: that it is man, therefore, who gives the devil being. But it by no means follows from this that man is his own devil: "it is another, a superhuman principle to which existence is imparted by man, a tempting, seducing, making-possessed, a d inspiring power, to which man lends himself as to a *non-ego*." And as to the Eden serpent, the legend of which is said to have been first united to the devil tradition in the Talmud about 200 A.D., Bishop Martensen says:—

It is the law of the cosmical principle to be subordinate to the kingdom of God; but, in order to become the foundation upon which service may rest, it must first act as an exciting power, must throw itself in man's way, and show him the possibility of rebelling against God, of saying no when God says yes. According to the moral explanation, the serpent is to be regarded as the symbol of this *impulse* toward independence, becoming active in man and inciting him to become free apart from his Creator. But this impulse toward independence could most assuredly never become active in man, if it had no foundation whatever *in the constitution of the creature*, if it had not its deepest root in a principle which is active in all created things. The serpent is the outward expression for this principle which creeps up to man to obtain an entrance... The forbidden fruit is the glittering world phenomenon which invites man to enjoy it and to make himself its possessor.—*Christian Dogmatics* (*Urwick's translation*), § 79.

Dr. Hedge, in his chapter on "Dualism and Optimism," says:—

From the Zoroastrian religion, the principle of dualism passed into Judaism, and thence into Christendom. The pseudo-Christian idea of the Devil is its lineal and legitimate fruit. I call it pseudo-Christian; for though Jesus employed the term, or, if you please, the conception, as a given article in the mental furniture of his time, he by no means accents it in a way to authorize its acceptance as a necessary constituent of the Christian creed. It is scarcely any longer regarded as such. Of Christian beliefs once universally received, and never so much as questioned, there is none which seems to have passed into such general discredit, none which is losing so fast its hold of the popular mind. The Devil is still a name to swear by, and still, as a figure of speech, represents a spiritual fact, but no longer stands for an ontological or statistical one. There is something very curious and not easily explained in this noiseless and imperceptible dropping out from the mind and creed of mankind of a once universal and rooted conviction. For nearly two thousand years, the belief in Satan was as fixed as any belief whatsoever in the mind of Christendom. For more than a thousand, the doctrine of the Atonement was not, as modern Orthodoxy conceives it, a satisfaction of divine Justice, but was understood as a satisfaction of Satan, to whom the world was supposed to have become forfeit by sin. The early Church, among its regular officials, had always one whose business it was to fight the Devil, in the person of any of his subordinates who might take possession of a human subject. In every church, the exorcist was as much a stated functionary as the deacon or the priest. The idea of Satan was not one of those which the Protestant Reformation repudiated. . . . Luther insisted, "We are but guests in a world of which the Devil is the prince and the god."

The real Devil, as figured in Mephistopheles, is "the spirit that denies," the opposing, unbelieving, bitter, mocking spirit,— the spirit whose idiom is sarcasm, whose life is a sneer. There is nothing more alien from Godhead, nothing more undivine, more antagonistic to all divineness, than such a spirit, whose natural symbol is the ape, and whose theological expression is "the sin against the Holy Ghost." — *Dr. Frederic H. Hedge* (*Ways of the Spirit*, pp. 239, 242).

> Thus through the world, like bolt and blast
> And scourging fire, the truth has passed.
> Clouds break; the steadfast heavens remain;
> Weeds burn; the ashes feed the grain!
>
> *Anon.*
>
> The low desire, the base design,
>   That makes another's virtues less;
> The revel of the ruddy wine,
>   And all occasions of excess;
> The longing for ignoble things;
>   The strife for triumph more than truth;
> The hardening of the heart, that brings
>   Irreverence for the dreams of youth;
> All thoughts of ill,— all evil deeds,
>   That have their root in thoughts of ill;
> Whatever hinders or impedes
>   The action of the nobler will,—
> All these must first be trampled down
>   Beneath our feet, if we would gain
> In the bright fields of fair renown
>   The right of eminent domain.
>
> *Henry W. Longfellow* (*The Ladder of St. Augustine*).

Another phase of the doctrine of a personal devil will be considered in the chapter on Damnation (xlii., *post*).

Chapter XIX.

TRANSGRESSION.

What are the Different Orthodox and Other Leading Metaphysical Views concerning the "Mystery of the Fall" and Christ's Teachings thereon?

KANT considered the fall and redemption of man to mean simply the necessary transition of Reason from the state of nature to that of culture. Schleiermacher propounded as an explanation of sin that the sensuous consciousness has obtained a *start* before man's consciousness of God; that this bondage of the higher intellectual consciousness must at last appear to man himself as a false relation, as something from which he must strive to be released. Fichte made the *ego* begin with being held in bonds by the *non-ego*, because the *ego*, from its very conception, must first conquer for itself its own liberty: he made evil the *vis inertiae*, in consequence of which the *ego* inclines to remain in its original state of nature instead of undertaking the labor of going out of and beyond itself.

Manes, a Persian who tried to combine the Oriental philosophy with Christianity, maintained that there are two supreme principles, light and darkness, the one good, the other evil, which produce all the happiness and calamities of the world. The Manicheans, accordingly, hold to an irreconcilable conflict between nature and mind.*

The Infralapsarians are those Calvinists who consider the decree of election to contemplate the apostasy as past, and the elect as being in a fallen and guilty state. The Supralapsarians consider this decree to contemplate the elect as persons to be created, and to apostatize with the rest of the race, and then to be recovered by divine grace. The former considered the election of grace as a remedy for an existing evil; the latter, as a part of God's original purpose in regard to men. Bishop Martensen, after adverting to the effort of Leibnitz and

---

* See *ante*, chap. xviii., Dr. Hedge on "Dualism."

other Supralapsarians to set forth the alleged fall as a *felix culpa*, says:—

The true optimism and the true Theodicy are to be looked for in the blending of the Supralapsarian and the Sublapsarian views. Christian optimism recognizes the unconditional necessity of the Incarnation; and, as upon this principle it regards human nature in the light of redemption, it can adopt the exclamation, *Felix culpa!* For, though sin was not willed by God, it could not occur beyond the range of his counsels: though God has not ordained it, it becomes a teleological force for the revelation of God's love. . . . History is the living drama of freedom, wherein all points are affected by the movement not only of divine thought, but also of holy will. . . . The pessimist views and subjective ideals regarding the world belong only to the stand-point of sinfulness itself.— *Christian Dogmatics (Urwick's translation),* § 89.

And yet, somehow, when one does take a survey of history or lifts his eyes out of the books of the metaphysicians to the world around, he is reminded of Bishop Francis Hare's aphorism: "Nothing is farther than earth from heaven, nothing is nearer than heaven to earth." And this suggests the aphorism of Nathaniel Hawthorne: "No fountain so small but that heaven may be imaged in its bosom"; and also the inquiry of Tulloch: "How happened it that Jesus' doctrine of sin escaped the taint of asceticism, and of that conception of evil, then not unknown within as well as without Palestine, which regarded matter as the abode of corruption?"

I see that good men are not so good as I once thought they were, and I find that few are so bad as either malicious enemies or censorious separating professors do imagine.— *Richard Baxter.*

> Who made the heart, 'tis He alone
>   Decidedly can try us:
> He knows each chord, its various tone;
>   Each spring, its various bias;
> Then at the balance let's be mute,
>   We never can adjust it.
> What's done we partly may compute,
>   But know not what's resisted.
>   *Robert Burns.*
>
> In men whom men pronounce as ill,
>   I find so much of goodness still;
> In men whom men pronounce divine,
>   I find so much of sin and blot,
> I hesitate to draw the line
>   Between the two when God has not.   *Joaquin Miller.*

Good has but one enemy, the evil; but the evil has two enemies, the good and itself.—*Julius Müller.*

Schleiermacher's averment, that sin comes from the sensuous consciousness having gotten the start of man's consciousness of God, recalls a conversation between a doctor of medicine and a doctor of divinity in a story written by a medical professor, the heroine of which met with a moral misfortune a few months before her birth, her mother being bitten by a rattlesnake. The medical side of the colloquy (marred by this abridging) is partly as follows:—

Ministers work out the machinery of human responsibility in an abstract kind of way: doctors have to study a child from the moment of birth upwards, and our algebra must constantly consider two factors,—friction and strength (or weakness) of material. We see him, for the first year or so, trained by his maker to pure selfishness, in order that he may be sure to take care of himself. When he comes to make his first choice between right and wrong, he is at a disadvantage from this *vis a tergo* of a whole year's life of selfishness. If stout, red, and lively, we expect to find him troublesome, noisy, and perhaps disobedient, more or less: if he is weak and pale-faced, he will be very likely to sit in the house and read books about other good children that were indifferent to the out-door amusements of the wicked little red-cheeked children. Some of the little folks we watch grow up to be young women, and occasionally one of them gets nervous, what we call hysterical; and that girl will begin to play all sorts of pranks,—to lie and cheat, perhaps in the most unaccountable way, so that she might seem to a minister a good example of total depravity. We don't see her in that light. We give her iron and valerian, and get her on horseback if we can, and so expect to make her will come all right again. By and by, we are called to see a baby threescore years and ten or more old. We find that this old baby has never got rid of that first year's teaching which led him to fill his stomach with all he could pump into it, and his hands with everything he could grab. People call him a miser. We are sorry for him; but we cannot help remembering his first year's training.

We see all kinds of monomania and insanity. We learn from them to recognize all sorts of queer tendencies in minds supposed to be sane, so that we have nothing but compassion for a large class of persons condemned as sinners by theologians, but considered by us as invalids. We have constant reasons for noticing the transmission of qualities from parents to offspring; and we find it hard to hold a child accountable in any moral point of view for inherited bad temper or tendency to drunkenness, as hard as we should to blame him for inheriting gout or asthma.

Ministers talk about the human will as if it stood on a high lookout, with plenty of light, and elbow-room reaching to the horizon. Doctors are constantly noticing how it is tied up and darkened by inferior organization, by disease and all sorts of crowding interferences, until they get to look upon Hottentots and Indians—and a good many of their own race—as a kind of self-conscious blood-clocks, with a very limited power of self-determination. That's the tendency, I say, of doctors' experience; but the people to whom they address their statements of the results of their observation belong to the thinking class of the highest races, and *they* are conscious of a great deal of liberty of will. So in the fact that civilization with all it offers has, on the whole, proved a dead failure with the aboriginal races of this country, they talk as if they knew from their own will all about that of a Digger Indian.— *Dr. Oliver W. Holmes* (*Elsie Venner*, chap. xxii.).

The doctor's expression "old baby" reminds us of John Dryden's lines : —

> Men are but children of a larger growth :
> Our appetites are apt to change as theirs,
> And full as craving too, and full as vain.*

Also of Coleridge's words, "In To-day already walks To-morrow"; and Huxley's, too, "A man's worst difficulties begin when he is able to do as he likes."

The doctor's declaration as to the effect of physical upon spiritual conditions reminds us of Lord Chesterfield's remark: "A light supper, a good night's sleep, and a fine morning have often made a hero of the same man, who, by indigestion, a restless night, and a rainy morning, would have proved a coward."

The doctor's remark on hereditary transmission of qualities is well illustrated by "Margaret the Criminal." She was a pauper child left adrift in one of the villages on the upper Hudson, about ninety years ago. There was no almshouse in the place, and she was made a subject of out-door relief, receiving occasionally food and clothing from the town officials, but was never educated nor sheltered in a proper home. She became the mother of a long race of criminals and paupers, which has cursed the county ever since. In one generation of her unhappy line there were twenty children, of whom seventeen lived to maturity. Nine served terms aggregating fifty years in the State Prison for high crimes, and all the others were frequent inmates in jails and almshouses. Of the 623 descendants of this outcast girl, 200 committed crimes which brought them upon the court records ; and most of the others were idiots, drunkards, lunatics, paupers, or prostitutes. Alas ! of how many it may be said as Mrs. Hale avers of Nell

---

* An exceptionally good illustration will be found in the character of Jedwort, in J. T Trowbridge's story, "The Man who stole a Meeting-house" (*Coupon Bonds, and Other Stories*, p. 369).

Gwynne: "'Poor Nellie' was the victim of circumstances, not the votary of vice."*

Society prepares the crime: the criminal commits it.—*Henry T. Buckle.*

> A pebble on the streamlet scant
> Has turned the course of many a river;
> A dew-drop on the baby plant
> Has warped the giant oak forever.
>
> *Charlotte Cossitt.*

> It is the little rift within the lute,
> That by and by will make the music mute,
> And, ever widening, slowly silence all.
>
> *Alfred Tennyson.*

As to the old Calvinistic view of the fall of Adam, it has lately been said:—

'Should a physician place a son of fifteen years in a plague hospital, expecting, nay, certain that he would incur the disease, and that he would propagate it to innumerable others, that he might show his skill in combating it, would not language fail to characterize the deed?—*Henry Ward Beecher* (*North American Review*, August, 1882).

And similarly as to the Anglican view:—

The burial service, a survival from barbarism, declared death to be sent by God's wrath in vengeance for the sin of Adam; when even the illiterate know that death made the earth beneath us a cemetery of animal form before man existed. In presence of weeping friends, it thanked God for taking the beloved historian Motley out of this wicked world, every tear giving the heart's lie to the lips' thanksgiving. The historian had been a philosopher, and every sentence of the ceremony was contradicted by the testimony of his life.—*Moncure D. Conway* (*Sermon in the Commonwealth*, Dec. 11, 1880).

As to the freedom of the will, we must concede something to Morell's theory; namely, that if what is termed a motive be not an objective reality, but merely the mind itself in a certain state of feeling, man, though under the necessity of acting in accordance with motives, is free. He cannot, it is true, alter the relation which God has established between emotions and volitions *generally*, but he may modify his own states of feeling, and through these his volitions also: just as a sine, being the function of an angle, if you require a sine of a different magnitude, the only possible way of obtaining it is by taking an angle of a different magnitude. Volition is a function of the

---

*See in Sarah J. Hale's *Biography of Distinguished Women*, p. 338, a portrait wherein Nell's face is not wanting in spiritual loveliness.

mind. Our mental states do not *solely* depend on external circumstances, but also upon our own spontaneity.*

This theory, of course, denies that all mental phenomena are derived from sensation. It considers them in three classes: (1) Intelligence, which creates conceptions, rules of action; (2) Sensibility, which supplies inducements, impulses; and (3) Will, which creates effort, the emission of voluntary power.

Faith and trust, and the pledging of ourselves to the infinite will and love, are qualities that cannot be created in us by the Almighty as natural forms of our inward constitution: they are results of the spiritual powers set in opposition to hardship, perplexity, sorrow, and the sight of things seeming to drift wrong.— *T. Starr King.*

---

* "Hist. and Crit. View Spec. Philos. of Europe," *Nineteenth Century*, p. 288. See also *post*, chap. xxviii., the consideration of the transcendental and experiential theories of right and wrong; also chap. xlv., various philosophical theories of the mind's knowledge of God.

Chapter XX.

INCEPTION.

Why did Jesus choose Capernaum for the Beginning of his Public Ministry, and how did the Associations of the Place affect his Discourses?

CAPERNAUM was a thriving village a little way from the head of the Sea of Galilee, where the western shore forms a small cape from which the view embraces the whole coast. The town was on the boundary between the territory of Philip and that of Herod Antipas, and accordingly had a custom-house and a garrison. The "highway to the sea," from Syria to the Mediterranean and Egypt, from Damascus to Ptolemais (Acre), ran through it, opening the markets of the coast to the rich yield of the neighboring farms, orchards, vineyards, and fisheries. Jesus would there have a better opportunity for intercourse with strangers than at Cana, Bethsaida, or Chorazin; would there find a more busy and less luxurious people than at Tiberias, Herod's capital; and possibly more docile than were his familiar neighbors at Nazareth. He made excursions to the neighboring villages, but appears to have become disgusted with his reception, and to have gone south, returning, however, occasionally.

Galilee, though less than thirty miles square, had, according to Josephus, two hundred and forty towns and villages and fifteen fortresses. Allowing for exaggeration, still its population was very dense, and its soil was of wonderful fertility.

The whole neighborhood of Capernaum is sacred to the memory of Jesus. There were the vineyards, on the hill slopes, round which their lord planted a hedge, and in which he built a watch-tower and dug a wine-press. There were the sunny hills, on which the old wine had grown and the new was growing, for which the householder would take care to provide the new leather bottles. The plain of Genesareth was the enamelled meadow, on which, in spring, ten thousand lilies were robed in more than the glory of Solomon, and where, in winter, the grass was cast into the oven. It was on such pastures as those around that the shepherd left the ninety-and-nine, to seek in the mountains the one that was lost, and bring it back, when found, on his shoulders, rejoicing. The ravens, that have neither storehouse nor barn, daily sailed over from the cliffs of Arbela, to seek their food on the shore of the lake; and from the same cliffs, from time to time, flew forth the hawks, to make the terrified hen gather her chickens under her wings. The orchards were there in which the fig-tree grew, on which the dresser of the vineyard in three years found no fruit, and in which the grain of mustard-seed grew into so great a tree that the birds of the air lodged in its branches.

Across the lake rose the hills of Gaulonitis, which the idly busy rabbis watched for signs of the weather. A murky red seen above them in the morning was a text for these sky-prophets to predict "foul weather to-day, for the sky is red and lowering"; and it was when the sun sank red and glowing behind the hills in the west that the solemn gossips, returning from their many prayers in the synagogue, made sure that it would be "fair weather to-morrow." It was when the sea-cloud was seen driving over the hilltops from Ptolemais and Carmel that neighbors warned each other that a shower was coming; and the clouds sailing north, toward Safed and Hermon, were the accepted earnest of coming heat.

The daily business of Capernaum itself supplied many of the illustrations so frequently introduced into the discourses of Jesus. He might see in the bazaar of the town or on the street the rich travelling merchant, who exchanged a heavy load of Babylonian carpets for the one lustrous pearl that had, perhaps, found its way to the lake from distant Ceylon. Fishermen, publicans, and dressers of vineyards passed and repassed each moment. Over in Julias, the favorite town of the tetrarch Philip, below in Tiberias, at the court of Antipas, lived the magnates, who delighted to be called "gracious lords," and walked in silk robes. The young Salome lived in the one town, her mother, Herodias, in the other; and the intercourse between the two courts could not have escaped the all-observing eye of Jesus as he moved about in Capernaum.—*Dr. Cunningham Geikie* (*Life and Words of Christ*, p. 342).

At first, Jesus probably lived with his mother and brothers and the few disciples he had already gathered. On his return from his first passover journey to Jerusalem, he appears to have made his abode when in town in the house of Peter, who lived with his brother Andrew and his mother-in-law.

Chapter XXI.

INAUGURATION.

In opening the Gospel Work, What were the Personal Habits of Jesus, and What the Order of Incidents, including the Choice of Disciples?

THERE was a judicious alternation of retirement and publicity, an adaptation of word and deed to circumstances. There continued communion with his own spirit, the quiet gathering in of all the lessons of life and nature around, deep study of the thoughts and dispositions of men, silent mastery of the religious ideas of the day, and a comprehensive knowledge of the religious parties of the people. He studied the Scriptures in the household or read them in the synagogues, until he absorbed and knew them better than did the scribes and Pharisees themselves.

Many reverential reasoners are of the opinion that for a time he preached and practised the Essene doctrines: this, as he did not marry, advocated continence "for the kingdom of heaven's sake,"* and taught non-resistance, baptism, and the selling of all one's possessions for the sake of the poor. Be this as it may, there is no doubt that he unfolded himself to his country gradually. "There was a twilight before the dawn, a dawn before the morning, and a morning before the day." But everything was meanwhile concentrated upon fulfilment of the grand and strange resolve: " I will build up a state by the mere force of my will, without help from the kings of the world, without taking advantage of any of the secondary causes that unite men together,— unity of interest or speech or blood-relationship. I will make laws for my state which shall never be repealed, and I will defy all the powers of destruction that are at work in the world to destroy what I build."

The Jewish theocracy had served its day. The new kingdom of God was to be a reign of holy love in the breast,

---

* Matt. xix., 12.

instead of a worthless service of rites and forms. Until then, outward priesthoods, local temples, the slaying of sacrifices, pompous rites and ceremonial laws, had been deemed essential. But the consecration of Jesus as the Messiah, not of the Jews alone, but of mankind, made the whole obsolete as incompatible with a universal religion. That he appreciated the immeasurable difficulties and dangers that beset his way, and was stepping with commensurate circumspection, detracts nothing from the real, ineffable grandeur of his position.

The precise order in which the incidents of the great work occurred cannot be satisfactorily drawn from the conflicting accounts. Dr. Strong* puts both the choosing of certain disciples and the Cana wedding before the "visit to Capernaum," and the call of Matthew (the fourteenth incident) afterwards. Probably, Judas of Karioth, Judea, was not chosen until after the first passover visit to Jerusalem. Perhaps two or more had been with Jesus at his visit to John the Baptist.

The list has sometimes been culled from Mark iii., Luke vi., and John i. as follows: Simon and Andrew Bar-Jona, John and James Bar-Zabdai, Thaddeus (or Lebbeus or Jude), Matthew (or Levi) and James Bar-Alpheus, Nathaniel Bar-Talmai, Philip, Simon (Zelotes), Thomas (or Didymus, "Twin," perhaps one of twin younger brothers of Jesus), and Judas (of Karioth). Perhaps James Bar-Zabdai was cut off early and James Bar-Joseph took his place. It was doubtless impracticable to get a representative from each tribe. The preponderance of the evidence, however, is affirmative of a choice of precisely twelve.

The sending of the seventy has been called "a dogmatic invention. As the twelve stand for the twelve tribes of Israel, so the seventy stand for the seventy nations of the world, as counted or imagined at that time. Luke, as the less Jewish Gospel, is not satisfied with a Jewish apostolate."

---

* In Harper's *Cyclopedia of Biblical, Theological, and Ecclesiastical Literature.*

Chapter XXII.

EXPANSION.

What Two Views *concerning the Development of Christ's Character and Mission?*

(1) THE supernatural; (2) The transitional.
The first embraces two theories: either that he was always omniscient, and his opinions unchangeable; or that he had a kind of omnipotence and omniscience which he so kept in abeyance as not to interfere with the conditions of his human nature.

Jesus might be hungry, thirsty, tired, and mistaken,—for instance, in the fig-tree. To the inquiry, "If he was omniscient, must he not have been so unlike mankind as to make his life unnatural and his character useless as an example?" the answer is that, judging from the history, his knowledge was limited by the usual conditions of usual experience, of which, however, his own special birth formed part. The only exceptions seem to be the two or three occasions on which he was elevated to superhuman knowledge, in order to carry on his beneficent work toward individuals,—for instance, the woman of Samaria. And if the question be asked, "Must he not as divine have known all things?" I answer these wearisome puzzles by another just as irrational: Being divine, cannot he be all things, and therefore limited in point of knowledge by voluntary self-surrender?— *Vicar T. W. Fowle* (*Reconciliation of Religion and Science*, p. 354).

Dr. Newman Smyth, in his chapter on "The Uniqueness of Jesus," remarks:—

Though he grew to manhood in a quiet Israelitish home, no man ever thinks of calling him a child of Abraham. Though living all his life among his father's people, he never became a Hebrew of the Hebrews. Though inheriting the traditions of Israel, the Son of David was known as the Son of Man.... The contrast between Jesus' character and the fixed Jewish type appears at once, when we view beside it the greatest of the prophets, who also came just before him, or the chief of the apostles who followed after him.— *Old Faiths in New Light*, p. 188.

(1) The transitional view is that Jesus had a natural growth intellectually and spiritually; and that possibly, after his intellect had expanded above the superstitions of his time and country, he still contented himself with simply approximative expressions of truth.

The real beauty of Christ's life is just that which is hid by the blind ascription of equal sanctity to all he did and said,— his growth. Slight as the authentic points are, they are points of fire. We see him steadily emerging from sectarian trammels and national prejudices: the smoke of Jewish tradition — Gehenna, devils, angels — mingling with, but never mastering the ever-mounting flame of his thought. It is a Jewish Messiah he sees coming in clouds of glory; but the Messianic costume is thrown off, when, descended, the judge says naught of Jew or Gentile, but parts to right and left men as they have or have not fed the hungry and clothed the naked. The hereditary conventional beliefs in his mind decrease until they linger only as superficial garb of his truth: he never makes any prevailing error his main point. It seems to me that some liberals concede too much to that Medusa, superstition, which turns every thought and emotion of Christ to dogmatic stone, when they admit his responsibility for the demonology, the devil, the eternal hell, incidentally mentioned without denial in his teachings. Under compulsion to fulfil the rôle of the Messiah, the Christ of Christendom is made to give an original and divine sanction to the cosmological notions of his age, which he held as we hold the law of gravitation.

The demonology, the great gulf fixed between heaven and hell were the best science of his age: the Darwins and Huxleys of his time, such as they were, believed them. He was not a dialectical or scientific sceptic engaged in questioning such things. In estimating a great man, we should surely look to that wherein he was unique, individual, exceeded his age and added to it. In raising to equal import Christ's mere hereditary mode of expression and the life that was in him, adoring alike body and raiment, the sects are really building as much upon the creed of Christ's crucifiers as on his own. Every scribe and Pharisee agreed with Christ about Gehenna and Satan.... What they did not believe was in a Father who sends his sunshine and rain on good and evil alike; a Father we may deduce at length not likely at any time to rain fires of hell upon his children. To the man who believed in such a Father, there must not be attributed an equally conscious and thought out agreement with the logical results of the conventional cosmogony which was sometimes the inevitable costume of his thought.

It is interesting to note how, from basing his opposition to falsities on the written Law, he more and more appeals to nature and reason. David's eating the shew-bread and man's superiority to the Sabbath are oddly connected for a time; but, at length, his protest against the Sabbath is based simply upon unresting nature and human liberty.

For his age and country, Christ was perhaps unique in his method of measuring usage and tradition by 'real principles. When he warned the youth to keep the commandments, and the young man asks *which*, he does not blindly reply, "The whole ten, of course": he names only five from the decalogue, all the real and human ones,— names none of those that protect Jehovah. For the Sabbatarian command, he substitutes, "Love thy neighbor as thyself." Instead of warning the youth against "graven images," which he is in no danger of worshipping, he touches his real idol,— his wealth; and, instead of exhorting him to do the work of Moses' time, he calls him to the great task of his own,— to come out there into the street, stand by his side, and toil for the right.

How far he carried this rationalism we cannot fully know; for his words come to us mingled with much that is irrational in his reporters. Nevertheless, to the careful eye, his pearl will not be confused with the shell enclosing it. We know that it was a great soul, far above any New Testament writer, which sends us those fine protests against prayer in public places, that relegation of the heart to the closet for its mystical communion with the Highest. Not one of those believers in popular marvels who report him could have invented those exalted poetic interpretations of nature which bid us learn of the sparrow and of the lily, more glorious than Solomon in his splendor, and appealed to men to discern the signs of their own time, as for the weather they watched the morning red and glow of evening. It was no believer in a fictitious providence who rebuked the notion that those on whom the tower of Siloam fell were worse than others. And, even in the Fourth Gospel, we can trace back to him that wonderful saying, that he would not pray for his disciples, because God needs no prompting of his love; and also that lesson of humility taught by his washing the feet of the humble workingmen who followed him. These things represent the integrity of a great mind,— the mind of a thinker, a reasoner, a poet. . . .

At one period, Christ says, "The scribes and Pharisees sat in Moses' seat: all things therefore whatsoever they bid you, do and keep; but do not ye after their works, for they say and do not." Here may be noticed the attitude of a youth in transition; for at another time he does what those occupants of Moses' seat tell him not to do, and repudiates them on principle. They tell him to keep the Sabbath; but he — casting, no doubt, a look on ever active nature around him — replies, "My Father ceases not his work on the Sabbath, nor do I."

At first, he evidently hoped to purify the ancient religion of his fathers from its later corruptions. In the ardor of this early aim, he may have made the violent attack on the tradesmen in the temple, ascribed to him. Before his attention was turned to the law itself, he attacked only the priests' hypocritical evasions thereof; for instance, their allowing a man to purchase an indulgence for not supporting — not honoring — his parents by paying a sum of money into the temple. But the time soon arrived when the conviction was forced upon him, that the Jewish Church could not be so purified or expanded as to answer the needs of mankind or represent his ideal; that, of all that edifice, not one stone should be left upon another.

Not without pangs was the transition completed. Those who have known what it is to wrestle with doubts and misgivings, who have known what it is to break the ties of love and friendship in order to follow truth and right, can best hear all the pathos of that lamentation that comes across the ages: "O Jerusalem, Jerusalem, that killest the prophets and stonest them that are sent unto thee, how often would I have gathered thy children as a hen gathers her chickens under her wings, and ye would not. Behold your house is left unto you desolate. For I say unto you, Ye shall not see me henceforth, till ye shall say, Blessed is he that cometh in the name of the Lord." The next sentence is significant: "And Jesus went out, and departed from the temple." That was just such a heart-broken man abandoning finally and forever the orthodox religion of his time as you, my friend, may have known in your pilgrimage.

Possibly also his mind passed through several phases of belief concerning his being the Messiah of the Jewish hope. From time to time after the Maccabean war, agitators had appeared, assumed to be the Messiah, raised revolts, and perished. As in modern times it has been the characteristic of religious radicals — Fox, Wesley, Swedenborg, Channing — eagerly to declare their faith to be the most genuine Christianity, so then was it felt necessary that a Jewish innovator should prove that he was setting up the only true and genuine Messiahship. This expected kingdom might be conceived variously, but it always involved the supremacy of the Jews over all other nations. Possibly a suggestion of claiming the Messiahship was thrust upon Christ by his friends, and afterward the Messianic idea was gradually translated into the larger spirit of his mind, and merged in his final conception of a regenerate humanity.— *Moncure D. Conway (Idols and Ideals, App. Essay, p. 22, ff.).*

> The outworn rite, the old abuse,
>   The pious fraud transparent grown,
> The good held captive in the use
>   Of wrong alone,—
> These wait their doom from that great law
>   Which makes the past time serve to-day;
> And fresher life the world shall draw
>   From their decay!
>
> Take heart, the master builds again;
>   A charmed life old goodness hath;
> The tares may perish, but the grain
>   Is not for death.
> God works in all things; all obey
>   His first propulsion from the night;
> Wake thou and watch! the world is gray
>   With morning light!
>
> *John G. Whittier.*

Chapter XXIII.

ADAPTATION.

What Other Explanation of the Fact of Christ's Use of Approximative Language?

ADAPTATION of utterance to his hearers' minds. Every reform imposes upon the reformer certain conditions to success. Christ's practice in this regard has been approved by the wise of all ages. Older than his era is the conservative maxim, not yet obsolete among radicals, politicians, and jurists: "The beaten path is the safe path" (*Via trita, via tuta*). Reforms come not in hurricane downfalls.

> Men must be **taught as** if you taught them not,
> And things unknown proposed as things forgot.

Dr. Matthew Arnold, in advocating concession to the use of certain expressions in the prayer-books or hymn-books, even when one's belief may not fully assent thereto, cites the practice of Jesus, who, though knowing that his use of the familiar language of his day — the language of poetry — would occasionally cause immense misapprehension, yet felt that it was not by introducing a brand-new religious language and by parting with the old and cherished images that the popular religion could be transformed, but by keeping the old language and images, and as far as possible carrying into them the soul of the new Christian ideal.* He then asks: —

When Jesus talked of the Son of Man coming in his glory with the holy angels, setting the good on his right hand and the bad on his left and sending away the bad into everlasting fire prepared for the devil and his angels, was he speaking literally? Did Jesus mean that all this would actually happen? Popular religion supposes so. Yet very many religious people even now suppose that Jesus was but using the figures of Messianic judgment familiar to his hearers, in order to impress upon them his main point,— what sort of spirit and of practice did really tend to salvation and what did not. And surely

---

* As to Christ's allusion to Jonah, see *post*, chap. xxxiv.

almost every one must perceive that when Jesus spoke to his disciples of their sitting on thrones, judging the twelve tribes of Israel, or of their drinking new wine with him in the kingdom of God, he was adopting their material images and beliefs, and was not speaking literally. Yet their master's thus adopting their material images and beliefs could not but confirm the disciples in them. And so it did, and Christendom, too, after them; yet in this way, apparently, Jesus chose to proceed.

But some one may say that Jesus used this language because he himself shared the materialistic notions of his disciples about the kingdom of God, and thought that coming upon the clouds and sitting upon thrones and drinking wine would really occur in it, and was mistaken in thinking so. Manifestly, his disciples thought — even the wisest of them, and after their master's death as well as before it — that this kingdom was to be a sudden, miraculous, outward transformation of things, which was to come about very soon and in their own lifetime. Nevertheless, they themselves report Jesus as saying what is in direct contradiction to all this. They report him describing the kingdom of God as an inward change requiring to be spread over an immense time, and coming about by natural means and gradual growth, not suddenly, miraculously. Jesus compares it to a grain of mustard-seed or a handful of leaven. The world must first be evangelized,— no work of one generation, but of centuries and centuries; not until then should the end, the new world, come.

True, the disciples also make Jesus speak as if he fancied this end to be as near as they did. But it is quite manifest that Jesus spoke to them at different times of two ends: one, the end of the Jewish state and nation, which any one who could discern the signs of that time might foresee; the other, the end of the world, the instatement of God's kingdom;— and that they confused the two ends together. Undeniably, therefore, Jesus saw things in a way very different from theirs, and much truer. And, if he uses their materializing language and imagery, then it cannot be because he shared their illusions. Nevertheless, he uses it.— *Last Essays on Church and Religion*, p. 45.

From a portion of this view, another eminent Free Religious writer dissents, deeming it likely that Jesus borrowed from Daniel the idea of a coming in the clouds of heaven; that his favorite designation of himself as the "Son of Man" made this almost inevitable, once he had assumed the rôle of the Messiah : —

Only this, however, is certain: that the Messianic self-consciousness of Jesus included the anticipation of his return to the earth after his death, to establish the kingdom of heaven. The criticism which endeavors to make it appear that the conceptions ascribed to Jesus here are entirely the reflection of the apostolic community is not thoroughly rational. It is necessary to ascribe these conceptions to

Jesus, in order to account for the hold they had upon the primitive Christian community.—*John W. Chadwick* (*The Man Jesus*, p. 160).

Still, the Christian, primitive or cultured, in discriminating on means and manners and locating the line of candor close to courtesy, must recognize Paul's idea of Christ's method: "I am made all things to all men, that I might by all means save some."

It may be a strange, deep question of science how our sun became established in the centre of his system, and reached that grandeur which marks him now,—eight great worlds, such as Earth, Mars, Saturn, Venus, Jupiter, moving ever around him and with him, held into being and harmony by his power, and adorned by his love; but, in spiritual directions, a similar scene appears, that of Christianity advancing and calling to her vast circle certain worlds of charity and brotherhood and purity and hope and beauty. In this large estimate of the scene, many of the variations of theologians, dead or still living, lose all their former significance, and a hundred names of worshippers blend into one worship, and a hundred ways of salvation meet in one path. On such a height, all vain janglings cease; and we see one God, one mediator, one human race, one worship; we hear one prayer, one hymn, and read one sublime creed,—"Fear God and keep his commandments, for this is the whole duty of man." —*David Swing.*

CHAPTER XXIV.

ALLOCUTION.

Where, When, and How were the Principal Discourses of Jesus delivered?

HE availed himself of every occasion that came in his way, especially of the admirable opportunities of the synagogue. His addresses and attached sayings have been preserved, collected, and handed down to us without any strict observance of time and place in their arrangement. The evangelists themselves make very free with the time and place of the discourses in fitting them into their own framework. For instance, in the fifth, sixth, and seventh chapters of Matthew, we possess an inestimable collection of short sayings and more extended discourses, which the first evangelist (or perhaps to a great extent the apostle from whom his Gospel takes its name) had woven together;[*] but they were really uttered at various times and under various circumstances, and have no connection with each other.

Matthew, however, represents Jesus as having delivered the whole collection at once on a mountain. Hence, the name of "Sermon on the Mount" is given to this precious monument of the teaching of Jesus; and the legend has fixed upon "the Horns of Chattin" as the place from which the sermon was delivered. Now, the evangelist had a special motive for fixing upon a mountain for this purpose. He intended to represent Jesus laying down the fundamental laws of the kingdom of heaven as the counterpart of Moses, who promulgated the constitution of the Old Covenant from Mount Sinai. Luke, however, on the other hand, not wishing Jesus to be regarded as a second Moses, or another lawgiver, just as deliberately makes the Master deliver this discourse on a plain.

The abruptness of the transitions is a noticeable feature. Probably many sayings which belong to the closing rather than the opening period of the ministry of Jesus have been put too early by the evangelists.... The Beatitudes may properly stand first as the express

---

[*] Matt. v., 1: sermon to the disciples; vii., 28, to multitudes [*ochloi*]. Perhaps the throng arrived after the disciples.

image of his life and character; yet they were probably uttered subsequently to his disciples privately, after persecution had come.

Whatever was more fitting to say to Nicodemus than to less intellectual persons was no doubt repeated in that interview. This would sum up approximately in: It is not enough, Nicodemus, that you have examined my credentials, and that, approving them, you own me as a teacher carrying a commission from on high. You must accept deeper results of my mission than any you have yet thought of, and must give your mind and spirit to be translated into the region of a new and better life.— *Dr. I. Hooykaas (The Bible for Learners,* vol. iii., p. 141, ff.).

Dr. Geikie, however, reconciles Matthew and Luke by suggesting that the "plain" was a terrace:—

Tradition has chosen the hill known as the "Horns of Hattin," two horn-like heights rising sixty feet above the plain between them, two hours west of Tiberias, at the mouth of the gorge which opens past Magdala into the wild cliffs of Arbela, famous in the history of the Zealots as their hiding-place, and famous also for Herod's battles in mid-air at the mouths of their caves, by means of great cages filled with soldiers let down the precipices. It is greatly in favor of this site to find such a writer as Dean Stanley saying that the situation so strikingly coincides with the intimations of the gospel narrative as almost to force the inference that in this instance the eye of those who selected the spot was rightly guided.

The plain on which the hill stands is easily accessible from the lake; and it is only a few minutes' walk from it to the summit, before reaching which a broad "level place" has to be crossed, exactly suited for the gathering of a multitude together. It was to this, apparently, that Jesus came down from one of the higher horns to address the people. Seated on some slightly elevated rock,—for the teacher always sat while he taught,—the people and the disciples sitting at his feet on the grass, the cloudless Syrian sky over them, the blue lake with its moving life on the one hand, and in the far north the grand form of Hermon glittering in the upper air, he began what is to us the Magna Charta of our faith, and to the hearers must have been the inauguration of the new kingdom of God.— *Life and Words of Christ,* p. 418.

A prominent characteristic of Christ's discourses is their parables. These were a most advantageous means of indoctrination. The images thus imprinted on the imagination, together with the lessons they taught, fixed themselves without effort on the memory, and were passed from mouth to mouth: they will go down through the centuries,

> Must throb in after-throbs till Time itself
> Be laid in stillness, and the universe
> Quiver and breathe upon no mirror more.

The dough standing to rise in the bread-trough illustrated the silent working of truth in society; the seeds falling on different kinds of soil, the degrees of receptivity of the human soul; the bird falling dead from the air, the perpetual, universal providence of God; the parent giving bread to his children at their meals, the influence of the Holy Spirit; the lightning seen all around the sky, at once the coming of a universal religion: by such illustration, Jesus perpetually appealed to the common sense of his hearers in support of his teaching. He also appealed sometimes to their scriptures, and occasionally he met reasoning by reasoning. But most frequently he taught by this reference to common life, so recognizing the analogy between God's laws in nature, in society, and in the soul.— *Dr. J. F. Clarke* (*Common Sense in Religion*, p. 12).

Thomas Fuller says of the good woman, "She makes plain cloth to be velvet by her handsome wearing of it." So Jesus made the parable, which up to his time had been only moderately efficient, a weapon with which he accomplished wonders. And here it is not improper to introduce an indorsement of Christ's practice as to poetic (or simile) license from an unexpected source:—

The most natural beauty in the world is honesty and moral truth. For all beauty is truth. True features make the beauty of a face, and true proportions the beauty of architecture, as true measure that of harmony and music. In poetry which is all fable, truth is still the perfection.— *Earl A. A. C. Shaftsbury.*

All my poetry is the poetry of circumstance. It wholly owes its birth to the realities of life.— *Goethe.*

Truth severe by fairy fiction dressed.— *Thomas Gray.*

Fiction may be much more instructive than real history.— *John Foster.*

The fainter lines are neglected, but the great characteristic features are imprinted on the mind forever.— *Baron Macaulay.*

One notable feature is the reutterances. Thenceforth, Jesus appears habitually to have employed himself in those kinds of word and deed which, repeated in substance over and over again in a large number of places and before great multitudes of witnesses, were to constitute the main ground of his appeal to the conscience of the world and the first basis of the general belief in him,— the basis upon which all the rest was in due time to be built up. But, while he thus wrought from day to day and from place to place, he was also at times employed in sowing a seed which was to lie longer in the ground before the time of germination.

Sometimes, he set himself to sow seed in capable minds and willing hearts, like those of the apostles or like that of Nicodemus; sometimes, to let it fall apart from the common beat of the chosen people, and where it could not be choked by their peculiar prejudices, as with the woman of Samaria. But also in Jerusalem itself, at least by one series of discourses, he was pleased to state sufficiently, in the hearing both of the people and of their guides, the dignity and claims of his person; so that the authentic declaration from his own lips of the truths which were to be developed in apostolic teaching might accredit that teaching to minds that would otherwise have stumbled at the contrast, or would have been unable to fill the void between such doctrine posthumously preached and the common tenor of our Lord's words and acts as they are given in the Synoptical Gospels. Some portions of St. John's Gospel may be regarded as the golden link between the Sermon on the Mount and the theology of the Apostolic Epistles.— *Hon. W. E. Gladstone (Review of Ecce Homo, p. 92).*

The key-note of Christ's discourse was self-abnegation. The Sermon on the Mount was an unfolding of that wide and deep word of John's message — " Repent ! " without rejection of any light from the established traditional lore of the listeners.

The principle may be described according to the side from which it is approached, as the worth of man or the love of God: " Man as man is called to and destined for the highest moral perfection, and as a consequence the purest blessedness." In the Roman Empire, the individual was of no importance except as a part of the great whole, as a citizen of Rome. In Israel, man had no rights, no hope, except as a member of the chosen race, a son of Abraham. But, for Jesus, man as man had sacred and inalienable rights, and a worth that nothing could transcend. And in the mind of Jesus, who brought all things straight into connection with God, this truth assumed this form. Man is by nature God's own child, is capable of bearing God's image, and is the object of his infinite affection. The Supreme Power, before which man bows in adoration, which has traced its indelible law upon his heart, is a power of love; and man's inmost nature is akin to it. Man is akin to God. God is our Father. And it is because man is so truly great that, as a spiritual being, he must trample down all that is material or push it altogether into the background, since it is too poor and worthless to be the object of his care.— *Prof. J. R. Seeley (Ecce Homo).*

The chief potency of the words of Jesus lay in the demonstration afforded by his example. It is the most hopeful and redeeming fact in history that Christ, by preference, associated with the meanest of our race. Indeed, the poor attracted him more than the rich: their vices seemed to him less dangerous. Injustice, cruelty, and oppression were more hateful to him than vices of passion or improvidence.

It was because the edict of universal love went forth to men whose hearts were in no cynical mood, but possessed with a spirit of devotion to a man, that words which at any other time, however grandly they might sound, would have been but words, penetrated so deeply, and along with the law of love the power of love was given. Therefore, also, the first Christians were enabled to dispense with philosophical phrases, and instead of saying that they loved the ideal of man in man, could simply say and feel that they loved Christ in every man. We have here the very kernel of the Christian moral scheme.

Few of us sympathize originally and directly with this devotion; few of us can perceive in human nature itself any merit sufficient to evoke it. But it is not so hard to love and venerate him who felt it. So vast a passion of love, a devotion so comprehensive, elevated, deliberate, and profound, has not elsewhere been in any degree approached save by some of his imitators. And, as love provokes love, many have found it possible to conceive for Christ an attachment the closeness of which no words can describe,— a veneration so possessing and absorbing the man within them that they have said, "I live no more, but Christ lives in me."

Now, such a feeling carries with it of necessity the feeling of love for all human beings. It matters no longer what quality men may exhibit: amiable or unamiable, as the brothers of Christ, as belonging to his sacred and consecrated kind, as the objects of his love in life and death, they must be dear to all to whom he is dear. And those who would for a moment know his heart and understand his life must begin by thinking of the whole race of man, and of each member of the race, with awful reverence and hope.— *Prof. J. R. Seeley* (*Ecce Homo*, p. 165 [178]).

Chapter XXV.

VENERATION.

Wherein and What the Regenerating Tendencies of the Indoctrination of Faith in Christ and in the Mutuality or "Solidarity" of the Human Race?

THERE are two facts, the converse of each other,— mutuality of blessing and mutuality of cursing. One is : —

There is no sort of wrong deed of which a man can bear the punishment alone: you can't isolate yourself, and say that the evil that is in you shall not spread. Men's lives are as thoroughly blended with each other as the air they breathe : evil spreads as necessarily as disease.— *George Eliot.*

As to the other, the existence of faith — of fidelity to an Unseen Power of Goodness — imports an exercise of the elemental power of sympathy and emotion, with the single, unalterable object of dying with Christ to the law of the flesh, to live with Christ to the law of the mind.

Justice is often but a form of pedantry, mercy mere easiness of temper, courage a mere firmness of physical constitution; but, if these virtues are genuine, then they indicate not goodness merely, but goodness considerably developed. A man may be potentially just or merciful, yet from defect of training he may be actually neither. We want a test which shall admit all who have it in them to be good, whether their good qualities be trained or not. Such a test is found in faith. He who, when goodness is impressively put before him, exhibits an instinctive loyalty to it, starts forward to take its side, trusts himself to it,— such a man has faith, and the root of the matter is in such a man. He may have habits of vice, but the loyal and faithful instinct in him will place him above many that practise virtue. He may be rude in thought and character, but he will unconsciously gravitate toward what is right. Other virtues can scarcely thrive without a fine natural organization and a happy training. But the most neglected and ungifted of men may make a beginning with faith. Other virtues want civilization, a certain amount of knowledge, a few books; but, in half-brutal countenances, faith will light up a glimmer of nobleness. The savage who can do little else can wonder and worship and enthusiastically obey. He who cannot know what is right can know that some one else knows, he who has no law may still have a master, he who is incapable of justice may be capable of fidelity, he who understands little may have his sins forgiven because he loves much.

Christ laid men under an immense obligation. He convinced them that he was a person of altogether transcendent greatness; one who needed nothing at their hands; one whom it was impossible to benefit by conferring riches or fame or dominion upon him, and that, being so great, he had devoted himself of mere benevolence to their good. He showed them that for their sakes he lived a hard and laborious life, and exposed himself to the utmost malice of powerful men. They saw him hungry, though they believed him able to turn the stones into bread; they saw his royal pretensions spurned, though they believed that he could in a moment take into his hand all the kingdoms of the world and the glory of them; they saw his life in danger; they saw him at last expire in agonies, though they believed that, had he so willed it, no danger could harm him, and that, had he thrown himself from the topmost pinnacle of the temple, he would have been softly received in the arms of ministering angels. Witnessing his sufferings and convinced that they were voluntarily endured, men's hearts were touched; and, pity for weakness blending strangely with wondering admiration of unlimited power, an agitation of gratitude, sympathy, and astonishment, such as nothing else could ever excite, sprang up in them; and when, turning from his deeds to his words, they found this very self-denial which had guided his own life prescribed as the principle which should guide theirs, gratitude broke forth in joyful obedience, self-denial produced self-denial, and the law and law-giver together were enshrined in their utmost hearts for inseparable veneration.—*Prof. J. R. Seeley (Ecce Homo*, pp. 66 and 50 [76 and 59]).

This universal adaptation of the faith test is quaintly mentioned by the old poet:—

> If bliss had lain in art or strength,
> None but the wise and strong had gained it;
> Where now by Faith all arms are of a length,
> One size doth all conditions fit.

And this "inseparable veneration" was to be the basis of a universal religion. Mankind were one family in the heart of Christ, and must become so in the hearts of his followers. A German poet and philosopher, after a long life of observation and reflection, testifies:—

The Religion which depends on reverence [*Ehrfurcht*, honor done without fear] for what is above us we denominate the Ethnic; it is the religion of the nations, and the first happy deliverance from a degrading fear: all Heathen religions, as we call them, are of this sort, whatsoever names they may bear. The Second Religion, which **founds itself on** reverence for what is around us, we denominate the **Philosophical;** for the philosopher stations himself in the middle, and **must draw down** to him all that is higher, and up to him all that is lower, and only in this medium condition does he merit the title of **Wise. Here, as** he surveys with clear sight his relation to his equals, and therefore **to** the whole human race, his relation likewise to all other earthly circumstances and arrangements necessary or accidental, he alone in a cosmic sense lives in Truth. But now we have to speak of a Third Religion, grounded on reverence for what is beneath us: this we name the Christian, **as in** the Christian religion such a temper is with most distinctness manifested: it is a last step **to** which mankind were fitted and destined to attain. But what a task was it, not only to be patient with the Earth, and let it lie beneath us, we appealing to a higher birthplace, but also to recognize humility and poverty, mockery and despite, disgrace and wretchedness, suffering and death,— to recognize these things as divine!— *Goethe* (*Wilhelm Meister's Travels*, chap. x., *Carlyle's translation*).

Religion is the human mind standing in reverence before the infinite energy of the universe, asking to be lifted into it,— opening itself to inspiration.— *Christian E. Luthardt.*

Religion is assent through conscience to God.— *James Martineau.*

And what say two leading American thinkers hereon?

As Humboldt says, "The finest fruit earth holds up to its Maker is a finished **man."** To ripen, lift, and educate a man is the first duty. Trade, **law,** learning, science, and religion are only the scaffolding wherewith to build a man. Despotism looks down into the poor man's cradle, and knows it can crush resistance and curb ill-will. Democracy **sees** the ballot in that baby hand; and selfishness bids her put integrity on one side of those baby footsteps and intelligence on the other, lest her own hearth be in peril. Thank God for His method of taking bonds of wealth and culture to share all their blessings with the humblest soul he gives to their keeping! The American should cherish as serene a faith as his fathers had. Instead of seeking a coward safety by battening down the hatches and putting men **back** into chains, he should recognize that God places him in **this peril** that he may work out a noble security by concentrating all **moral forces to** lift this weak, rotting, and dangerous mass into sunlight and health. The fathers touched their highest level when, with stout-hearted and serene faith, they trusted God that it was safe to leave men with all the rights he gave them. Let us be worthy of their blood, and save this sheet-anchor of the race — universal suffrage,— God's church, God's school, God's method of gently binding men into commonwealths, in order that they may at last melt into brothers.— *Wendell Phillips* (*The Scholar in a Republic*, p. 20).

The other leading American utterance is in the concluding discourse of Dr. James Freeman Clarke's recent series on the "Ideas of Paul":—

Paul had an idea of the steady outward progress of the whole Christian community. All rested on one deep principle,— faith in Jesus as the Christ. It would not come — this growth — from science or philosophy, from conscience or reason, from circumstances or environment: it would only come from faith in this divine ideal,— Christ, the fulness of the manifestation of God.

Observe now how men seek and need ideals, in order to grow. Every man, who is making progress, does so because he is pursuing an ideal aim. Every one has some leader, master, some one who represents to his imagination the best thing he knows. Students in science have their masters, their ideal chiefs,— Humboldt or Tyndall, perhaps; students in philosophy theirs,— Plato, Aristotle, Stuart Mill; students in literature theirs,— Shakspere, Bacon, Emerson; ardent, aspiring politicians theirs. Amid the dangers of a democratic government, what a blessing that we have in this country an ideal of perfect patriotism, of pure love of country, in our Washington! He stands as an ideal of purity in public affairs, and so he is regarded by the world. So, for example, speaks Byron,—

> Where may the wearied eye repose
>   When gazing on the great?
> Where neither guilty glory glows,
>   Nor despicable state,—
> Yes, one,— the first, the last, the best,—
> The Cincinnatus of the West,
>   Whom envy dared not hate.
> Bequeathed the name of Washington
> To make men blush there was but one.

So, also, Macaulay testifies, speaking of Hampden: "When the vices and ignorance which the old tyranny had generated threatened the new freedom with destruction, then it was that England missed that sobriety, self-command, perfect soundness of judgment, perfect rectitude of intention, to which the history of revolutions furnishes no parallel, or furnishes a parallel in Washington alone."

What an immense disaster it would be to this nation to lose this ideal of patriotism. Suppose some destructive critic should succeed in convincing us that Washington, after all, was no better than other vulgar conquerors,— no patriot, but a self-seeker, a demagogue, a cunning partisan: could any greater misfortune than that befall our country? Such a misfortune, only infinitely greater, would befall the human race, if it could be made to appear that Jesus was not the divine ideal, the perfect man, the image of the divine goodness, truth, and love.

It was by faith in this ideal Jesus that Paul lived and worked. All his hope for human progress flowed from this faith. "Speaking the truth in love," said he, "let us grow up in all things into him who is our head, even Jesus Christ. Till we all come, in the oneness of faith and the knowledge of the Son of God, unto a perfect man, into the measure of the stature of the fulness of Christ." It was not any abstract philosophic truth which Paul trusted in as the source of human progress, but truth made real in the life of Jesus; truth become a part of human experience; truth shown to be possible by one great example. This is the difference between speculative truth, which only moves the reason, and living truth, which awakens the whole soul.— *Boston Saturday Evening Gazette,* May 21, 1881.

No man or woman of the humblest sort can really be strong, gentle, pure, and good, without the world being better for it, without somebody being helped and comforted by the very existence of that goodness.— *Phillips Brooks.*

The foregoing allusion to Macaulay recalls his lay of Horatius, which recurred to General D. McCook when facing death at Kenesaw Mountain, as told by General Garfield in an after-dinner conversation:—

"Why, they were men who went into battle inspired by all the heroism of antiquity. They marched into the fight with Miltiades and Themistocles and all the heroes of history in the air above them. There was that glorious soldier, General Dan McCook; he was storming the heights of Kenesaw Mountain at the head of his troops; the summit was crowded with rebel troops; the ascent was precipitous; the troops had to lift themselves up by the bushes and branches; he knew it was almost certain death. In a momentary pause in the ascent, he was heard to utter, as if speaking to himself, but in calm, clear tones, those words from Macaulay's *Lays of Ancient Rome:* —

> Then outspoke brave Horatius, the captain of the gate:
> "To every man upon this earth death cometh soon or late.
> And how can man die better than facing fearful odds,
> For the ashes of his fathers and the temples of his gods?
> And for the tender mother who dandled him to rest,
> And for the wife who nurses his baby at her breast?"

The rough soldiers all around felt the full meaning of these words, and remembered them. A moment afterward, McCook rushed up the heights, and in two minutes fell dead

> For the ashes of his fathers and the temples of his gods.

And now," said General Garfield, "could man die better?" I have given you the words, but I cannot give you the grand, glowing manner with which Garfield recited them.— *John L. Hayes.*

And Garfield himself!

And here, too, lies reason for our treasuring the sign to worship therein the thing signified,— the image of the cross, the torn banners in the rotundas of our capitols.

> Brave battle-flags from wild war's bloody waves
> Dashed quivering back upon Time's echoing strand,
> To tell the tale of dauntless souls and true.

Here will be recalled Carlyle's remark as to hero-worship: "Religion, I find, stands upon it,—not paganism only, but far higher and truer religions, all religion hitherto known. Hero-worship, heart-felt, prostrate admiration, submission, burning, boundless, for a noblest, godlike form of man,—is not that the germ of Christianity itself? The greatest of all heroes is one whom we do not name here. Let sacred silence meditate that matter: you will find it the ultimate perfection of a principle extant throughout man's whole history on earth." Whereupon George McCrie says, "Christianity stands not upon this as its mainstay: it stands upon the supernatural doctrines of justification through the blood of Christ and regeneration by the Holy Ghost."* And to a reviewer of this reviewer has this favorite predicate, "stands upon," suggested Seneca's aphorism, "Religion worships God; superstition profanes that worship." All of which recalls the more modern maxim, "Thou holdest not the root, but the root thee."

But no one will be disposed to deny that a glorious company of martyrs reflect praise on what is divinest in man: and this, too, outside the list given by the author of the Epistle to the Hebrews, of them that wrought righteousness through fidelity to conviction of an unseen power. Time will fail me, if I tell of Gideon, Socrates, Leonidas, the Roman sentinel at Pompeii's gate, Winkelreid, Gustav Adolphus, Latimer, Raleigh, Maynard, John Brown, and so forth.

We may admit that the reverence paid to them in former days was unreasonable and excessive; that credulity and ignorance have, in many instances, falsified the actions imputed to them; that enthusiasm has magnified their numbers beyond all belief; that, when the communion with martyrs was associated with the presence of their material remains, the passion for relics led to a thousand abuses, and the belief in their intercession to a thousand superstitions. But why, in uprooting the false, uproot also the beautiful and the true? Surely, it is a thing not to be set aside or forgotten, that generous men and meek women, strong in the strength and elevated by the sacrifice of a Redeemer, did suffer, did endure, did triumph for the truth's sake, did leave us an example which ought to make our hearts glow within us in admiration and gratitude.— *Anna Murphy Jameson (Sacred and Legendary Art).*

---

* *The Religion of our Literature,* p. 64.

A "cloud of witnesses" indeed, recalling and supplementing the familiar "Proposition I." of Archbishop William Paley's *Evidences:* "Many professing to have been the original witnesses of Christ's miracles, crucifixion, and resurrection, passed their lives in labors, dangers, and sufferings, voluntarily undergone in attestation of the accounts which they delivered, and solely in consequence of their belief in the truth of those accounts." Whether or not we partially dissent from both " I." and " II.," we must assent to what underlies,— call it, if you please, the sentiment of the ages : —

"My will, not thine, be done," turns Paradise into a desert. " Thy will, not mine, be done." turns the desert into a Paradise, and makes Gethsemane the gate of heaven.— *Edmond de Pressensé.*

> Thy native home is whereso'er
> Christ spirit breathes a holier air,
> Where Christ-like faith is keen to seek
> What truth or conscience freely speak,
> Where Christ-like love delights to span
> The rents that sever man from man,—
> Where round God's throne his just ones stand,
> There, Christian, is thy Fatherland.
>
> *Dean A. P. Stanley.*

Still must we apostrophize our ideals : —

> Angels of growth! . . .
> Did ye descend, what were ye more than I ? . . .
> Wait there,— wait and invite me while I climb;
>   For, see, I come ! — but slow, but slow!
> Yet ever as your chime,
> Soft and sublime,
>   Lifts at my feet, they move, they go
> Up the great stair of time.
>
> *David A. Wasson.*

> We have not wings, we cannot soar ;
>   But we have feet to scale and climb
> By slow degrees, by more and more,
>   The cloudy summits of our time.
>
> *Henry W. Longfellow.*

Chapter XXVI.

EVOLUTION.

What is meant in the Beatitudes by the "Kingdom of Heaven," and What the Progress of its Development?

THE dominion of the higher in human character, attained by individual conformity of conduct to the law of love, through an evolution wherein the morally, intellectually, and religiously fittest — the permanently strongest — survives the mere ephemerally strongest. The weak — the temporarily weak — shall ultimately inherit the earth. Mammoth and megalosaurus, mere moving mountains of monster force, have perished from the planet. The lions have decreased before the lambs. Man, weakest of all animals at birth, has been awarded the sceptre of the world, because he was fittest, through his power to love, to consider, to deny himself for others.

It is the very evangel of our time that knowledge is shadowing out the moral essence of the world. It has shown mere physical power steadily decreasing, and the power of thought and love increasing; and it has thus discovered for the humane a new basis for their hope, a new spur for their effort. Ferocity is a weakness; fanaticism is feebleness; selfishness is suicidal. Turkey feels it; Spain feels it; Rome is learning it. Love, justice, knowledge, lead the world, and human hearts may now sing unto their Lord a new song. A new song! and yet that which is now a matter of knowledge was of old felt out by the intuition and faith of great hearts.

It was felt out by Christ, who estimated things by their sentiment, — by their spirit,— and not by their outward size and seeming strength. He anticipated the whole story of moral evolution. To the lowly, he said, is given the kingdom of heaven: humility shall inherit the earth. He had faith that ideas could level the loftiest temples, stone by stone, and perfect faith move mountains. He could see a vast property in a widow's mite, and emptiness in the costliest offering. He valued the sympathy of a woman whom others scorned more than the gifts of the proud. A cup of cold water given for truth's sake carried with it a divine virtue. He looked not to the thing done, whether it were large or little, but to the heart and worth put into it: nothing could be large that had no soul in it, nothing small which had in it one spark of love and truth.

Is there no philosophy in all this? Why, modern knowledge has almost abolished distinctions of great and small. It reads one law in the rounding of a world or a tear; it sees in the smallest improvement of plant or animal the essence of a new kingdom. It discovers the power of leasts.... When all the world is smiting the unpopular cause, what is implied, if one approaches with hand extended, not to smite, but to clasp and bless? Out of all, that one hand alone represents the divine life and purpose of nature; that one alone acts for no selfish end, is guided by no low interest, bribed by no mean desire, not terrified by public odium. That heart which brings its love and devotion to the true and right has brought with it the might of every law,—the forces of destiny. When Dr. Johnson was once loudly defending some strange principle of his against a company of gainsayers, all opposed him, it seemed. One man present alone said to him, "I believe you are right." The man who said that was John Wesley. Johnson lowered his voice and said, "To have convinced such a man as you is all I can desire." With the one best man on his side, Johnson felt he was in the majority.

That cause is not weak which has won the faith of the wise and the love of the pure in heart, though the wise be few and poor, and the lovers able to give but a cup of cold water. Its star is in the east, its day will not recede: it moves with steadfast planets in their courses.— *Moncure D. Conway* (*Idols and Ideals*, p. 95).

This incident of Dr. Johnson may have suggested to Beaconsfield the remark, "I prefer to belong to the intellectual rather than to the numerical majority."

The simile of the mustard-seed and the parable of the sower suggest yet another illustration of this "moral evolution":—

The law of the harvest is to reap more than you sow. Sow an act, and you reap a habit; sow a habit, and you reap a character; sow a character, and you reap a destiny.— *George D. Boardman.*

And not one destiny merely. It is declared in the "Papyrus Prisse" (found, says Mrs. L. M. Child, in a very ancient Egyptian tomb, and supposed to be the oldest writing in the world, 2000 B.C.) that "what a man has to do is to teach his children wisdom. After he has finished the lot of man, their duty consists in going up the ladder which he has set for them."

Mr. Conway's remark that nothing could be small, etc., recalls that of Michael Angelo, "Trifles make perfection, but perfection is no trifle."

Recently, it was a bold thing to say that conduct was three-fourths of life. It is beginning to be seen that it is all of life,— not doing simply, but knowing and being. Never before have men been so conscious that every study and every art ultimates in this. "The invention of new crimes in politics," as it has been called,— what is it but a perception of the higher law? Political economy is seen to be not a national, but an international question ; and the solution of its problems lies in the translation of its terms into the language not of local, but of human interests. How all literature is analyzed for its light on moral questions! Fiction fails to interest us, if it does not involve the situations, perils, victories of the moral sense. Theology is but the tragedy of conscience told in rhetoric. Art must awaken the sense of universal relation. And science, tracing the process of creation from atom to orb, from monad to man, consciously or unconsciously pours all its treasures, gives all the force of its infinite facts, to establish the authority of the moral law.—*J. C. Learned* (*Saratoga Sermon*, 1882).

In the gradual establishment of dominion of the higher self, two lines of tendency have been noted as affecting the harmonious expansion of all the powers which make the beauty and worth of human nature. Two individuals or two nations, placed in different circumstances, would have diverse views of the relative importance and value of reason as a guide and some other authority as the controller of conduct, whence would result the usurpation of the function of one faculty by the over-development of another.

At the bottom of both the Greek and the Hebrew notion is the desire, native in man, for reason and the will of God, the feeling after the universal order,— in a word, the love of God. But while Hebraism seizes upon certain plain, capital intimations of the universal order, and rivets itself, one may say, with unequalled grandeur of earnestness and intensity on the study and observance of them, the bent of Hellenism is to follow with flexible activity the whole play of the universal order, to be apprehensive of missing any part of it, of sacrificing one part to another, to slip away from resting in this or that intimation of it, however capital. An unclouded clearness of mind, an unimpeded play of thought, is what this bent drives at. The governing idea of Hellenism is *spontaneity* of *consciousness;* that of Hebraism, *strictness* of *conscience*.

Christianity changed nothing in this essential bent of Hebraism to set doing above knowing. Self-conquest, self-devotion, the following not our own individual will, but the will of God,— *obedience*,— is the fundamental idea of this form, also of the discipline to which we have attached the general name of Hebraism. Only as the old law and the network of prescriptions with which it enveloped human life were evidently a motive power not driving and searching enough to produce the result aimed at,— patient continuance in well-doing, self-conquest, — Christianity substituted for them boundless devotion to that inspiring and affecting pattern of self-conquest offered by Christ ; and by the new motive power, of which the essence was this, though the love and admiration of Christian Churches have for centuries been employed in varying, amplifying, and adorning the plain description of it, Christianity, as St. Paul truly says, "establishes the law," and, in the strength of the ampler power which she has thus supplied to fulfil it, has accomplished the miracles we all see of her history.— *Dr. Matthew Arnold (Culture and Anarchy*, p. 147).

And here may be noted another feature in the philosophy of the progress of Christianity :—

The mighty change which Christ achieved in the whole frame and attitude of the human mind with respect to divine things was transmitted from age to age, but not by effort and agony like his, or like the subordinate but kindred agency of those who were chosen by him to co-operate in the great revolution. Sometimes, it was, indeed, both sustained and developed by the great powers and by the faith and zeal of individuals, and by a constancy even unto death; but, in the main, it passed on from age to age by traditional, insensible, and unconscious influences. As the ages grew, and as the historic no less than the social weight of Christianity rapidly accumulated, men, by no unnatural process, came to rely more and more on the evidence afforded by the simple prevalence of the religion in the world, which was in truth a very great one; less and less upon the results of any original investigation reaching upward to the Fountain-head. The adhesion of the civil power, the weight of a clergy, the solidity and mass of Christian institutions, the general accommodation of law to principles derived from the Scripture, that very flavor of at least an historic Christianity which, after a long, undisputed possession, pervades and scents the whole atmosphere of social life,— all these in ordinary times seem to the mass of men to be as proofs so sufficient that to seek for others would be a waste of time and labor. If there be unreason in this blind reliance, probably much more unreason is shown when the period of reaction comes.— *Hon. W. E. Gladstone (Review of Ecce Homo*, p. 115).

According therewith comes an eloquent answer to the inquiry, the peroration of the concluding discourse of Dr. J. F. Clarke's series on the *Ideas of Paul :* —

In an age full of tendencies to materialism, and yet full of the spirit of enterprise and progress, what is needed but a new influx of this faith in a divine spirit, not miraculous and arbitrary, but like an ocean of love, in which all are borne along, and which will flow into every heart and mind which opens to receive it? In a day which is full of intellectual activity, what better than to add the joy of faith and hope, the sight of a divine future? In an age of humanity and philanthropy, what is needed but a heavenly love to be joined with earthly sympathy, a divine impulse to bear us on toward human charity? In an age when this life is growing happier, when the old wrongs and abuses are disappearing, what is more needed than the sight of immortality, of the world to come, a continuation of all that is best in this, a place of reunion of loving hearts, of greater peace and joy, where there shall be higher tastes, more generous love, keener insight, and where we shall see and know more of the great Master, the dear Friend, Jesus Christ? These are the ideas of Paul. Can we find any better?—*Boston Saturday Evening Gazette*, May 21, 1881.

I would give nothing for a young man who did not begin life with an enthusiasm of some kind: it shows at least that he had faith in something good, lofty, and generous from his own stand-point.—*George L. Le Clerc, Comte de Buffon.*

Morality is but the vestibule of religion.—*Dr. E. H. Chapin.*

One shall not say: Every fall is a fall upward, and I will fall as much as I please. On the contrary, we read everywhere the doom of the shiftless, the disobedient, and the frivolous. The work of God goes on: the lines of right and truth become with each age plainer; the pressure toward just and pure living is heavier to fight against; and history is a record of the ruin, in some shape, of every individual, dynasty, trade, party, or nation which persisted in withstanding the progress of good.—*Charles F. Dole (Sermon on Ezek.* xxi., 27).

>Here patriot Truth her glorious precepts draw,
>Pledged to Religion, Liberty, and Law.
>
>*Joseph Story.*

Another phase of this topic will be incidentally considered in the next two chapters.

Chapter XXVII.

INDOCTRINATION.

What is the most Important Characteristic of the Sermon on the Mount, and What the First Four Precepts against Selfishness?

Its concreteness. This has been remarked by thinkers of every denomination. Witness widely indorsed aphorisms:—

Christianity, which is always true to the heart, knows no abstract virtues, but virtues resulting from our wants, and useful to all.— *François R. A., Vicomte de Chateaubriand.*

Do the duty that lies nearest to thee.— *Goethe.*

All bow to Virtue, and then walk away.— *J. De Finod.*

Aim above morality. Be not simply good. Be good for something.— *H. D. Thoreau.*

What we need most is not so much to realize the ideal as to idealize the real.— *Dr. F. H. Hedge.*

How unlike those old scholastics that were forever busily idle over such worthless abstract questionings as "What's Matter?" "How many million angels can dance on a needle's point?"— *Dr. Marcellus A. Herrick.*

What is mind? No matter. What is matter? Never mind. What is the soul? It is immaterial.— *Thomas Hood.*

The passage from the physics of the brain to the corresponding facts of consciousness is unthinkable.— *John Tyndall.*

What I object to in Scotch philosophers in general is that they reason upon man as they would upon a divinity, they pursue truth without caring if it be useful truth.— *Sydney Smith.*

The negative precept of the Grecian sage, and of the most human of the rabbis,* Jesus makes the golden rule of the world. . . . The

---

* In the sayings of Hillel, Dean Stanley hears "faint accents of a generous and universal theology" (*The Jewish Church*, iii., p. 507).

philosophers brought much beaten oil; but Jesus, by the power of his spirit, converted the oil into light.*... In him was Yea.† This unbroken and undoubting "Yea" of Jesus' self-consciousness manifests itself throughout his teaching. His doctrine is never a question and a weary doubt.—*Dr. Newman Smyth* (*Old Faiths in New Light*, pp. 199, 217).

Having considered the manner, etc., of Christ's teaching,‡ it in part remains to consider the *matter* thereof. This embraces two themes: (1) Reverence and (2) Love. The former has just been considered.§ Of the latter, two interacting phases have already been predicated: (1) the subjective phase, or a certain *condition of the soul* induced by introspection and self-renunciation; (2) the objective phase, or a certain *conduct of life* in all the various relations of each to other and to the community. The conformity of this conduct to certain rules of natural justice laid down by Moses, Confucius, Socrates, Jesus, and ethical writers ancient and modern, constitutes morality. Religion has sometimes been defined to be morality affected by emotion. Thus, when Cicero says, "Hold off from sensuality; for, if you have given yourself up to it, you will find yourself unable to think of anything else," this is morality. But when Jesus says, "Blessed are the pure in heart, for they shall see God," this is religion. But, as has been well remarked, emotion has no value in the Christian system, save as it stands connected with the right conduct as cause thereof.

Emotion is the bud, not the flower; and never is it of value until it expands into a flower. Every religious sentiment, every act of devotion which does not produce a corresponding elevation of life, is worse than useless: it is absolutely pernicious, because it ministers to self-deception, and tends to lower the line of personal morals.—*W. H. H. Murray.*

The world is beginning to apprehend that, after all our disputes and discussions upon dogmatic Christianity, religion consists of love to God and love to man, and has its final result and grand consummation in character.—*Dr. J. G. Holland.*

The world wants the gold standard of righteousness rather than the fictitious and fluctuating paper currency of creeds.—*Rush R. Shippen.*

Ritual does not produce religion, but religion produces ritual.—*Dr. James F. Clarke.*

---

* See Neander's thorough discussion of "The Relation of the Hellenic to Christian Ethics," *Wissenschaftliche Abhandlungen.*
† II. Cor. i., 19.   ‡ *Ante*, chap. xxiv.
§ Directly in chap. xxv. and incidentally in chap. xi.

It is possible for a man to stand high in the Church, to obtain preferment and honor in it, on account of his zeal and success as an ecclesiastical propagandist, and yet not be a follower of Christ. It is time men learned to discern between the Christian spirit and the ecclesiastical spirit.— *Anon. (The Interior).*

The whole business of religion is not merely to insure a man against fire in the other world, but to create an insurable interest in him.— *Henry W. Beecher (Response at the Herbert Spencer Dinner).*

It is not proposed here to consider at any length the trite points of Christ's law of love, but to advert to some features that he therein emphasized that have not always received the attention requisite to the symmetry of culture already mentioned in considering Harmonization, etc.*

The Beatitudes, since they relate directly and explicitly to condition, and only generally to conduct, would perhaps more appropriately form the peroration than the introduction of the Sermon on the Mount, and were probably so placed by Jesus; and no doubt they were more or less repeated by him in his private farewell discourses with his disciples. They would, however, form no inapt premonition to fortify the disciples' minds against what must be encountered in their southward journey. The watchword of the Beatitudes is THE KINGDOM OF HEAVEN.

Oh, what a theme! How it brings back voices forevermore silent! Nay, "he being dead yet speaketh." And how the testimony of the long line of faithful monitors to whom any of us have listened concur hereon,— Catholic or Protestant, orthodox or other! Three decades ago, the writer listened lovingly to a venerable Methodist clergyman † who with earnest persuasiveness set forth the conditions of admission into this kingdom. A few days ago, he heard a young Unitarian clergyman set forth the same conditions with the same simple earnestness, and quoting the same Scriptures. Each was informally addressing a small Bible-circle of honest truth-seekers. The latter said : —

To John the Baptist, the kingdom of heaven was a new order of things external; to Jesus, it was a new state of the soul. One might be, said Jesus, very little therein, and yet be greater than John. Paul gloried only in *Christ's* ideal. "The kingdom of God is within you." The conditions of entering the state were: (1) *Humility.* A little child would be greatest. (2) *Sincerity.* Pharisaic righteousness

---

* *Ante,* chap. xvii.
† The late Rev. Benjamin Burnham, of Groton., Vt.

would avail nothing. (3) *Earnestness.* "There is no man that hath left house or wife or brethren or parents or children for the kingdom of God's sake who shall not receive manifold more in this time, and, in the world to come, eternal life." (4) *Gradual Growth.* A mustard-seed planted in cherishing soil is a good emblem of the gradual growth and marvellous development of this kingdom in the heart and in the world. (5) A *new* principle. One must be born anew, said Jesus to Nicodemus. (6) A *present* principle. It is not merely future and afar off. "This is life eternal, that they should know thee, the only true God, and him whom thou didst send, even Jesus Christ." And, to know Christ, we must know experientially what is declared in the Beatitudes promote the kingdom of God in the heart. Well, if one hath felt sorrow,— been really "*acquainted* with grief,"— one must have had self-examination until the inmost soul plainly sees and is thoroughly sick of the unrest that comes of slavery to the lower nature, is famishing with feeding on husks, hungers and thirsts after righteousness, renounces all base allegiance. — *J. Frederick Dutton* (Hawes Place Church, South Boston).

Ah, sorrow! "The saddest thing under the sky," exclaimed the Countess de Gasparin, "is a soul incapable of sadness." And not individually alone do we verify these principles. "Nations," declares Mazzini, "are educated through suffering, mankind is purified through sorrow. The power of creating obstacles to progress is human and partial. Omnipotence is with the ages." To nations no less than to individuals applies the quaint aphorism of George Herbert, "Prosperity lets go the bridle." And, as to pride and humility, the proverbial philosophy of all peoples is an infinite confirmation of that of the Hebrew sages of the era of David and Solomon.

To be able under all circumstances to practise five things constitutes perfect virtue. These five things are gravity, generosity of soul, sincerity, earnestness, and kindness.— *Confucius.*

Of the precepts to love there stand prominent directions to cultivate: —

(1) The kindness of imparting knowledge. Let your light shine by word and by deed, and thereby draw folks to follow and glorify the Divine. What though it bring you envy, misrepresentation, unpopularity, discomfort, ostracism? There's a beatitude in it. Only thus can the human family progress upward. As to all things, therefore, whatsoever you (imagining yourself in the place of one ignorant, narrow, conceited, and Pharisaical) would be admonished and instructed in, admonish and instruct.

(2) The kindness of reconciliation. Of course there can be no kingdom of heaven — no dominion of the higher — so long

as the cruel and malevolent lower is predominating. What though patience under a wrong be difficult? There's a beatitude in it. Only thus can the human family progress upward.

As to all things, therefore, whatsoever you, if having trespassed or been spiteful, would that the wronged person should do unto you by way of restitution or forgiveness, do you even so unto him or her. " Love is the loadstone of love."

Good will, like a good name, is got by many actions, and lost by one.— *Baron Francis Jeffrey.*

To persevere in one's duty and to be silent is the first answer to calumny.— *George Washington.*

I have never seen anything in the world worth getting angry about. —*Henry J. Raymond.*

(3) **The kindness of** promoting chastity. The procreative instinct is a necessary, a beneficent one. "The preservation of the species was a point of such necessity that nature has secured it at all hazards by immensely overloading the passion at the risk of perpetuating crime and disorder."* But of course there can be no kingdom of heaven — no dominion of the higher, the home sacrament — so long as the base, the brutish, unrestrained lower is obtruding, usurping, and dominating. Just outside of Jerusalem burns the offal-fire, Gehenna. Would it not be fool hardiness, insanity, madness, to let any propensity put and keep you in Gehenna? The rather have no mind or body at all. Amputation and cauterization are better than blood-poisoning; and prevention is better than amputation. What though self-continence be sometimes difficult? It will be easy enough after you have habitually reined in your imagination, unless you are hopelessly insane. When unaverted was David's gaze from Bathsheba, *then* unaverted was the assassination of Uriah. There's a beatitude in purity and chivalrous honor. Only thus can the human family progress upward. As to all things, therefore, whatsoever you, if happy in the possession of wife, daughter or sister, husband, son or brother, would that another should do (or refrain from) to promote that happiness, do you yourself do (or refrain from). This is the scope of the seventh commandment, this the *ad hominem* of Nathan's parable.

He who indulges sensual passions is like a person who runs against the wind with a lighted torch in his hand. Foolish man! If he does

---

* R. W. Emerson (*Conduct of Life*, p. 107).

not let go the blazing torch, he must needs have the pain of a burnt hand. Just so it is with respect to the poison of lust, anger, covetousness, and envy.... Is a woman old? Regard her as your mother. Is she of honorable station? Regard her as your sister. Is she of small account? Regard her as your younger sister. Is she a child? Treat her reverently.—*Buddha Sakya.*

The man who tells me an indelicate story does me an injury.—*James T. Fields.*

<blockquote>
Immodest words admit of no defence,
For want of decency is want of sense.
</blockquote>

W. Dillon, Earl of Roscommon.

It is one of the heaviest penalties of wrong thinking and of wrong living that they blur, if they do not obliterate, the very perception of good and evil.—*Mary Clemmer.*

What troubles the man is a confusion of the head arising from corruption of the heart.—*Robert Burns.*

John Milton explained the alleged precept of Christ concerning divorce to refer solely to what was really asked of him as he knew the matter to lie in the mind of his questioners,—namely, whether a man might put away a wife who adhered to him and discharged her duties as wife; and he said that for no cause but for her adultery (which might be committed while she still discharged her duties directly to her husband) could she be rightfully divorced, leaving entirely out of contemplation the case of one who refused to conduct as wife to her husband. "A peculiar and inferior precept must not be expounded against the general and supreme rule of charity." "By so strict a sentence against divorce, Christ meant through counter sway of restraint to curb the wild exorbitance of over-weening rabbis almost into the other extreme, as when we bow things the contrary way to make them come to their natural straightness." *

Paul's advice †—to let the unbelieving husband depart, etc.—has been explained to mean: She that will not dwell with her husband is not put away by him, but goes herself. Refusal to be a meet help, open misdemeanors resulting in incurable impotency, etc., unfit her to be by the higher law esteemed a wife. And this appears to be the view of enlightened legislators and jurists generally. Thus much for the beatitude of chastity: the curse inevitable upon unchastity needs no comment.

---

* *The Doctrine and Discipline of Divorce.* Prose Works, vol. i., book ii., chap. i.
† I. Cor. vii., 15.

Woe him that cunning trades in hearts contrives.
Base love good women to base loving drives.
If men loved larger, larger were our lives ;
And woed they nobler, won they nobler wives. *Sidney Lanier.*

To lead sweet lives of purest chastity,
To love one maiden only, cleave to her,
And worship her by years of noble deeds
Until they won her; for indeed I know
Of no more subtle master under heaven
Than is the maiden passion for a maid,
Not only to keep down the base in man,
But to teach high thoughts and amiable words,
And courtliness and the desire of fame,
And love of truth, and all that makes a man.
  Alfred Tennyson.

The saddest thing that can befall a soul
Is when it loses faith in God and Woman.
Lost I those gems,
Though the world's throne stood empty in my path,
I would go wandering back into my childhood,
Searching for them with tears.
  Alexander Smith.

Woman! with that word,
Life's dearest hopes and memories come ;
Truth, beauty, love, in her adored,
And earth's lost paradise restored
In the green bower of home. *Fitz-Greene Halleck.*

A guardian angel o'er his life presiding,
Doubling his pleasure and his cares dividing.
  Samuel Rogers.

O woman! lovely woman! nature made thee
To temper man ; we had been brutes without you.
Angels are painted fair, to look like you :
There's in you all that we believe of heaven,—
Amazing brightness, purity, and truth,
Eternal joy, and everlasting youth. *Thomas Otway.*

Love is never lasting which **flames** before it burns.—*Owen Feltham.*

A woman's whole life is a history of the affections. The heart is her world.... She sends forth her sympathies on adventure, she embarks her whole soul in the traffic of affection, and, if shipwrecked, her case is hopeless,— for it **is a** bankruptcy of the heart.—*Washington Irving.*

(4) The kindness of simple manners. Superfluous **asseverations are** the product either of vanity or of mental indolence. **If, instead** of clear and simple expressions of affirmation or **denial, one resorts** to needless appeals to what should be kept **sacred from** the familiarity that breeds contempt, half the bene**fits of** social **converse** are undermined and neutralized. Of course, there can **be no** kingdom of heaven—no dominion of the higher, the decent—so long as the indecent and profane predominate in speech or gesture. Even as to that whose end is to hold the mirror up to nature, there are tacit canons of

reverence. What though it be hard sometimes for an unfortunately bred person to refrain from uttering hot, incisive epithets,— "exclamations that savor more of strength than righteousness,"— or incongruous bombast, and from listening to inane, sensational trash, instead of refined literature and unassuming communication. There's a beatitude in the consciousness of not being an intellectual sluggard, an obliquitous bore, or the swaggering fool portrayed in the proverbs cherished in every sensible person's mind. As to all things, therefore, whatsoever ye would that another in his or her talk or manners to yourself or to your friend, pupil, son, or daughter, should refrain from in perjury, profanity, vulgarity, clownishness, solecism, unintelligibility, innuendo, importunity, or hoggishness, therefrom yourself refrain. This is the scope of every seer's inspired words in behalf of the true, the beautiful, and the good. Nothing is beautiful but truth. Whatsoever things are true, honorable, just, pure, lovely, or of good report, think of. Introspect your motives. Be sincere. Meanwhile, keep circumspecting. The shams, the affectations, the hypocrisy, the nonsense, the idiosyncrasies, that you despise and deprecate in another man or woman or boy or girl, eradicate and exterminate forever from your own disposition and dealings. As to what is "of good report," study the prophets, the sages, the wits. The existence of a custom or conventionality is only presumptive — not conclusive — of its being the correct thing. What is the ephemeral admiration or applause of a shallow coterie or a silly rabble, when weighed against the Well-done of Supreme Eternal Conscience?

Good breeding is surface Christianity.— *Dr. Oliver W. Holmes.*

A moral, sensible, and well-bred man
Will not affront me, and no other can. *W. Cowper.*

With the sweet charity of speech,
Give words that heal and words that teach.
Lydia Huntington Sigourney.

Old cunning stagers
Say fools for arguments use wagers. *Samuel Butler.*

A large mass of error is easily embalmed and perpetuated by a little truth.— *Charles Mackay.*

No man is hurt but by himself.— *Diogenes.*

Be wisely worldly, but not worldly wise. *Francis Quarles.*

We laugh to see a whole flock of sheep jump because one did so: might not one imagine that superior beings do the same by us, and for exactly the same reason? — *Fulke Greville, Lord Brooke.*

Chapter XXVIII.

REALIZATION.

What Three Leading Experiential Precepts in the Sermon on the Mount?

(1) **The** kindness of preserving resources of kindness. Your life is short, and your physical and mental forces limited. Waste no time nor energy.

> Hours are golden links, God's token,
> Reaching heaven; but one by one
> Take them, lest the chain be broken
> Ere thy pilgrimage be done. — *Adelaide A. Procter.*

Squander no voice upon deaf ears. Exercise discernment. **Beware of** false prophets. Test before you fully confide. A **premium** bestowed on a pretender or charlatan is an injustice to modest merit. Don't give pearls to pigs. Help ingratitude **punish** itself. Keep **your** equanimity. Don't destroy your **nerves** by needlessly fussy anxieties about your future. Don't **borrow** morrow-trouble. You can't cross Jordan before you **get to it.** Look at these lilies! They simply fulfil the conditions of their existence; and what more beautiful! Seek only **to be at one with your** environment, and all will come around right eventually.

If any one say that he has seen a just man in want of bread, I answer that it was in some place where there was no other just man. — *St. Clement.*

It is **the** slowest pulsation which is the most vital. The hero will, then, know how to wait **as** well as to make haste. All good abides with him who waiteth wisely.— *H. B. Thoreau.*

Liberality consists less in giving profusely than in giving judiciously.— *John de la Bruyère.*

(2) The **kindness** of considerate judgment of your neighbors' motives, opinions, or conduct. Recollect the grief it causes **yourself** to find yourself prematurely and wrongfully censured

by folks who have ignored premises that would, if pondered, have led to a conclusion in your favor. " Love . . . taketh not account of evil." *

Before the birth of love, many fearful things took place, through the empire of necessity; but, when this god was born, all things arose to men.—*Socrates.*

Think on thy wants, on thy faults. Recollect all the patience, all the kindness, all the tenderness which has been shown thee.... Think how the power of affection can make all things right.— *Frederika Bremer.*

The few records that we possess of the personal intercourse of Jesus with those around him show great insight into character. He seemed to understand every one,— John the Baptist, Peter, Thomas, Nicodemus, Pilate, Paul, the Pharisees, Judas,— and the peculiarity of his judgment of them was its liberality. He was only harsh toward the Pharisees, and his harshness to them consisted simply in describing them as they were.— *Dr. James F. Clarke.*

The highest exercise of charity is charity toward the uncharitable. —*Joseph S. Buckminster.*

The best of us are but poor wretches just saved from shipwreck: can we feel anything but awe and pity when we see a fellow-passenger swallowed up by the waves?— *George Eliot.*

Never does a man portray his own character more vividly than in his manner of portraying another.—*J. P. F. Richter.*

> When dunces are satiric,
> I take it for panegyric. *Dean Jonathan Swift.*

> You cannot gather back the scattered seeds
> Which far and wide will grow to noxious weeds,
> Nor can the mischief once by scandal sown
> By any penance be again undone.
>   *Mary E. C. Johnson (Montreal Witness).*

The precept against prejudging is perhaps most often ignored in the opinion of one partisan or sect against another.

Early Christians painted the saints of other religions as demons,— sculptured them as gargoyles. Some later Christians have substituted slander for argument, and to prove conventional theories have set forth for theologic gargoyles the "infidel" on a death-bed surrounded by horrors, the "materialist" as given up to sensuality, or "man of science" living in an arctic sea of negation, perishing without hope.... Very few persons are competent to pursue those philosophical studies which underlie the various conclusions called nominalism, realism, intuitionalism, utilitarianism, idealism, material-

---

* I. Cor. xiii., 5.

ism.* But the latter word has a familiar sound: materialism is related to matter, and matter plainly means the earth and flesh and blood, food and drink. Consequently, a materialist must mean a gross, fleshly character, a man who believes in nothing he cannot bite; and, as opposed to the idealist, he must be a man without ideas.— *Moncure D. Conway* (*Idols and Ideals*, p. 16).

Minds of ordinary calibre ordinarily condemn everything that is beyond their range.— *Duc de Rochefoucauld.*

Remember that what you believe will depend very largely upon what you are.— *Dr. Noah Porter.*

> Stiff in opinions, always in the wrong, . . .
> So over-violent or over-civil
> That every man with him was God or Devil.
>
> *John Dryden.*
>
> Grunt up a solemn lengthened groan,
> And damn a' parties but your own.
>
> *Robert Burns.*
>
> Compound for sins they are inclined to
> By damning those they have no mind to,
> And one another clapper-clawing.
>
> *Samuel Butler.*
>
> That frown upon St. Giles' sins, but blink
> The peccadilloes of all Piccadilly.
>
> *Thomas Hood.*

On the precept as to kindness of judgment, another point remains to be noted. In contradistinction from that tendency to mere moralism, which sacrifices the concrete, the practical, to one-sidedness or egotism (which tendency, for want of an exact name, we defectively designate sometimes "Puritanism," sometimes "Pharisaism," or sometimes "Asceticism"),† Jesus was pre-eminently — in the better and reverent sense of the term — a man of the world. He was no cynic or pessimist. He never stood aloof from any proper festivities to which his friends invited him, never questioned the motives of other participants therein, never chided the cheer of child or youth or maiden or elder with croakings of everlasting torments. He rejoiced with those that were rejoicing. He wept with those that were weeping. He would do himself and others all the good he could on any day of the week whatever, any abstract old inhibitions and conventionalities to the contrary notwithstanding. He would help himself to a handful of lunch from a friend's wheat-field, whenever sure his friend would rejoice to know he had done so.

---

* The younger reader will see in the unabridged dictionary the true meaning of these words, "nominalism," "realism," etc., as used by metaphysicians.
† See *ante*, chap. xvii., "Harmonization."

Doubtless, he listened indulgently to all the pleased prattle of Mary or Martha about the progress of the lilies and the roses she had been cultivating to charm his anticipated visit. If afterwards any affliction came to her household, he gave what solace he could; and this, with no such reprimand as Sheridan — or some other mirror-holder — represents given to a cheerful, blind youth by a severe matron, "When tribulation is sent to us, we ought to 'tribulate.'" He never encouraged us to be hypercritical in scanning our neighbors' methods of promoting piety. Piety might enter at the eye or ear. He gave no warrant for the proceeding, rather forcibly mentioned by James R. Lowell, "The Puritans thrust beauty out of the meeting-house, and slammed the door in her face."

The Puritans who decapitated statues and broke the superb windows of stained glass did not do this to wage a warfare with art, but with what art represented. It covered a lie, it made a beautiful exterior to falsehood, it represented what was not true; and they, sturdy men, honest and upright, hated lies and deceit, and would have none of it. But we in a later generation, grown wiser with the ages, see differently· we know that the mission of art is to beautify, to soften, to elevate, to refine; that it broadens men's ideas, that it makes them better.... The words that applied to Palestine eighteen centuries ago —" A rich man cannot inherit the kingdom of God "—apply to us only in a modified sense. If men win money honestly, they have every right to do with it what they will, so they do not subvert its uses, and make it pander to their animalism, but develop instead the more spiritual portions of their nature, which have been growing ever since the world began.— *Henry Ward Beecher.*

> A thing of beauty is a joy forever
> Its loveliness increases: it will never
> Pass into nothingness, but still will keep
> A bower quiet for us, and a sleep
> Full of sweet dreams, and health and quiet breathing.
> Therefore on every morrow are we wreathing
> A flowery band to bind us to the earth,
> Spite of despondence, of the inhuman dearth
> Of noble natures, of the gloomy days,
> Of all the unhealthy and o'er-darkened ways
> Made for our searching; yes, in spite of all,
> Some shape of beauty moves away the pall
> From our dark spirits.
>
> *John Keats.*

To contemplate things lovely is always an ascent.— *David Swing.*

Yet the Puritans' meeting-house was a true sanctuary. To their Sabbath home applied the adage, "Home is home, be it never so homely."

> Home's not merely four square walls,
>   Though with pictures hung and gilded :
> Home is where affection calls,
>   Filled with shrines the heart hath builded.
>
> *Queen.*

While there is not a single passage in the New Testament from which it can be inferred that, under Christianity, there is such a duty as Sabbath-keeping or such a sin as Sabbath-breaking, certain champions are continually crying out for stricter penal laws enforcing the observance of the first day of the week. The worst effect of such demands is that they inevitably provoke opposition to a custom which is of great value to society. The practice of devoting one day in seven to moral, religious, and social uses stands firmly upon its own merits, and, like Sunday-schools, needs no other support.— *Samuel J. Barrows.*

An eye-witness of the Pilgrims' departure from Holland testifies that they were not without the right sort of cheerfulness:—

And when the ship was ready to carry us away, the brethren that stayed having again solemnly sought the Lord with us and for us, and we further engaging ourselves mutually as before,—they, I say, that stayed at Leyden feasted us that were to go, at our pastor's house, being large; where we refreshed ourselves, after tears, with singing of psalms, making joyful melody in our hearts, as well as with the voice, there being many of the congregation very expert in music; and indeed it was the sweetest melody that ever mine ears heard. . . . So lifting up our hands to each other, and our hearts for each other to the Lord our God, we departed, and found his presence with us; in the midst of our manifold straits He carried us through.— *Edward Winslow.*

And, right here, we must never forget that we can infinitely better dispense with all of a certain kind of art beauty than "endure, then pity, then embrace" some of the concomitants thereof that characterized the court of Charles II. And a word may be added as to the martyrdom of Mrs. Stowe's Uncle Tom for construing the precept, "Servants, obey your masters," to justify his refusal to disclose to Legree the hiding-place of Emeline and Cassy; also as to the nun's lie to the inspector in Victor Hugo's *Les Misérables*. An editorial, referring to M. J. Savage's critique on Frances Power Cobbe's new book, elucidates this great moral problem of the ages as follows:—

In the example that Mr. Savage adduces, in which the Sister of Charity tells a lie to Javert, to save Jean Valjean from an unjust return to the galleys, we readily condone the falsehood, and may even join in Victor Hugo's rhapsody upon it. But on the other hand, when, in Scott's *Heart of Mid-Lothian*, Jeanie Deans refuses to tell a lie to save the life of her own sister, we are struck with the moral grandeur of the Scotch girl; and so far from thinking, as Mr. Savage implies, "that she ought to have been herself the victim," on that account we cry "Amen!" to her truthfulness, and think the angels in heaven are weak in their ethics, if they do not join in the benediction.

Now, each of these cases seems perfectly good as against the other, and together they seem to furnish a practical antinomy in morals. It must be noted, however, in the first case, that the elevation which belongs to the act comes from the fact that it is some sacrifice to the nun not to tell the truth, and that the lie is told to promote the cause of justice as well as mercy. If the nun were a habitual liar, the story would have no more effect upon us than the lie of any common perjurer. Yet, even with this clearly in mind, the two examples stand out as illustrations of moral contradictions, each of which seems just in itself, but which stand in bold opposition to each other when we bring them together. They seem to indicate that each of the two moral theories which they are adduced to support needs the help of the other. The transcendental theory of absolute right must be held as practically a relative one, when it is exercised, as in every human life, under finite and relative conditions. On the other hand, the experiential theory would be viciously weak, if it could be characterized as Mahaffy characterizes the society described in Hesiod, "where private interest is the paramount object and the ultimate test of morals." It needs to make its generalizations of happiness as broad and high as the heavens, and to recognize not merely the provisional, the expedient, and the "useful," but the universal and eternal side of human relations.

The theory of evolution in morals throws great light upon most difficult ethical problems. It shows us the growth of human conceptions of right and wrong, truth and falsehood. But it does not prove to us that right and wrong, truth and falsehood, are merely human creations. If human experience proves anything, it proves indubitably that man is conditioned morally as he is physically, and that he can only develop healthfully along certain lines which are implicated in his primal constitution and revealed by experience, but which are no more the creation of his experience than the planet on which he stands, or the laws which hold the worlds in perfect order on their courses. It is the Truth that determines humanity, and not alone humanity that determines the Truth. And when Jeanie Deans refused to tell a lie, we may be positive that the noble girl was not thinking alone of her own advantage, or of her sister's advantage, or the welfare of the race, or the authority of the court, but of the authority of the Truth, which was as real to her as God himself. And no one would more readily agree with Mr. Savage than Jeanie Deans,—that "all the happiness of the world comes from keeping God's laws of life, and all the misery from breaking them."— *Samuel J. Barrows* (*Christian Register*, June 16, 1881).

To this, Mr. Savage replied : —

... Our only possible standard of judgment is not any personal whim, but *the race experience* as to those courses of conduct that conduce to human well-being. If there is any *absolute* or *transcendent* reason for doing one thing and not doing another, we can never know it. We have no *absolute* knowledge of anything. And to say that a thing is transcendent is to say that it transcends knowledge. There may be a transcendent reason for the action of gravitation or electricity, but it does not concern us in any practical way. We can only study them in their effects.— *Christian Register,* June 23, 1881.

The comment as to the nun reminds us of R. Brinsley Sheridan's witticism, "I never scruple to tell a lie to help a friend, but it hurts my conscience awfully to be found out." It did not hurt Sheridan's principles much, forsooth, whenever the friend he fibbed for was himself. When picked up intoxicated, he answered the police officer's demand for his name, "Wilberforce!"

The dilemma of Hugo's nun, Uncle Tom, Jeanie Deans, etc., recalls Fichte's argument:—

The well-known illustration of the schools may make our thoughts clearer: A man pursued by his enemy with a drawn dagger hides himself in your presence. His enemy comes up, and asks you where he is. If you tell the truth, an innocent man is murdered: therefore, so some conclude, you must tell a lie. But how is it that these hasty reasoners rush so quickly to the crooked way, when so many possibilities are open to them on the straight path? In the first place, why should you tell the questioner *either* the *truth or* a lie? Why not some third alternative? *e.g.,* that you are not bound to give him any answer; that he seems to have a very evil purpose in his question; that you advise him in all kindness to give it up; that, besides this, you will take the part of the pursued and defend him at the risk of your own life, which, moreover, it is your absolute duty to do. But in that case, you urge, his rage would be turned against you. And how, I pray, does it happen that you calculate only upon this one result? Since a second one is certainly among the possibilities,— namely, that your adversary, struck with the justice and the boldness of your resistance, may withdraw from the pursuit of his enemy, allow his feelings to grow cooler, and be willing to come to terms with him. But suppose that he should attack you. Why will you at all events avoid that? For it is your unquestionable duty to protect the fugitive with your own body, since, whenever human life is in danger, you no longer have any right to think of the security of your own. And now it plainly appears that the immediate object of your lie was not to save your neighbor's life, but only to come out of this affair with a whole skin; and, moreover, yours was no actual danger, but only one of two possible cases. It seems, then, that you were willing to lie merely to avoid the remote possibility of coming to harm!

Suppose, however, that he attacks you, does it necessarily follow that you are overpowered by the attack, and that no other alternative is possible? According to the supposition, the fugitive has hidden himself in your immediate vicinity: *you* are now in danger, and he is obliged by gratitude, as well as by general sense of duty, to hasten to your assistance. What right have you to assume decidedly that he will not do this? Or suppose he does not come to your help, yet you have gained time by your resistance, and it may chance that others will come to support you. If, after all, nothing of the kind happens, and you must fight alone, why, then, are you so sure of being defeated? You do not allow for the strength which even your body may receive from the firm resolution to tolerate absolutely nothing that is wrong, as well as from the enthusiasm of a righteous cause; nor do you take into account the weakness which may come over your adversary, through his confusion and a consciousness that his cause is unjust. In the worst case, you can only die; and death releases you from all further obligation to the assailed man, while at the same time it saves you from the danger of a lie.—*Johann G. Fichte.*

Legislators, however, are agreed that you *always* have a "right to think of the security of your own life."

Mr. Savage's replication recalls the words of a devout veteran thinker: —

Tyndall's deistical work, *Christianity as Old as the Creation, or the Gospel a Republication of the Law of Nature*, admits in its title the strongest ground, nay, the only ground, on which we can believe or defend Christianity. To suppose it a divine after-thought, a supplementary creation, an excrescence upon nature, is to dishonor it under shelter of pretended advocacy,— nay, more, it is to impugn the divine immutableness, the integrity of those attributes which underlie all religion. The highest view of Christianity is that which regards it as the religion of nature, as the constitutional law of the spiritual universe, as corresponding to the mathematical laws which are embodied in the material universe,— absolute, necessary, eternal truth, that which always was and ever will be. Revelation did not create it any more than Newton created the law of universal gravitation, or Kepler the laws of planetary motion.— *Dr. A. P. Peabody.*

Last, though not least, may be cited two counsellors on the supremacy of "the Inner Light."

Right and duty in the hearts of men have for a long time been the same in their essence under all systems, or under no system. The fatalist Zeno scourged the doctrine of moral responsibility into his thievish slave, and Spinoza, the pantheist, at whose doctrine the Christian teachers shudder, exhibited in his life the Christian virtues in their full effulgence. Legislators do not inquire into the grounds of "liberty and necessity." Laws are made and administered according to the needs of society, as viewed by the most enlightened in their day. The ethical teaching changes from age to age, because morals is a progressive science. We should hang Drakes and Cabots to-day as pirates; but the Christian Queen Elizabeth fêted them and went shares with them in the loot of Philip's treasure-ships. Negro slavery was not odious to Whitfield. As time goes on, many things we now endure will surely pass into the category of crimes.— " U." (*Boston Daily Advertiser*, Aug. 12, 1881).

Man is more than constitutions.—*John G. Whittier.*

<blockquote>
All must be false that thwart this one great end,
And all of God that bless mankind or mend.   *Alexander Pope.*
</blockquote>

(3) The kindness of systematic charities. Dr. Stephen H. Tyng's idea and plan of operations, as exemplified in the church whereof he is pastor in New York, is delineated in his pamphlet report thereof under three heads,— Ingathering, Training, and Work : —

The ingathering goes on through popular Sunday services, with evangelistic services during the week, prayer-meetings, meetings for inquirers, etc. There is a temperance organization among the young men that gives six o'clock Sunday-evening teas. Each member has a ticket for a friend, and becomes responsible for him; and in this way last winter a very low and degraded class of men, a hundred and fifty or more, were drawn in, so that at first it was necessary to station detectives in different parts of the room. After the tea, a prayer-meeting is held.

The basement of the church has a regular kitchen and dining-room, and all the appliances for entertainments. Among the women there is a society composed of shop-girls, servants, etc., that meets one evening in the week for social and religious intercourse. Some of the members of the church bake bread regularly, and there is a stated distribution of it to the poor from the basement of the church. The church dispensary furnishes medicines gratis, and there are six physicians who visit at stated times and seasons. Legal questions are settled for the poor without charge, and a burial society provides for their interment. My idea is to have an agency adapted to every department of need. Like the prophet, we desire to stretch ourselves on the man, eye to eye, hand to hand, feet to feet,— to reach him in his want, whatever that may be.

This recalls the " Associated Charities " of Boston and other cities, wherein by personal visits of local voluntary agents cases of want are remedied, employment furnished, and imposition prevented.* Each a little — a little well alive — presents a telling aggregate.

In thirty years, the Children's Aid Society has taken out of New York City 67,000 children, many of whom have become farmers, lawyers, merchants, physicians, judges, teachers, and

---

* See suggestions by Abby W. May, Bella C. Barrows, Eliza T. Sunderland, and others, in the report of the Women's Auxiliary Conference, *Christian Register* of Oct. 12, 1882.

good men's wives. In the newsboys' lodging-houses, such attention is paid to health that, out of 187,000 who have been in them, only one death has occurred. In the girls' lodging-houses, 100,000 girls have been lodged and taught. The result has been that, while New York has grown from 800,000 to 1,200,000 inhabitants, youthful crime has decreased. The records of the courts show that, between 1859 and 1881, the annual commitments of female vagrants have diminished from 5,700 to 1,800; the commitments of girls for petty larceny, from about 1,000 annually to about 300. Organized crime has been met by organized Christian influence. The only hope of the community is in the co-operation of its individuals for the true and the right.

It is not growing like a tree,
In bulk, doth make men better be;
Or standing like an oak three hundred year,
To fall a log at last, dry, bald, and sere.
A lily of a day is fairer far in May,
    Although it fall and die that night,—
    It was the plant and flower of Light.
In small proportions we just beauties see,
And in short measures life may perfect be.

Ben Jonson.

" Write me as one that loves his fellow-men."
The angel wrote and vanished. The next night
He came again with a great wakening light,
And showed their names whom love of God had blest.
And, lo! Ben Adhem's name led all the rest.

Leigh Hunt.

Though no siegeless rampart guard us,
    There's no peril shall appall,
Be one bulwark not debarred us
    When the foe shall threaten thrall:
    TRUTH and faithful front in all!
When we falter from *her* altar,
    Heaven heed not blind Error's call!
    Make the traitor's mad arm fall!
Rise for Truth, when hordes assault her,
    Phalanx firm as Cathay's wall!
Bigot folly scorning,
TRUTH our ways adorning,
    Like our sires we'll crown her
    With our lives and honor.
Cherish we the trust,
Hallowing the Fathers' dust!
    Truth and the Right forever!
    Heart and home shall never
    Hope and Freedom sever.
We will be true. We'll dare and do.
Peal on from sea to sea
The song, "We stand, the Free!"

B. F. B. (Centennial Ode, 1876).

Chapter XXIX.

SUPPLICATION.

What Three Views of Christ's Precepts on Prayer?

(1) THE supplicational, which looks mainly to an objective blessing from prayer; (2) the aspirational, which aims chiefly at a subjective benefit; and (3) the intermediate, which takes for model the combination of the two found in the Lord's Prayer.

The Lord's Prayer contains the sum total of religion and morals.— *Duke of Wellington.*

In its seven petitions, it expresses the whole course of religious experience: in the first three, the unhindered flight of the spirit to God; in the next three, the hindrances opposed to this aspiration by the sense of dependence on earthly circumstances, and by the conflict with sin; while the last petition expresses the solution which harmonizes this conflict.— *W. M. De Wette.*

I desire no other evidence of the truth of Christianity than the Lord's Prayer.— *Baronne de Staël-Holstein.*

Only in the mouth of the Christian does the Lord's Prayer obtain its full meaning, since only the Christian can call God Father in the full sense of the word, only he can pray with right intelligence for the coming of God's kingdom, and only he can say, Forgive us our debts as we forgive our debtors.— *F. A. G. Tholuck.*

Tholuck says the Greek word [*epiousion*] translated "daily" (in the N. R. margin "for the coming day") occurs nowhere else in the New Testament, nor in any of the twelve hundred works of Greek literature that remain to us. Some say it means "necessary," and that the expression is a figurative petition for whatever we need — whether of temporal or spiritual things — to make us strong for the day's occasions.

Solicitude is the audience chamber of God.— *Walter S. Landor.*

The supplicational view is that of all nations in their primitive condition. The Jews prayed seven times a day. In all Mohammedan countries, all men pray at fixed hours. The sacred books of the Hindus and of the Parsees are one long liturgy of supplication. In Buddhist countries, the people assemble in the streets of the city at sunset for prayer. The walls of the Egyptian tombs are covered with supplications to Osiris and Amun. In the retreat of the ten thousand Greeks, their general in command, Xenophon, before each day's march, offered public prayer to the gods of Olympus. Among enlightened peoples, however, as Mr. Conway remarks,—

> No one prays that the sun may stand still and lengthen his day, or that his water tank may yield pure wine, or a fish just purchased hold a coin large enough to pay his tax, or for restoration of the dead. But the movements of the clouds seem so irregular that an arbitrary power is associated with them, and some persons yet pray for rain or sunshine. But there are fewer and fewer, as meteorology becomes more and more developed as a science. That which a man soweth he shall not by prayer escape reaping.— *Idols and Ideals*, p. 65.

A poetic phase of the supplicational view is presented by Dr. John Ryland, an English (Baptist) clergyman: —

> Prayer has divided seas, rolled up flowing rivers, made flinty rocks gush into fountains, quenched flames of fire, muzzled lions, disarmed vipers and poisons, marshalled the stars against the wicked, stopped the course of the moon, arrested the sun in its rapid race, burst open iron gates, recalled souls from eternity, conquered the strongest devils, commanded legions of angels down from heaven. Prayer has bridled and chained the raging passions of man, and routed and destroyed vast armies of proud, daring, blustering atheists. Prayer brought one man from the bottom of the sea, and carried another in a chariot of fire to heaven. What has not prayer done?*

Herewith may be classed many poetic aphorisms like that of Martin F. Tupper, "Prayer is the slender nerve that moves the muscles of Omnipotence." In a low condition of society, a supplicational and a meditative view has each presented an abuse so identical that extremes appear to meet. Thus alleged answers to prayer have been explained: —

---

* For a similar "daring" belief (expressed without "blustering"), see Dr. S. I. Prime's *Five Years of Prayer, with the Answers*. Also the newspaper reports of Rev. D. L. Moody's Tabernacle Services, whereat were read requests for prayers for specific objects. Also, *The Wonders of Prayer*, by H. T. Williams, drawing from certain coincidences certain inferences. Thus, upon the death of a cow belonging to Rev. C. H. Spurgeon's grandfather, a neighboring missionary society sent the loser £20. A reviewer, imagining himself logical, questioned whether the cow would have died, had the society been out of funds.

A German savant discovered the long-venerated bones of a saint to be those of a donkey, but on this account they had not been a whit less remedial. "Any state of the body earnestly expected," says a learned physiologist, " is very likely to ensue." There is a man in Belgium whose hands and feet bleed every Friday, as it were from nails driven into them. The priests say it is a miracle like unto the famous stigmata of St. Francis of Assisi. A commission of medical men, appointed by the government, say it is the result of morbid expectation, the whole energy of the victim's nature being directed to this end, so flattering to his ecclesiastical pretensions. There is a Consumptives' Home in Boston supported entirely by prayer. It has its contribution-boxes in scores of public places, conspicuously labelled with the name *and policy* of the institution. When a people are wasted with famine, it is not even necessary to *over*hear their prayers for succor. It is sufficient for those who can help them to hear of the fact....

One shattered train, one sinking wreck, offsets all the imaginary interferences that have ever been recorded, and remands them at once and forever to the province of coincidence or overhearing or exaggeration. Of what avail the baby-house suggestion that God, anticipating human prayer, left certain openings in the network of his laws through which he can reach out handfuls of benefits and immunities,— winds out of some Æolian cave, or showers of needed rain, and quiet of the sea or of the heart? Law is an armor so compact that there is not a joint which any interfering touch can penetrate....To pray for so much interference as would quell one coming storm, or squeeze one rain-drop out of a reluctant cloud, is to pray that the entire history of the universe up to date may be revised, and that God may change the essence of his nature with a view to our imaginary comfort or advantage.—*John W. Chadwick* (*The Faith of Reason*, pp. 174, 179).

A writer in the London *Telegraph*, commenting on the mistake of the rector at Rhyl, North Wales, in opening his Prayer-Book at the "Prayer for Rain" and supplicating "rain on the inheritance," when the Primate's circular had invited prayers for fair weather, commends the simple earnestness of the Orkney minister who, being asked to pray for better weather, prayed, "Lord, send us braw weather, and a bit sough of breeze that will dree the stra' and winna harm the heads; but, if ye blaw us a tearin', rivin', bletherin' gale, like what we've been ha'ing, ye'll play the vera mischief wi' the aits, and fairly spoil a'." At least, the criticism would not here apply of "pumping prayers for the ineffable, though all the valves of memory gasp and wheeze." This tendency to mingle advice with supplication was exemplified in the case of the colored preacher who assumed to remind the Omniscient that the Republican party were letting "our breddren in de Souf be 'timidated by de wicked Democrats. Dey done bust de Freedmen's Bank. Lord, hold 'em in de holler ob dy han', ober de mouf of hell, an' scorch 'em, an' scorch 'em, but don't let 'em drop in!" Or in that of another who, on learning that the assassinator of President Lincoln was hiding near in Maryland, prayed, "Lord, cotch him, and when dou hast cotcht him, don't be so mercifu' as dou art too apt to be,— gen'r'ly speakin'." This addressing God from an anthropomorphic stand-point recalls the rather blunt lines : —

> Just then there came another voice,
> In supplicating tones,
> "Oh! may the grave be late to close
> O'er Neighbor David's bones!"
> "There's surely one for me at last!"
> But Satan cried, "Not yet!
> He merely wants the man to live
> Until he pays a debt."

In the case of prayers from diverse minds (instanced by Mr. Clemens in *The Innocents Abroad*, where persons on ships going in opposite directions pray each for winds to favor his own ship), Dr. Nehemiah Adams was wont to say that the Holy Spirit would lead each, etc., if sought aright. But his son, Capt. Robert C. Adams, declared —

Intercourse with numerous Christians, many of whom I was convinced prayed earnestly for the guidance of the Spirit, showed me that the Holy Spirit led each man to different and often opposing views, though one devout and highly educated Christian assured me that no one ever studied the Bible prayerfully without believing as he did; but I found that his present adherents numbered only two.— *The Index*, November, 1881.

And the writer of another open letter suggests :—

You say, if we had Daniel's faith, we, too, might venture into the lions' den without fear of harm. Is this teaching true to life? Are the righteous saved from physical injury,— from sickness and from sudden death? Had the moral quality of the passengers on the train that broke through the bridge at Ashtabula anything to do with the disaster? Did the fire or frost spare the body of the sweet singer [P. P. Bliss] whose death all good people deplore? — *Dr. W. H. Ryder (Open Letter to D. L. Moody).*

Though President Garfield died, the prayers for his restoration were not, in every sense, futile. Supplications for blessings are now superseding imprecatory, clannish prayers, the world over, still slowly.*

---

* See M. J. Savage's *Religion of Evolution*, p. 150.

We are all tattooed in our cradles with the beliefs of our tribe. The record may seem superficial, but it is indelible. You cannot educate a man wholly out of the superstitious fears which were implanted in his imagination, no matter how utterly his reason may reject them.—*Dr. O. W. Holmes.*

The tribe or individual that lets in vindictive imaginings of a neighbor's vexatious doings, and thereupon burns to get a shoe cast out over Edom, hurts one's own self more than Edom. So, too, as to a prayer that one's neighbor's wife be left a widow, and his children be fatherless, "be continually vagabonds and beg"* An excess of solitary reflection brings morbid brooding and melancholy. The living may too much lay to heart the great truth enunciated by the old Hebrew, "It is better to go to the house of mourning than to the house of feasting"; or by Shakspere, "My desolation doth begin to make a better life." Where "spiritual moods," meditations, and rhapsodies, instead of being a part of life become its all,

That way madness lies.

The Presbytery of Edinburgh, in 1853, petitioned Queen Victoria to appoint a day of national fasting and prayer for the extermination of the Asiatic cholera then raging there. The Home Secretary, Lord Palmerston, replied that the affairs of this world are regulated by natural laws, on the observance or neglect of which the weal or woe of mankind depends; that one of those laws connects disease with the exhalations of bodies, and it is by virtue of this law that contagion spreads, either in crowded cities or in places where vegetable decomposition is going on; that man, by exerting himself, can disperse or neutralize these noxious influences, and the appearance of the cholera proves that he has not exerted himself. Knowing that such a fast would in Scotland be sure to be rigidly kept, and by causing mental depression and physical exhaustion prepare thousands of delicate persons, before twenty-four hours had passed, to receive the deadly poison already lurking around them, he advised the petitioners to employ their time in planning and executing measures for purifying the localities of the poorer classes from those sources of contagion which, if allowed to remain, would "infallibly breed pestilence and be fruitful in death, in spite of all the prayers and fastings of a united but inactive nation."

But the fact that some men pray unreasonably does not controvert the fact that men cannot help praying. And Dr. E. H.

---

* Ps. cix., 10.

Chapin says, "We may be sure that that which is so spontaneous and ineradicable in human nature has its fitting objects and methods in the arrangements of a boundless Providence." And S. Taylor Coleridge is not the only witness that

He prayeth best who loveth best.

The properly intermediate view of prayer may be well represented by the cry of a new-born babe. This cry means: I am in pain and weakness and hunger and ignorance and fear. I know nothing. What? Ah! I think: therefore I am.* There is an *Ego* and a *non-Ego*. I have but one impulse, a yearning to find in all this not-me — in all this strange, new environment — a Somewhat that shall relieve, shield, nourish me. Nothing more? Ah! that Somewhat will never satisfy this yearning unless it also have consciousness,— be a part of, or in alliance with, the me sufficiently to sympathize with my soul-want. Nevertheless, my bodily want is the more immediately exigent of the two; and, in the process of its becoming satisfied, I have a glimmering sense of adaptation of means to end. With the comfort there comes to be associated a pallid face and two sweet, half-sad, half-glad, loving eyes, longing down at mine. My solace is just in proportion to my earnest that the new found, responsive Somewhat is able and willing to bear my sorrow and to supplement my void, my perishing need of knowledge, strength, and communion. Soon, I peacefully slumber. On awaking, I experience the same sense of want; I find myself apprehensive that I am alone. Suppose Reason (or any other third unknown entity) were to say to me that the original Somewhat, the no longer "*x*," the Being that had demonstrated herself to my spirit as a power not myself that makes for sweetness and light, would not forsake my cradle, and that therefore my crying would be very impertinent, what should I immediately answer? It would be a cry: "I *must* cry! I *want* to cry!" And would not the answer be a sound one?

Years elapse, and after I have learned a little of good and evil, right and wrong, and feel that there is a Power not myself — yet in some sense a part of myself, my ideal — that makes for sweetness and light and righteousness, a Somewhat having sensibility, intelligence, and will, I find myself in a like condition of spiritual want, and with the same lonesome yearning. If now I cry out a supplication to that Being, and Reason intervenes a Wherefore, I can only reply: "Mind thine own proper business, O Reason! Do not usurp the function of Faith and Feeling."

---

* "Cogito, ergo sum."— *René Descartes.*

Hence the adage that the only sensible prayer is the earnest prayer. And right here is found the point of the parable of the unjust judge,* the "because this widow troubleth me"; also that of the loaves loaned at midnight,† the "because of his importunity [*anaideia*], his 'cheek.'"

> So runs my dream; but what am I?
> An infant crying in the night,
> An infant crying for the light,
> And with no language but a cry.
>
> *Alfred Tennyson* (*In Memoriam*, liii.).

And here be it observed that the name of that Somewhat is, in one regard, of no consequence,— whether "Ma," "Mother," "Mater" or "Pater." The entity, "the rose," is just "as sweet," the growth of gratitude, of jurisdiction, just as sure.‡

As the mother comes and bends by night over her sick and sleeping child, all unconscious of her presence, so the Lord comes and looks on us with tenderest pity when we think nothing of him. Yet sometimes the sick and sleeping child may half arouse itself, and stretch up its little drowsy arm to its mother, and put it round her neck, drawing her face close down to his, and giving her a little sleepy kiss; and the mother is well pleased. So I think that God is well pleased when we, half-awakening from our drowsy sleep in sense and sin, just look up a little moment, and cry out of our heart, though it may be only a single cry of longing, or one unuttered whisper of vague hope. — *Dr. J. F. Clarke* (*Sermon on Acts* ix., 11, *Boston Saturday Evening Gazette*, June, 1881).

> Sometimes from troubled dream in fear he starts:
> One word in glad or piteous tones I hear,—
> "Mamma!"— his childish lips can add no more.
> "What is it, dear? What does my darling want?"
> I fondly ask. But "Mamma! mamma!" still
> His only answer, till I e'en must guess
> The unspoken want by love's divining art.
>
> Thou Love divine, who knowest the things we need
> Before we ask, the word upon the tongue
> Before 'tis spoken, who of old didst say,
> "As one a mother's love soft comforteth,
> So will I comfort thee; they may forget,
> Yet will not I,"— we know not what we want,
> Or, knowing, find no words to utter it.
> Hear thou our cry when from the shows of life
> We weary turn, or shrink from threatening ills.
> No word but *Father* we may speak, yet hear,
> And read the want too deep for words to tell.
> We know not what to pray for as we ought;
> Help our infirmities. Fold us within
> Thine everlasting arms. Make us to know
> All things together work for good to us.

---

* Luke xviii., 5.   † Luke xi., 8.
‡ See in chap. xi., *note*, Goethe hereon.

SUPPLICATION

Thy children dear; that neither life nor death,
Nor angels, principalities, nor powers,
Nor things that are, nor things to come, nor height,
Nor depth, nor aught besides, shall ever part
Thy children from thee. And when breaks the cry
Of *Father!* from our glad or troubled lips,
Whisper sweet words of peace: "Dear child, I know.
Abide in me. My love is over thee."

H. D. Catlin ("*Love's Divining*." *Christian Register*, May 26, 1881).

All that I feel of pity thou hast known
Before I was; my best is all thy own
From thy great heart of goodness mine but drew
Wishes and prayers; but thou, O Lord, wilt do
In thy own time, by ways I cannot see,
All that I feel when I am nearest thee.

Anon.

Keep me from mine own undoing,
  Help me turn to thee when tried,
Still my footsteps, Father, viewing,
  Keep me ever at thy side.

Anon. (*H. and T. B. for C. and H.*, 57).

The way is dark, my Father. Cloud on cloud
Is gathering thickly o'er my head, and loud
The thunder roars above me. See, I stand
Like one bewildered. Father, take my hand,
And through the gloom lead safely home thy child.

The day goes fast, my Father, and the night
Is drawing darkly down. My faithless sight
Sees ghostly visions; fears, a spectral band,
Encompass me. O Father, take my hand,
And from the night lead up to light thy child.

The way is long, my Father, and my soul
Longs for the rest and quiet of the goal.
While yet I journey through this weary land,
Keep me from wandering. Father, take my hand :
Quickly and straight lead to heaven's gate thy child.

The path is rough, my Father. Many a thorn
Has pierced me, and my weary feet, all torn
And bleeding, mark the way. Yet thy command
Bids me press forward. Father, take my hand :
Then, safe and blest, lead up to rest thy child.

The throng is great, my Father. Many a doubt
And fear and danger compass me about,
And foes oppress me sore. I cannot stand
Or go alone. O Father, take my hand,
And through the throng lead safe along thy child.

The cross is heavy, Father. I have borne
It long, and still do bear it. Let my worn
And fainting spirit rise to that blest land
Where crowns are given. Father, take my hand,
And, reaching down, lead to the crown thy child.

Anon. (*The Appeal*).

Chapter XXX.

ASPIRATION.

What generally Indorsed Sentiments of Experienced Thinkers upon best promoting the Aspirational Element of Prayer?

WITH these, hymnology overflows. The Buddhist priests are said to have responded to the French missionaries, Huc and Gabet: "We ought to respect all prayer. Men of prayer belong to all countries: they are strangers nowhere. Such is the doctrine taught by our Holy Books."

Under the intermediate thesis just considered, one may commend the objective theory of "help from on high," even while having in view only the subjective good of self-help, aspiration, and exertion. The father in La Fontaine's fable has never been deemed at all disingenuous for directing his sons to keep the heritage and dig for a concealed treasure. The "treasure" was in the digging itself, and in the consequent health, harvests, and habits of industry,— a prosperity which an immediate attainment of the object directly longed for would have defeated.

> "Labor is worship," the wild bee is ringing.
> Listen! that eloquent whisper upspringing
> Speaks to thy soul out of nature's great heart.
> Labor is life! 'tis the still water faileth;
> Idleness ever despaireth, bewaileth;
> Keep the watch wound, or the dark rust assaileth.
> Frances S. Osgood

Labor is nature's physician.— *Galen.*

I have fire-proof, perennial enjoyments called employments.— *Jean P. F. Richter.*

The reward of doing one duty is the power to perform another.— *Ben Azai.*

> Be good, sweet maid, and let who will be clever;
> *Do* noble things, not dream them all day long,
> And so make life, death, and that vast forever
> One grand, sweet song.
> Charles Kingsley.

Joy's soul lies in the doing.— *William Shakspere.*

> The reward is in the doing,
> And the rapture of pursuing
> Is the prize.
>
> Henry W. Longfellow.

Evidently there are two extremes, each having its peculiar evil. The man who never sequesters himself (or, as the New Revision beautifully renders it, enters into his "inner chamber"), and, when he has shut the door against the overbearing pressure of secular pursuits, contemplates his higher destinations, becomes a grovelling earthworm rather than

> A glorious thing
> Of buoyant wing.

The woman's mind that is always in a giddy whirl of frivolities remains inane. "As one thinketh in his heart, so is he." If he longs to be submissive, patient, modest, liberal, considerate of his relations to his moral environment, such must he tend to become. To be godlike, he must meditate upon God; to make any part of the attributes of Deity his own, he must aspire to the true, the beautiful, and the good.

Is virtue a thing remote? I wish to be virtuous, and, lo! virtue is at hand.— *Confucius.*

> Thrice blest whose lives are faithful prayers,
> Whose loves in higher love endure;
> What souls possess themselves so pure,
> Or is there blessedness like theirs?
>
> <div align="right"><i>Alfred Tennyson</i> (In Memoriam, xxxii.).</div>

You need but *will*, and it is done. But if you relax your efforts, you will be ruined; for ruin and recovery are both from within.— *Epictetus.*

Use the temporal; desire the eternal.— *Thomas à Kempis.*

Learn as if you were to live forever; live as if you were to die to-morrow.— *Ansalus de Insulis.*

Accordingly, many who hold only to the aspirational view take supplication simply as a means of aspiration. This appears to be the gist of the averment of George Eliot:—

The most powerful movement of feeling with a liturgy is the prayer which seeks for nothing special, but is the yearning to escape from the limitations of our own weakness, and an invocation of all Good to enter and abide with us; or else a self-oblivious lifting up of gladness, a *Gloria in Excelsis* that such Good exists; both the yearning and the exultation gathering their utmost force from the sense of communion in a form which has expressed them both for long generations of struggling men.— *Daniel Deronda,* p. 333.*

This recalls the prayer of another noble soul, Phœbe Cary: —

> I ask not that for me the plan
> Of good and ill be set aside,
> But that the common lot of man
> Be nobly borne and glorified.
> I know I may not always keep
> My steps in places green and sweet,
> Nor find the pathway of the deep
> A path of safety to my feet;
> But pray that when the tempest's breath
> Shall fiercely sweep my way about,
> I make not shipwreck of my faith
> In the unfathomed sea of doubt.
>
> *H. and T. B. for C. and H.*, 565.

A like model prayer is that of James Merrick: —

> Author of good, we rest on thee:
> Thine ever watchful eye
> Alone our real wants can see,
> Thy hand alone supply.
> In thine all-gracious providence
> Our cheerful hopes confide;
> Oh, let thy power be our defence,
> Thy love our footsteps guide.
> And since, by passion's force subdued,
> Too oft with stubborn will
> We blindly shun the latent good,
> And grasp the specious ill,—
> Not what we wish, but what we want,
> Let mercy still supply:
> The good unasked, O Father, grant;
> The ill, though asked, deny.
>
> *Methodist Hymns,* 633; *H. and T. B. for C. and H.*, 583.

There is truth in Jeremy Taylor's aphorism: "Every man can build a chapel in his breast, himself the priest, his heart the sacrifice and the earth he treads on the altar." But just how far a liturgy is a help to that "powerful movement of feeling," just quoted from George Eliot, is a trite theme. Perhaps no more advanced thought can be found thereon than in a recent discourse by Dr. J. F. Clarke, on Jer. xxiii., 28, "What is the chaff to the wheat?" —

The Gentiles worshipped a God of power from fear and hope, deprecating divine vengeance, invoking divine favor. The Jews worshipped a God of Justice, seeking pardon for their sins, and thanking God for his help. No doubt, both Jew and Gentile saw

---

* For a rather exceptional illustration of "the theological paradox," "In order to pray for grace, we must have grace to pray," see J. T. Trowbridge's story, "Preaching for Selwin," in *Coupon Bonds, and Other Stories,* p. 329.

something higher, but this is the essence of the two kinds of prayer. They were both prayers of form,— of days, times, hours, methods. These have come down to us, for they have their origin in human weakness. But the divinest worship of all, the worship of the Father, needs no ritual nor liturgy, no sacred place nor sacred hour, no outward expression, no uttered prayers, even though they may have been consecrated by the associations of three thousand years. All these are helps, useful, and sometimes necessary; but they are not the essence of prayer. "Neither in this mountain, nor yet at Jerusalem, shall men worship the Father." The highest worship of all is to carry with us evermore the sense of that heavenly protection, that divine tenderness. It is to look in and look up, at all times, sure that he is near, that he is ready to pour his love into our soul. It is to feel, as Jesus felt, that we can do nothing of ourselves, and therefore to have our church, our oratory, our liturgy, in our heart, wherever we are. In the midst of work, of conversation, of amusement, of daily care, we may thus walk in the Spirit and live in the Spirit. The Christian world is gradually passing into this highest style of prayer. It will not then pray less, but more; for God will then write his law in the heart, and all shall know him, worship him, and love him.— *Boston Saturday Evening Gazette*, May 28, 1881.

Free prayer is natural, personal emotional: formal prayer is weighty, stately, reflective. It is hopeless to try to mingle the two. The personal prayer which would be dignified is merely ponderous: the formal prayer which would be emotional is merely sentimental. But under our flexible methods there should be room for both.— *Francis G. Peabody*, (*Saratoga Sermon*, 1882).

Similarly testifies another devout thinker: —

That God is most discerned when we are at our best, in our most favored moments of spiritual collectedness and intensity, or in our most anguished moments of penitential self-knowledge in the light of his countenance, makes it impossible for prayer to be without effort. To draw nigh to him by withdrawing from all that does not bring him near cannot be effected without a sustained uplifting of ourselves. When we purposely resort to this as a religious duty for the sake of the blessings which we know will come upon us if we attain to a communion with him, there is no other act of our nature of so absolute a self-devotion. In the great outward deeds and sacrifices which fellowship with God inspires, all the human sympathies mingle with and sustain the service. In the act of communion which goes before, in which the Holy Spirit offers the service and apparels for it, the soul is "alone with the Alone." The world's supreme act of self-sacrifice was serene and calm in the moments of its performance, anguished and awful in the moments of its preparation. It was always in the intensity of prayer that our Lord saw what the Father willed him to do; and the natural weakness which trembled and shrunk was poured into the bosom of the communing Comforter and replaced by his strength, so that the real trial was over before the outward trial came; and then no defeat was possible, for every element of infirmity had been brought to the Light in which is no darkness, and before him had passed away.—*J. H. Thom.*

This recalls the aphorism of Richter, "**Prayer** purifies: it is a self-preached sermon." Especially so, when supplemented with Dr. Clarke's earlier utterance: —

Supposing the main purpose and aim of life to be directed toward truth and right, the main current of the heart to be setting toward God and heaven, still it will happen that there will be eddies here and there running the other way. Often it will happen that we shall find ourselves for the time estranged from God, and then we shall often make the discovery of our estrangement by its effect upon our prayers. We find it difficult to pray,— we have nothing to say; we pray from our memory of past needs rather than from a sense of present ones. Our words mount up, our thoughts remain below. This state of mind indicates the estrangement of our heart from God, and warns us to return. Then, a special preparation becomes necessary. We pray God to teach us how to pray. We reflect on our real needs till the desire for pardon, peace, the restoration of inward life, returns. We examine our past thoughts and actions till we discover what it is which has led us away from the true path. And so, out of a genuine humility, there springs up once more a sincere desire, and our prayer again becomes the utterance of the heart.— *The Christian Doctrine of Prayer*, p. 126.

Does not this accord with the experience of every Christian? Let us see how far the aspirational view is held by the oracles of every sect and people, Catholic, Protestant, and "Gentile," bound thinker or free thinker. All will be found to indorse Thomas Fuller's admonition, "Leave not off praying to God; for either praying will make thee leave off sinning, or continuing in sin will make thee desist from praying."

Prayer is the contemplation of the facts of life from the highest point of view. It is the soliloquy of a beholding and a jubilant soul. It is the spirit of God pronouncing his works good. . . . As soon as the man is at one with God, he will not beg. He will then see prayer in all action. The prayer of the farmer kneeling in his field to weed it, the prayer of the rower kneeling with the stroke of his oar, are true prayers heard through all nature, though for cheap ends.— *R. W. Emerson (Self-reliance, Essays*, I., p. 67).

From this view, Dr. Clarke dissents: "Prayer does 'look abroad and ask for some foreign addition.'" Accordingly, he takes for the legend of the title-page of *The Christian Doctrine of Prayer* what may be translated from the Greek of

Plotinus, "The Flight of One Alone to the Only One," or, more freely, "The Fleeing of the Lonely to the Only." [Φυγὴ μόνου πρὸς τὸν Μόνον.] And, in a sermon on Acts ix., 11, he adds:—

First of all, then, in prayer is the sense of a divine presence, the consciousness of a divine power, wisdom, and love above all, through all, and in us all. Nature without this all-pervading sense of Deity is cold and dead. Life without it has no sufficient aim and purpose. Sorrow and disappointment without it have no secure consolation. Without it there is no unity to the world, no meaning in existence. Without it, science itself would soon lose its interest; for why study the facts and laws of a universe which came from nothing and is going nowhere?

In the Psalms there is this very striking petition, "Unite my heart to fear thy name." The soul needs the unity which comes from devotion to something infinite, perfect, the ideal beauty and goodness of things. This unites the heart and life, and prevents it from being wasted and distracted in the endless variety of nature.—*Boston Saturday Evening Gazette,* June 18, 1881.

This may be supplemented by Mr. Emerson's observation: "Is not prayer a study of truth, a sally of the soul into the unfound infinite? No man ever prayed heartily without learning something."

> One adequate support
> For the calamities of mortal life
> Exists,—*one only:* an assured belief
> That the procession of our fate, howe'er
> Sad or disturbed, is ordered by a Being
> Of infinite benevolence and power,
> Whose everlasting purposes embrace
> All accidents, converting them to good.
> The darts of anguish fix not where the seat
> Of suffering hath been thoroughly fortified
> By acquiescence in the Will Supreme
> For time and for eternity, by faith,
> Faith absolute in God, including hope,
> And the defence that lies in boundless love
> Of his perfections, with habitual dread
> Of aught unworthily conceived, endured
> Impatiently, ill-done, or left undone
> To the dishonor of his holy name.
> Soul of our souls and safeguard of the world!
> Sustain thou only canst the sick of heart,
> Restore their languid spirits, and recall
> Their lost affections unto thee and thine.
>   .   .   .   .   .
> How beautiful this dome of sky!
> And the vast hills in fluctuation fixed
> At thy command, how awful! Shall the soul,
> Human and rational, report of thee
> Even less than these? Be mute who will, who can;
> Yet I will praise thee with impassioned voice.
> My lips that may forget thee in the crowd

> Cannot forget thee here, where thou hast built
> For thy own glory in the wilderness ...
> Come labor when the worn-out frame requires
> Perpetual Sabbath; come disease and want,
> And sad exclusion through decay of sense!
> But leave me unabated trust in thee,
> And let thy favor to the end of life
> Inspire me with ability to seek
> Repose and hope among external things,
> Father of heaven and earth! and I am rich,
> And will possess my portion in content.
>
> *Wm. Wordsworth* ("*The Excursion,*" *Works,* p. 557).

The same key-note, "Leave me unabated trust in thee!" It reminds us of Horne's metaphor, "Prayer is the voice of Faith," or Bulwer-Lytton's hyperbole, "Faith builds in the dungeon and the lazar-house its sublimest shrines; and, up through roofs of stone that shut out the eye of heaven, ascends the ladder where angels glide to and fro,— prayer."

> No human eyes thy face may see,
> No human thought thy form may know,
>   But all creation dwells in thee,
> And thy great Life through all doth flow.
>   And yet — oh, strange and wondrous thought!
> Thou art a God who hearest prayer,
>   And every heart with sorrow fraught
> To seek thy presence aid may dare
>   And though most weak their efforts seem
> Into one creed these thoughts to bind,
>   And vain the intellectual dream
> To see and know the eternal mind,
>   Yet thou wilt turn them not aside
> Who cannot solve thy life divine,
>   But would give up all reason's pride
> To know their hearts approved by thine.
>
> *Thomas W. Higginson.*

This recalls the words of J. G. Whittier, "The simple heart that freely asks in love obtains." There is a world of meaning in Buddha's aphorism, "The greatest prayer is patience."

It may happen that two men shall profess the same religion, hold the same Bible, and call God by the same name, but one of them shall be a believer in the true God, and one not; one shall keep the first commandment, and the other break it. For one may pray in this way: "O Lord, I pray thee to save my soul. I know thou art a hard man, reaping where thou hast not strewed; and so, though thou hast made me so that I am born totally depraved, and unable to do any good thing, thou dost require of me to obey and **love thee**. I am wholly selfish and an enemy to thee, and am unable to love anything truly; but I admit I ought to love thee, notwithstanding. I **do** not see how I am guilty in doing wrong, when I cannot do **right**; but I am told that I ought to confess myself a **sinner**, and **so** I do: I confess myself to be the vilest of sinners.

Thou hast said that the righteousness of the righteous shall be upon *him*, and the wickedness of the wicked be upon *him ;* and yet I hope to be saved, not by any merits, or by becoming good myself, but by the merits and goodness of Jesus Christ. Amen."

Now, that is one prayer. Here is another, uttered perhaps by a poor ignorant slave, who has never been allowed to read the Bible, and whose theological notions are therefore very simple and childlike: "O Lord, I do not know thee very well, but I believe thou art a good Master, and I want to be a good servant. O Master, show me how to do right. Help me, O Lord, to-day not to be angry, nor idle, nor to tell any lies, but to be faithful in everything. If I am beaten or ill-used unjustly, help me to bear it, as the good Master Jesus bore it patiently when they beat him. Amen." Now, these two both say, O Lord, but they are not worshipping the same being. . . .

We believe in God when we believe in that which is divine in all things; when we see in men something divine and noble in the midst of all that is evil; when we see in childhood something divine, and revere the innocence yet unstained by the world. So, too, we believe in God when we love our friends, not because they are of use to us, not because our tastes and theirs happen to agree just now, but because we see and admire in them some innate beauty which God stamps on each soul when he makes it; some carnate and inborn charm of spontaneous sweetness or courage or honor or aspiration or reverence or humility or conscience which God gave them in his counsel before the foundation of the world. And we see God when we love all his creatures, whether they are sympathetic with us or antipathetic, when we overlook their faults and pardon their offences, and care for their souls as God and Christ care for their souls. This is divine love, true love, which sees God; which whosoever has dwells in God and God in him. He may have many faults, vices, follies, sins, but this generosity in his heart is the redeeming element; this is Christ born within him, the hope of glory; this gives him a solid inward peace and satisfaction, and makes him assured and confident before God.— *Dr. J. F. Clarke* (*Common Sense in Religion*, pp. 66, 71).

When a pump is frequently used, the water pours out at the first stroke, because it is high; but, if the pump has not been used for a long time, the water gets low, and when you want it you must pump a long while, and the water comes only after great efforts. It is so with prayer. If we are instant in prayer, every little circumstance awakens the disposition to pray, and desire and words are always ready; but, if we neglect prayer, it is difficult for us to pray, for the water in the well gets low.— *Felix Neff.*

Heaven is never deaf but when man's heart is dumb.— *Francis Quarles.*

"Prayer," says St. Jerome, "is a groan." Ah! our groans are prayers as well. The very cry of distress is an involuntary appeal to that invisible Power whose aid the soul invokes.... Prayer has a right to the word "ineffable." It is an hour of outpourings which words cannot express, of that interior speech which we do not articulate even when we employ it.— *Anna S. S. Swetchin.*

Certain thoughts are prayers. There are moments when, whatever be the attitude of the body, the soul is on its knees.— *Victor Hugo.*

Prayer is the wing wherewith the soul flies to heaven, and meditation the eye wherewith we see God.— *St. Ambrose.*

In prayer, it is better to have a heart without words than words without a heart.— *John Bunyan.*

<pre>
        Prayer is the soul's sincere desire,
          Uttered or unexpressed.   James Montgomery.
</pre>

The Christian life is a long and continual tendency of our hearts toward that eternal goodness which we desire on earth. All our happiness consists in thirsting for it. Now, this thirst is prayer. Ever desire to approach your Creator, and you will never cease to pray. Do not think it is necessary to pronounce many words.— *Archbishop Francis de S. Fénelon.*

Prayer is not eloquence, but earnestness; not the definition of helplessness, but the feeling of it; not figures of speech, but compunction of soul.— *Hannah More.*

Prayer among men is supposed a means to change the person to whom we pray: prayer to God does not change him, but fits us to receive the things prayed for.— *Bishop Edward Stillingfleet.*

<pre>
          At first I prayed for Light:
            Could I but see the way,
          How gladly would I walk
            To everlasting day!
          I asked the world's deep law
            Before my eyes to ope,
          And let me see my prayer fulfilled,
            And realize my hope.
          But God was kinder than my prayer,
          And darkness veiled me everywhere.

          And next I asked for strength,
            That I might tread the road
          With firm, unfaltering pace
            To heaven's serene abode;
          That I might never know
            A faltering, failing heart,
          But manfully go on
            And reach the highest part.
          But God was kinder than my prayer,
          And weakness checked me everywhere.

          And then I asked for faith:
            Could I but trust my God,
          I'd live in heavenly peace,
            Though foes were all abroad.
</pre>

His light thus shining round,
  No faltering should I know;
And faith in heaven above
  Would make a heaven below.
But God was kinder than my prayer,
And doubts beset me everywhere.

And now I pray for love,
  Deep love to God and man,—
A love that will not fail,
  However dark his plan;
That sees all life in him,
  Rejoicing in his power,
And faithful, though the darkest clouds
  Of gloom and doubt may lower.
And God is kinder than my prayer:
Love fills and blesses everywhere.
Ednah D. Cheney (Riverside Record).

I cannot find thee. Even when, most adoring,
  Before thy shrine I bend in lowliest prayer;
Beyond these bounds of thought, my thought, upsoaring,
  From furthest quest comes back: thou art not there.

Yet high above the limits of my seeing,
  And folded far within the inmost heart,
And deep below the deeps of conscious being,
  Thy splendor shineth: there, O God, thou art.

I cannot lose thee. Still in thee abiding,
  The end is clear, how wide soe'er I roam;
The law that holds the worlds my steps is guiding,
  And I must rest at last in thee, my home.*
Eliza Scudder (H. and T. B. for C. and H., 278).

Deep unto deep may call, but I
  With peaceful heart can say,
Thy loving-kindness hath a charge
  No waves can take away:
Then let the storm that speeds me home
  Deal with me as it may.
Anna L. Waring.

O thou, who art the secret source
  That rises in each soul,
Thou art the ocean too,— thy charm,
  That ever-deepening roll.
William C. Gannett.

---

* See lines from Derzhavin's "Ode to God," chap. xliii., *post.*

Chapter XXXI.

ALLEVIATION.

What Two Views of the Curative Ministrations of Jesus to Minds and Bodies diseased?

(1) That the cures were wholly supernatural. (2) That they were entirely natural, or at least merely preternatural,* and that the record thereof was made from exaggerated oral narrations. Thus, for instance, the little daughter of Jairus was only in a comatose condition,— "not dead, but sleeping,"— to rise up at the tender, familiar tones of her friend, "Talitha, cumi!"— "My pet lamb, rise up!"

There are modern cases of both febrile and nervous affections amenable to control by moral power; for instance, by the ascendency of any one commanding the patient's respect, or by any agency that arouses his own dormant energy of self-control. At the Faith Convention, Old Orchard Beach, Me., Aug. 1, 1881, several persons testified to having been physically healed "by faith." And, in a sermon on "Faith Cures," citing that of the wife of Rev. S. L. Gracey, after prayer of Dr. C. Cullis, Dr. Withrow mentions the case of a friend who had long suffered agonies under sciatica, to whom a friend said, "I will cure you," uttering the words in a tone of emphatic assurance. He procured a lump of alum, and commanded the sufferer to put it into the pocket of his pants, and not to remove it, and he would certainly have no more pain. Neither did he have any to speak of, for years afterward. Another friend suffering from the same disease was confidently assured that thousands had been cured by placing a potato in the skirt pocket of the coat. He did it, and the pain vanished as by magic. These were not cases of hysteria, imaginary pains that only needed the patient to count himself free, and he would be. And surely there was nothing miraculous or medicinal in the manner of their cure.

---
* In the sense adopted in Mr. A. Bronson Alcott's *Conversations*.

Dr. Benjamin Rush tells of an old man who for several years had suffered an annual attack of gout. He was lying in one of these paroxysms when his son accidentally drove the shaft of a wagon through the window of his room, making a terrible noise and smashing of glass. The sufferer leaped from his bed with the agility of a boy, forgetting either crutch or cane, which from that time on were not needed. . . . A moral wretch may match the achievements of the most righteous man in making marvellous cures. No monarch, in the seven centuries that "the king's evil" was cured by the royal touch, equalled the perfidious and profligate Charles II. A full hundred thousand patients are said to have come under his hand.—*Dr. J. L. Withrow (Golden Rule,* Sept. 30, 1882).

Dr. William A. Hammond publishes the case of a Catholic patient, who for many months had suffered from a distressing spasmodic affection of certain muscles of her neck. One morning, she expressed regret at being unable to go to Lourdes. He told her that he had some of the water of Lourdes, and another water which had produced marvellous results, and in his opinion was preferable to the other. This last was called *Aqua Crotonis.* Both were at her service, but she was strongly advised to use the latter. She evinced the greatest joy, and begged hard for the water of Lourdes, but consented to try the Croton water first. The genuine Lourdes water was given her, labelled *Aqua Crotonis.* This was rubbed on the affected part vigorously for two days, with no result. Croton water was then given her, labelled " Water of Lourdes, Feast of the Annunciation, 1879." The patient received it about 11 A.M. At half-past one, she rushed into the consulting room, exclaiming, " I am cured! I am cured! See what the Holy Virgin has done for me !" And she *was* cured. The contracted muscles were relaxed, and she could turn her head as well as ever.

Similar was the case of a sick German Protestant at Washington, whose husband, on viewing the remains of President Garfield at the Capitol, picked from the wreath presented by Queen Victoria a loosened flower, thinking it a partially opened tuberose. He put it in water by her bedside, and it blossomed out, disclosing the form of a dove in the centre. It seemed miraculous to her, as she did not know there was such a flower (the flower of the Holy Spirit). She began to mend from the moment she saw it, calling it the Christ flower, sent from the dead President's bier to heal her. Where the disease was regarded as the effect of demoniacal possession, the sufferer's belief that Jesus had some secret means of cure, or was especially favored by God with power of casting out the devil. would act as a strong ally to that sense of moral power and "authority" which his commanding presence inspired. And this, too, whether Jesus merely addressed the supposed demons in accordance with the needs of the patients, or was himself so far a child of the times as to attribute their sufferings to actual evil spirits dwelling in them.

Dr. John Brown, of Edinburgh, once gave a laborer a prescription, saying, "Take that, and come back in a fortnight, when you will be well." The patient came at the fortnight's end, with a clean tongue and happy face; he had made a pill of the paper, and faith in his physician's skill had done the rest.

In the case of the pre-natal *crotalus* bite already mentioned,* the physician remarks that occasionally a girl gets hysterical and "begins to play all sorts of pranks,—to lie and cheat, perhaps in the most unaccountable way, so that she might seem to a minister a good example of total depravity. We don't see her in that light. We give her iron and valerian, and get her on horseback if we can, and so expect to make her will come all right again."

On this and on cognate subjects upon which human science is yet in its creeping infancy, no intelligent student feels in any presumptuous mood of proffering very positive affirmation or denial. To predicate of man or of the lower animals or of migratory birds the possession of a sixth sense is a mere alternative of convenience. "One thing is sure," says Goethe, "under certain conditions, our soul, through the exercise of mysterious functions, has a greater power than reason; and the power is given it to antedate the future,—ay, to see into the future." It is well authenticated that Swedenborg, when hundreds of miles from his Stockholm home, was conscious of a conflagration there going on and imperilling his own house. So, also, is well authenticated the phenomenon of mind-reading, as demonstrated by a Yale student and others. So, also, that of the American girl who, when blindfold, reads a book printed in a foreign language.

Of Stuart C. Cumberland, who in London, New York, Boston, and other cities, has given wonderful demonstrations in thought-reading, it is said:—

He blindfolded himself, and taking Rev. H. W. Beecher by the hand, asked him to think of some object in the room. When the clergyman said he had done so, Mr. Cumberland placed Mr. Beecher's hand to his own forehead, and then, seemingly in a state of high nervous excitement, ran across the room and took the eye-glasses from Dr. Meredith Clymer's nose. At the same time, Mr. Beecher shouted,

---
Ante, chap. xix.

"Right." Then, the thought-reader was taken out of the room by Dr. G. M. Beard and Rev. G. H. Hepworth; while Mr. Beecher handed a small silver trinket to Dr. A. B. Ball, who concealed it in his shoe. Mr. Beecher also marked two tiny spots on different parts of the wall with a lead-pencil. Mr. Cumberland was then brought in, and, seizing the hand of the Plymouth pastor, he wandered about the room, stopped in front of Dr. Ball, and finally knelt down and took the trinket from the shoe. He also, while still blindfolded, put his finger upon the two spots upon the wall.— *New York Herald*, Nov. 29, 1882.

This power of Mr. Cumberland, Charles Foster, and others, has been by Dr. Crookes and other scientists attributed to induction. "The act of volition or of concentration of thought affects strongly the entire muscular and nervous system. To a person of acute mental perception, this excitement or mental impulse can be communicated by induction, exactly as the current passing along one telegraph or telephone wire will induce a similar current upon another wire running parallel with it."

In this connection, some writers have adduced a theory concerning certain metaphysical phenomena in conversions at colored camp-meetings; and that of Paul. Sampson Staniforth, a Methodist soldier in the campaign of Fontenay, relates his conversion in words which bear plainly marked on them the very stamp of good faith:—

From twelve at night until two, it was my turn to stand sentinel at a dangerous post. I had a fellow sentinel, but I desired him to go away, which he willingly did. As soon as I was alone, I knelt down and determined not to rise, but to continue crying and wrestling with God till he should have mercy on me. How long I was in that agony I cannot tell; but, as I looked up to heaven, I saw the clouds open exceedingly bright, and I saw Jesus hanging on the cross. At the same moment, these words were applied to my heart, "Thy sins are forgiven thee." All guilt was gone, and my soul was filled with unutterable peace. The fear of death and hell was vanished away. I was filled with wonder and astonishment. I closed my eyes, but the impression was still the same; and for about ten weeks, while I was awake, let me be where I would, the same appearance was still before my eyes, and the same impression upon my heart, "Thy sins are forgiven thee."*

It is often a phenomenon of an insanity in one direction that the mind is preternaturally keen in another.

"Second sight" is a flag over disputed ground. But it is matter of knowledge that there are persons whose yearnings, conceptions

---

* See *St. Paul and Protestantism*, by Dr. Matthew Arnold; also *Visions: a Study of Pseudopia*, by Dr. E. H. Clarke.

—nay, travelled conclusions—continually take the form of images which have a foreshadowing power: the deed they would do starts up before them in complete shape, making a coercive type; the event they hunger for or dread rises into vision with a reed-like growth, feeding itself fast on unnumbered impressions. They are not always the less capable of the argumentative process, nor less sane than the commonplace calculators of the market. Sometimes it may be that their natures have manifold openings, like the hundred-gated Thebes, where there may naturally be a greater and more miscellaneous inrush than through a narrow, beadle-watched portal.—*George Eliot* (*Daniel Deronda*).

So, too, as to cases of "unconscious cerebration." The wonderful movements of some somnambulists are well attested, reminding us of the delicate feats of Japanese prestidigitation, or of the wingings of a bat, eluding an interstrung lace-work of wires in a darkened room. Buni, lately giving mesmeric exhibitions in the larger cities of Hindostan, it is said, invites the public to bring thereto ferocious wild beasts. Like "Rarey, the horse-tamer," Buni "holds them with his glittering eye." In a few seconds, they subside into a condition of cataleptic stiffness, from which they can only be revived by certain passes, which he solemnly executes with his right hand. A snake in a violent state of irritation was brought to Buni by a menagerie proprietor, enclosed in a wooden cage. When deposited on the platform, it was writhing and hissing fiercely. Buni bent over the cage and fixed his eyes upon its occupant, gently waving his hand over the serpent's restless head. In less than a minute, the snake stretched itself out, stiffened, and lay apparently dead. Buni took it up and thrust several needles into its body, but it gave no sign of angry activity. Subsequently, a savage dog, held in a leash by its owner, was brought in, and at Buni's command let loose upon him, bristling with fury. He raised his hand, and in a second the fierce brute dropped upon its belly as though stricken by lightning. It seemed absolutely paralyzed by some unknown agency, and was unable to move a muscle until released from the magnetizer's spell by a majestic wave of his hand.*

The patient's intercourse with Jesus appears to have been a matter of instantaneous recognition and sympathy. This would not be uncommon. Nothing is truer than the remark of Alexander Knox † that, "in this frail and corrupt world, we

---

* See two papers by Mrs. A. H. Leonowens, in the *Youth's Companion*, December, 1882, concerning the Nojai jugglers at the Island of Serpents in the Volga River.
† In Southey's *Life of John Wesley*.

sometimes meet persons who in their very mien and aspect, as well as in the whole habit of life, manifest such a signature and stamp of virtue as to make our judgment of them a matter of intuition rather than the result of continued examination." Dr. Thomas Chalmers calls it "a beauty of holiness which effloresces on the countenance, the manner and the outward path."

It is recorded that occasionally there was, however, a failure to heal "because of their unbelief."

> The deaf may hear the Saviour's voice,
>   The fettered tongue its chain may break;
> But the deaf heart, the dumb by choice,
>   The laggard soul that will not wake,
> The guilt that scorns to be forgiven,—
> These baffle e'en the spells of heaven.
> In thought of these, his brows benign
> Not e'en in healing cloudless shine.
>
> Come while the blossoms of thy years are brightest,
>   Thou youthful wanderer in a flowery maze;
> Come, while the restless heart is bounding lightest,
>   And joy's pure sunbeams tremble in thy ways;
> Come, while sweet thoughts, like summer buds unfolding,
>   Waken rich feelings in the careless breast;
> While yet thy hand the ephemeral wreath is holding,
>   Come and secure interminable rest.
>
> Soon will the freshness of thy days be over,
>   And thy free buoyancy of soul be flown;
> Pleasure will fold her wing, and friend and lover
>   Will to the embraces of the worm have gone;
> Those who now love thee will have passed forever,—
>   Their looks of kindness will be lost to thee:
> Thou wilt need balm to heal thy spirit's fever,
>   As thy sick heart broods over years to be.
>
>   *Willis Gaylord Clark* (*Literary Remains*, p. 438).

Chapter XXXII.

TRANSFIGURATION.

What Three Views concerning the Transfiguration?

(1) THAT there was a supernatural occurrence, literally as described in Matt. xvii. and Mark ix.

(2) That the scene is a mere allegory of the conception that the authority of the law and prophets must be superseded,— Moses and Elijah disappear, leaving Jesus alone singled out as the son of God's good pleasure.

(3) That the account is a traditional exaggeration of a precious interview between Jesus, Peter, John, and James,— the latter perhaps a brother of Jesus that had taken the place of a deceased son of Zebedee.

"We are shaped and fashioned," says Goethe, "by what we love." These three are not the only disciples, who, when once on the height of lofty communion with the True, the Beautiful, and the Good, fondly linger and yearn to "abide" there forever, nevermore to descend to life's petty, hampering, commonplace concerns; who have to be reminded that there are other elements of our spiritual nature demanding a fair chance for symmetrical development; that it is only required of us that we be faithful to the pattern shown us up there. Apprehension — comprehension — of the upward often comes of apprehensiveness of the downward.

The most difficult thing in life is to keep the heights which the soul has reached.— *David Riddle, Jr.*

> And looks commercing with the skies,
> Thy rapt soul sitting in thine eyes.
>
> Thyself amid the silence clear,
> The world far off and dim;
> Thy vision free, the Bright One near,
> Thyself alone with him.
>
> *John Milton.*

Is it entirely fanciful to believe that these favored disciples then and there began to see the world as Jesus saw it? There is an Arabian proverb, "Get close to the seller of perfumes, if you want to be fragrant." John Bunyan says, "Old truths are new to us, if they come with the smell of heaven upon them." We know that everything became lovely as Jesus looked at it. God was a being of divine loveliness,—not a stern king or judge, as the Jews too often regarded him. Did he appear to these rapt contemplators a mere law of nature or order of the universe? So science frequently regards him. Piety, what is it? A devout and advanced thinker, after adverting to the ceremonial, the emotional, the doctrinal, and other kinds of piety, says:—

If these varieties of piety could be combined in one kind, omitting their defects, we should have the highest kind of all. If we could have a solemn awe and fear of sin and its consequences, as the basis of religion; beautiful, harmonious rites and ceremonies, as the helps to piety; the sympathy of human hearts, social meetings, brotherly fellowship, as the daily food of piety; and the broadest science brought into the Church instead of being left in the college, teaching us to see God in the majestic movements of the stars, in the delicate anatomy of the flower, in the molecular motions and forces of chemical atoms, in the long processes of geology,— by such a combination, we should have the highest piety of all. This can only come through the piety taught us and given to us by Jesus Christ. Its essence is the life of God in the soul, personally communicated through Jesus, the providential mediator, and redeeming us by its power from all evil. It finds God within us as well as around us. It is childlike. The child is not in the least afraid of its parents, if they are what they ought to be; but it looks up to them with reverence, and is afraid of offending them. That is all the fear there is in it. . . .

God in Christ is a loving order, a fatherly law, a personal friend, yet of unknown depth and height. He is serenely majestic as the central power in the universe, holding all worlds in the hollow of his hand. Yet he is inwardly present to the heart of his humblest child, whenever, in sincere prayer and penitence, his child opens his heart to him. . . .

All the love we have learned in this world only needs to take a new direction to become divine love. The greatest scientific discovery of the present time is said to be that of the correlation and conservation of forces. It means that there is one force underlying all forces, now taking one form, now another. It is now motion, then heat, then electricity, then magnetism, then chemical affinity. So in the spiritual world, all forces of the soul are the same, and he who has one can have the rest. Therefore it is that, in the New Testament, faith is sometimes made the whole of religion, and sometimes hope is said to be the source of salvation, and sometimes we are told if we obey the Commandments we shall enter into life, and then we are taught that love is the fulfilling of the law. They are all one and the same. They take different forms according to the position of the soul. But who has really one has all. If a man can really trust God, then he can obey him. If he can really obey, then he can believe. If he can love his brother as himself, he can love God. If he can love God, then he can love his brother.—*Dr. J. F. Clarke (Common Sense in Religion*, pp. 281, ff.).

>The world's great altar stairs
>That slope through darkness up to God.

>I keep the holy faith in God, in man,
>And in the angels ministrant between;
>I hold to one true Church of all true souls,
>Whose churchly seal is neither bread nor wine,
>Nor laying on of hands, nor holy oil,
>But only the anointing of God's grace.
>
>*Theodore Tilton.*

The Christian Church,—as old as the centuries and as young as the future.—*Bulwer-Lytton.*

>More of truth and more of might,
>More of love and more of light,
>More of reason and of right.
>
>*Sir John Bowring.*

In an Appendix, *post*, will be narrated one or two well-authenticated cases of death-bed transfiguration, not attributable to any physiological derangement: suggesting that, at least figuratively,

>The discord that involveth
>Some startling change of key
>The Master's hand resolveth
>In richest harmony.
>
>*Anon. (Youth's Companion*, Feb. 22, 1883).

Cases where there seem to be gleamings from another world, and the spirit's dissolving tenement, like the dungeon of Chillon, is momentarily lit up

>Dim with a dull imprisoned ray,
>A sunbeam which hath lost its way.
>
>*Lord George Gordon Byron.*

>How sweetly did they float upon the wings
>Of silence, through the empty-vaulted night.
>At every fall smoothing the raven down
>Of darkness till it smiled!
>
>*John Milton.*

Chapter XXXIII.

AGGRESSION.

What Three Views concerning Christ's ejecting Traders from the Temple; and What generally as to his Self-assertion or Aggression?

(1) THAT there was a miraculous feat, as described, Matt. xxi., Mark xi., Luke xix., John ii.; "due," as St. Jerome says, "to the starry light which shone from his eyes, and to the divine majesty which beamed from his features."

(2) That such success of one not very muscular man against a rough crowd was not miraculous, but simply due to the weakness, product of a guilty conscience, on the one side, and the grandeur of a supreme enthusiasm on the other. Dr. Geikie says that "all were under a spell for the moment. It was an act such as Matthias or Judas Maccabæus might have done; and, prophet-like as it was, in such a place, and in such a cause, its unique heroism secured its triumph. Dr. J. F. Clarke imagines* that "Jesus entered the Court of the Gentiles, accompanied by the great multitude, who had formed a triumphal procession around him. Indignation seized him when he saw the place of worship for the nations of the world treated with such contempt by the priesthood, who ought to have welcomed the Gentiles to the worship of the one true God. The divine anger of the prophet of old seized him; and, like as ancient seers spoke to the sight of men by outward actions, he took a whip and drove from the court these traffickers."

(3) That the legend is a traditional exaggeration of the circumstance that Jesus administered a rebuke to some one of the desecrators, who thereupon confessed conviction of error, and forthwith abandoned the business. Accordingly, that Jesus invariably exemplified his own precepts upon non-aggression; that in this, as well as in the rebuke administered to the hypocritical Pharisees, he "must be cruel only to be kind."

---

* In *The Legend of Thomas, called Didymus.*

There is a tradition that this was the view of Benjamin Franklin. But the tradition is hardly so well authenticated as his aphorism, "Christianity commands us to pass by injuries; policy, to let them pass by us." But as to just when and to what extent meekness is policy, there is a great contrariety of opinion.

> Those who bear misfortunes over-meekly
> Do but persuade mankind that they and want
> Are all too fitly matched to be disjoined,
> And so to it they leave them.
>
> *Joanna Baillie.*

> Tender handed, stroke a nettle,
>   And it stings you for your pains:
> Grasp it like a man of mettle,
>   And it soft as silk remains.
> 'Tis the same with common natures:
>   Use 'em kindly, they rebel;
> But be rough as nutmeg-graters,
>   And the rogues obey you well.
>
> *Aaron Hill.*

There is a nearly equal diversity of opinion as to the reasons for the peculiar entry into the city just before the ejection of the traders.

Apparently, this triumphal entry was a spontaneous outburst of enthusiasm confined within narrow limits. It may be that Jesus hoped that these limits would extend until they should comprise an effective majority of the population of the city, and that so, perhaps without a struggle, the hierarchy would be overthrown and his own kingdom set up in its place. It may be he had spoken of these things with them so frequently that he allowed himself to think that his disciples were completely disabused of their materialistic notions of his Messiahship; but, from all that we can glean concerning them, we may be sure that they were not. Already they imagined themselves sitting on twelve thrones, judging the twelve tribes of Israel. Jesus is made to promise them this honor in one of the worst distortions of the New Testament tradition. It was their triumph quite as much as his own that they were celebrating as they spread their garments in his way.—*John W. Chadwick (The Man Jesus,* p. 167).

The record of another instance of self-assertion savors more especially of dignity. Standing arraigned before the malignant, bigoted priests, Jesus gives them a rational answer, courteous, but not cringing. Some poor, pompous fool, "dressed in a little brief authority," imperiously hisses out, "Is that the way you answer a *high priest?*" and strikes him. Jesus makes no movement to repel the violence, but, fixing his clear and brave, but sad and sweetly pitying eye full and square and immovable upon the leering features of the loathsome upstart, replies, "If I have answered in any wrong way, *show* *wherein.*" Jesus pauses for an answer. Everybody's attention is concentrated on the wincing, contemptible bully. In that long moment of silent suspense culminates the defeat of the ashamed assailant. Jesus clinches the lesson to the self-made culprit — yea, to the whole crowd of abashed claquers — with, "If there was nothing wrong in my answer, why did you strike me, sir?"* This, uttered with a countenance more in sorrow than in anger, thenceforth in all the remaining years of that man's life was an ever present monitor that would not down. Too happy he if his heat-oppressed brain had, in its retrospect, the poor warder of one little memory,— that, instant upon the reproof, the parting glance of Jesus at the rash wretch was one of tender forgiveness.

In dealing with a dolt, everybody — Jesus not excepted — must be justified in speaking incisively. Call it "showing spirit," if you please. Euphemisms would be wasted. "I love clamor," said Edmund Burke, "when there is an abuse. The alarm-bell disturbs the inhabitants, but saves them from being burnt in their beds." Of course, if it is a case where neither mild nor sharp words can avail, the only alternative is silence. Accordingly, the deportment of Jesus in the next two scenes cannot be called inconsistent therewith. Luke says † the company then arose, took Jesus before Pilate, and charged him with having declared himself an anointed king [*christon basilea*]. Pilate asked him, "Art thou king of the Jews?" Jesus answered, "Thou sayest." Pilate, finding no fault in him, and ascertaining he was a Galilean, and consequently of Herod's jurisdiction, sent him to Herod, who happened then to be stopping at Jerusalem. Herod had long wished to see Jesus: he hoped to see some sign [*sēmeion*] achieved by him. Herod questioned him in many words, but Jesus answered him nothing. The priests stood there vehemently accusing him. Herod with his soldiers set him at naught, mocked him, arrayed him in gorgeous apparel, and sent him back to Pilate. Pilate finally succumbed to the clamor for crucifixion.

The proper discrimination — the right generalization to be deduced from the whole record of Christ's life — appears to be well summed up in Dr. Alexandre R. Vinet's aphorism: "Duty does not consist in suffering everything, but in suffering everything for duty. Sometimes, indeed, it is our duty not to suffer." It is a trite proverb that "He who puts up with insult invites injury"; or, as Auguste Préault says, "To pardon an old injury is to invite a new one,"— sometimes. Confucius asks,

---

* John xviii., 23. † Luke xxiii.

"If doing what ought to be done be made the first business, and success a secondary consideration, is not this the way to exalt virtue?" And Mary Lyon used to say, "There is nothing in the universe that I fear, but that I shall not know my duty, or shall fail to do it." Dr. J. F. Clarke says:—

When resistance can do no good, when we have uttered our protest and it is ineffectual, then it is often more dignified to bear evil in silence. Then our silence is perhaps the loudest protest. Jesus was patient in this way before the Jewish Sanhedrim, and his silence troubled them more than if he had spoken. "Why do not you answer?" said the high priest. "Do not you hear what these men accuse you of?" Still he stood silent. Imagine the scene. All his enemies are around him; he is helpless in their midst. They bring witnesses to prove him guilty of death. He hears all the charges and makes no reply. His mind is far away. His work is done. He sees not the haggard, stern faces of his enemies, not the base looks of the witnesses. He sees, perhaps, his own Galilean lake sleeping in its beauty among the hills; he sees the scenes of his childhood where he first met God in the solitude and serenity of nature. He sees the place where he knew first the greatness of his mission. Calm, strong, indifferent to what was passing around him, he stood in the silence of his own thoughts. What they chose to accuse him of, how they meant to bring him to his cross, was nothing to him now. He had passed beyond all that, and so he was silent. "As a sheep before its shearers is dumb, so he opened not his mouth." But even that silence was not the passive, meek, unresisting patience which we commonly attribute to Jesus. It was the golden silence which speaks louder than words. It told them that he knew that his fate was already sealed, and that they had already determined that he should die. "Why go through the form of a defence? This is nothing to me: this is your affair." ...

True patience is not passive, but active. It is holding on. It is to be not weary in well doing, though there seems to be no success. It is not to draw back or give up, but to persevere, whether men bear or whether they forbear. It is—to use an old word and a good one, though somewhat passed by—longanimity, which is the sister of magnanimity. Magnanimity is greatness of soul which aims at vast and noble ends, rising above all things base and mean. Longanimity is the persevering purpose which keeps to its idea, without rest and without haste, not making a pause nor leaving a void. The purpose is so strong that it is not disturbed by difficulty, nor terrified by danger, nor chilled by neglect. It holds on. That is the meaning of patience.—*Common Sense in Religion*, pp. 394-396.

> Men who their duties know,
> But know their rights, and, knowing, dare maintain,
> Prevent the long-aimed blow,
> And crush the tyrant while they rend the chain.
> These constitute a State.
>
> *Sir William Jones.*

CHAPTER XXXIV.

MINISTRATION.

What is the Common Enumeration of the Miracles alleged in the Four Gospels to have been performed by Christ; and What the Present Different Leading Views of the Accounts thereof?

SOME commentators reckon only thirty miracles to be distinctly set forth. They would identify Luke's draught of fishes with John's, would exclude from the category Luke's mention of the healing of Malchus' ear, and would consider the account in Matthew and Mark of a disappointing fig-tree as only setting forth a parable.* Ewald thinks there was but one feeding of the multitude.† Archbishop Richard Trench sets down thirty-three, and as occurring in the following order:—

Making wine from water (John ii.).
Curing a nobleman's son (John iv.).
First draught of fishes (Luke v.).
Stilling a tempest (Matt. viii., Mark iv., Luke viii.).
Curing a Gadarene lunatic (Matt. viii., Mark v., Luke viii.).
Raising from death Jairus' daughter (Matt. ix., Mark v.).
Curing a woman's issuance (Matt. ix., Mark v., Luke viii.); two Galilean blind men (Matt. ix.); a paralytic (Matt. ix., Mark ii., Luke v.); a Galilean leper (Matt. viii., Mark i., Luke v.); a centurion's servant (Matt. viii., Luke vii.); a Capernaum lunatic (Mark i., Luke iv.); and Peter's mother-in-law (Matt. viii., Mark i., Luke iv.).
Raising from death a widow's son (Luke vii.).
Curing a Bethesda invalid (John v.).
Feeding 5,000 men, etc. (Matt. xiv., Mark vi., Luke ix., John vi.).
Walking on water (Matt. xiv., Mark vi., Luke vi.).
Curing a man born blind (John ix.); a man's withered hand (Matt. xii., Mark iii., Luke vi.); an infirm woman (Luke xiii.); a dropsical man (Luke xiv.); ten lepers (Luke xvii.); a Syro-Phœnician woman (Matt. xv., Mark vii.); and a deaf and dumb man (Mark vii.).
Feeding 4,000 men, etc. (Matt. xv., Mark viii.).

---
* See *post*, chap. xxxv.   † *Life of Jesus Christ* (Glover's translation, p. 198).

Curing a Bethsaida blind man (Mark viii.); and a boy (Matt. xvii., Mark ix., Luke ix.).
Coin in a fish's mouth (Matt. xvii.).
Raising Lazarus from death (John xi.).
Curing two Jericho blind men (Matt. xx., Mark x., Luke xvii.).
Withering a fig-tree (Matt. xxi., Mark xi.).
Curing Malchus' ear (Luke xxii.).
Second draught of fishes (John xxi.).— *Notes on the Miracles, etc.*

The principal different views concerning these accounts may perhaps be most conveniently considered in the following order:—

(1) The "*a priori*" theory. God, says Spinoza, is immanent in nature and does not transcend it. He has made its laws so unchangeable and yet so elastic that they shall prove, under every circumstance and in every need, the adequate organs and servants of his will. He never contradicts himself when he has once made a law, he is not such a victim of caprice as to violate it by a miracle.*

(2) The "orthodox" theory. "The government of a world," says Carl A. Hase,† "actuated by human freedom, is only possible by means of an inworking of divine freedom. This inworking gives us the philosophical notion of a miracle, which therefore can only be denied with the denial of Providence itself." Dr. Jonathan Edwards in substance declares that the Supreme Being is not so much a God of nature as a God of men; the world is chiefly a workshop for the making of men; a miracle is not disorder, but a new order; the shifting of order is not a makeshift of whim, but a condescension of grace to induce, as essential to a specific blessing, a belief in respect to a certain vicegerency, etc., indispensable to any effectual repairing of a jar that got into the machinery of the universe through the exigency of leaving man a free moral agent. That a change of order surprising to man is not disorder may be illustrated by the aloe. The order of the development of the century plant is not established in ninety-nine years: the "miracle of bloom" in the hundredth year is no disorder.

A miracle is a surprise, but to whom? Not to higher intelligences who see the interiors of nature and know what is about to be from the unbroken links of the ascending series; not to Him who fills those interiors with reality and floods them with his life; but to us who see but one link of the chain, who are ignorant of the long line of antecedents, and who stand where the result first breaks upon

---

*See Theodore Parker's sermon, "Theism."   † *Lehrbuch der Dogmatik*, § 130.

human sight.— *Edmund H. Sears* (*The Fourth Gospel the Heart of Christ*, p. 21).

(3) A "*quasi*-orthodox" theory is that the alleged wonders were merely relative miracles,— miraculous only to those in regard of whom they were first done,— as when a savage believes that a telescope has the power of bringing the far instantaneously near, or a tropic islander is informed by a trustworthy missionary that in a Northern clime the surface of a river has grown so hard that an elephant can safely walk thereon.* Schleiermacher avers that Jesus was able to evoke — as from nature's hidden recesses, from her inward sanctuary — powers which none other could. These facts, which seem exceptional, were deeply laid in the first constitution of the law, and, at a certain turning-point in the world's history, by the providence of God, who had arranged all things from the beginning of the world for the glory of his son, emerged at his bidding. Dr. Furness would postulate,— Given a man of the character of Jesus, and miracles for him are just as natural as our ordinary occupations and works are for us.

(4) The "Hume" theory is that the fact of any miracle is a case of conflicting evidence,— that of the testimony of narrators, and that of human experience; that, in balancing the two, the only case in which the evidence for the miracle could be admitted as prevailing would be that in which the falseness or error of the attesting witnesses would be a greater miracle than the miracle which they affirm; and that there is no case in which the evidence for any one miracle is able to outweigh the *a priori* evidence which is against all miracles.

(5) The "Mill" theory is that, if the evidence produced is such that it is more likely that the set of observations and experiments upon which the law rests should have been inaccurately performed or inaccurately interpreted than that the evidence in question should be false, we may believe the evidence; but then we must abandon the law. And since the law was received on what seemed a complete induction, it can only be rejected on evidence equivalent, as being inconsistent not with any number of approximate generalizations, but with some other and better established law of nature. The doctrine must prove the miracles, not the miracles the doctrine. St. Paul expressly warned the churches, if any one came to them working miracles, to observe what he taught, and, unless he preached

---

*See some rather exceptional illustrations in Mr. J. T. Trowbridge's "Story of a Monomaniac," *Coupon Bonds, and Other Stories*, pp. 336, 348, 355.

Christ and him crucified, not to listen to the teaching. **And Mr. Mill adds:** —

There is no reason, therefore, that timid Christians should shrink from accepting the logical canon of the Grounds of Disbelief. And it is not hazarding much to predict that a school which peremptorily rejects all evidences of religion except such as, when relied upon exclusively, the canon in question irreversibly condemns,— which denies to mankind the right to judge of religious doctrine, and bids them depend on miracles as their sole guide,— must, in the present state of the human mind, inevitably fail in its attempt to put itself at the head of the religious feelings and convictions of this country, by whatever learning, argumentative skill, and even in many respects comprehensive views of human affairs its peculiar doctrines may be recommended to the acceptance of thinkers.— *John Stuart Mill's Logic*, Part II., chap. xx., "Grounds of Disbelief."

Archbishop Trench reiterates the same remark: "A miracle does not prove the truth of a doctrine, or the divine mission of him that brings it to pass. The doctrine must first commend itself to the conscience as being good."* And he is also careful to distinguish from the New the Old Testament alleged miracles: the cleaving of the sea, Ex. xiv., 21; of a river, Josh. iii., 14; of the earth, Num. xvi., 31; a rock, Num. xx., 11; fire from the sky, II. Kings i., 12; fire made harmless, Dan. iii., 25; and beasts, vi., 22; Jonah ii., 10. As to the Egyptian plagues, Dr. S. Davidson remarks that national traditions account for all that appears miraculous therein †

Similarly, Dr. Rufus P. Stebbins remarks ‡ that the Book of Jonah — written after the captivity, and perhaps three hundred years after Jonah lived — indicates, by its subject and the manner of treatment, that it was of the type of "Bel and the Dragon," "Susannah," "Tobit," "Judith," and "Daniel," written to edify patriots. The writer did not intend his readers to believe saints endured just such trials, no more than Bunyan's are to believe that Christian was locked up by a real giant in a real castle, or had a hand-to-hand fight with Apollyon, or Mrs. Stowe's that an Uncle Tom was whipped to death by order of a Legree. Jesus would naturally make a classical allusion to Jonah, as we speak of Christian and Giant Despair, or of Uncle Tom, or of what Æsop's fox did and said. The hymn that Jonah (ii., 1) "prayed unto the Lord his God out

---

* *Notes on the Miracles*, etc., p. 25.
† As to the alleged increase, in 430 years, of the 70 Israelites who went down to Egypt to 600,000 fighting men, implying an entire population of 2,500,000, see the *Encyclopædia Britannica* thereon.
‡ See *Christian Register*, Oct. 19, 1882.

of the fish's belly " is composed of scraps of poetry gathered from different psalms and strung together with little connection or taste, the writer not being skilful enough to give even the right tenses not to betray the late origin of the composition, " Out of the belly of hell cried I, and thou heardest my voice."

Dr. Matthew Arnold remarks: —

To engage in an *a priori* argument to prove that miracles are impossible against an adversary who argues *a priori* that they are possible, is the vainest labor in the world.... The human mind, as its experience widens, gets acquainted with the natural history of miracles; it sees how they arise, and slowly, but inevitably, puts them aside.— *God and the Bible*, p. 42 [72].

As to the familiar argument of Archbishop Butler,*—that there is no presumption from analogy against some operations which we should now call miraculous, particularly none "against a revelation at the beginning of the world," etc.,— Vicar James B. Mozley thinks it "has not been interfered with by anything that science has brought to light since Butler's time." †

But the vicar omits to define the exact scope of his use of the word "science." ‡

Pertinent here comes a criticism by Mr. Tyndall: —

Mr. Mozley says the death of Arius was not miraculous, because the coincidence of the death of a heresiarch taking place when it was peculiarly advantageous to the orthodox faith ... was not such as to compel the inference of extraordinary divine agency; but it was a special providence, because it carried a reasonable appearance of it. The miracle of the Thundering Legion was a special "providence, but not a miracle, for the same reason, because the coincidence of an instantaneous fall of rain in answer to prayer carried some appearance, but not proof, of preternatural agency.". . . In other words, if a special providence could be *proved* to be a special providence, it would cease to be a special providence, and become a miracle.... But, instead of speaking of it as a doubtful miracle, he calls it " an invisible miracle." He speaks of the point of contact of supernatural power with the chain of causation being so high up as to be wholly or in part out of sight, whereas the essence of a special providence is the uncertainty whether there is any contact at all, either high or low. By the use of an incorrect term, however, a grave danger is avoided.

---

* *Analogy*, etc., ii., chap. ii.
† *Bampton Lectures on Miracles* (2d ed.), p. 313.
‡ See Dr. J. W. Draper's *History of the Conflict between Religion and Science*, F. D. Maurice's *Claims of the Bible and of Science* and Dr. Matthew Arnold's review thereof, and *Last Essays on Church and Religion*, chap. ii., "Bishop Butler and the Zeitgeist."

For the idea of doubt, if kept systematically before the mind, would soon be fatal to the special providence as a means of edification. The term employed, on the contrary, invites and encourages the trust which is necessary to supplement the evidence.... Whenever the evidence of the miraculous seems incommensurate with the fact which it has to establish, or rather when the fact is so amazing that hardly any evidence is sufficient to establish it, he invokes "the affections." They must urge the reason to accept the conclusion from which unaided it recoils. The affections and emotions are eminently the court of appeal in matters of real religion, which is an affair of the heart; but they are not, I submit, the court in which to weigh allegations regarding the credibility of physical facts. These must be judged by the dry light of the intellect alone, appeals to the affections being reserved for cases where moral elevation, and not historic conviction, is the aim. It is, moreover, because the result, in the case under consideration, is deemed desirable that the affections are called upon to back it. If undesirable, they would with equal right be called upon to act the other way. Even to the disciplined scientific mind, this would be a dangerous doctrine....

Mahometanism has lived and spread without miracles; and to assert, in the face of this, that Christianity has spread *because* of miracles, is not more opposed to the spirit of science than to the common sense of mankind.—*John Tyndall* (*Fragments of Science for Unscientific People*, pp. 47, 50).

In this connection must not be omitted **Thomas Carlyle's** illustration:—

To the minnow, every cranny and pebble and quality and accident of its little native creek may have become familiar. But does the minnow understand the ocean tides and periodic currents, the tradewinds and monsoons and moon's eclipses, by all which the condition of its little creek is regulated and may from time to time (unmiraculously enough) be quite overset and reversed? Such a minnow is man: his creek this planet earth, his ocean the immeasurable all; his monsoons and periodic currents the mysterious course of Providence through æons of æons.— *Sartor Resartus*, Book II., chap. viii.

This last expression will **recall** another, but perhaps rather unpleasantly (lest unjustly), ironical utterance by Carlyle, which, if not an admonition right in point, should here be excluded for "idiosyncrasy":—

> The Builder of this universe was wise;
> He formed all souls, all systems, planets, particles.
> The plan he formed his worlds and æons by
> Was— Heavens!— was thy small nine and thirty articles!

In applying to accounts of miracles the logicians' "Canons of Disbelief" just referred to, one fact as to the testimony of experience concerning individual and national credulity must not escape consideration ; namely, the predominance of feeling over judgment, of fancy over reason; or rather the tendency to seek a bit of reason as — to borrow a word from the apothecaries — a "medium" for swallowing marvels. A little gypsy girl, when asked why the lions did not eat up Daniel, answered, "I guess God told the lions that Daniel was not good to eat." A child never asks itself whether the chimney-flue is large enough to take in Santa Claus and his pack. "Grandmother says so" is proof enough. To every people, the sun has been a god; each has its "folk-lore"; to one or another there have been spirits of the earth, of the air, of the water,— angels, bargeists, boggarts, brownies, bug'ears, cat-witches, demigods, demons, devils, dryads, erl-kings, elves, fairies, fauns, gnomes, goblins, gorgons, hag-hurts, hamadryads, imps, kelpies, mermaids, naiads, nixies, nymphs, ogres, plutos, plutuses, pucks, quat-bringers, raven-rooks, satyrs, sprites, tritons, undines, voodists, warlocks, wizards,— indeed, as M. J. Savage remarks, "the whole universe one wild, strange scene of phantasm."* Even the intellectual Kepler believed that the order of the motions of the heavenly bodies could only be explained on the supposition that an angel inhabited and guided each planet in its course. Even the eminent jurist, Sir Matthew Hale, honestly condemned to death certain persons as witches.

At the trial of two widows of Lowestoft in Suffolk, named Rose Callender and Amy Duny, at Bury Saint Edmunds, at the spring assizes in 1664, on a charge of bewitching two children of Samuel Pacy, Sir Matthew Hale instructed the jury that witches do exist: "for, firstly, the Scriptures have affirmed so much; secondly, the wisdom of all nations hath provided laws against such persons, which is an argument of their confidence of such a crime." The sentence of death was executed.— *See, in Dr. M. Arnold's Last Essays on Church and Religion, "A Psychological Parallel."*

If this could be true of the mental operations of the Chief Justice of the King's Bench, the author of *The Primitive Origination of Mankind considered and explained according to the Light of Nature, The History of the Pleas of the Crown*, and *Contemplations, Moral and Divine*, etc.,— shall we say that, as to the common people,— their loose habits of observation and narration,— Shakspere's averment is at all hyperbolical? —

---

* *Talks about Jesus*, p. 27.

> No natural exhalation in the sky,
> No scape of nature, no distempered day,
> No common wind, no customed event,
> But they will pluck away the natural cause,
> And call them meteors, prodigies, and signs,
> Abortive presages and tongues of heaven.
>
> *King John*, Act III, Scene 4

> No evil thing that walks by night
> In fog or fire, by lake or moorish fen,
> Blue meagre hag, or stubborn unlaid ghost
> That breaks his magic chains at curfew time,
> No goblin or swart faery of the mine,
> Hath hurtful power o'er Truth and Purity.
>
> *John Milton.*

> A thousand fantasies
> Begin to throng into my memory,
> Of calling shapes, and beckoning shadows dire,
> And airy tongues, that syllable men's names
> On sands, and shores, and desert wildernesses.
>
> *John Milton.*

The world has never had enough monitors like Fisher Ames, proclaiming that, in order "to study nature or man, we ought to know things that are in the ordinary course, not the unaccountable things that happen out of it."

Every nation on earth affords illustrations of seeming inability to abandon some unreasoning prejudice or silly superstition. Charles R. Mills, for nearly a quarter of a century a Presbyterian missionary in China, mentions a custom in Shantung of letting accumulate on the floor of the house a "luck hillock"— in one inn, three feet high — of the dirt scrapings from the shoes, etc. This was to conciliate the "Yang," the force that has to do with life, light, warmth, prosperity, as against the "Yin," the opposite,— the former strong, the latter effeminate. When some Dutchman proposed to make the river Manzanares navigable to the Tagus, and that to Lisbon, the Council said if it had been the will of God that the rivers should be navigable, he would have made them so.*

A people who are charmed by a horseshoe whim, who do not practise the decimal system of weights and measures, nor give their children a decent orthography, and who levy on the chattels of widows and spinsters, but deny them suffrage representation as to expenditure of the tax, have not far to go for examples of senseless aversion to new and rational ideas. Dr. Zabdiel Boylston introduced inoculation for the small-pox in

---

* The London *Telegraph* announces that Dr. Otto Kuntze has explored Palamaran, the Death Valley, and finds it as healthy as any other part of Java. The legends of death from the upas tree were wholly propagated by Javanese superstition.

Boston in 1721, and tried it at first on his son Thomas and other members of his family. The municipal government prohibited its practice, and the people would have torn him to pieces had he not retired from the city.* This was of a piece with a certain unreasoning bigotry:—

> Exclusion is in their mouths and supremacy in their hearts. These are the essence of sectarianism, call it by what denomination you will.— *Lady Sidney Owenson Morgan.*

This recalls the conversation mentioned in the life of J. S. Buckminster, that occurred many years ago, concerning a new, but now influential, sect. Said one, "Well, they do manage to set a fair example in their lives." "That is true," answered the other; "but, do you know, I believe the devil helps them to do this, that we may be the more easily blinded to the damnable nature of their doctrines." Isaac Pitman tells us that, not a half century ago, an English clergyman warned his hearers against "mesmerism, phrenology, and stenography." "All are bigots," says Margaret Fuller, "who limit the Divine within the boundaries of their present knowledge." Sadi Gul is generally conceded to have made a hit in his parable of Abraham's aged Parsee guest: "Abraham, for a hundred years hath the divine bounty flowed out to this man in sunshine and rain, in bread and life. Is it fit for thee to withhold thy hand from him, because his worship is not thine?"

Especially were the Jews, at the time of Jesus, given to all sorts of demonological whims concerning prodigies, exorcisms, amulets, and dreams,— so says an eminent scholar, Dr. John Lightfoot. *Credat Judæus,*—"Let the Jew believe that!"— was a Roman proverb. The gospel narratives bear the stamp of the spirit that prevailed, and show us the conditions with which the preaching of Christianity had to comply, or rather the price it had to pay in order to gain a hearing. Prodigies, it was imagined, were necessary to mark Jesus as the Christ. "Truly thou art the Son of God!" "Is not this the Son of David?" cry out the astounded multitudes; and demons prove again and again that they are well aware of his dignity. One writer's words, "Unless you see signs and wonders you will not believe," taken in connection with Paul's declaration, "The Jews require a sign," might be paraphrased, "The reason why the Jews

---

*See Dr. J. M. Jones' *History of Inoculation,* etc., *passim*. As to the credulity of the ancient Mexicans, who divided the world's life into five ages with five successive suns, see Montaigne's *Essays,* iii., p. 207. As to African and other superstitions, see the (1881) Index of (volumes of) *Harper's Magazine,* p. 653.

never believed in Jesus was that they never saw him do expected signs and wonders."

As to the credulity of a later age, ecclesiastical history says two hundred miracles of Ignatius Loyola were laid before the Pope when Loyola's canonization was in question, including walking in the air, raising the dead, etc.; and that it was hardly less common for Francis Xavier to raise the dead than to heal the sick. St. Dunstan,* Cotton Mather, Salem, Boston Common,— *verb. sap.*

And as to the present day, there is much to remind of Goethe's aphorism, "Miracle is the pet child of Faith," if not also of Renan's remark, "A miracle was never wrought in the presence of savans." In Ireland, as recently as the last famine there, we find — what?

... As usual, the new miracle was first perceived by a poor woman, in the shape of an apparition of the Virgin, St. Joseph, and St. John, close to a Catholic church. Other women and children rapidly began to see it, too; then the housekeeper of an archdeacon saw it; and then the archdeacon himself saw it,— or something very like it. As soon as the fame of it got abroad, cripples and diseased persons began to come in, in great numbers, to get the benefit of it; and now the restoration of sight to the blind, hearing to the deaf, walking to the lame, by merely sitting round the church or in contact with it, has occurred so frequently that the individual cases have ceased to be reported. . . . In no instance have they been efficacious upon any sceptic or Protestant.— *The (N.Y.) Nation*, March 25.

An apparition can be produced by a paint composed chiefly of sulphide of calcium, now used in some tunnel cars.†

In studying the record of the resurrection, ‡ we shall have occasion further to consider the subject of infectious visions.

The so-called liberal application of Mill's rule will be considered in the next chapter.

---

* See Dickens' *Child's History of England*, chap. iv.
† As to the optical illusion known as "the conjurer's ghost," see in *Harper's Magazine*, lv., p. 822 (November, 1877), a well-illustrated article entitled "The King of the Conjurers."
‡ Chap. xxxvi.

CHAPTER XXXV.

VERIFICATION.

What is the Present Tendency of the Age in applying the Rule of Paul, "Make the Doctrine prove the Miracle," and the Converse Rule of Trench and Mill, that "No Miracle proves a Doctrine"?

NEITHER to affirm nor deny the possibility of what is called a miracle; to concede with Aristotle the averment of Agathon, that "it is a part of probability that many improbable things will happen"; and merely to declare that "the burden of proof is on the affirmative,"—that the proponent of an extraordinary allegation must support it by extraordinary proof. It were idle to ask such questions as, Why silent as to miracles of Christ is Philo, the learned Alexandrian Jew, born before Christ and surviving him; or Josephus, the learned Jew, born A.D. 37; or Paul; or his co-worker Clement, who left a genuine Epistle; or Ignatius, who died A.D. *c.* 107; or Pliny and Tacitus, though they mention Christ? Or whether the feeding of the multitude be not a reminiscence of II. Kings iv., 43?

It is becoming the "*Zeitgeist*," the time-spirit of the Occident, to trace a truth-sense in every enunciation of the Orient; to find God revealing himself most majestically in the apparently orderly,— in the objective which accords rather than discords with the soul's subjective ideal of the True, the Beautiful, and the Good; to enjoy the development of a blooming plant more than stories of fairies that passed over the earth and left flowers in their pathway. Mr. Lowell's prophet, on returning from the mountain whither he had gone in quest of a sign from God, meets his little daughter with an equal sign and wonder in her hand, which, as he says,—

<blockquote>Beside my very threshold
She had plucked and brought to me.</blockquote>

One fruit of this truth-seeking spirit is to discover a rich emblematic significance in many of these wonder-accounts, or in their probable originals. The Orientals conveyed truth by concrete figures of speech, and not, like Occidental scholars, in ratiocinative, articulated abstractions. It would not be impossible in the East for an oral picture-statement of the calling of four disciples who were fishermen to become, by shifts of coloring from one of its features to another, transformed in the lapse of half a century into the story of a miraculous draft of fishes. But, in this western world, such a transformation would of itself be a "miracle," even in the developments of the most enterprising pantomime troupe, or in the varied activities of a sewing-circle. No less a supernaturalist than Archbishop Trench utilizes the fig-tree story for an apt moral:—

Jesus did not attribute moral responsibilities to the tree when he smote it because of its unfruitfulness, but he did attribute to it a fitness for representing moral qualities. The tree vaunted itself to be in advance of all the other trees, challenged the passer-by that he should come and refresh himself with its fruit. Yet, when the Lord accepted its challenge and drew near, it proved to be but as the others, without fruit as they; for indeed, as the Evangelist observes, the time of figs had not yet arrived. The sin of Israel symbolized by the tree was not so much that they were without fruit as that they boasted of so much. Their true fruit would have been to own they had no fruit,— without Christ could do nothing.— *Notes on the Miracles*, etc., p. 349.

The "improvement" of allegory is especially apparent in the Strauss or Tübingen School. Many beautiful illustrations are given by the Dutch School. Thus Dr. Hooykaas remarks, as to the Cana wine transmutation, that when the Israelite community of God lamented to her great Son that there was nothing left but the water of religious forms, he told her to fill the vessels of stone that stood at hand to meet the requirements of Levitical purity, and the water was turned into wine. Instead of forms, he gave the spirit; for life according to the law, he substituted that free love of God which is the life of the spirit. The joy of the wedding-feast was now secure; the kingdom of God would win its way.*

Again, Jesus, with the slenderest means at his command, fed the souls of countless multitudes: this bread of the spirit increases when it is consumed, and increases still more when imparted to others.† And again, in a tempest, in the midst of dire agitation and distress, Jesus was absolutely at rest. How many storms broke loose upon him in his own personal

---

* See *The Bible for Learners*, vol. iii., p. 233.
† *Id.*, p. 149. Or, as Milton says, "Good, the more communicated more abundant grows."

experiences and the frenzied indignation of others,— in the passionate opposition and dark schemes of his antagonists! Yet, in the might of his faith in God, he maintained his own unruffled serenity, and quieted many a storm which the opposition he met had raised in the bosoms of the terrified disciples.

The pilot of the Galilean lake.   *John Milton.*

To the widow at Nain, to Jairus, to the sisters at Bethany,— in the house of mourning everywhere,— he sweetly whispered: "Weep not! you shall see the dear departed again. This apparently final sleep shall be succeeded by a glorious waking." And another solacing thought may we think, that expressed by James R. Lowell: —

> With every anguish of our earthly part,
> The spirit's sight grows clearer. This was meant
> When Jesus touched the blind man's lids with clay.

Rather than to insist that a sign shall signify too much, it were better to "let well enough alone." *

Back over the course which his fame had travelled came certain Pharisees from Jerusalem, apparently sent out to spy into his teachings and entrap him into dangerous admissions. They succeeded perfectly. From henceforth it was war to the knife. As if to gather up his energies for the encounter, Jesus betook himself beyond the borders of Galilee, into the vicinity of Tyre and Sidon. Returning to the lake shore, he found his enemies awaiting him with a new stratagem. They wanted a sign from heaven. Was not their wanting it itself a sign that his cures of the possessed were too near akin to the cures of their own exorcists to pass with them for genuine miracles? But these were all he had to offer; and he did not offer these. If miracle had played the part in the economy of Jesus which modern Orthodoxy claims, there would have been no excuse for his not performing such a miracle as would have silenced every demur at his prophetic office. What he did was to blast the Pharisees, and, with them, the pedlers in Christian evidences from that day to this, with the assertion, "A wicked and adulterous generation seeketh after a sign, but there shall no sign be given them." — *J. W. Chadwick* (*The Man Jesus*, p. 144).

In further answer to the main question, it may be observed that the tendency of modern liberals is like that of a "more-or-less liberal," born A.D. 1483, who said : —

I have seen two miracles lately. I looked up, and saw the clouds above me in the noontide; and they looked like the sea that was hanging over me; and I could see no cord on which they were sus-

---

* See, in the Commentaries of Paulus, ingenious harmonizations of the constancy of nature with truths of Scripture.

pended, and yet they never fell. And then, when the noontide had gone and the midnight came, I looked again; and there was the dome of heaven, and it was spangled with stars; and I could see no pillars that held up the skies, and yet they never fell. Now, he that holds the stars up and moves the clouds in their course can do all things, and I trust him in the sight of these miracles.— *Martin Luther.*

The life of Jesus was both supernatural and natural. It was natural because it was a pure development of humanity, uncorrupted, undepraved, as God made it, and as he means it to be. It was supernatural as showing the perpetual presence in his soul of the higher world, the world of eternal truth and infinite goodness.— *Dr. James F. Clarke (Boston Sat. Ev. Gazette,* March 18, 1883).

> We may not climb the heavenly steeps
> To bring the Lord Christ down;
> In vain we search the lowest deeps,
> For him no depths can drown.
>
> Hush every lip, close every book,
> The strife of tongues forbear;
> Why forward reach, or backward look,
> For love which clasps like air?
>
> In joy of inward peace, or sense
> Of sorrow over sin,
> He is his own best evidence,
> His witness is within.
>
> No fable old, nor mythic lore,
> Nor dreams of bards and seers,
> No dead fact stranded on the shore
> Of the oblivious years;
>
> But warm, sweet, tender, even yet
> A present life is he,
> And faith has yet its Olivet,
> And love its Galilee.
>
> We faintly hear, we dimly see,
> In differing phrase we pray;
> But, dim or clear, we own in Thee
> The Life, the Truth, the Way.

John G. Whittier.

Chapter XXXVI.

RESURRECTION.

What Two Views concerning a Resurrection of the Body of Jesus?

(1) THE supernatural: that, on the third day after the crucifixion, it became reanimate, and, after he had walked on earth nearly forty days, ascended into the sky. The "Acts of Pilate," * after stating the arraignment nearly as in Matthew, proceeds: "Then Pilate commanded Jesus to be brought before him and spake to him the following words: 'Thine own nation hath charged thee as making thyself a king. Wherefore, I, Herod, sentence thee to be whipped, according to the laws of former governors, and that thou be first bound, then hanged upon a cross in that place where thou art now a prisoner; and also two criminals with thee, Demas and Gestas.'" In the next chapter, the account of the crucifixion is given very much as in Matthew; save, after stating that the soldiers cast lots and divided his garments, no mention is made of fulfilling any prophecy. The name of the soldier who inserted the spear is said to be Longinus. In chapter xiii., a soldier reports in a synagogue the earthquake, the rolling away of the stone from the sepulchre he was guarding, and the appearance of the angel, very much as in Matthew; and Christ is stated to have appeared to Joseph of Arimathea. In chapter xiv., it is stated that Phineas, a priest, Ada, a schoolmaster, and Agens, a Levite, came from Galilee to Jerusalem and told the priests that Christ had been seen talking with the eleven disciples.

Jacques Saurin thinks nobody doubts that the tomb was fastened after the interment, and that it was found vacant; and he adduces thence a dilemma, one horn of which is a theft (or a removal by Joseph) and the other the miracle.

The Fourth of the Thirty-nine Articles declares "Christ did

---
* *Ante*, chap. ii.

truly rise again from death, and took again his body, with flesh, bones, and all things appertaining to man's nature; wherewith he ascended into Heaven," etc. It should, however, here be stated (as Rev. R. H. Newton has remarked of said Articles) that the American Episcopal Church "left them as no more part of the Prayer Book, save for the printer's binding, than the other general legislation of the General Convention."

(2) The rationalistic view is that there is no such external fact of history as the alleged *post mortem* materialization; that the resurrection is simply a form of belief assumed by the faith of Christ's surviving friends, and thus the whole is a chapter of their inner life and not of this outward life,— especially after fleeing in haste from the hostile Orthodoxy of Jerusalem to their own native land. For instance, the record says not that he rose from death or from the grave, but from "the dead," — that is, from the realms of the dead, the place where the majority of Jews, Babylonians, Greeks, Romans, etc., believed the shades of the departed abide. Thus Virgil says of Turnus,

> Death's chill
> Unnerved the limbs, but the undying soul
> Sighed its contempt and flitted to the shades. *

The apostles could not endure the thought that their Master was left in the abyss, a powerless shadow. They were convinced that he must be living in heaven in glory; and, as when thus waked to life there must be a body, the conclusion was inevitable that he had risen from the realm of the shades. Perhaps there can be no better statement of the grounds of the latter view than that presented by Dr. I. Hooykaas : —

The contradictions in the narratives themselves, though so great as to lay insuperable difficulties in the way of a literal interpretation, no longer surprise us when we know that we are dealing with a product of the religious imagination, gradually amplified and embellished by tradition. . . . No such place as Emmaus has been found within two leagues of Jerusalem. There is an Emmaus (or Nicopolis) at a distance of six or seven leagues from the City of the Temple, but this cannot be the place intended. There is a bathing-place of the same name on the Sea of Gennesareth; and this tempts us to ask whether the scene was not originally laid in Galilee,— which really witnessed the reviving faith of the disciples,— and subsequently transferred to Jerusalem without change of names. Finally, we may note that Jesus appears in different places — to the two travellers and to Simon — at the same time. But, in spite of all these traces of composite origin, the background and general outline of the picture still furnish us with

---

* Gov. John D. Long's translation

precious materials for retracing the origin of the belief of the disciples in the resurrection; for we must never forget that a powerful imagination, supported by the symbolical forms of expression then current, might well translate reminiscences into present facts, suspense or other emotions into external events.

The friends of Jesus — so we read this story — were bitterly disappointed in their fairest hopes by the cross of Jesus. And yet they still regarded their Master as a mighty prophet, and their hearts and mouths still overflowed with him. And while they thought and spoke of him, — at one in burning love, but often widely severed in opinions and expectations, — Jesus himself came to them. Not the glorified Christ from heaven, but the Jesus they had known on earth. They did not perceive or did not notice it; but he was there, drawn to their sides by the magic power of loving and reverent remembrances. He was with them, speaking to them, drawing out their thoughts, and then correcting and instructing them, until at last, in the light of the event, they began to understand his teaching of the last few weeks, so fruitless at the time. They saw how the Scripture pointed out, in many a special utterance and in the common lot of prophets, what the sad end must be, and how the temporal defeat would lead to victory and would win the Messianic crown. When rightly looked into, the Scripture was full of hints and predictions of the event. How could they be so slow of heart! They would fain prolong those moments of his presence, hardly realized in the life of reminiscence, — they would not let him go. And then, as they lay down to meat and broke the bread, that symbolic action on the last evening of the Master's life started back into their minds, the impression of that last meeting was renewed. They remembered all he told them, and above all that clear announcement of his death and of his triumph ["She poured this ointment on my body to prepare me for the burial," etc.]; and then the scales fell from their eyes, he was the Promised One once more! And now he is gone from their bodily sight; but, henceforth, nothing can disturb their faith. He is the Christ. He cannot be a prey to the realm of shades. He lives! He will come again! ...

Paul, in a letter to the community at Corinth, in the year 58 A.D., reminds them what he had told them a few years before, in accordance with what he himself had heard from eye-witnesses many years before, — not long after the death of Jesus. It was "that Christ died for the forgiveness of our sins, according to Scripture; and was buried and was raised up the third day, according to the Scripture; and appeared to Cephas (Peter), and afterwards to the Twelve. Then he appeared to more than five hundred brethren at once, most of whom are still living, but some have fallen asleep. Then he appeared to James, and afterwards to all the apostles, and last of all to me also."

Now, on the assumption that it comes from the hand of Paul, this enumeration, which evidently aims at completeness, deserves our confidence; for Paul would certainly take care to inform himself accurately in such a matter. In speaking of the "resurrection," he does not mean the reanimation of the body of Jesus; and, indeed, he expressly excludes such a thought by ascribing to the Christ a glorified and spiritual body not made of flesh and blood. It is equally certain that he thinks of the Christ as having appeared *from heaven*; and his ranking the appearance to himself — unquestionably the product of his own fervid imagination — as parallel with those which preceded it seems to indicate that they were all visions alike. And, indeed, the return to earth of one already dead and glorified, or the veritable apparition of a spirit, is a thing which far transcends the limits of credibility. The Israelites, though well aware of the difference between a vision and something seen under ordinary conditions, **were** yet firmly convinced that what they saw in the ecstasy of a **vision** had an objective reality corresponding to it. It may deserve our attention also that in this passage Paul first supports the faith in the resurrection of Jesus by an appeal to the Scripture, and subsequently confirms it by a *reductio ad absurdum*. In other words, he is more inclined to demonstrate that Christ *must* have risen than to build upon adequate testimony to the fact that he *had* risen. . . . Even the appearance to five hundred believers offers no insuperable difficulty; for, when we remember how infectious the excited condition favorable to visions sometimes is, it seems far from impossible that the whole of a numerous gathering of disciples might believe themselves to see the Master. History furnishes other instances not less striking of a number of people in a state of spiritual exaltation seeing one and the same image before their eyes.* . . .

Peter is mentioned as the first who saw his Master. Peter's fervent and excitable temperament, acting upon his deep sense of the injury he had done to his beloved Master and his longing to receive assurance of forgiveness, might well throw him into just such a state of exaltation as might make him see the form he loved rise up before him, **with an** expression of exalted tenderness and generous forgiveness, as a mighty incentive and a glorious consolation.

But it ought to be mentioned that, according to another tradition preserved in our Gospels, it was not Peter, but the faithful friends who had seen Jesus die, — the two Marys, whom we left in speechless agony at the sepulchre, — to whom the first assurance was vouchsafed that their Master had arisen. It was an angel, or Jesus himself, who brought the proclamation to them (with or without their companion, Salome), and told them to carry the great news to the disciples, and especially to Peter. In itself, this account is at least as credible as the other. The tried attachment and touching fidelity of these women to Jesus, working upon the more sensitive female system, would make them eminently susceptible of such impressions as we are discussing; and it seems more probable that tradition would gradually substitute **Peter** for the women than that they should have usurped his place. In fact, we find the women, in this version of the events, specially charged to take the glad news to Peter, and may fancy that we see therein the first indication of a feeling that gradually gave the place of honor to

---

* See *ante*, chap. xxxiv., p. 188, and Appendix, *post*, pp. 290, 293.

the apostle to the exclusion of the women. On the other hand, great doubt is thrown upon the whole picture of the women and their vision by its unhistorical setting,—representing Jerusalem as the locality, the Sunday morning as the time, and the empty tomb as the scene of the vision; whereas, all these three traits are of much later origin. . . . The very fact that it was in Galilee the disciples saw the Master is itself a proof that ample time intervened to admit of the power of recollection bringing them completely under his influence again. The uniform tradition as to the third day refers to the time of his leaving the realms of death for heaven, not to that of his appearance to his friends. It is perhaps an inference from Scripture, Hosea vi., 2, and perhaps grew out of an expression used by Jesus himself; in either case, probably due to the misunderstanding of proverbial expression. . . .

The fact that, after some of the disciples had in a state of transport seen Jesus, others were in doubt and were only subsequently swept down the stream of general conviction, appears to us a genuine historical trait, and never quite disappears from the later stories. Finally, we may observe that the provisional assumption of Jesus into heaven, where he would at once receive from God the office of Messiah in anticipation of his return to earth, was needed to satisfy the demand of the disciples for their Master's complete restoration from the shame of his death upon the cross. . . .

In general, we may be pretty sure that the oldest tradition, whether preserved in the Epistle to the Corinthians or in Matthew, knew nothing of any words pronounced by the risen Christ when he appeared. All these belong to the later transformations of the story, and form but one of many deviations and accretions. In fact, the original story is gradually disguised past all recognition. The appearances of Jesus are transferred to Jerusalem, obviously with the view of making the scene of the Messiah's defeat that of his restoration and triumph also; they are placed upon the third day, as taking place while Jesus passed on high from the shadow land; they are robbed of their true character, and become more and more material, after the general manner of legends. A variety of special occasions, circumstances, and sayings were from time to time added, unconsciously or by design, till the whole was expanded into a second life upon earth of several weeks' duration.— *The Bible for Learners*, vol. iii., p. 466, ff.

The morbid condition thus described will not seem quite impossible to any one who has carefully studied J. Bastien-Lepage's great painting, "The Vision of Joan d'Arc." Coleridge once remarked that he had no doubt that Dr. Johnson saw the Cock-Lane ghost: he only doubted whether the ghost was there for him to see.

The averment of Dr. Hooykaas, as to the contagiousness of this ideational state of mind of the bereaved and trembling friends of Jesus, reminds us of an incident at the burning of the

Crystal Palace. Hundreds of persons watched for an hour the agonies of an escaped animal upon the roof; but, all the time, the animal which they were pitying was safe, and what they saw was a piece of tin roofing shrivelled in the flames.* For explanation of some of the alleged discrepancies, reference may be had to the commentaries of Dr. Adam Clark, Matthew Henry, and others. Thus, Luke says Jesus "vanished out of sight" of Cleopas and the other traveller, on the very day † of the resurrection; in Acts, the *ascension* is placed forty days after the resurrection. Matthew does not claim that any one witnessed the resurrection. An angel requests the women to go quickly and tell the disciples that Jesus is risen and "goeth before you into Galilee; there shall ye see him." ‡ Mark says, "Neither said they anything to any man," *i.e.*, any stranger they might happen to meet § As to this alleged angel, it has been remarked:—

> That God should send an angel to hasten the disciples to Galilee to meet Jesus there, and that afterward they should see him in Jerusalem, gives God the appearance of a person who does not know his own mind, or the angel the appearance of not being well informed. This story must have been current in circles where an appearance in Jerusalem was no part of the tradition. . . . An angel in a story is as sure a proof that the story is a legend as a trout in the milk that the milk has suffered from adulteration. The angel causes an earthquake. A very little knowledge of the nature of an earthquake is sufficient to discredit this one, mentioned only by Matthew, among whose "properties" earthquakes particularly abound. He introduces one at the moment of Jesus' death, in the course of which "the graves were opened, and many bodies of the saints which slept arose and went into Jerusalem and were seen by many"; but the Gospels do not mention any such occurrence, though it is sufficiently impressive for a passing word. The guard at the tomb is another trait peculiar to the First Gospel. It was evidently placed there ideally, to rebut any charge that the body of Jesus was secretly removed by his disciples, not actually to prevent such removal. That Pilate would detail a Roman guard for such a purpose is incredible; that the guard, to please the Sanhedrim, would risk their lives by confessing that they fell asleep, is unspeakably absurd. The account also suggests the question, What was the need of an earthquake to roll away the stone when Jesus was already risen?—*J. W. Chadwick (The Man Jesus, p. 201)*.

The story of the deputation of priests to the procurator, the sealing of the tomb, the apparition, the flight and bribing of the

---

* As to apparitions, etc., see *ante*, chap. xxxiv   † Luke xxiv., 13.
‡ Matt. xxviii., 7.   § Mark xvi., 8.

sentinels, as worked out elaborately in the "Gospel of Nicodemus," Dr. Hooykaas deems to be quite absurd. "Is it," he asks, "likely that the enemies of Jesus would have heard a prophesy of his rising again when his very friends never dreamed of it for a moment, and when he had never once spoken of his resurrection in public? Is not the conduct here ascribed to the councillors and the soldiers — the latter of whom would have needlessly exposed themselves to the heaviest punishment — so clumsy and childish as to be impossible? But once set aside these difficulties and accept the picture as emblematic, and how fine and true its strokes appear!"

The powers of Church and State have combined against the Nazarene and brought him to his fall. On the one side, the high priests and Pharisees defending the Law, the temple, and last, not least, their own authority and influence, against the sacrilegious blows of this seducer of the people; on the other side, the procurator, who cherishes no personal hostility to him, but overcomes his own indifferent toleration, and sacrifices the Nazarene in the interests of order. The new religious movement is crushed forever by this combination. Both Church and State combine to keep it down. The one puts its seal upon the stone, the other sets its watch before the grave, — in vain! As by the finger of God the seal is broken and the watch is smitten down. Jesus stands up! Though hurled to the ground, he rises again: his momentary defeat was but a step to his abiding triumph. The alliance of ecclesiastical and civil authorities is powerless against the truth, against the kingdom of God, against the Christ. The triumph is his. It has its witnesses in every age, in our age, in our hearts, whenever the principles of Jesus vanquish the obstinate resistance of routine and prejudice, of impurity and selfishness; whenever his ideal conquers the commonplace reality. Of this triumph, every Easter that Christians observe is the grateful record and "the joyful promise." In this the truest sense, "Christ has arisen" indeed!

Another lesson in the premises has most eloquently been set forth by Mr. Chadwick: —

There was another burial of Jesus than that in the fresh rockhewn sepulchre of the New Testament tradition. It was in a tomb where thousands were already buried, — buried alive under the forms and ceremonies of an effete religion. Into this tomb, the friends of Jesus, the apostles, and the brothers who, in his lifetime, had given him no countenance, made haste to carry him; not his emaciated form, not his nail-wounded flesh, but the real man, — his thought, his spirit. But from this burial of Jesus there was indeed a resurrection;

and the angel who rolled away the stone of the sepulchre was no supernatural being, with his countenance like lightning, and his raiment white as snow. No! but a man who, according to his own description, was "in bodily presence weak, and in speech contemptible." Nevertheless there was that in him which was sufficient for the burden that was laid upon him. With mighty, ringing strokes, he hewed his way through manifold obstructions, straight to the spirit of Jesus,— his inmost thought and life,— and bade it rise up and come forth; and even so it did. And Christianity, that might else have been a Jewish sect, losing itself in arid wastes of pedantry and ritual after a few generations, entered upon a career of universal influence. This was the real resurrection of Jesus, the triumph of his essential spirit over the Judaizing narrowness of the Church of the Apostles; and it was a resurrection of infinitely greater significance than any impossible resuscitation of his mortal body. And Paul of Tarsus, the man through whom it was accomplished, was of such mind and heart and will that, in comparison with him, all bent with toil and scarred with battle though he was, the dazzling brightness of any legendary angel is "no light, but rather darkness visible." — *John White Chadwick* (*The Man Jesus*, p. 221).

The emotions of the faithful women have suggested still another lesson:—

> And like them, too, I am troubled
>   As I tread my way alone,
> While my faithless heart is wondering
>   Who will roll away the stone.
> Stones are lying in the pathway
>   Duty tells me I must tread,—
> Hope and love together buried,
>   With a stone at foot and head.
> But there cometh a glad morning,
>   When all stones shall roll away,
> And the spirit rise triumphant
>   Into God's eternal day.
>
> *Anon.*

> In the grave, yet not to earth,
>   Wholly sink heroic lives,
> While the memory of their worth
>   In the heart of man survives.
> See with joy his spirit rise,—
> Rise triumphant from its dust,
>   Rise again to save and bless,
> Spirit of immortal trust,
>   Breath of truth and holiness.
>
> *Seth C. Beach.*

Chapter XXXVII.

ELECTION.

*What Two Views as to " Divine Election and Fore-ordination,"
and the Teachings of Christ and Paul thereon ?*

(1) THE Calvinistic : that God, being absolute sovereign, has from the beginning predestined some angels and men to eternal life and joy, and fore-ordained others to everlasting death and punishment.*

(2) The Free-will view: that election and predestination are only temporal ; that this is the meaning in each of the places where Paul uses the word [pro-orizo];† that both in the physical and moral universe there is an eternal reign of law, in one sense without variableness or shadow of turning; and that, in Paul's argument, ‡ God's showing his " wrath " means his letting the evil consequences of sin be made known.

The evolutional phase of the latter view is that we are what we are because the universe is what it is ; if it acts upon us, we react upon it. Thus Herbert Spencer has defined life to be "the definite combination of heterogeneous changes, both simultaneous and successive, in correspondence with external coexistence and sequences." The hypothesis of evolution in its scientific aspect presents three factors,— heredity, environment, and adaptation. By heredity is meant the tendency of our organism to develop in the likeness of its progenitor; by environment, the sum total of the physical conditions by which the developing organism is surrounded,— the ambient world; and by adaptation, the disposition so to modify as to bring an organism and its environment into harmony. This may be accomplished either by progression or retrogression.

Mr. Spencer elsewhere defines evolution as " a change from an indefinite, incoherent homogeneity to a definite, coherent heterogeneity, through continuous differentiations and integrations."

---

* As to the "Supralapsarian" and "Infralapsarian" Calvinistic views, see *ante*, chap. xix.
† Rom. viii., 29, 30; I. Cor. ii., 7; Eph. i., 5, 11.   ‡ Rom. ix., 22.

How happened it that, amid the grotesque myths which were the current beliefs of antiquity, this one clear, authoritative assertion of creation by law **sprang** up and maintained itself in Israel? How happened it that **the** doctrine of an ascending order of life was put into the religious primer of Israel? How did it come to pass that a Jewish patriarch and lawgiver knew to some extent the fact of the orderly development, "the increasing differentiation," the progress from type **to** type, and **to** ever higher forms of the creation? And that, too, centuries before the accumulated results of the laws of heredity in **the** brain of a Herbert Spencer had recorded themselves, through his physiological organization, **and** for the wonder of a late age, in his *First Principles.*— *Dr. Newman Smyth (Old Faiths in New Light,* p. 171).

Attach what weight we may to the physical causes which have brought about this evolution, I cannot see how it is possible to conceive of any but a moral **cause** for the endowments that made the primordial germ susceptible of their action. And, in the so-called *laws* of organic evolution, I see nothing but the orderly and continuous working out of the original intelligent design.— *Dr. William B. Carpenter, F.R.S.* (*Modern Review,* October, 1882).

As Rev. W. R. Alger has remarked, " Man now living on the **earth** is a focalizing epitome of the typical cosmic forces whose play **has** produced the entire series of existences from the first reactionary molecule **or** simplest sentient thing up to the perfected human organism which is in itself a concentrated universe." Thus much as to physical evolutional election.*

So, not inaptly, did Paul say the potter may mould one lump of clay to humbler uses than another. A good illustration of the operation of the like law in the moral world is given by Dr. J. F. **Clarke, in** his tenth discourse **on** the " Ideas of Paul " : —

Here are two brothers; **we will** call them Esau Brown and Jacob Brown. When they were boys, Esau was careless, generous, brave; **he** did not learn his lessons very well, but he was a great favorite with the other boys. He often got them into scrapes, but he never betrayed them. He honestly owned up, and took the punishment himself. He was a great plague at home, and his mother did not love him as much as she loved Jacob. Jacob was always ready to help her about the house; he was thoughtful and careful. He brought his mother little presents on her birthday; but Esau, though he loved **her, never** remembered to do anything of the sort. Jacob **used to trade with** his companions, and had a money-box full of half-**dollars and dimes. At** last, as they grew to be young men, Esau got **into a serious scrape,** and his father scolded him severely; and he

---

*And see M. J. Savage's *Religion of Evolution, passim*; also Dr. John Cleland's *Evolution, Expression, and Sensation, passim.*

concluded to go West, but had no money to go with. Then Jacob offered to give him two hundred dollars, if Esau would sign away his share in their father's property; and he did so.

Jacob Brown went into business, and became a prosperous man, and, when he died, left half a million dollars to the Hospital for Women and Children. Esau Brown moved from Ohio to Iowa, from Iowa to California, and from California to Oregon, and never seemed to accomplish much in any place; and, when he died, he left his widow and children to the care of his brother, who, I am glad to say, made them comfortable. So people said, "What a mysterious providence that the Lord should have done so much better for Jacob Brown than for Esau Brown, when, really, Esau was as good-hearted a man as you ever saw, and Jacob was a little close." And Rev. Moses Gilead, preaching the funeral sermon, took his text from the first chapter of Malachi, second verse,— "Was not Esau Jacob's brother? saith the Lord; yet I loved Jacob, and I hated Esau, and laid his heritage waste." But the real truth of the matter was that Jacob Brown was prosperous, not because he was good, but because he was prudent, industrious, economical, and had good business habits. The Lord did not really love him more than he loved his brother. The Lord did not elect him to everlasting life in the other world, but he elected him to be the man to endow the Women's Hospital in this world; and to be able to do that was something.

Just so the Lord elected the Patriarch Jacob and his descendants, the Jews, to establish the doctrine of Monotheism in the world. He elected them to teach mankind faith in God as a Ruler, Judge, and Personal Providence. The Jews were like their father Jacob. They inherited from him his undoubting faith in one God, *his* God, and the God of his children. They inherited his pacific habit, his tendency to trade rather than to war, his tenacity to his convictions, his sagacity, and knowledge of men. Therefore, they were the right people to receive and preserve the Mosaic Law, and that has been their business in the world. They were the chosen people; chosen for *that* because their character fitted them for that. They were not chosen to possess an exclusive heaven hereafter, but to do a special work here. They were chosen, elected, predestinated for that work when they were born and before they were born. They were chosen when they were so constituted as to be the right persons to do the work. When the Lord made them so, he chose them. Their election and calling was written in their organization, in the shape of their brains, and the temper of their character.— *Boston Saturday Evening Gazette*, April 9, 1881.

And it is in the nature of things that brain shall conquer brawn. This common-sense view seems best for mere mortals who cannot afford to waste time in coming to the result of Milton's angels, who on a hill apart discoursed

<blockquote>Of fate, free-will, foreknowledge absolute,
And found no end in wandering mazes lost.</blockquote>

Chapter XXXVIII.

REDEMPTION.

What Two Views of Redemption of the Soul from Consequences of Sin?

(1) THE intercessional, and (2) the evolutional.

The former particularly emphasizes as essential thereto, **repentance, intercession,** "justification by faith" in and reliance upon a certain "plan of salvation," etc. This plan or scheme of salvation is commonly considered to comprise a thesis of five points or dogmas: (1) a "**fall** of man,"—a corruption of his nature whereby every person has incurred the penalty of eternal anguish; (2) a vicarious atonement by Christ, who through his sufferings and death satisfied the divine law, and opened a way of escape from the penalty and anguish to all who by faith accept the benefit of his sacrifice; (3) the deity of Christ, which alone could have made his atonement satisfactory in lieu of the whole human race; (4) the publication of this danger, **and of** the plan of redemption, in an inspired revelation authenticated by miracles; and (5) the eternal blessedness of all who accept and believe in this "plan of salvation," and the everlasting torment of those who reject and disbelieve it.

The "covenant of redemption" and "justification by faith" have sometimes been stated to import that, "before the creation of **the human** race, God stipulated with Christ that the sins of the redeemed should be imputed to the innocent Christ, who should be condemned and **put** to death, that whoever should heartily consent to the covenant of reconciliation offered through Christ should, by the imputation of his obedience unto them, be justified and holden righteous before God."

> Five bleeding wounds. . . . "Forgive!" they cry,
> "Nor let the ransomed sinner die!"
> The Father hears him pray — his dear anointed one:
> He cannot turn away the presence of his Son.
> The Spirit answers to the blood,
> And tells me I am born of God.
>
> *Charles Wesley.*

> Jesus paid it all, all the debt I owe,
> And nothing either great or small remains for me to do.
> Hallelujah, 'tis done! I believe on the Son!
> I am saved by the blood of the crucified One.
>
> *Elvina M. Hall.*

> With mine own heart I am in constant strife.
>   What shall I do?
> Remembrance of past errors blights my life.
>   What shall I do?
> Though kindly Thou, O Lord, my sins forgivest,
> Their mem'ry still within my heart is rife.
>   What shall I do?
>
> *Omar Khayyam.*

The human sense of weakness — of dependence on some higher power for rescue from woes — will be recalled, not wholly without analogy, in the passage in *The Light of Asia* where Gautama is represented as becoming the Buddha: —

> The veil is rent
> Which blinded me. I am as all these men
> Who cry upon their gods and are not heard
> Or are not heeded, — *yet there must be aid!*
> Perchance the gods have need of help themselves,
> Being so feeble that, when sad lips cry,
> They cannot save. *I* would not let one cry
> Whom I *could* save! How can it be that Brahm
> Would make a world and keep it miserable,
> Since if, all powerful, he leaves it so,
> He is not good; and, if not powerful,
> He is not God?
>
> *Edwin Arnold.*

Poetic portraiture — as in case of Milton and some others — has even represented the "Covenant" as having been executed between two persons and attested by a third person in a sort of Trinity-council.

Calvin's view* is: (1) God was an enemy to man until Christ died; (2) Christ satisfied the justice of God, and paid our debt; (3) he was a substitute who suffered God's wrath and all the punishment due to sinners; and (4) he thus reconciled God to man, and made it possible for God to forgive our sins, which he could not have done otherwise, even though man repented.

In support of Calvin's view, Paul's words are appealed to, — "enemies," "reconciled," "ransom" "redemption," etc. To which the "free-will" advocates reply that Paul declared God to be not an enemy, but the opposite: God, "by his great love wherewith he loved us even when we were dead in sin, hath quickened us together with Christ, and saved us by free grace"; † that the words "ransom," "sacrifice," etc., were

---

* *Institutes*, Book ii., chap. xvi., §§ 2 and 10.   † Eph. ii., 5.

Paul's most natural nomenclature in his answer to the amazed questionings of Jews, Greeks, and Romans,—"How can there be a religion without ritual, temple, or victim?"—namely, "Christ is our sacrifice, our passover, our lamb slain from the foundation of the world."

The Assembly's "Confession"* says: "Our first parents sinned," etc. "They being the root of all mankind, the guilt of this sin was imputed and the same death in sin conveyed to all their posterity." In support of this view, three statements of Paul have been cited: (1) Rom. v., 12, 18; (2) I. Cor. xv., 22; (3) Eph. ii., 3. These have been *otherwise* explained to mean: (1) "The influence of one man's sin hath extended itself over all men. Why should not the influence of one man's goodness extend itself over all men?" (2) "Since moral death entered the world by the disobedience of a single man and has spread itself over the race, why should not moral life enter the world by another single man, and also spread over the whole race?" (3) "Death passed upon all men because"—Adam? no— themselves "all have sinned." A law is not broken: a man transgresses the law, and the law breaks him. "By nature children of wrath" means by race or by natural position, etc. By their position in the midst of a carnal race, the life of that race flowed into them, so that they were also estranged from God, and under a sense of divine wrath.†

(2) The evolutional view of the redemption of the soul will be considered in the next two chapters.

---

*Chap. vi.
† As to the necessity of an incarnation for the completion of the creative purpose, see Dorner's *History of the Doctrine of the Person of Christ, passim*; also Ullmann's *Reformatoren von der Reformation*, ii., pp. 339-401.

Chapter XXXIX.

TRANSITION.

What Transitional Condition is implied in the "Free-will" Explanation of Paul's Words, "All be made alive," etc.?

THAT Paul set forth two transitions — first, from the "carnal" man, under dominion of the animal propensities, to the psychical (or "natural") man, under dominion of the law; secondly, from this merely moral man to the spiritual man, from the law to the gospel, from effort to impulse, from duty to love. A sense of bondage, of want, is the subjective condition of redemption; the gospel of Christ the objective condition. So long as a soul is struggling up through transition and refusing evil, it is not guilty for what it does; "not I, but sin."

This new life, this trust, this hope, was the leaven mingled in the meal till all should be leavened. Thus, while the Calvinistic view considers men in only two classes, it has been found more convenient for free-will expression to demark three. Dr. J. F. Clarke, in his eighth discourse on the "Ideas of Paul," — text, I. Cor. xv., 22, "As in Adam all die, so also in Christ shall all be made alive," — concludes: —

Christ introduces a tendency to good by making God, duty, and immortality realities to the soul. Philosophy gives them to us as probabilities for the thought; Christianity introduces them into our life. Philosophy and theology theorize; religion realizes. One rests on speculation, the other on experience. By inward intuition, inward experience, — call it what you will, — Christ came in contact with truth, saw it, felt it, knew it. Christianity and science rest on the same basis, — experience. Christianity is a perpetually new demonstration of the reality of God, duty, and immortality, in each generation, in each soul. Accordingly, to the religious man, God is as real as the world; laws of duty as absolute as the laws of nature; immortality, or eternal life, or spiritual existence, flowing from God, now and always, as real as bodily life, or temporal existence, flowing from the outward through the senses.

To sum up what we have said: The carnal man dislikes and shuns God; the moral man fears and obeys him; the spiritual man loves and lives for him. The carnal man is his enemy; the moral man his servant; the spiritual man his friend. The carnal man is led by animal desires; the moral man by conscience; the spiritual man by love. The carnal man is moving downward toward death; the spiritual man upward, toward life and peace; the moral man, even when standing still, is looking in the right direction. In the carnal man there is no conflict: he is at harmony with himself, for his higher nature sleeps, and his soul obeys his lower nature. In the spiritual man, again, there is no conflict, but a higher and truer harmony of all his powers; for body serves the soul, and soul the spirit. But in the moral man there is a constant struggle and conflict; for the flesh and spirit are both active, and the flesh lusteth against the spirit, and the spirit against the flesh, and these are opposite one to another, so that ye cannot do the things ye would.

Thus we see the truth of Paul's saying, "We are saved by hope," and how it is connected with his whole system of thought. It is a hope full of immortal life. Hope gives courage, and helps us forward. The great gift of hope came to the world through Christ. He taught mankind to see an infinite Love surrounding all being, guiding all events, inspiring all hearts, and leading all things on toward an infinite and perfect good. With this hope in our souls, we can face evil and conquer it. Evil is real, it is in us, it is around us; but it is not supreme. Good is higher and stronger. Sin may abound, but grace more.— *Boston Saturday Evening Gazette*, March 26, 1881.

The old in religion dies out,— the old error, the old dispensation, the old superstition; but not the old religion. For this there is no decline, no decay; for it is the life of God in the soul.— *Orville Dewey*.

These words — "we are saved by hope" — recall those of Dr. Hedge, in his chapter on "Dualism and Optimism":—

Optimism is the true solution of the problem of evil, a doctrine with which that of Theism must stand or fall. If this world is not the best possible world, then the God of Theism is not that world's creator; the best possible, not as a present finality, but as means and method of the perfect good. This is the only optimism which reason can legitimate. The time will never come when evil shall wholly cease from the earth, when all wrong shall be expunged, suffering unknown, and

> Fear and sin and grief expire,
> Cast out by perfect love.

Neither in this world nor in any future world is such a state possible. Evil there must always be. Old evils may be abolished, but new evils will spring. The health of humanity requires the existence of evil as incentive to effort and topic of action. Progress is better than all perfection. Finding is good, but seeking is better, if finding is to end with rest in the found. The kingdom of heaven must be always coming; but hope would expire were it fully come.

And the saying remains forever true, that "by hope we are saved."— *Frederic H. Hedge (Ways of the Spirit*, p. 251).

In this connection, it will be edifying to note the famous utterance of the late Thomas Carlyle, who had been educated a Calvinist; and this, though one cannot help being reminded of the remark Mr. Emerson made in 1848, "Carlyle is a trip-hammer with an Æolian attachment": —

Our Life is compassed round with Necessity; yet is the meaning of Life itself no other than Freedom, than voluntary Force. Thus have we a warfare; in the beginning, especially, a hard-fought battle. For the God-given mandate, *Work thou in Well-doing*, lies mysteriously written in Promethean Prophetic characters in our hearts, and leaves us no rest till it be deciphered and obeyed; till it burn forth in our conduct, a visible, acted Gospel of Freedom. And as the clay-given mandate, *Eat thou and be filled*, at the same time persuasively proclaims itself through every nerve,—must there not be a confusion, a contest, before the better influence can become the upper?... Our Wilderness is the wide World in an Atheistic Century; our Forty Days are long years of suffering and fasting. Nevertheless, to these also comes an end....

The hot Harmattan wind had raged itself out; its howl went silent within me, and the long-deafened soul could now hear. I paused in my wild wanderings, and sat me down to wait and consider; for it was as if the hour of change drew nigh. I seemed to surrender, to renounce utterly, and say, "Fly, then, false shadows of Hope. I will chase you no more, I will believe you no more. And ye, too, haggard spectres of Fear, I care not for you; ye, too, are all shadows and a lie. Let me rest here, for I am way-weary and life-weary." ... The first preliminary moral act, Annihilation of Self, had been happily accomplished; and my mind's eyes were now unsealed, and its hands ungyved.... Often, also, could I see the black Tempest marching in anger through the distance. Round some Schreckhorn, as yet grim-blue, would the vapor gather, and there tumultuously eddy, and flow down like a mad witch's hair; till after a space it vanished, and in the clear sunbeam your Schreckhorn stood smiling, grim-white, for the vapor had held snow. How thou fermentest and elaboratest in thy great fermenting-vat and laboratory of an Atmosphere, of a World, O Nature! Or what is Nature? Ha! Why do I not name thee God? Art not thou the "living garment of God"? O heavens, is it, in very deed, He, then, that ever speaks through thee, that lives and loves in thee, that lives and loves in me?

Fore-shadows — call them rather fore-splendors — of that Truth and beginning of Truths fell mysteriously over my soul. Sweeter than Dayspring to the Shipwrecked in Nova Zembla; ah! like the mother's voice to her little child that strays bewildered, weeping, in unknown tumults; like soft streamings of celestial music to my too-exasperated heart,— came that Evangel. The Universe is not dead and demoniacal, a charnel-house with spectres, but god-like, and my Father's!

With other eyes, too, could I now look upon my fellow-man with an infinite Love, an infinite Pity. Poor, wandering, wayward man! Art thou not tried and beaten with stripes, even as I am? Ever, whether thou bear the royal mantle or the beggar's gabardine, art thou not so weary, so heavy-laden? and thy Bed of Rest is but a Grave. O my Brother, why cannot I shelter thee in my bosom, and wipe away all tears from thy eyes! Truly, the din of many-voiced Life, which, in this solitude, with the mind's organ, I could hear, was no longer a maddening discord, but a melting one; like inarticulate cries and sobbings of a dumb creature, which in the ear of Heaven are prayers. The poor Earth, with her poor joys, was now my needy Mother, not my cruel Step-dame. Man, with his so mad Wants and so mean Endeavors, had become the dearer to me; and, even for his sufferings and his sins, I now first named him Brother. Thus was I standing in the porch of that "*Sanctuary of Sorrow*"; by strange, steep ways had I, too, been guided thither; and ere long its sacred gates would open, and the "*Divine Depth of Sorrow*" lie disclosed to me. . .

There is in man a *Higher* than Love of Happiness: he can do without Happiness, and instead thereof find Blessedness. . . . Which God-inspired Doctrine art thou also honored to be taught, O heavens! and broken with manifold merciful Afflictions, even till thou become contrite, and learn it! Oh, thank thy Destiny for these. Thankfully bear what yet remain: thou hadst need of them; the Self in thee needed to be annihilated. By benignant fever-paroxysms is Life rooting out the deep-seated chronic Disease, and triumphs over Death. On the roaring billows of Time, thou art not engulfed, but borne aloft into the azure of Eternity. Love not Pleasure, love God. This is the *Everlasting Yea*, wherein all contradiction is solved; wherein whoso walks and works, it is well with him. . . . Conviction, were it never so excellent, is worthless till it convert itself into Conduct. Nay, properly, Conviction is not possible till then. . . . Most true is it, as a wise man teaches us, that "Doubt of any sort cannot be removed except by Action." On which ground, too, let him who gropes painfully in the darkness or uncertain light and prays vehemently that the dawn may ripen into day, lay this other precept well to heart, which to me was of invaluable service, "*Do the Duty which lies nearest thee*," which thou knowest to be a Duty! Thy second Duty will already have become clearer. . . . The Situation that has not its Duty, its Ideal, was never yet occupied by man. Yes, here, in this poor, miserable, hampered, despicable Actual wherein thou even now standest, here or nowhere is thy Ideal; work it out therefrom; and, working, believe, live, be free.— *Sartor Resartus (passim)*.

Of many Calvinist replications to the foregoing, a prominent one is that of Rev. George McCrie, who says: "If it be true that 'God loves in me,' it must be equally true that 'God hates in me'; and, by the same logic, he is all hatred to sin, and indignation against sinners." *

---

* *The Religion of our Literature*, London, 1875, p. 51.

Carlyle's admonition, "Love not pleasure," brings to mind that of Charles W. Wendte, "Pleasure may fill up the interstices of life, but it is poor material to build its framework of."

In the choice of amusements, a business man should patronize out-of-door exercises; any diversion which keeps one up nearly until midnight in a crowded hall and unhealthy atmosphere, is not in the better sense recreative or improving. . . . He should not be completely absorbed in business; he should ride *on* the harrow, not *under* it.— *C. B. Patten (Lecture before the Boston Young Men's Christian Union).*

Dean Stanley tells us * that Thomas Erskine, of Linlathen, once meeting a shepherd in a lonely path in the Highlands, greeted him with the question, " Do you know the Father ? " and, without waiting for the reply, passed on his way. Years afterwards, he met the same shepherd among the same hills, who recognized him, and gave him the answer as he passed, " I know the Father now." That knowledge he had found in the experience of a human life.

It comes to us, if it comes at all, through those years of learning and of waiting in which our human hearts are both humbled and exalted, both made empty and enriched. That knowledge is the knowledge in which all moral experiences sum up their wisdom of life; and it cannot be taught, for it is a revelation coming through the life of man, through all his affections, needs, trials, satisfactions,— a knowledge of the heart which cannot be taken away. Thus the Bible sums up its revelations of the Father in one intensely human word, God is love.— *Dr. Newman Smyth (Old Faiths in New Light,* p. 277).

> Habitual evils change not on a sudden,
> But many days must pass and many sorrows.
> Conscious remorse and anguish must be felt,
> To curb desire, to break the stubborn will,
> And work a second nature in the soul,
> Ere virtue can resume the place she lost.
>
> *Nicholas Rowe.*

---

* *Lectures on Hist. Church of Scotland,* p. 184.

Chapter XL.

REGENERATION.

What is the Evolutional View of Regeneration, and What concerning Emotion, Subordination, and Profession, as Factors or as Results?

THAT which particularly emphasizes as essential thereto introspection, self-renunciation, aspiration, and "at-one-ment with God." This view, no less than the intercessional, considers that Christ "gave himself for us, that he might redeem us from all iniquity,"— but not in the same sense. The thesis how and wherein has been presented in four points: (1) He rendered an unbroken obedience to the law of the spirit; he served the spirit of God; he came not to do his own will, but the will of God. (2) The law of the spirit making men one (it being only by the law in our members that we are many), Christ had an unfailing sense of the *mutuality* (or "solidarity") of men,— that it was not God's will that one of his human creatures should perish. (3) Christ persevered in this uninterrupted obedience to the law of the spirit,— in this unfailing sense of human solidarity,— even to the death, although everything befell him which might break the one or tire the other. (4) He had in himself, and in all he said and did, that infallible force of attraction which doubled the virtue of everything said and done by him,

> And made it the beacon toward sweetness and light,—
> The beacon to beauty,
> The beacon to duty,
> The beacon that brightens all tempest and night.
> *Celeste Shute Burnham.*

The inworking and outworking of our consequent reverence and sense of obligation toward him are already considered.*

Dr. Horace Bushnell's view of the death of Christ was that he died to reconcile man to God, not God to man; that there

---

*Chap. xxv. See Dr. M. Arnold's *St. Paul and Protestantism*, passim.

is no antagonism between justice and mercy which makes an "atonement" (in the dogmatic sense of the word) necessary or even possible. The opinion long and generally held that the Scripture sacrifices import expiation, he thought might be accounted for by the fact that there is a natural tendency in all worthy ideas of religion to lapse into such as are unworthy,— repentance, for instance, into doing penance; that the sacrifices could easily be corrupted in this manner, and, in fact, were by all the pagan religions; and then that there was imported back into the constructions of Scripture a notice of expiation as pertaining to sacrifice under the plausible but unsuspected sanction of classic usages and associations.*

Dr. William E. Channing's view was that the blood of Christ is emblematic: "Our liberty was purchased and our country saved by the *blood* of patriots."† "I regard Jesus as the Shekinah to us."‡ Similarly, Dr. Emanuel Swedenborg.§

In becoming acquainted with Jesus as one of ourselves, we are unconsciously learning to have faith in the highest ideal, and a new sense is formed within us of the worth and sacred destiny of the race which has produced such an instance of what it may become. It is not from any theological propositions, however logically sound, it is not from any verbal precepts, however wise and pure, that we can draw the strength that we greatly need amidst the impenetrable mystery of life. There is no religion that is of any value, however venerable its doctrines and its ceremonials, that is not rooted deep in faith in human virtue; that does not create an ever-growing trust in rectitude, in unselfishness, in whatever is good and noble. There can be no faith in God unless there is faith in man. If we do not hold our brother sacred whom we see, how can we revere God whom we do not see? There is no divine goodness for us if we do not believe in human virtue.— *Dr. W. H. Furness (Jesus).*

We have changed the Master's summary, "Repent, for the kingdom of heaven is at hand," into another, "Repent, for the kingdom of hell is not far off." Instead of making men afraid to sin, we have tried to make them afraid to die. Even in that we have not greatly succeeded. . . . Make a man understand that there is no happiness for him except in being merciful, meek, Christ-like, and you make him realize that he must be born again.— *William B. Wright.*

Death-bed repentance is burning the candle of life in the service of the devil, then blowing the snuff in the face of heaven.— *Lorenzo Dow.*

The permanence of the blessing of regeneration is entitled

---

* *The Vicarious Sacrifice grounded in Principles of Universal Obligation, passim.*
† *The Perfect Life,* p. 279.   ‡ *Memoirs,* etc., p. 438.
§ *The True Christian Religion,* n. 706.

to further consideration. In a discourse on Eccl. iii., 14, "What God gives, he gives forever," Dr. J. F. Clarke says:—

When God has once given us to know himself, this greatest of all gifts he gives forever. After years of trivial, outward life, life empty of any solid satisfaction, there comes some day of trial, of sorrow, of great and bitter disappointment; some day in which remorse seizes us for our wasted years, or our hardness and indifference toward our friends, or our life empty of any great purpose. Then, perhaps, in the midst of our sense of utter helplessness, we are led to see that God loves us still; that his arms are around us; that he can forgive to the uttermost all our folly, and in that sight we begin a new life. After this, no matter what comes, we have something we can never lose again; a faith in God's love which nothing can quench; one anchor which holds fast in every storm. "Now abides faith," says Paul, telling how belief changes and opinion passes away. If we have ever once really trusted the Supreme Goodness, that will always remain in the depths of the soul, a seed of hope and love. When God gave me that, he gave it forever. I suppose this is what is really meant by the Calvinistic doctrine of "the perseverance of the saints." Not that the saints may not do wrong and go wrong, may not forget their best purpose sometimes, forget God's love sometimes. But there remains that experience in their heart always, ready to bring them once again to their Father. That which brought the Prodigal Son back to his father was the remembrance of his father's liberality. "How many hired servants of my Father have bread enough!"—*Boston Saturday Evening Gazette,* March 12, 1881.

In either view, it is evident that Paul considered Christ to have entered into his glory when he had made his physical death itself a crowning witness to his obedience to righteousness. The author of the Epistle to the Hebrews * represents the death as analogous to the Jewish system of sacrifices; but his powers of combining, type-finding, and expounding seem somewhat to have dominated his religious preceptions. What the true expiation was has been well stated by Paul.† Christ has to step between us foolish transgressors and the destructive natural consequences of our transgression, and, by a superhuman example, a spending himself without stint, a more than mortal scale of justice and purity, to save the ideal of human life and conduct from the deterioration with which men's ordinary practice threatens it. In this way, Christ truly "became for our sakes poor, though he was rich," he was truly "bruised for our iniquities," he "suffered in our behalf," "bore the sin of many," and "made intercession for the trans-

---

* Perhaps Apollos, "mighty in the Scriptures," Acts xviii., 24.
† II. Cor. v., 21; Titus ii., 14.

gressors." In this way, he was sacrificed as a blameless lamb to redeem us from the vain manner of life that had become our second nature. In this way, he who knew no sin was made to be sin for us.

With Goethe's Elder, in the Hall of the Past, would we "draw a veil over those sufferings, because we reverence them so highly: . . . those mysterious secrets in which the divine depth of sorrow lies hid," we would not "fondle them and trick them out until the most reverend of all solemnities appears vulgar and paltry." *

As to this characteristic of self-subordination, similarly testifies that earnest evangelist, Dwight L. Moody: "It is a good deal better to live a holy life than to talk about it. . . . Lighthouses don't ring bells and fire cannons to call attention to their shining: they just shine." And this coincides with the reverence — not to say self-respect — of those who have at all reflected on the growth of character. No sincere man very often mentions that he loves his wife and children. "Special ecstatic experiences in the direction of soul-delirium, vented in rhapsodies and loud agonizings, do not appear to be the lot of most men of deep religious conviction." This anonymous comment † recalls other current aphorisms as to intellection, emotion, annunciation, and repression: —

The heart of man is older than his head. The first-born is sensitive, but blind: his younger brother has a cold, but all-comprehensive glance. The blind must consent to be led by the clear-sighted, if he would avoid falling.— *W. C. L. Ziegler.*

Some people carry their hearts in their heads: very many carry their heads in their hearts. The great difficulty is to keep them apart, and yet both actively working together.— *John P. Durbin, Jr.*

Mere sensibility is not saving. Many are affected by the tragedy of the cross, who will not deny themselves a single indulgence for his sake who hung on it.— *George Punchard.*

Discretion and hardy valor are the twins of honor, and nursed together make a conqueror; divided, but a mere talker.— *Beaumont and Fletcher.*

The mark of the man of the world is absence of pretension. He does not make a speech; he takes a low business tone, avoids all brag, is nobody, dresses plainly, promises not at all, performs much, speaks in monosyllables, hugs his fact. He calls his employment by its lowest name, and so takes from evil tongues their sharpest weapon.— *Ralph W. Emerson.*

---

* *Wilhelm Meister's Travels,* chap. xi.
† Of the Springfield *Republican* on the Northfield prayer-meeting.

Striking manners are bad manners.— *Robert Hall.*

He who gives himself airs of importance exhibits the credentials of impotence.— *John Gaspar Lavater.*

Honest and courageous people have very little to say about either their courage or their honesty. The sun has no need to boast of his brightness, nor the moon of her effulgence.— *Hosea Ballou.*

Who think too little and who talk too much.— *John Dryden.*

I do suspect you grievously, ... you promise me so infinitely.— *William Shakspere.*

Words are women, deeds are men.— *George Herbert.*

To indulge a consciousness of goodness is the way to lose it.— *Shu-King (Ancient sacred book of the Chinese).*

As the traveller entered that ancient city [Busyrane], he read on the first gate, "Be bold"; and on the second gate, "Be bold, be bold, and evermore be bold"; and then he paused as he read on the third gate, "Be not too bold!" A man's strength should be like the momentum of a falling planet, and his discretion like the return of its due and perfect curve.— *Ralph W Emerson.*

Much of the charm of life is ruined by the exacting demands of confidence. Respect the natural modesty of the soul: its more delicate flowers of feeling close their petals, when they are touched too rudely.— *Stopford A. Brooke.*

I am sick of opinions. Give me a humble, gentle lover of God and man; a man full of mercy and good fruits, "without partiality and without hypocrisy," a man laying himself out in the work of faith, the patience of hope, and the labor of love.— *John Wesley.*

One feels the best things without speaking of them.— *Berthold Auerbach.*

Silence is the sanctuary of prudence.— *Balthasar Gracian.*

They that govern most make least noise.— *John Selden.*

Macaulay ... has occasional flashes of silence, that make his conversation perfectly delightful.— *Sydney Smith.*

Silence is the virtue of the feeble.— *Auguste Préault.*

And do a wilful stillness entertain, ... reputed wise for saying nothing.— *William Shakspere.*

What we say in secret is known to Him who made our interior nature. He who made us is present with us, though we are alone.— *The Papyrus Prisse* (2000 B.C.).

Thought is deeper than all speech,
  Feeling deeper than all thought:
Souls to souls can never teach
  What unto themselves is taught.
Christopher P. Cranch.

Approve
The depth and not the tumult of the soul.
Soft is the music that would charm forever.
The flower of sweetest smell is shy and lowly.
William Wordsworth.

The man that blushes is not quite a brute.
Dr. Edward Young.

Man lives apart, but not alone;
  He walks amid his peers, unread;
The best of thoughts that he hath known,
  For lack of listeners, are never said.
Jean Ingelow.

Of every noble work, the silent part is best,
Of all expression that which cannot be expressed.
William W. Story.

Words that weep and tears that speak.
Abraham Cowley.

Passions are likened best to floods and streams:
The shallow murmur, but the deep are dumb.
Sir Walter Raleigh.

Remember aye the ocean deeps are mute;
  The shallows roar:
Worth is the ocean, fame is but the bruit
  Along the shore.
John F. C. Schiller (translated by A. H. Clough).

Our whitest pearl we never find;
  Our ripest fruit we never reach;
Thy flowering moments of the mind
  Drop half their petals in our speech.
Dr. Oliver W. Holmes.

My name is Pride. . . .
Love softly whispered, "I will be the guide."
"Not so," I laughed in gay disdain,
  "For Love is blind.".
And on we wandered through the summer weather,
  Crushing the fragrant flowers beneath our careless feet,
Unheeding all the glory, only feeling "Life is sweet,"
  Love and I together.
Hope sang for us, and we were glad and gay;
But I was guide, and so we lost our way.
A. Abbott.

Chapter XLI.

SALVATION.

What is the Evolutional View concerning the Later as compared with the Earlier Teachings of Paul upon the Scope of the Life and Death of Christ with Reference to our Salvation?

THAT while Paul from first to last preached the redemption, transition, and regeneration just considered,* there was a progressive modification of the doctrine of "the appearing of the glory," etc.†

By nature and habit, and with his full belief that the end of the world was nigh at hand, Paul used these words to mean a Messianic coming and kingdom. Later Christianity has transformed them, as it has transformed so much else of Paul's to a life beyond the grave; but it has by no means spiritualized them. Paul, as his spiritual growth advanced, spiritualized them more and more: he came to think in using them, more and more, of a gradual inward transformation of the world by a conformity like Christ's to the will of God than a Messianic advent. Yet, even then, they are always second with him, and not first: the essence of saving grace is always to make us more righteous, to bring us into conformity with the divine law, to enable us to "bear fruit to God."—*Dr. Matthew* **Arnold** (*St. Paul and Protestantism*).

Elsewhere, Dr. Arnold, adverting to introspection and self-renunciation, admits with Paul that the world [*kosmos*] knew not God (or the true order of things) by wisdom [*dia tēs sophias*],—that is, by or through the isolated preponderance of its intellectual impulses,—but insists that it is yet necessary to set up a sort of converse to this proposition, and to say

---

* See last three chapters.

† For the grace of God hath appeared, bringing salvation to all men, instructing us, to the intent that, denying ungodliness and worldly lusts, we should live soberly and righteously and godly in this present world [age, *aiōni*], looking for the blessed hope and appearing of the glory of our great God and Saviour Jesus Christ; who gave himself for us, that he might redeem us from all iniquity, and purify unto himself a people for his own possession, zealous of good works.—*Titus* ii. 11–14.

likewise (what is equally true, taking for want of a better term a certain word in a technical sense, and without disparaging its nobler associations): "The world by *Puritanism* knew not God. A clew to sound order and authority we can only get by going back upon the actual instincts and forces which rule our life, seeing them as they really are, connecting them with other instincts and forces, and enlarging our whole view and rule of life."*

An impulse to do a thing is in itself no reason why we should do it, because impulses proceed from two sources, quite different and of different degrees of authority. St. Paul contrasts them as the inward man and the man in our members, the mind of the flesh and the spiritual mind. Jesus contrasts them as *life*, properly so named, and *life in this world*,— the former full of light, endurance, felicity, in connection with the higher and permanent self. And the means by which a man might be placed in the former was by dying to the latter. "Whosoever would come after me, let him renounce himself,"— let him die as regards his old self, and so live. This was what Paul meant by bearing about the dying [*necrosis*] of the Lord Jesus that the *life* of Jesus may be made manifest in our body. By the "himself" to be renounced — the "old man" to be put off, the life in this world — was meant "doing the desires of the flesh and of the thoughts" [*thelēmata tōn dianoiōn*, Eph. ii., 3] which Jesus had already put his disciples in the way of sifting and scrutinizing, and of trying by the standard of conformity to conscience.— *St. Paul and Protestantism, passim.*

Similar testimony upon the necessity of the dying of the lower self in order that the higher may live, comes from witnesses of every assortment of antecedents. Goethe sings out,—

> [Stirb und werde!
> Denn so lang du das nicht,
> Bist du nur ein trü Gast,
> Auf der dunkeln Erde.]

"Die and re-exist! for so long as this is not accomplished, thou art but a troubled guest upon an earth of gloom."

Selfishness, . . . the most inhibited sin in the canon.— *Shakspere*.

A covetous man does not possess his wealth: his wealth possesses him.— *Bias (One of the "Seven")*.

Dr. J. F. Clarke, in his ninth discourse on the "Ideas of Paul" (text, II. Cor. v., 19: "God was in Christ reconciling the world unto himself"), concludes:—

All theories of the atonement fall into two classes, mythological and moral. The mythological theory teaches that it was some trans-

---

* *Culture and Anarchy*, p. 66.

action in the supernatural world, some work done to satisfy the divine justice, or to make peace between the unreconciled attributes of God,— to make it possible for God to forgive his penitent child.

The other theories are moral. They teach that Christ died to manifest the eternal love of God,— not to create it, but to make it known; and that his death is the supreme example of a power which comes down from heaven into human hearts, to purify, redeem, and save the world. It teaches that we all can live and act in this same spirit, all be mediators of this divine life, all can unite with Jesus in reconciling men to God and to each other.

Paul said that he rejoiced in his sufferings, which enabled him "to fill up that which was behind in the sufferings of Christ" (Col. i., 24). This text has much perplexed the theologians, whose theories declare that Christ's sufferings were a full and perfect satisfaction for the sins of all mankind. Paul seems to declare that his own sufferings supplied that which was deficient in those of Christ. The truth is that human self-sacrifice carries on the work of Christ. All sufferings generously endured for the sake of our brothers partake of the nature of Christ's sufferings, and do the same atoning work. They make it easier to believe in a Divine Love, because we have seen the same love in man. If men forgive us, we believe God can forgive us. Man's love, therefore, like that of Christ, reconciles the world to God; and all the blood of martyrs has the same redeeming power with that of Jesus.— *Boston Saturday Evening Gazette*, April 2, 1881.

On this theme of salvation,— of growth into at-one-ment with our moral environment, through the method of Jesus (introspection and self-renunciation),— Mr. Whittier has sung in a strain whose key-note of sweet reasonableness must have been derived from the Master himself. The extrinsic topic was the (sometimes) silent meeting of the Friends or "Quakers."

> So to the calmly gathered thought
> The innermost of truth is taught,
> The mystery dimly understood,
> That love of God is love of good,
> And, chiefly, its divinest trace
> In Him of Nazareth's holy face;
> That to be saved is only this,—
> Salvation from our selfishness,
> From more than elemental fire
> The soul's unsanctified desire,
> From sin itself, and not the pain
> That warns us of its chafing chain;
> That worship's deeper meaning lies
> In mercy and not sacrifice,
> Not proud humilities of sense
> And posturing of penitence,
> But love's unforced obedience;
> That Book and Church and Day are given
> For man, not God,— for earth, not heaven,—
> The blessed means to holiest ends,
> Not masters, but benignant friends;

> That the dear Christ dwells not afar
> The king of some remoter star,
> Listening at times with flattered ear
> To homage wrung from selfish fear,
> But here amidst the poor and blind,
> The bound and suffering of our kind,
> In works we do, in prayers we pray,
> Life of our life, he lives to-day.
>
> *Among the Hills, and Other Poems: "The Meeting."*

But how as to those poor souls that have little or no power to think? To whom little has been given, little will be required. Not the worst misfortune in the world was that of the "Daft Catechumen": —

> He wore the cowl, he kissed the cross,
>   He handled book and beads:
> The friars plied his stupid head
>   With litanies and creeds.
> 'Twas vain. Though lines on lines they taught,
>   He could learn only three:
> I love the Lord, I trust the Lord,
>   I hope the Lord to see.
>
> *Anon.*

And how as to those who have a few additional glimmerings?

> With wider view come loftier goal!
>   With broader light, more good to see!
> With freedom, more of self-control!
>   With knowledge deeper reverence be!
> Anew we pledge ourselves to Thee,
>   To follow where thy truth shall lead;
> Afloat upon its boundless sea,
>   Who sails with God is safe indeed.
>
> *Samuel Longfellow.*

Chapter XLII.

DAMNATION.

What Three Views concerning Christ's Intendment in the Use of the Words "Gehenna," "Condemnation," etc.?

(1) The literalist, (2) the moderate orthodox, and (3) the evolutional.

The first is expressed in Rev. John Brown's "Catechism" (still extensively used) as follows:—

> Hell is a place of endless torment, being a lake that burns with fire and brimstone. . . Wicked men's companions in hell are their father, the devil, and all other evil angels. . . They will continue in hell forever and ever. . . . They will roar, curse, and blaspheme God. — *Two Shorter Catechisms United*, p. 14.

And a prominent orthodox professor writes of retribution:—

> In few things is the superlative wisdom of inspiration, and especially that of our Lord, more obvious than in the unmitigated, the peremptory, the absolute revelation of eternal woe. . . The popular mind must hold it with firm, close grip, or it cannot long hold it at all. It never can live subject to the law of chances.— *Dr. Austin Phelps (The Congregationalist*, November, 1882).

Whereupon, a keen editorial observer comments:—

> A largely increasing number of Christians to-day in all the Churches think "the superlative wisdom of inspiration" is more obvious in what is withheld concerning that doctrine than in what is revealed. Positive revelation being denied, the sentiments of hope, faith, and our confidence in the justice of God assert themselves; and the old doctrine of everlasting punishment goes to the limbo of obsolete dogmas.— *Samuel J. Barrows (Christian Register*, Nov. 30, 1882).

The second view considers the word "Gehenna" (the name of the offal-depository fire-place near Jerusalem) to be used simply figuratively, as being the only adequate emblem of a soul in a condition of endless loathing, remorse, and despair.* The

---

* As to the various words translated "hell," see Canon Farrar's *Mercy and Judgment*, chap. xiv.

parable of the shepherd's **goats**, the expressions traceable to Babylonian mythology, etc., **are** considered to refer to an irremediable ultimate local segregation of the finally impenitent.*

The third view considers all those utterances attributed to Jesus that would indicate any belief in the superstitions of his time and country to be either the distortions of successive narrow-minded but adoring reporters, or else mere early and temporary beliefs which finally became very essentially modified. It declares that **sin's** punishment is sin's effect. Dr. Matthew Arnold says: —

> Jesus employed as **sanctions** of his doctrine his **contemporaries'** ready-made notions **of hell** and judgment, just as Socrates did. He talked of the outer **darkness** and the unquenchable fire, as Socrates talked of **the** rivers of **Tartarus.** . . . It is not to be supposed that a rejection of all the poetry of popular religion is necessary or advisable now, any more than when Jesus came. But it is an aim which may well indeed be pursued with enthusiasm, to make the true meaning of Jesus, in using that poetry, emerge and prevail. For the immense pathos, so perpetually enlarged upon, of his life and death, does really culminate here,— that Christians have so profoundly misunderstood him.

And, in this connection, it has been mentioned, as not without significance, that Luke (iv., 19, 20) says that Jesus, upon quoting Isaiah lxi., 2, "to preach the acceptable year of the Lord," "closed the book and sat down"; probably without adding the rest, "and the day of vengeance of our God."

The "cosmical principle symbolized by the serpent" has already been considered in one phase, in the chapter on Demonization.† As to a personal devil, Moncure D. Conway says: —

> The doctrine of a personal spirit of evil, originating in Persia, had invested some centuries **before** the birth of Christ an Assyrian angel of Accusation,— **Satan** ; and he had become degraded from a retributive agent of **God into** a fiend. There was no philosophy of evil at the time to secure even the mind of Christ against this idea. And, indeed, however repulsive it may be now, at that period it seemed essential **to the growth** of a pure ideal of God, as Infinite Love, with whom the **origination of** evil could not be associated. The world was recoiling from **the** worship of demons under guise of deities, and the new ideal **was** secured by attributing all phenomena of evil to imps, furies, dragons, all of which were ultimately generalized by Christianity into Satan, whose works it was the mission of Christ to destroy.— *Idols and Ideals, App. Essay*, p. 54.

---

* As to purification by fire, etc., see Lydia M. Child's *Progress of Religious Ideas*, chap. ii., p. 160. (See chap. xlv., *post*, near the end.) See also *The Rosicrucians, passim*.   † See chap. xviii.

As to the future state, **it is a trite** hyperbole that the libraries **of the world** groan under the ponderous mass of matter directly devoted to this great theme. Some of the best thoughts bearing **logically** or collaterally thereon have been incidentally preserved in books treating mainly of other subjects. Thus, the eloquent passage in one of Horace Greeley's popular addresses, "Who shall say then that Nebuchadnezzar on his throne is happier than Daniel in his prison?" etc., may be found in *Recollections of a Busy Life, App. Essay,* p. 524.

Not alone in Mr. Whittier's lines,

> Of all sad words of tongue or pen,
> The saddest **are** these, "It might have been,"

or in Tennyson's,

> This is truth the poet sings,
> That a sorrow's crown of sorrow
> Is remembering better things,

do we alight upon reminders of **Dante's**

> [Nessun maggior dolore
> Che ricordarsi del tempo felice
> Nella miseria.]
>
> No penitence and no confessional:
> No priest ordains it, yet they're forced to sit
> Amid deep ashes of their vanished years,

or of Cicero's **burning** utterance against Piso: —

Think **not** that guilt requires the burning torches of the Furies to agitate **and** torment it. Frauds, crimes, remembrances of the past, terrors **of** the future,— these are the domestic Furies that **are** ever present to the mind of the impious.

Whoever sins against **light** kisses the lips of a blazing cannon.— *Jeremy Taylor.*

Punishment is lame, but it comes.— *George Herbert.*

Guilt is a spiritual Rubicon.— *Jane Porter.*

There is an aching that is worse than any pain.— *George MacDonald.*

> The good he scorned
> Stalked off reluctant, like an ill-used ghost,
> Not to return; or, if it did, in visits
> Like those of angels, short and far between.
>
> *Robert Blair.*
>
> He that has light within his own clear breast
> May sit in the centre and enjoy bright day;
> But he that hides a dark soul and foul thoughts
> Benighted walks under the midday sun.
>
> *John Milton.*

> Untainted by the guilty bribe,
> Uncursed amidst the harpy tribe;
> No orphan's cry to wound my ear,
> My honor and my conscience clear;
> Thus may I calmly meet my end,
> Thus to the grave in peace descend.
> *Sir William Blackstone.*

Hell is the infinite terror of the soul, whatever that may be, . . . to be conscious of having done another an injury that through eternity never can be undone,—infinite, maddening remorse.—*F. W. Robertson.*

Eternal punishment is the consolidation and perpetuation of evil character, projecting itself into the eternal world, and reaping its own self-prepared consequences.—*Dr. R. S. Storrs.*

"Lockhart, I may have but a minute to speak to you. My dear, be a good man, be virtuous, be religious: nothing else will give you any comfort when you come to lie here."—*Sir Walter Scott.*

Harmonization with our environment is the indispensable condition of peace of soul: our environment in this world and the next consists unalterably of God, conscience, and our own record.—*Joseph Cook.*

An eminent essayist, referring to the effect of narcotics upon his dreams, indorses the common view that the "book of account" is the mind itself of each individual:—

Of this at least I feel assured, that there is no such thing as forgetting possible to the mind: a thousand accidents may and will interpose a veil: but alike, whether veiled or unveiled, the inscription remains forever; just as the stars seem to withdraw before the common light of day, whereas, in fact, we all know that it is the light which is drawn over them as a veil, and that they are waiting to be revealed when the obscuring daylight shall have withdrawn.—*Thomas De Quincey* (*Confessions of an English Opium-eater*, p. 149).

Upon an asseveration in one of Joseph Cook's lectures that the maxim, "It is never too late to mend," is false, and that every conscience will regret sin's existence, Adoniram J. Paterson animadverts, as importing from the premise that regret is pain, the sequence that—

The St. Pauls and the St. Johns will suffer more than the Neros and the Caligulas. Christ, having infinite tenderness, will have infinite suffering. . . . There may be pertinence in the simile of Mr. Cook: "This planet moves through space enswathed in light. The radiance of the sun billows away to all quarters of infinity. Behind the globe, a shadow is projecting, diminishing, indeed, and lost at last in the immeasurable vastness of the illuminations of the scene." But the effect of sin—the shadow—never falls toward the sun, never upon the face of God. To say that it is to "darken the sea of glass, and cast its shadow across the great white throne," is irreverent. To say that the sin of a thousand years ago exists to-day is as unscientific as to affirm that the pains from which some martyr died will be active forever. Sin is not a distinct entity. Fed by evil desires, it lives; apart from these, it dies. . . .

A reformer, expecting a judgment "at hand," is not necessarily declaring the eternal permanence of evil, when he cries, "He that is unjust, let him be unjust still": he means: "You cannot now save the city, give it to its fate." Sin is an awful thing in any age, in any world. Conformity of the soul to God is the only condition that can give peace, here or hereafter. God knew this from the beginning, and adjusted his universe accordingly. Evil is transient and incidental. As God lives and reigns, evil is doomed. Good is permanent and essential. As God lives and reigns, it shall gain the victory. Hallelujah! the Lord God omnipotent reigneth.

Another writer propounded the inquiry, "Suppose a man, who on earth repented at the age of eighty, had died at fifty: how does Mr. Cook happen to know that at the age of thirty years more, in the other world, it is utterly impossible for the same man to turn and go upward?" This recalls an unpublished sermon * of one of the ripest thinkers upon this theme, the late Rev. Herman Bisbee (text, Matt. v., 20: "Except your righteousness shall exceed," etc., "ye shall in no wise enter into the kingdom of heaven"). The following, gathered from a crude report of it, will be found excellently in point: —

Every candid reader of the New Testament has observed that the discourse of Christ abounds in warnings of some imminent danger to the human soul,—something to be shunned at the cost of property, standing, friends, and life itself. As to the character of this danger, the indefiniteness of his expressions leaves a large margin for honest differences of opinion. To foretell all that constitutes heaven, one must be omniscient; and the same is true as to hell. Language fails to exhaust these themes, just as the eye fails to take in the universe when it looks at the stars. And this infinitude of the concerns of the soul has afforded ground for the play of imagination, until exaggerated fantasies have superseded simple facts. And then, as with everything else in life, the revolting aspect of one extreme has caused a reaction to the opposite.

But the fact that heaven means the sum of human blessedness is not affected by the limitations of our knowledge how far that blessedness may go, what varieties it has, what laws of unfoldment, or what places for realization. So, also, what Christ calls destruction or hell has a clear and solemn meaning, although no man may paint its outlines or describe its sorrows. One who looks out upon the sea has a clear and magnificent idea of Ocean, although he sees but its begin-

---

* Delivered in the Hawes Place Church, South Boston, Mass., Dec. 10, 1876.

nings. So far as we do behold human life, there stand out the two great possibilities. In Buddha, in Socrates, in Mohammed, in Swedenborg, in all nations and peoples, have these two ideas lain side by side, as we see them in the New Testament. By every analogy which we know, the two ways of human life that Jesus pointed out — one broad, leading to loss, the other narrow but to gain — extend into the immortal world: there, as here, each soul will pursue what it loves, and seek that which it enjoys. If here we learn to love intrigue and power and falsehood and excitement, we shall seek them over there, as certainly as we shall seek honesty and purity and peace. Nor do the two roads less diverge, merely because the beginnings of divergence are often imperceptible. . . .

The finite cannot comprehend the infinite. We are to judge of what is to come by what is,— not by the goodness of God. Any theologian could prove from the goodness of God that no such world as this could ever be,— that no such thing as evil or imperfection could exist; but facts would refute him. We can only reason from what is, to prove in the first place the goodness of God. In this life, we see good men sometimes become evil, and evil men break off and grow good. I know of no warrant for saying that those who continue to increase in evil during this life will increase in evil forever, or that those who here increase in good will so increase forever. We may speculate, but conjecture is not knowledge. We know the tendency: we know the momentum of habit is such that Christ's words are true, that there is danger in one way, safety in the other. All heroic and consecrated effort is based on the possibility of being overcome by temptation, and the counter possibility of overcoming and experiencing the ineffable glory. . . .

If eternity has no finality, we cannot speak of what will finally happen. The doctrine that the righteous and the wicked are to be assembled and separated — the righteous welcomed to heaven, and the wicked sentenced and driven to everlasting torments — is probably an error made originally by interpreting certain expressions too literally. The awful fact is not that God ever sentences a man to be where he does not wish to be, but that a human being should ever choose dark and debased surroundings. . . . Christ has sometimes been spoken of as carrying in his person the sins of the whole world. He evidently carried upon his spirit a load of mountain weight. But we may reasonably say it was a clear and sympathetic perception of the two kinds of life possible to man; of the joy, peace, and glory consequent upon the one, and the unrest, remorse, and darkness attendant upon the other. . . . No feebler terms than "hell" and "condemnation," "heaven" and "joy of the Lord" could fully express his idea of the destinations.

Mr. Bisbee's "warnings of some imminent danger to the human soul" recall Milton's,—

> Long is the way,
> And hard, that out of hell leads up to light.

His words, "There, as here, each soul will pursue what it loves," etc., were in a subsequent discourse explained as follows: —

Even if it were possible, as Swedenborg asserts, for a man to gain a preponderating love of good or ill, so that he could but choose to go in one direction or the other, I do not see why he should never be able to reject the evil love, and gain the good in the future.... I have never yet met a man so degraded that he did not *believe* in the good, and wish his children trained to its love and practice. There is great variety of opinion as to what will bring highest good; but the faith of the vile is in the good, as well as that of the good themselves. I have seen men going into greater evils, as long as I saw them at all: the miserliness of the miser grows upon him; the sottishness of the sot deepens with years; the hardness of the hard-hearted is stonier, the longer it continues; the lust of the lustful is more shameless and accursed. I see enough to appall me at the thought of going in that direction. At the same time, I do not see that a human being can reach that condition in which there is no hope of his deliverance. So far as I *know*, there is a protest of the nature against the corruption practised, a protest that can never be entirely silenced.

In studying the laws of God as I see them operating here, I find that the whole race is slowly lifting. The cruelty of the vicious is less cruel than it was: the lower and the higher classes rise together. I do not see any tendency in this life for one great body of people to go into deeper and deeper barbarism, and another class to go into higher and higher enlightenment; but all humanity mounts step by step into a better condition. I judge of the future by what I see in the present. The law of unfoldment which links the highest to the lowest, which will not let the few ascend, unless they take others with them, which makes every soul neighbor to every other soul,— that law will accomplish greater and greater things forever.

I have not the slightest idea that the time will come when all men will be free from further desire, activity, struggle, and sorrow. As we rise in the scale of being in this world, we learn to see certain things as evil which once were not evil to us. The state that I am in now will look to me like a terrible state to be in, though now it is pleasing and delightful. If two men are ascending a mountain and keep at equal distance apart, one will see the other as being below him all the way, though both ascend. As that which was once comfortable in homes is now looked upon as poverty, so that which is comfortable now will in some future day be looked upon as poverty. And this has always been and will forever be, so far as appears. There will be that below us to shun, that above us to woo us to sublimer endeavor. To me, heaven and hell are relative terms: that below is hell, and that above is heaven; but the movement is universal and eternal. So far as I see, there will be always, as there is now, and as there always was, something to shun, something more to win; yet the vast multitude, children of the same Infinite, rising into wider, higher, sweeter, and more blissful reception of that Infinite. As I expect to be the same soul or being there as here, so I expect God will be the same, and conditions of advancement the same. The separation of the righteous and the wicked there will be only by the laws that separate them here; and there will be no fixed state in which one must stay there more than here.

Let him, then, who would learn how to live a life of bliss by and by learn to live a life of cleanliness, temperance, usefulness, courage, and efficiency here. The scholar who understands best the grade which he is in is best prepared for the grade into which he shall be promoted.

The child opens his eyes upon the wonder of the world, and comes to a knowledge of his powers little by little. In myself, I was never more a child, never more on the threshold of all possible good, than I am to-day. That which I have attained gives me no greater sense of completeness than that which I had as a child. The power to comprehend only reveals more and more to comprehend. The power to enjoy but reveals more and more to enjoy. The little country town* of my childhood was as much to me as all New England to-day; and the New England of my childhood was as much as all the world of to-day. Slowly, by toil and pain, there has come to me a more sacred friendship, a deeper worship, a vaster thought, a more abundant delight. If this may continue; if the way may still conduct me into higher sensations, into greater knowledge, into more divine love; if the future shall open and open and open; if I may ever pursue something, as I have here; if joy shall forever go with good, and pain with evil, as here; if I may draw closer to better hearts, and draw out more of the fathomlessness of my being; if this may be, just this, step by step, little by little,— I shall not ask, for I cannot conceive, a more glorious destiny.†

In confirmation of Mr. Bisbee's testimony upon the relations between desire, activity, and happiness, comes Cowper's : —

> Lives spent in indolence, and therefore sad. . . .
> Absence of occupation is not rest,
> A mind quite vacant is a mind distressed.

In idleness there is perpetual despair.— *Thomas Carlyle.*

If I may speak of myself (the only person of whom I can speak with certainty), *my* happy hours have far exceeded, and far exceed, the scanty numbers of the Caliph of Spain; and I shall not scruple to

---

*West Derby, Vt., overlooking an unusually grand landscape of lake, mountains, hills, and villages.

† To those who have heard the above discourse (of whom the writer was one) there is a peculiarly touching pathos in the peroration, "If this may continue," etc. A few months after its delivery, on the eve of an anticipated vacation, Mr. Bisbee preached with equal eloquence on a collateral theme, abridged the closing exercise including the benediction, descended the pulpit stairs, was stricken with apoplexy, and soon the meek and noble spirit was released to its "more glorious destiny."

add that many of them are due to the pleasing labor of the present composition.— *Edward Gibbon.*

The reference is to "Abdalrahman, the Just," who, not long before his death, A.D. 790, had assumed the title of King of Cordova. He testified : —

I have now reigned above fifty years in victory or peace, beloved by my subjects, dreaded by my enemies, and respected by allies. Riches and honors, power and pleasure, have waited on my call; nor does any earthly blessing appear to have been wanting to my felicity. In this situation, I have diligently numbered the days of pure and genuine happiness which have fallen to my lot: they amount to *fourteen.* O man, place not thy confidence in this world!

Gibbon's testimony is well supplemented by two women's : —

For ages, happiness has been represented as a huge precious stone, impossible to find, which people seek hopelessly. It is not so. Happiness is a mosaic, composed of a thousand little stones, which separately and of themselves have little value, but which, united with art, form a graceful design — *Mme. Emile de Girardin.*

The happiest women, like the happiest nations, have no history.— *George Eliot.*

Another ripe reasoner hereon, after defining heaven to consist of "heavenly knowledge, love, and action," says of hell : —

Suppose that each man is tested by a sliding scale, arranged, not only according to his goodness and wickedness, but also according to his opportunities and advantages. Then, it would follow that a pretty bad man, who had had no opportunities or poor opportunities, would go to heaven; and a pretty good man, who had not made equal use of his better opportunities, would go to hell. Then, hell would contain many people much better than those in heaven. This is the dilemma. If only good people are to go to heaven, and only the bad to hell, then those will be punished for not being good who have never had any opportunity of being so and who could not help being bad. But, if each man is rewarded or punished according to his efforts to do right, taking into account all the circumstances, then good and bad people will be mixed together in heaven, and other good and bad people will be mixed together in hell. If heaven be a place and hell another place, it is impossible to escape this difficulty. But if heaven be inward happiness and peace, and hell be inward dissatisfaction and unrest, then the difficulty disappears. Just so far as a man is true to his conscience and his heart, he enters into an inward heaven; just so far as he is false to it, he goes into an inward hell. The worm that never dies is conscience. . . .

The conception Jesus had of God as a father is utterly opposed to the usual doctrine of probation. Could a good earthly father put his children on trial in this way? Could he take his little ones and test them as a manufacturer tests his goods, and, fixing an arbitrary mark of excellence, reject all that do not come up to it? No! ten times no! Those who are low down and far off are the very ones the good earthly and heavenly Father cares for the most. The Son of God comes to seek and to save those who are lost. . . .

The sight of a heavenly Father who keeps bringing up the rearguard of humanity, and goes out to seek and save the lost sheep, has worked on the world to create a different civilization. It tends to unite men in a common mode of life. Out of the fatherhood of God comes the brotherhood of man. The new heavens make the new earth.— *Dr. J. F. Clarke* (*Common Sense in Religion*, p. 150).

A still more emphatic "No!" has been uttered as follows: —

This avenging God, rancorous torturer, who burns his creatures in a slow fire! When they tell me that God made himself a man, I prefer to recognize a man who made himself a god.— *Alfred de Musset.*

One horn of the dilemma propounded by Dr. Clarke recalls the declaration of "Father" Edward Taylor that, if Mr. Emerson was sent to perdition, the best people would migrate with him. Mr. Spurgeon's remark, "He that believeth shall be saved, let his sins be ever so many; he that believeth not shall be damned, let his sins be ever so few," suggests a passage in a Chicago clergyman's open letter to an earnest literalist: —

You say that no sinner can be saved who does not actually appropriate the blood of Christ with the conscious acceptance of the imputed righteousness which he possesses; and this, though honest of purpose and doing the best he knows. Take the saved on these terms, even in this very city as a basis, and you will have to figure very liberally to make in Europe and America more than 40,000,000, — the present population of the United States. Now, America is said to contain about 85,519,000 human beings; Europe, 309,178,000; Asia, 824,548,000; Africa, 199,521,000; Australia and Polynesia, 4,748,000. In view of these figures, who rules the universe, God or the devil? Is this the best that the grace of God can do for mankind?— *Dr. W. H. Ryder* (*Open Letter to Dwight L. Moody*).*

Which recalls the remark reported to have been made by H. W. Beecher in a sermon at St. Paul, Minn., about the same date: "As to worshipping a God who damns men through all creation, I cannot worship the devil, and that is only a demoniacal God." Nevertheless, nobody who has lived through his (or her) teens will deny that a single folly — not to say sin — will for a lifetime remind one of the princess who could not

---

* See Art. xviii. of the Thirty-nine Articles as to who "are to be had accursed."

sleep on a hundred **beds** of **down** because of the little pebble underneath **them** all. There **is a** sense in which the Scotch literalist was not very illogical, though he may have chosen his premises inadvertently. "But," said **his** friend, "according to your statement, nobody is likely to be saved except yourself and your brother Alexander!" "Aweel, I'm nae sae sure aboot Sandy, neither." This **view** of "the Eternal Goodness" reminds New Englanders of **the** Hopkins "logic linked and strong" that made the test of a condition of salvation the being willing to be damned.* Welcome, Whittier!—

> I see the wrong that round me lies,
>   I feel the guilt within;
> I hear with groan and travail cries
>   The world confess its sin.
>
> Yet in the maddening maze of things,
>   And tossed by storm and flood,
> To one fixed stake my spirit clings;
>   I know that God is good!
>
> Not mine to look when cherubim
>   And seraphs may not see;
> But nothing can be good in him
>   Which evil is in me.

---

*See in the *Christian Register* of Jan. 4, 1883, p. 5, an article by Dr. J. L. Withrow, on "The Unknown Number of the Lost," which perhaps indicates the most advanced "orthodox" thought on the subject. See also at page 2 therein an editorial by Samuel J. Barrows, quoting old "orthodox" utterances of Drs. Lewis Du Moulin, Nathanael Emmons, Jonathan Edwards, Enoch Pond, Charles Hodge, and others, and especially Krauth's "Acta" of the Synod of Dort.

Chapter XLIII.

PERPETUATION.

What are the Five Principal Arguments in Behalf of the Immortality of the Soul?

(1) **The** metaphysical based on the immateriality, etc. Consciousness teaches that the soul is one and indivisible,— not made up of parts like the body. The body is multiform, the soul uniform.

The soul is never so hampered by its enthralment within the body as when it loves.— *O. S. Fowler.*

Some have conceived a metaphysical argument from our notions of time and space.

Eternity is a negative idea clothed with a positive name. It supposes in that to which it is applied a present existence, and is the negation of a beginning or of an end of that existence.— *Archbishop William Paley.*

(2) The teleological, based on the fact that the soul is adapted to perpetual progress, and has a corresponding desire and expectation. Not to Milton alone is welcome

> White-handed Hope,
> Thou hovering angel girt with golden wings!
> — *John Milton.*

> No man may say at night
> His goal is reached; the hunger for the light
> Moves with the star; our thirst will not depart,
> Howe'er we drink. 'Tis what before us goes,
> Keeps us aweary, will not let us lay
> Our heads in dreamland, though the enchanted palm
> Rise from our desert; though the fountain grows
> Up in our path, with slumber's flowing balm:
> The soul is o'er the horizon far away.
> — *John James Piatt.*

> And as I watch the line of light that plays
>   Along the smooth wave toward the burning west,
> I long to tread that golden path of rays,
>   And think 'twould lead to some bright isle of rest.
> — *Thomas Moore.*

> The soul on earth is an immortal guest
> Compelled to starve at an unreal feast;
> A spark which upward tends by nature's force;
> A stream diverted from its native source;
> A drop dissevered from the boundless sea;
> A moment parted from eternity;
> A pilgrim panting for the rest to come;
> An exile anxious for his native home.
>
> Hannah More.

If man has a capacity for a continued existence, and no continued existence has been provided for him, this is the only exception we know to the rule that every power planted in the nature of God's creatures has its appropriate sphere already designed and prepared for it in the very structure of the universe. "The human heart," says Kant, "refuses to believe in a universe without a purpose." A recent anonymous writer believes with Mr. Whittier that,

> Since he who knows our needs is just,
> Somehow, somewhere, meet we must,

with even the children who have loved us here. Of angels, in the old sense, celestial beings come down out of the sky, we know nothing, believe nothing. But they are creatures of love, working through the imagination. The word, in Greek, means messengers. And, no doubt, messengers of love, in human form, have been transfigured by the loving vision of those who have been helped. All this and the whole growth of religion on the earth goes to show that the greatest reality we know, our own soul, is not a combination of material substances, but partakes of the divine nature.

> Thou wilt not leave us in the dust;
>   Thou madest man, he knows not why;
>   He thinks he was not made to die;
> And thou hast made him: thou art just.
>
> Alfred Tennyson.
>
> So sinks the day-star in the ocean-bed,
> And yet anon repairs his drooping head,
> And tricks his beams, and with new-spangled ore
> Flames in the forehead of the morning sky.
>
> John Milton.

Heaven may have happiness as utterly unknown to us as the gift of perfect vision would be to a man born blind.... Mutual love, pure and exalted, founded on charms both mental and corporeal, as it constitutes the highest happiness on earth, may, for anything we know to the contrary, also form the lowest happiness of heaven. And it would appear consonant with the administration of Providence in other matters that there should be such a link between earth and heaven; for, in all cases, a chasm seems to be purposely avoided, *prudente Deo.* Thus, the material world has its links, by which it is made to shake hands, as it were, with the vegetable, the vegetable with the animal, the animal with the intellectual, and the intellectual with what we may be allowed to hope of the angelic.— *Caleb C. Colton.*

> All served, all serving; nothing stands alone;
> The chain holds on, and where it ends unknown.
> *Alexander Pope.*

This argument has been well presented in a sermon on Gen. i., 31, "God saw everything was very good," preached in the Broadway Unitarian Church, South Boston, Oct. 12, 1879:—

There is no alternative but to assume that even crime and brutality are serving the higher order of the universe in some way we cannot fathom, but in God's way. To make a devil responsible for the bad and God only accredited with the good is not the way in which matters are disposed in earthly courts. "He who does wrong through another does it himself," says a legal proverb. Who made and takes care of Satan?

The solution that was the fancy of the childhood of our race settled nothing. But to grapple with the fact that God permits wrong of every sort, and to set it beside the fact that as we look backward we find the orderly and beautiful ever rising out of the chaotic and hideous, is to give solid foundation for the only creed the wise man can entertain, that the perfect God can be trusted in his dark deeds as in his bright ones, in clouds and tempests as with mid-day glory of the sun. Yes, over all, through all, in all, is the beneficent power whose march is devious and perplexing, but whose plan and final results are eternally good. And man may go to his work, and study the world with full hope and serenity.— *George A. Thayer.*

> For right is right, since God is God;
> And right the day must win.
> To doubt would be disloyalty;
> To falter would be sin.
> *George Stanley Faber.*

> Come what will, then, I will trust thee,
> For I know that thou art true;
> And the ill that often must be
> Shall not hide the good from view.
> With thy tender arms enclosing
> And thy pitying eye on mine,
> In its light and love reposing,
> Never let my soul repine.
> *Virtue Hall Burnham.*

> The soul, how can she but immortal be,
> When with the motions of both will and wit
> She still aspireth to eternity,
> And never rests till she aspire to it?...
> At first, her mother earth she holdeth dear,
> And doth embrace the world and worldly things:
> She flies close by the ground, and hovers here,
> And mounts not up with her celestial wings;
> Yet, under heaven, she cannot light on aught
> That with her heavenly nature doth agree;

> She cannot rest, she cannot fix her thought,
>   She cannot in this world contented be.
> For who did ever yet, in honor, wealth,
>   Or pleasure of the sense, contentment find?
> Who ever ceased to wish when he had health,
>   Or having wisdom was not vexed in mind?
> Then, as a bee that among weeds doth fall,
>   Which seem sweet flowers with lustre fresh and gay,
> She lights on that and this, and tasteth all,
>   But pleased with none doth rise and soar away.
> So, when the soul finds here no true content,
>   And, like Noah's dove, can no sure footing take,
> She doth return from whence she first was sent,
>   And flies to Him that first her wings did make.
> Sir John Davies.

> The minstrel's strain may swell or bend
>   To chances of his mood or lyre,
>   But, if 'tis kindled with true fire,
> A theme of purpose thrills from end to end!
>
> We may not scan like mortal's lay
>   The mighty metres that rehearse
>   The Epos of the Universe,
> But yet the Great *Poietes* makes alway!
>
> Our grandsires sang in pious lauds,
>   "God moves in a mysterious way;
>   Yea, wondrous far beyond what they
> Conceived! Is it *too* wondrous to be God's?
> Marcus Paulus Venetus (The Spectator).

(3) The inchoatal, based on the fact of insoluble problems. We are all, in our mind and our life, brought face to face with questions to which no sufficient answer can be found.

Every generation of men comes in turn to look at these paradoxes, these antinomies of the reason. How can an infinite being create a finite world? What is the origin of evil? What is the relation between freedom and law, liberty in man and the providence of God? We are obliged by the law of our thought to ask these questions, and are unable to answer them. Do they not then vindicate an hereafter, where the solution will be found? Are they not like the sentence written at the foot of an unfinished story,—"To be continued in our next"?—*Dr. J. F. Clarke (Common Sense in Religion, p. 207).*

> The lyfe so short, the craft so long to lerne,
> Th' assay so hard, so sharpe the conquering.
> Geoffrey Chaucer.

> God's greatness flows around our incompleteness;
> Round our restlessness, his rest.
> Elizabeth Barrett Browning.

God, who keeps his word with the birds and fishes in their migratory instinct, will keep his word with man.—*Ruth Prescott Hall.*

Our dissatisfaction with any other solution is the blazing evidence of our immortality.—*Ralph W. Emerson.*

The truest end of life is to know the life that never ends.— *William Penn.*

Heaven will be the sweet surprise of a perfect explanation.— *Dr. Robert Price.*

To God shall ye all return, and he will enlighten you concerning the subjects of your disputes.— *Mohammed.*

(4) **The rejuvenatal, based on the fact of mental rejuvenation.** How often, while the body grows older, does the spirit seem to grow younger, fresher, more active! Goethe said of Schiller, "He went on and on, for thirty-eight years, never resting, never ceasing from new activity and fresh accomplishments." Meanwhile, the body of Schiller was steadily decaying. The cases of Wesley, Channing, J. Q. Adams, and a multitude of others, show that death may take possession of the feeble body and yet have no dominion over the ascending soul. They recall Francis Joubert's remark, "He seemed to be a soul that had met with a body, and tried to make the best of it." Such a one reminds Dr. J. F Clarke of a seal with the device of a sky-rocket, and the motto *Dum vivo, volo,*— "While I live, I ascend."

He was one of a lean body and visage, as if his eager soul, biting for anger at the clog of his body, desired to fret a passage through it.— *Thomas Fuller.*

Drawing near her death, she sent most pious thoughts as harbingers to heaven; and her soul saw a glimpse of happiness through the chinks of her sickness-broken body.— *Thomas Fuller.*

> The soul's dark cottage, battered and decayed,
> Lets in new light through chinks that time has made.
> Stronger by weakness, wiser men become,
> As they draw near to their eternal home.
> *Edmund Waller.*

> **Death had** illumined the Land of **Sleep**;
>   And his lifeless body lay
> A worn-out fetter, that the soul
>   Had broken and thrown away.
> *Henry W. Longfellow.*

(5) **The absolute, based** on the significance of our personality. This, however, may be considered to combine the four others, and possibly also certain arguments from analogy; for instance, the suspension of consciousness during sleep, the spring awakening, the chrysalis, etc. But, after all the arguing, Dr. James Martineau's remark is not without truth,— "We do not believe immortality because we have proved it, but we forever try to prove it because we believe it." The wish begets

the thought. Not Fichte alone has exclaimed, "As often as I hear of some undeserved wretchedness, my thoughts rest on that world where all will be made straight, and where the labors of the sorrowful will end in joy." We clutch and cherish every straw thereon in the poets. *Some* of the *Night Thoughts* are not " parsed and passed."

> Look nature through; 'tis revolution all;
> All change, no death. . . All sinks to reascend,
> Emblems of man who passes, not expires. . . .
> Still seems it strange that thou shouldst live forever?
> Is it less strange that thou shouldst live at all?
> This is a miracle, and that no more.
>
> *Dr. Edward Young.*

> Man, thou shalt never die! Celestial voices
> Hymn it unto our souls.
>
> *Richard H. Dana.*

> It may be
> The thoughts that visit us we know not whence,
> Sudden as inspiration, are the whispers
> Of disembodied spirits speaking to us,
> As friends, who wait outside a prison wall,
> Through the barred windows speak to those within.
>
> *H. W. Longfellow* (*Atlantic Monthly*, February, 1883).

> 'Tis the divinity that stirs within us,
> And intimates eternity to man.
> Aye, thou shalt flourish in immortal youth,
> Unhurt amidst the war of elements,
> The wreck of matter and the crush of worlds.
>
> *Joseph Addison.*

> Life,— the childhood of Immortality!
>
> *Goethe.*

> And death is a low mist which cannot blot
> The brightness it may veil, when lofty thought
> Lifts a young heart above its mortal lair,
> And love and life contend in it.
>
> *Percy B. Shelley.*

> To die is landing on some friendly shore,
> Where billows never break nor tempests roar.
> Ere well we feel the friendly stroke, 'tis o'er.
>
> *William Garth* (1670–1719).

What is death? To go out like a light, and in a sweet trance to forget ourselves and all the passing phenomena of the day as we forget the phantoms of a fleeting dream; to form as in a dream new connections with God's world; to enter into a more exalted sphere, and to make a new step up man's graduated ascent of creation.— *J. Heinrich D. Zschokke.*

Our great thoughts, our great affections, the truths of our life, never leave us. Surely, they cannot separate from our consciousness, shall follow it whithersoever that shall go, and are of their nature divine and immortal.— *William M. Thackeray.*

There are treasures laid up in the heart,— treasures of charity, piety, temperance, and soberness. These treasures a man takes with him beyond death, when he leaves this world.— *Buddha.*

Whatsoever that be within us that feels, thinks, desires, and animates, is something celestial, divine, and consequently imperishable. — *Aristotle.*

All men's souls are immortal, but the souls of the righteous are immortal and divine.— *Socrates.*

What springs from earth dissolves to earth again, and heaven-born things fly to their native seat.— *Marcus Antoninus.*

> The look of sympathy, the gentle word
> Spoken so low that only angels heard,
> The secret act of pure self-sacrifice,
> Unseen by men, but marked by angels' eyes,
>   These are not lost.
>
> The happy dreams that gladdened all our youth,
> When dreams had less of self and more of truth,
> The childhood's faith, so tranquil and so sweet,
> Which sat like Mary at the Master's feet,
>   These are not lost.
>
> The kindly plan devised for others' good,
> So seldom guessed, so little understood,
> The quiet, steadfast love that strove to win
> Some wanderer from the ways of sin,
>   These are not lost.
>
> Not lost, O Lord! for in thy city bright
> Our eyes shall see the past by clearer light;
> And things long hidden from our gaze below
> Thou wilt reveal, and we shall surely know
>   These are not lost.
>
>   *Richard Metcalf.*

And as to the later prose literature on immortality, perhaps few riper thinkers thereon can be found than Emerson, Bellows, and one or two others now to be quoted, each supplementing the other as to our personality's blending with God.

We cannot prove our faith by syllogisms. The argument refuses to form in the mind. A conclusion, an inference, a grand augury, is ever hovering; but attempt to ground it, and the reasons are all vanishing and inadequate. You cannot make a written theory or demonstration of this as you can an orrery of the Copernican astronomy. It must be sacredly treated. Speak of the mount in the mount. Not by literature or theology, but only by rare integrity, by a man permeated and perfumed with airs of heaven,— with manliest or womanliest enduring love,— can the vision be clear to a use the most sublime. And hence the fact that in the minds of men the testimony of a few inspired souls has had such weight and penetration. You shall not say: "O my bishop, O my pastor, is there any resurrection? What do you think? Did Dr. Channing believe that we should know each other? did Wesley? did Butler? did Fénelon?" What questions are these! Go read Milton, Shakspere, or any truly ideal poet. Read Plato, or any seer of the interior realities. Read St. Augustine, Swedenborg, Immanuel Kant. Let any master simply recite to you the substantial laws of the intellect, and in the presence of the laws themselves you will never ask such primary-school questions.

Is immortality only an intellectual quality, or, shall I say, only an energy, there being no passive? He has it, and he alone, who gives life to all names, persons, things, where he comes. No religion, not the wildest mythology, dies for him; no art is lost. He vivifies what he touches. Future state is an illusion for the ever-present state. It is not length of life, but depth of life. It is not duration, but a taking of the soul out of time, as all high action of the mind does: when we are living in the sentiments, we ask no questions about time. The spirit world takes place,—that which is always the same. But see how the sentiment is wise. Jesus explained nothing, but the influence of him took people out of time, and they felt eternal. A great integrity makes us immortal; an admiration, a deep love, a strong will, arms us above fear. It makes a day memorable. We say we lived years in that hour. It is strange that Jesus is esteemed by mankind the bringer of the doctrine of immortality. He is never once weak or sentimental; he is very abstemious of explanation; he never preaches the personal immortality; while Plato and Cicero had both allowed themselves to overstep the stern limits of the spirit, and gratify the people with that picture.

How ill agrees this majestical immortality of our religion with the frivolous population! Will you build magnificently for mice? Will you offer empires to such as cannot set a house or private affairs in order? Here are people who cannot dispose of a day; an hour hangs heavy on their hands; and will you offer them rolling ages without end? But this is the way we rise. Within every man's thought is a higher thought; within the character he exhibits to-day, a higher character. The youth puts off the illusions of the child, the man puts off the ignorance and tumultuous passions of youth; proceeding thence, puts off the egotism of manhood, and becomes at last a public and universal soul. He is rising to greater heights, but also rising to realities; the outer relations and circumstances dying out, he, entering deeper into God, God into him, until the last garment of egotism falls, and he is with God,— shares the will and the immensity of the First Cause.— *Ralph Waldo Emerson* (*Letters and Social Aims*, p. 280, ff.).

Mr. Emerson's pithy " not length of life, but depth of life " well supplements Dr. Samuel Johnson's remark, " A peasant and a philosopher may be equally *satisfied*, but not equally *happy:* happiness consists in the multiplicity of agreeable consciousness." Also Dr. James Martineau's, "He whose heart beats the quickest lives the longest." And others: —

> We live in deeds, not years; in thoughts, not breaths;
> In feelings, not in figures on a dial.
> We should count time by heart-throbs. He most lives
> Who thinks most, feels the noblest, acts the best.
> *Philip J. Bailey.*

> One crowded hour of glorious life
> Is worth a world without a name.
> *Sir Walter Scott.*

Mr. Emerson's averment as to the final blending with God reaffirms one or two of the Persian sage: —

Taking the first footstep with the good thought, the second with the good word, and the third with the good deed, I entered paradise. ... All flows out from the Deity, and all must be absorbed in him again.— *Zoroaster.*

And this recalls Derzhavin's "Ode to God," which has been translated from Russian into Chinese and Japanese, by order of the emperors, and hung up, embroidered in gold, in one of their principal temples. The following extract is from Sir John Bowring's translation thereof: —

> What am I?
> Nought! But the effluence of thy light divine,
> Pervading worlds, hath reached my bosom too.
> Yes, in my spirit doth thy spirit shine,
> As shines the sunbeam in a drop of dew.
> Nought! But I live, and on Hope's pinions fly
> Eager toward thy presence; for in thee
> I live and breathe, and dwell, aspiring high,
> Even to the throne of thy divinity.
> I am, O God, and surely thou must be!

The next seer presents most eloquently all the four arguments combined, but emphasizes the teleological: —

No one thing in this universe can be of a deeper moment to a whole man than his own proper personal life. You may talk to him until doomsday about being lost in the Infinite, but he clings to himself as the true factor. Nay, the very angels are well enough; but he would not be an angel, and why should he? Angels have no mothers to croon over them,— by what he can make out,— or fathers to romp with them, ... nor fell in love, ... or made homes, ... or fought strong battles with human brain and hands, or wept over graves, or were stormed by grand utterances or great books. ...

Nor would he be Abraham or Moses or John the beloved. He has solved the problem of his own personal identity, and would not have it *re*solved into the grandest presence that ever trod the earth. These years with their clustering memories, mingled as they are with sin and sorrow and pain, are still his years. They stand out clear and free from the vast and awful mystery of the past, and reveal to him his own life. A poor thing, he says, but mine own; full of mistakes, but mine own; haunted with shadows that shake the heart, but mine own, so that I would not even have it lost in God. I want to keep track of myself. Send me where you will, but let me be aware that I am still this man who is now living a human life, and that those who are living human lives with me will be there in the mystery, not unclothed but clothed upon; then I shall rest in hope.

He will tell you also that this seems to be, of all things, fair, as between God and man. He has given me a nature, he says, so like his own that I cannot give it up. He could not do that, and stand justified before his own universe, if there was no other life to round this out and clothe it with perfection. The tree in my garden loses nine blossoms where it ripens one apple, but that does not trouble the tree. The dumb things let their young go forth to live or die, and forget them. The flocks and herds neighbor with each other: one is taken and another left, and to-morrow it is all the same. Nor do they regret their mistakes or sorrow for their sins, as I do: their life rounds itself, and is complete when they die. The insect of an afternoon, the organism of a hundred years, they have no hauntings of a life before this, and no premonitions of the life hereafter. But the blossoms fall from the tree of my life, he says, yearlings die out of my flock, my children go forth from my home, old friends are taken from my side. I cannot lose or leave them, or prevent this eternal longing after them. They are part of myself, and I am only shards and shreds of the whole fair circle my nature demands, if, being once mine, they are not mine forever. Or, in looking into my own life, I see where I have missed it, and want to try again. I find I am only a learner, and want to learn, and then to put the lesson to some noble use. What can all this incompleteness mean which haunts me, but a promise of completeness. Have I not a right to demand another life which will link itself close into this, or declare to the heavens this is a broken trust, and bid them see to it who have seen to me, or remand the race to an existence that pays as it goes?

Now, it seems clear to me that this claim is founded in fair reason. We hold this right to see the account come out square on this simple ground, if on no other. These searching sorrows and regrets are the vouchers for it, their long enduring the assurance that they hold good. And this deep love for the life we live here, great and good in proportion to the worth of it to the world, with the unslain desire that what we gain through this life may not be lost when we have done with these bodies,—what is all this, though there were no higher word about it, but the hold of the human soul on its own, now and forever? And this is the mind of Christ touching these mysteries of life and death,—that it will be all right, and right in the line of our longing. The solution of the problem lies where it has always lain,—in the Gospels, and in our power to catch their noble meanings and make the truth they tell our own. So, to feel the powers of the world to come, we must come close to this Christ who brought life and immortality to light, and said: "Let not your heart be troubled: ye believe in God, believe also in me. In my Father's house are many mansions: if it were not so, I would have told you."—*Robert Collyer* (*Unity Pulpit*, ii., No. 20, p. 7, ff.).

Nature has created something more glorious even than mind. Her highest, brightest, divinest work is that which binds us to one another, that mysterious emotion we call sympathy, in the widest sense, the feeling for and with one another, the delighting in one another, the working with one another, the coming ever and ever nearer to one another. I say that is nature's most wonderful work, and that is purely spiritual; and for that earth and time provide no adequate sphere, either of growth or exercise. Shall there not be for that a resurrection? Is there, as the men of science tell us, is there an unseen universe into which myriads upon myriads of atoms pass in the ceaseless flow of matter, and is there no unseen universe to which the lord and master of matter goes? Is there a resurrection for molecules and not for memory, continuity for the unconscious and annihilation for the conscious? Does persistent and forceful nature work for life through all the lower stages and never fail, and then at the climax break down and work only for death? Does the unerring energy through countless ages pursue its conquering course of development, working through great processes of evolution, and with mighty, far-seeing laws aim at the preservation of the fittest, and then, having at such vast expenditure got the fittest, does the gigantic work break down, and all end, at last, in the *fiasco* of a grave?—*John Page Hopps* (*Beside the Still Waters*).

To respect the person of woman in her weakness, of the citizen in his poverty, of the humblest man in his own inability to protect his rights,—this is the triumph of public morality, of law and social freedom. Is this blessed, elevating, ennobling principle, which really makes the *person* of man sacred, not an irresistible voice in defence of the precious significance and prophecy of personality? Will God, who planted this principle, allow the mere death of the body to loosen the very centralizing principle of man's soul? Will his moral and intellectual faculties disperse into thin air as the gases fly when the bubble bursts, or will that sacred polarity of his being hold them to his central, self-conscious essence, and continue to clothe his Ego, himself, in their beautiful spiritual folds? I cannot doubt what the answer of a true philosophy must be. But again, the sense of personality and faith in immortality have been inseparably connected and proportioned to each other. A weak sense of personality, a weak feeling of right and duty, a weak feeling of responsibility, leave a weak hold upon, a feeble longing for, a doubtful or apathetic state of mind in regard to, immortality. A powerful sense of personal rights and duties is equivalent to a strong sense of personality. And this sense has always gone with the thirst, expectation, and prophecy of immortality.—*Dr. Henry W. Bellows* (*Christian Register*, March 27, 1880).

These " truths that wake to perish never " remind us of Mr. Collyer's boyhood neighbor of Rydal Mount : —

> O joy that in our embers
> Is something that doth live,
> That nature yet remembers
> What was so fugitive!
> The thought of our past years in me doth breed
> Perpetual benediction. Not indeed
> For that which is most worthy to be blest,
> Delight and liberty, the simple creed
> Of childhood, whether busy or at rest,
> With new-fledged hope still fluttering in his breast,—
> Not for these I raise
> The song of thanks and praise,
> But for those obstinate questionings
> Of sense and outward things,
> Fallings from us, vanishings,
> Blank misgivings of a creature
> Moving about in worlds not realized,.
> High instincts before which our mortal nature
> Did tremble like a guilty thing surprised ;
> But for these first affections,
> These shadowy recollections,
> Which, be they what they may,
> Are yet the fountain light of all our day,
> Are yet a master light of all our seeing,
> Uphold us, cherish, and have power to make
> Our noisy years seem moments in the being
> Of the eternal silence ; truths that wake
> To perish never;
> Which neither listlessness, nor mad endeavor,
> Nor man, nor boy,
> Nor all that is at enmity with joy,
> Can utterly abolish or destroy!
> Hence, in a season of calm **weather**,
> Though inland far we be,
> Our souls have sight of that immortal sea
> Which brought us hither ;
> Can in a moment travel thither,
> And see the children sport upon the shore,
> And hear the mighty waters rolling evermore.
>
> *William Wordsworth (Intimations of Immortality,* ix *).*

The soul is never satisfied with any explanation of its future which, at any present moment, it can fully understand. We desire a future which can be fully comprehended only in that future. We must grow to the revelation. The moment it is all made plain, it becomes substantially like the present or the past, and all progress is precluded. We lose interest in what is to come. We wander ever after upon a level plain, with no mysterious heights to inspire us and lead us on.— *J. Frederick Dutton.*

Consolation for the death of Louis Blanc must be sought in the belief of his immortality; for the law of heaven wills that such men shall live forever. If a light has spent itself, the source of that light is not quenched.— *Victor Hugo.*

As to the comparative weight of the foregoing arguments, it has been said: —

The Platonic idea that the soul is an indivisible unit has played a distinguished part in the argument for immortality, as a ground for the belief. So, too, has the idea that the soul is immaterial and therefore indestructible. But the immortal hope has seldom taken counsel with either of these ideas. Men "beholding the bright countenance of truth in the quiet and still air of delightful studies" have strengthened their belief by these considerations; but men and women who have seen the light of life go out in faces strong or fair have nourished their hopes upon a different diet. No indivisible unit was the man or woman or the little child whom we forever miss — nay, but a unit infinitely divisible, having for us an infinite variety of gleaming lights and tender shadows. No immaterial subject was it that we loved and that we hope to.

> Communion in spirit? Forgive me,
> But I who am earthy and weak
> Would give all my incomes from dreamland
> For the touch of her hand on my cheek.

Over against the philosopher's indivisible unit and his soul's immateriality, the natural man has set such poems as that little one [by Adaline D. T. Whitney] which sings: —

> God does not send us strange flowers every year;
> When the spring winds blow o'er the pleasant places,
> The same dear things lift up the same fair faces,
> The violet is here.
>
> It all comes back,— the odor, grace, and hue,
> Each sweet relation of its life repeated;
> Nothing is lost, no looking-for is cheated;
> It is the thing we knew.
>
> So after the death-winter it will be:
> God will not put strange sights in heavenly places;
> The old love will look out from the old faces;
> Veilchen, I shall have thee.
>
> *John W. Chadwick* (*The Commonwealth*, 1882).

There is a great mistake in teaching children that they have souls. They ought to be taught that they have bodies, and that their bodies die, but they themselves live on.

> Weep not for death!
> 'Tis but a fever stilled,
> A pain suppressed, a fear at rest,
> A solemn hope fulfilled.
> The moonshine on the slumbering deep
> Is scarcely calmer — wherefore weep?
>
> Weep not for death!
> The fount of tears is sealed;
> Who knows how bright the inward light
> To those shut eyes revealed?
> Who knows what peerless love may fill
> The heart that seems so cold and still?

One of the sweetest passages in the Bible is this one: "Underneath are the everlasting arms." It is not often preached from; perhaps because it is felt to be so much richer and more touching than anything we ministers can say about it. But what a vivid idea of infancy is resting in arms which maternal love never allows to become weary. Sick-room experiences confirm the impression when we have seen a feeble mother or sister lifted from the bed of pain by the stronger ones of the household. In the case of our heavenly Father, the arms are felt but not seen. The invisible secret support comes to the soul in its hours of weakness or trouble; for God knoweth our feebleness, he remembers that we are but dust.— *Theodore L. Cuyler.*

Transported May!
Thou couldst not stay;
Who gave, took thee away.
Come, child, and whisper peace to me.
Say, must I wait, or come to thee?
I list to hear thy message clear.

"Cease, cease new grief to borrow!"
Last night I heard her say,
"For sorrow hath no morrow,
'Tis born of yesterday.
Translated thou shalt be,
My cloudless daylight see,
And bathe, as I, in fairest morrows endlessly."

A. Bronson Alcott.

I have no power to look across the tide,
To know, while here, the land beyond the river;
But this I know, I shall be God's forever.
So I can trust.

Anon.

And you shall shortly know that lengthened breath
Is not the sweetest gift God sends his friend,
And that sometimes the sable pall of death
Conceals the fairest boon his love can send.
If we could push ajar the gates of life,
And stand within, and all God's workings see,
We could interpret all this doubt and strife,
And for each mystery could find a key.

But not to-day. Then be content, poor heart!
God's plans, like lilies, pure and white unfold.
We must not tear the close-shut leaves apart,
Time will reveal the calyxes of gold.
And if, through patient toil, we reach the land
Where tired feet, with sandals loose, may rest,
When we shall clearly know and understand,
I think that we will say, "God knew the best!"

May Riley Smith.

We know in part; the other part
Is hid in God, and only shines
In points of glory on the heart
That moves toward him in Love's straight lines.

Benjamin F. Larrabee (Zion's Herald, 1878).

We see but dimly through the mists and vapors:
  Amid these earthly damps,
What seem to us but sad, funereal tapers,
  May be heaven's distant lamps.
There is no Death! What seems so is transition.
  This life of mortal breath
Is but a suburb of the life elysian,
  Whose portal we call Death.

. . . .

Thus do we walk with her, and keep unbroken
  The bond which nature gives,
Thinking that our remembrance, though unspoken,
  May reach her where she lives.
Not as a child shall we again behold her;
  For when, with raptures wild,
In our embraces we again enfold her,
  She will not be a child;
But a fair maiden in her Father's mansion,
  Clothed with celestial grace,
And beautiful with all the soul's expansion
  Shall we behold her face.

Henry W. Longfellow.

    When for me the silent oar
      Parts the silent river,
    And I stand upon the shore
      Of the strange forever,
    Shall I miss the loved and known?
    Shall I vainly seek mine own?

    Can the ties that make us here
      Know ourselves immortal
    Drop away like foliage sere
      At life's inner portal?
    What is holiest below
    Must forever live and grow.

    He who plants within our hearts
      All this deep affection,
    Giving when the form departs
      Fadeless recollection,
    Will but clasp the unbroken chain
    Closer when we meet again.

    Therefore dread I not to go
      O'er the silent river. . . .

*Lucy Larcom.**

---

* Set to a sweet German melody, in *The Sunnyside*, p. 102.

Chapter XLIV.

EXALTATION.

What Two Views as to Christ's Intendment concerning Heaven?

(1) THE localizing theory. (2) The evolutional.

The first — seeking to realize, materialize, or localize heaven — is expressed in the hymn said to be translated from a Latin one of the ninth century, first in 1616, and since variously, — a portion as follows: —

> Jerusalem, my happy home, ...
> O happy harbor of the saints,
> O sweet and pleasant soil!
> In thee no sorrow shall be found,
> No death, no care, no toil.
> Apostles, martyrs, prophets there
> In holy converse stand;
> And soon my saintly friends below
> Will join the glorious band.

The first view interprets the simile of the shepherd and goats,* as indicating a second advent of Christ, a day of judgment, and a segregation of the righteous and the wicked; so also as to the declaration † that they who are in their graves shall hear the voice of the Son of Man and shall come forth, they that have done good unto the resurrection of life, etc.

There is a suggestion in Dr. Thomas Young's *Natural Philosophy* that there may be a sphere of life, an order of existence, still material, as distinct from the purely spiritual, and yet possessed of some specific property, which distinguishes it from the matter of atomic constitution, of which our senses alone can take cognizance; there may be supersensible, yet not purely immaterial, existences.

Certain phenomena of the visible universe suggest the supposition of an unseen universe, related to the present, yet of a different kind or order, out of which came the things which appear, and into which they shall be dissolved, enriching it as they pass into it, — the new heavens

---

* Matt. xxv.   † John v., 29.

and the new earth of revelation.... They do not demonstrate its existence, for physical science never can prove the supersensible. — *Dr. Newman Smyth (Old Faiths in New Light,* p. 298).

When clouds which hid the sun all day minister to his last glory with colors of ineffable tint and brilliancy, it seems a proclamation that, come what will in a world of gloom and tempest, beauty and visible glory still exist for man, and are a sign of him who made them. We could live without the sunset, but its delight pleads with our spirit.— *Thomas Tyrwhitt.*

The second view is that the gospel writers (or redactors) colored some of the earlier utterances of Jesus with the lore of the current poetic literature of the day; for instance, the words, "an holy one coming down from heaven"; * also, "and many of them that sleep in the dust of the earth shall awake, some to everlasting life"; † also "the judgment was set and the books were opened." ‡ The doctrine of progress through this life and the next — of gradual abandonment to the Highest, and so a sharing of his perfection — has already been presented in the extract from a sermon by Rev. Herman Bisbee, § and in the passage from Mr. Emerson's essay on "Immortality." ‖

Dr. Wm. E. Channing says : —

As in the child we view the future man, so in man we are taught by the gospel to view the germ of the future angel. We are taught there is no height of excellence in the universe to which the human mind in the progress of eternity may not attain....

We shall be the same beings in heaven as on earth. We shall retain our present faculties. We shall probably, too, have bodies,— the eye to behold creation and receive its beauties, the ear to hear the voice of friendship and to receive the pleasures of harmony, and every sense refined and purified.—*Memoirs,* ii., pp. 22, 48.

In this regard, Dr. Emanuel Swedenborg's views ¶ were very like those of Dr. Channing. And so we keep appealing to the seers. What was remarked in the last chapter, of our grasping and hoarding every proof of immortality will apply to our yearnings for assurances of a blissful one. How every available analogy is watched and studied and cherished !

> In the leaves that blow and perish
> In the space of a single hour,
> As the loves that most we cherish
> Die like the frailest flower,—
> In the living things whose living
> Withers or ere they bloom,
> He reads of the great thanksgiving
> Which breathes from the open tomb.

---

* Dan. iv., 23. † Dan. xii., 2. ‡ Dan. vii., 10.
§ Chap. xlii , p. 228. ‖ Chap. xliii., p. 240. ¶ N. J. D., *n.* 224.

The bright spring leaves returning
  To the stem whence autumn's fell,
And the heart of summer burning
  To change the winter's spell,
The year that again repasses,
  The grain that again revives,
Are signs on the darkened glasses
  That bar and bound our lives.

I know how the glass must **darken**
  To my vision more and more,
When the weak ear strains to hearken,
  When the faint eye glazes o'er;
But the glass shall melt and shiver,
  Once kissed by the fighting breath,
And the light beyond the river
  Shine full in the face of Death.

Strong set in a strong affection,
  We look to the golden prime
When a mightier resurrection
  Shall burst on the doubts of Time;
And the thoughts of all the sages,
  Like the waves of the fretful main,
At the base of the Rock of Ages
  Shall foam and fume in vain.
          Herman Merrivale (The Spectator).

Shall I be left forgotten in the dust
When fate relenting lets the flower revive?
No! heaven's immortal spring shall yet arrive,
And man's majestic beauty bloom again,
Bright through the eternal year of love's triumphant reign.
          James Beattie.

  Like herb and flower, like sun and star,
    To gracious God akin;
  Still more beloved and nearer far,
    In spite of death and sin,
  And when the flesh shall pass away,
    My summer will begin.
          Angus Fairbairn.

'Twas sown in weakness here,
  'Twill there be raised in power;
That which was sown an earthly seed
  Shall rise a heavenly flower.
          Horace Bonar.

  I can but trust that good shall fall
    At last,— far off,— at last to all,
  And every winter change to spring. . . .
  The wish that of the living whole
    No life may fail beyond the grave,
    Derives it not from what we have
  The likest God within the soul?
          Alfred Tennyson (In Memoriam, liii.).

Faith views the tempest passing by,
Sees evening shadows quickly fly,
And all serene in heaven.
          William B. Tappan.

There is nae sorrow there,
There's neither cold nor care:
The day is aye fair, John,
In the land o' the leal.
Lady Carolina O. Nairne.

There joys unseen by mortal eyes
  Or reason's feeble ray,
In ever blooming prospect rise,
  Unconscious of decay.
Anne Steele.

How blest the sacred tie that binds
In union sweet according minds! . .
Nor shall the glowing flame expire
When droops at length frail nature's fire;
For they shall meet in realms above,
A heaven of joy, because of love.
Anna L. Barbauld.

My soul is full of whispered song,
  My blindness is my sight;
The shadows that I feared so long
  Are all alive with light.
The palace walls I almost see,
  Where dwells my Lord and King:
O grave, where is thy victory!
  O death, where is thy sting!
Alice Cary.

The oak strikes deeper as its boughs
  By furious blasts are driven;
So life's tempestuous storms the more
  Have fixed my heart in heaven.
Beyond this vale of tears
  There is a life above,
Unmeasured by the flight of years;
  And all that life is love.
James Montgomery.

There truth forever shines, and love forever burns.
Isaac Watts.

How brave a prospect is a traversed plain
  Where flowers and palms refresh the eye,
And days well spent like the glad east remain,
  Whose morning glories cannot die.
Henry Vaughan.

Oh, if no other boon were given
  To keep our hearts from wrong and stain,
Who would not try to win a heaven
  Where all we love shall live again!
Thomas Moore.

My sprightly neighbor gone before
To that unknown and silent shore,
Shall we not meet as heretofore
  Some summer morning?
When from the cheerful eyes a ray
Hath struck a bliss upon the day,
A bliss that will not go away,
  A sweet forewarning.
Charles Lamb.

Shalt thou not teach me in that calmer home
  The wisdom that I learned so ill in this,—
The wisdom which is love, till I become
  Thy fit companion in that land of bliss?
William C. Bryant.

If the fair face of violets should perish
  Before another springtime had its birth,
Could all the costly blooms that florists cherish
  Bring back its April beauty to the earth?

And so with souls we love: they pass and leave us;
  Time teaches patience at a bitter cost;
Yet all the new loves which the years may give us
  Fill not the heart-place aching for the lost.
                                                    Anon.

The shadows of death o'er my path have been sweeping;
  There are those who have loved me debarred from the day;
The green turf is bright where in peace they are sleeping,
  And on wings of remembrance my soul is away.
It is shut to the glow of this present existence,
  It hears from the Past a funereal strain;
And it eagerly turns to the high-seeming distance,
  Where the last blooms of earth will be garnered again;
Where no mildew the soft damask-rose cheek shall nourish,
  Where Grief bears no longer the poisonous sting;
Where pitiless Death no dark sceptre can flourish,
  Or stain with his blight the luxuriant spring.
              Willis Gaylord Clark (A Song of May).

I shall join the lost, the loved of earth, and meet each kindred breast,
Where the wicked cease from troubling, and the weary are at rest.
        Willis G. Clark (Last Prayer of Mary, Queen of Scots).

And we wept that one so lovely should have a life so brief;
Yet not unmeet it was that one like that young friend of ours,
So gentle and so beautiful, should perish with the flowers.
                                          William C. Bryant.

And glance to glance and hand to hand in greeting,—
  The past with all its fears,
  Its silence and its tears,
  Its lonely, yearning years,
Shall vanish in the moment of that meeting.
                                  Elizabeth Stuart Phelps.

Heaven is heavenly knowledge, love, and action. . . . The tragedies of life on earth, . . . persons are brought together by birth, by habit, and by natural affection, who yet do not meet intimately, who have no real intimacy of mind and heart. Perhaps the homes hereafter will be arranged according to deeper affinities than these. Those who belong to each other will come together. . . . It is the nature of Christian love to be able to come down in deeper sympathy with all below, as it ascends in fulness of life to loftier attainment above. . . . The mysteries of theologies are usually very poor things, very mean and small matters; but God's mysteries are grand and noble. They lift the soul to conceptions of something higher than this world can give; they open the golden gates of the great hereafter; they give us glimpses of the eternal city of God, wherein all the beauty and love of this life shall be transfigured into something higher:—

Upon the frontier of this shadowy land
  We pilgrims of eternal sorrow stand:
What realm lies forward with its happier store

Of forests green and deep,
    Of valleys hushed in sleep,
And lakes most peaceful?   'Tis the land of Evermore.
    Dr. J. F. Clarke (Common Sense in Religion, p. 27).

New born, I bless the waking hour;
    Once more, with awe, rejoice to be;
My conscious soul resumes her power,
    And springs, my guardian God, to thee. . . .

That deeper shade shall break away,
    That deeper sleep shall leave mine eyes;
Thy light shall give eternal day,
    Thy love the rapture of the skies.
                                    John Hawkesworth.

And yet, as angels in some brighter dreams
    Call to the soul when man doth sleep,
So some strange thoughts transcend our wonted themes,
    And into glory peep.
                                    Henry Vaughan.

            . . . Beyond
That belt of darkness still the years roll on
More gently, but with not less mighty sweep.
They gather up again and softly bear
All the sweet lives that late were overwhelmed
And lost to sight,—all that in them was good,
Noble, and truly great and worthy of love,—
The lives of infants and ingenuous youths,
Sages and saintly women, who have made
Their households happy,—all are raised and borne
By that great current in its onward sweep,
Wandering and rippling with caressing waves
Around green islands, fragrant with the breath
Of flowers that never wither.   So they pass
From stage to stage along the shining course
Of that fair river broadening like a sea.
As its smooth eddies curl along their way,
They bring old friends together; hands are clasped
In joy unspeakable; the mother's arms
Again are folded round the child she loved
And lost.   Old sorrows are forgotten now,
Or but remembered to make sweet the hour
That overpays them; wounded hearts that bled
Or broke are healed forever.   In the room
Of this grief-shadowed Present there shall be
A Present in whose reign no grief shall gnaw
The heart, and never shall a tender tie
Be broken,—in whose reign the eternal change
That waits on growth and action shall proceed
With everlasting concord hand in hand.
        William C. Bryant (The Flood of Years).

Here may thy storm-beat vessel safely ride;
    This is the port of rest from troublous toil,
The world's sweet inn from pain and wearisome turmoil.
                                    Edmund Spenser.

And there in Abraham's bosom — whatever it be which that bosom signifies — lives my sweet friend. For what other place is there for such a soul? — *St. Augustine.*

Finally, one who, after such a halo-cloud of witnesses, can lay no claim to be seer or psalmist, would fain add some testimony of his own, albeit a tiny mite,—a thought or two penned a quarter of a century ago in the album of a friend, in response to her challenge for "a chain of rhyme" upon the theme. "Labor for the meat which abideth unto eternal life."

> Time still, as he flies, brings increase to her truth,
> And gives to her mind what he steals from her youth.
> *Edward Moore.*
>
> Adieu! Adieu! 'twere hard to part,
>   If parting were forever,
> Nor whispered true the trusting heart,
>   " 'Tis but for time we sever";
> Nor a gentle voice once heard on earth
>   Had charmed the soul to cherish
> The pleasures choice of heavenly birth
>   Which never, never perish.
>
> Roam as we may to find delight
>   Amid the bowers of Beauty,
> Or work by day and watch by night
>   At the sceptre-beck of Duty,
> The soul will turn from riches reft
>   In passing Death's dire portal,
> And fondliest yearn for some sweets left
>   Enlinked with the immortal.
>
> In starlit space we proudly pause
>   The rapt and revelling Reason,
> And subtly trace the mystic laws
>   That guide each circling season;
> But when we seem by visioned sight
>   To have searched and known the Eternal,
> 'Tis but a gleam of the golden light
>   That glads the powers supernal.
>
> The dulcet symphonies we hear
>   In grove and grot resounding,
> The brooklet's hymn, the carol clear,
>   Sweet echo's voices bounding,
> The melody of human tongue,—
>   All harmonies terrestrial
> Are but the prelude of the song
>   Of choristers celestial.
>
> The fairy form that flits in grace
>   Through festive hall resplendent,
> The witching charm of woman's face,
>   With rose-tint wreath transcendent,
> Age shall transmute, the spell be o'er,
>   And dimmed the bright eye's flashes,
> As the fabled fruit of the Dead Sea shore
>   In the pilgrim's grasp is ashes.
>
> But the sunny cheer of Virtue meek
>   That shines through the spirit-keeper,
> Though time besere and blanch the cheek,
>   Shall lovelier glow and deeper;
> Aye, the mind may woo and the heart may cull
>   An Eden fading never,
> For the High, the True, the Beautiful,
>   Are wed to the soul forever.
> B. F. B.

Chapter XLV.

INTELLECTION, EMOTION, VOLITION.

Supplementary to the Teachings of Socrates, Plato, Christ, and Paul, what are the Four Principal Philosophical Theories of the Mind's Knowledge of God?

(1) THE Greek (" Aristotelian " or " Kantian "), (2) the German (or " Schellingian "), (3) the French (or " Cousinian "), and (4) the Scottish (or " Hamiltonian ").

It has been observed* that "man is a microcosm, ... the image of God," also † that the mental phenomena have been classified (by Stewart, Reid, etc.) under "the Intellect, the Sensibilities, and the Will." It may be useful in conclusion hereon briefly to append an historical summarization.

Aristotle (born B.C. 384) identifies the human with the divine mind, designating one as the absolute Form or Idea, the active Reason, or "Self-knowledge of Reason," and the other as the passive Reason. In deducing the *objective* elements in human knowledge, he arranged the *matter* of our thoughts in ten categories; namely, Substance, Quantity, Quality, Relation, Action, Passion, Place, Time, Posture, Habit.

Immanuel Kant (b. 1724), deducing the *subjective* elements, arranged the *forms* of our thoughts in three great faculties: (1) the Sensational perception, which gives the matter of our notions; (2) the Understanding, which gives the form; and (3) the pure Reason, which brings unity and connection to the whole exercise of the Understanding. His categories of Sensation are two, (1) Time and (2) Space: everything perceived must have a when and a where. His general categories of the Understanding are four, under each of which he has four sub-categories: under (1) Quantity, we have Unity, Plurality, and Totality; under (2) Quality, we have Affirmation, Negation, and Limitation; under (3) Relation, we have Substance, Causality, and Reciprocity; and under (4) Modality, we have Possi-

---

* *Ante*, chap. xl. † Chap. xix.

bility, Actuality, and Necessity The pure Reason, according as it is directed to substance, or to phenomena, or to the ideal of perfection, leads to the three irreducible ideas of (1) the Soul (the absolute subject), (2) the Universe (the totality of all phenomena), and (3) of God (the all-perfect essence).

Victor Cousin [Koozan] (b. 1792) would reduce all our thoughts to the two primitive ideas of (1) Action and (2) Being; the one giving the category of causality, the other of substance; the one implying the relative, the contingent, the particular, the phenomenal; the other implying the absolute, the necessary, the universal, the infinite. His third general category is the relation between the two former, or rather between their sub-categories, namely: Unity, Multiplicity; Absolute Space, Bounded Space; Absolute Existence, Dependent Existence; Eternity, Time; Infinite, Finite; Primary Cause, Secondary Cause; Substance, Phenomena; Mind, Thoughts; Beau-Ideal, Beau-Real; The Perfect, The Imperfect; Contraction, Expansion; Subject, Object.

René Descartes (b. 1596), having taken for the fundamental principle of his philosophy the fact that conscious being is postulated in thinking ("cogito, ergo sum"), John G. Fichte (b. 1762) developed a system based on two categories: (1) an absolute Affirmation: The Me is the Me, wherein the mind views itself as the absolute *subject;* and (2) an absolute Negation: The Not-me is not the same as the Me, wherein the mind views itself as *object.* Fichte died without completely deducing the absolute unity of thought and existence as attained in the infinite Being, leaving this doctrine of identity to be developed by his pupil, W. J. Schelling (b. 1775), who lays down three movements, or " Potencies ": (1) of Reflection, or the attempt of the Infinite to represent itself in the Finite; (2) of Subsumption, or the attempt the absolute makes, having embodied itself in the Finite, to return to the Infinite; and (3) of Reason ("Potenz der Vernunft"), the union or indifference point of the two former, wherein the expansive and attractive, the subjective and objective movements are blended.

George W. F Hegel (b. 1770) considered God to be the universal personality, which realizes itself in every human consciousness as so many separate thoughts of one eternal mind. God, therefore, is, in Hegel's philosophy, the whole process of thought, combining in itself the objective movement as seen in nature with the subjective as seen in logic, and fully realizing itself only in the universal spirit of humanity. He made pure self-existence answer to the Father, the objectifying of this pure existence answer to the *Logos prophorikos*, the **Son**, and the complete reunion of the two in the Church to answer to the **Spirit**. Indeed, his whole system is a more or less fanciful arrangement of threes.

Hegel's general division is: (1) **Logic**, (2) Philosophy of Nature, and (3) Philosophy of Mind. Logic embraces (1) Being, or Thought in its immediacy; (2) **Essence**, or Thought in its communication; and (3) **Notion**, or Thought in its regress, in which it forms a complete idea in itself.

Hegel considers Being under three categories: (1) Quality, having three sub-categories, — Being [" Seyn "], Existence [" Daseyn "], Independent existence [" Für-sich-seyn "]; (2) Quantity, having three sub-categories, — Pure Quantity, Divisible Quantity, and Degree; and (3) Measure (or Mass), the union of quality and quantity. He considers Essence under three categories: (1) Ground of Existence, embracing Pure notions of essence, Essential existence, and Thing; (2) Phenomenon, embracing Phenomenal world, Matter [" Inhalt "] and Form and Relation [" Verhältniss "]; and (3) Reality, or Union of the two, embracing Relation of Substance, Relation of Cause and Action and Reaction. He considers Notion under three categories (1) Subjective Notion, embracing Notion as such [" Begriff "], Judgment [" **Urtheil** "], and Inference [" Schluss "]; (2) Object, embracing Mechanical **powers**, chemical powers, and Design [" Teleologie "]; (3) Idea, embracing Life, Intelligence [" Erkennen "], and absolute Idea.

Hegel's second general division, Philosophy of Nature, comprehends three categories: (1) Mechanics, (2) Physics, and (3) Organism, each embracing three sub-categories. His third general division, Philosophy of Mind, comprehends three categories: (1) Mind viewed subjectively, under three sub-categories, Anthropology, Psychology, and Will; (2) **Mind** viewed objectively under Jurisprudence, Morals, and Politics; and (3) Absolute Mind, under three sub-categories, Æsthetics, Religion, Philosophy.

Thus, it will be seen that Hegel's method — the " genetic " he terms it — is the developing method, termed by Plato, in the sixth book of the *Republic*, the " dialectic." As Prof. W. T. Harris remarked in his Concord lecture, July 27, 1881 : " The genetic method differs from the inductive in the fact that it recognizes universal and necessary principles as the basis of empirical experience and of the phenomena of observation. Ordinary induction professes to arrive at general results which are not seen as necessary and universal, but only as 'invariable experience.' The genetic method differs from the deductive method in the fact that it deals with the world of experience,— the world of man and the world of nature,— and seeks to find in the objects which it investigates the ultimate rational principles which are presupposed."

Sir William Hamilton has reduced the philosophical hypotheses, which have obtained respecting our knowledge of the absolute or unconditioned, to four distinct heads: —

(1) *The Absolute is altogether inconceivable*, every notion we have of it being simply a *negation* of that which characterizes finite and conditioned existence. This opinion Hamilton himself holds in common with the English and Scottish schools of modern times.

(2) *The Absolute, though not an object of real knowledge, yet exists subjectively within our consciousness as a regulative principle.* Thus, Kant believed that pure Reason necessarily gives rise to the *notion* of the infinite and unconditioned, which notion we view under the threefold type of the soul, the universe, and the Deity; but he did not admit the objective reality of these conceptions. He regarded them merely as personifications of our own subjective laws or processes.

(3) *The Absolute cannot be comprehended in consciousness and reflection; but it can be gazed upon by a higher faculty, that of intellectual intuition.* This is Schelling's doctrine.

(4) *The Absolute can be grasped by reason, and brought within the compass of our real consciousness.* This is the theory of Cousin.

Concerning these four theories,— the Scottish, or Hamiltonian, the Aristotelian, or Kantian, the German, and the French,— Mr. J. D. Morell says: —

We cannot divest our minds of the belief that there is something *positive* in the glance which the human soul casts upon the world of eternity and infinity. Whether we rise to the contemplation of the Absolute through the medium of the true, the beautiful, or the good, we cannot imagine that our highest conceptions of these terminate in darkness, in a total negation of all knowledge. So far from this, there seem to be flashes of light, ineffable it may be, but still real, which envelop the soul in a lustre all divine, when it catches glimpses of *infinite* truth, *infinite* beauty, and *infinite* excellence. The mind, instead of plunging into a total eclipse of all intellection, when it rises to this elevation, seems rather to be dazzled by a too great effulgence; yet still the light is real light, although to any but the strongest vision the effect may be to *blind* rather than to illume. It is not by negations that men are governed, but it is before the idea of eternity and infinity that our fiercest humanity is softened and subdued.—

Historical and Critical View of Speculative Philosophy in Europe, Nineteenth Century, p. 656.

And here, very pertinently and instructively, may be appended a brief, if not less abstruse, comparison of the more ancient beliefs upon the relation of God to the human soul, particularly Hindu, Babylonian, Egyptian, and Hebrew: —

The most spiritual portion of the Hindu sacred books teach the existence of one invisible God whom they call Brahm. They make no images of him, and build no temples for his worship. His name is never uttered by a pious Hindu. None of their traditions represent him as incarnated in any form, because they believe him to be utterly above human comprehension, and altogether incapable of the slightest change in his existence. Nature is the inferior passive portion of him. All things emanate from him; all is he, and all returns to him. His action upon nature and upon human souls is through a variety of spirits, presiding over the planets, the elements, and all the forces of nature. All in the scale of being are emanations from him in successive gradations. The highest of these emanations are Brahma, the Creator, Vishnu, the Preserver, and Siva, the Destroyer, who is likewise the reproducer of forms. . . . Genesa, god of wisdom, is greatly revered. They never commence any important business without offering him flowers or sprinkling his image with oil.— *L. Maria Child* (*Progress of Religious Ideas*, I., p. 10).

Every ancient nation of which any historical records remain believed in one Invisible Being, the Centre and Source of all things. Orientals conceived of him as inactive, serenely contemplating the glory of his own essence, radiating from himself all the vitality of the universe by inherent necessity, not by any exercise of his will, having no superintendence over creation, no interest in the affairs of men. These views perhaps originated partly in the prevailing Asiatic notions that anything like activity or labor was degrading to the character of a monarch. But a much stronger influence doubtless proceeded from the general idea that evil was inherent in matter. The human soul was unwilling to admit that the Supreme Being could be in any way connected with evil. Perceiving the material world to be full of apparent evils, men inferred that it could not have been produced by the one pure essence. Consequently, they imagined that a great Spirit or Power emanated from the Eternal One, and by the agency of this second god worlds were created. Hindus named this first emanation Brahma; Egyptians, Amun; Persians, Ormuzd; all regarded him as the Creator.

The religion of the Hebrews differed from other prior and contemporary systems in representing the One Source of Being as himself the Creator and Sustainer of all things, by his own direct agency and the active exertion of his will. But in later times, after their captivity in Babylon and their settlement in Alexandria, when Oriental, Egyptian, and Grecian theories became mixed with the written doctrines ascribed to Moses, they also taught that God created the world by the agency of a second power whom their writers called "the First Adam," "the Lord of heaven," "the Wisdom of God," "the Word of God," "the first begotten Son of God," "the Esteemed the Same as God." ...

Man seems to have made God after his own image. Hindus invested Brahm with their own love of contemplation and repose. The Chinese Chang-ti was exactly according to their pattern of a wise and beneficent emperor. The Jehovah of the Hebrews was jealous of his own pre-eminence, great in slaughter of Philistines, stern but placable to his chosen people. The Greeks, lively and intellectual, conceived of Deity as an active, enterprising, intriguing, and amorous being. Philosophers thought of him as the mind of the universe. Socrates and Plato rose to the idea of a Universal Father.... It seems likely that the title of God and the Devil [D'Evil] applied to the great contending Powers, supposed to sway the universe, originated in the old Persian ideas concerning Ormuzd, the Prince of Good, and Arimanes of Evil.

There was universally a sacred and mystical number representing Deity in his completeness. One of the most ancient symbols in Hindustan and Egypt was a triangle with an eye in the centre, to represent the All-seeing. Hindus represented their three great gods in one image. Egyptian deities were usually in triads. Plato taught a Trinity of divine attributes, Goodness, Wisdom, and pervading Life. Cabalists appear to have expressed the same ideas in Hebrew style, when they wrote of Jehovah, the Wisdom of Jehovah, and the Habitation of Jehovah. Hindus, Egyptians, Platonists, and Cabalists, supposing man to be an image of God, all represented him as a triune being consisting of a rational soul and a material body. In all countries, philosophers and mystics expressed more or less vaguely that the Deity was one in three.

It was a very prevalent theory, conspicuous in various religions, that the ideas pre-existing in Deity took form by the utterance of a word. In Persian and Hebrew sacred books, it is declared that God spoke, and light sprang into existence, followed successively by all the other objects of creation. Persians called this word Honover, and invoked him as the great Primal Spirit. Hebrews called the word Memra, and regarded him as a representative of Jehovah to the mind of man. With Hindus, the creative Word was Aum, called Om. They believed it included within itself all the qualities of Brahma, and reverenced it next to him. The general idea evidently was that the Word existed with God from all eternity, and when spoken became a glorious form, the aggregate embodiment of all the divine ideas, including them all within itself, and thus by development becoming God's great agent in the work of creation....

Hindus, Persians, Hebrews, Greeks. all believed in a great company of spirits, who mediated between man and the higher deities. They carried up the prayers of mortals, and brought down blessings in return. Generally, some one spirit was supposed to be pre-eminent in the kindly offices of intercession and propitiation. Persians named Mithras "the Mediator." Cabalists called the angel Metraton the mediator between God and man. They said he led the children of Israel through the wilderness and gave the law to Moses. Platonized Jews in Alexandria described the Logos or Word the "Mediator and Intercessor between God and man." They supposed he appeared under various angelic forms to the patriarchs, that he dictated to Moses, and inspired the prophets; for it had become a universal idea that no man had seen God at any time.

The same tendencies which made men try to bring the Creator nearer to them, by the intervention of intermediate agents, naturally led them to worship the mediums in preference to the higher Deity, whom they represented and served. Thus, Brahma gave place to Vishnu in various forms; Osiris eclipsed Amun; Mithras superseded Ormuzd; and Apollo received much more worship than Jupiter....

In most nations, a belief prevailed that the return of the Golden Age would be brought about by the advent of a just and holy man, through whose agency all discords, moral and physical, would be harmonized, and the world restored to order. Hindus believed such a personage would appear, and bring all nations under guidance of the Brahmins. Chinese expected a holy one would appear on their sacred mountain, and bring all the world into subjection to the Chinese empire. Persians believed such awaiting comer would convert the whole world to the religion of Zoroaster. The Hebrews had the strongest assurance that a Prince and Deliverer would come in the royal line of King David, who would exterminate all nations and individuals, except those who adopted the Jewish religion....

Hindus, Persians, Greeks, and Jews, all supposed sinners would be subjected to purification by fire. Persians believed that all spirits, even the Devil himself, would finally do homage to goodness, and thus become happy. Jews supposed the wicked of their own nation would be tormented with fire hereafter, but merely for purposes of purification. At the end of the world, they would be summoned to rise from the dead, and share in the bliss of the Messiah's kingdom. They supposed that other nations would have no resurrection....

At a very early period, the ascribing of evil to the imperfection of matter introduced civil war into the house of life, by teaching men to regard the body as an enemy to the soul. Passions and instincts given for usefulness and enjoyment were considered spiritual snares. A healthy body and a good appetite were hindrances in the way of holiness; and to feel sexual attraction was yielding to the instigation of the Devil. In order to become angels, men tormented their poor material forms. They reduced themselves to skeletons by midnight watchings and prolonged fasts; they scourged themselves till the blood flowed; they tore their flesh with hooks and burned it with fire. They spent their wealth in sacrifices and their time in prayers, to atone for the sin of having any bodily wants. From this horror of natural instincts arose the traditions of various nations that their holy teachers were born of virgins, this being necessary to disconnect them with the alleged impurity of human passions....

The idea of one representative of evil, named Satan, did not appear in Jewish writings till after their residence in Babylon. A host of inferior evil spirits swarmed in all religions, and were everywhere supposed to produce diseases by taking possession of human bodies. Sudden and violent attacks of illness, such as insanity or fits, were peculiarly attributed to their agency. It was the general belief that they could be expelled by invoking a good spirit or uttering a holy name. In all the ancient nations, people were in the constant habit of resorting to priests and sanctified men to cast out demons by reciting sacred words. And they nearly all had traditions concerning spirits who rebelled against the highest Deity, were expelled from paradise, and kept chained in lower regions. . . .

One feature common to ancient nations was to deem unpremeditated speech prophetic, especially so the exclamations of insane people. It was a common thing to excite prophetic frenzy by music. The Grecian Pythoness, before she uttered oracles, inhaled a kind of vapor which put her into a nervous and bewildered state. Various records tell of men who prophesied in trances; who could read the interior thoughts of others; whose souls occasionally left their bodies for a while, and at such times could give information concerning the most distant places. Of the oracles of the Sibyls, Heraclitus (B.C. 500) said, "Their unadorned, crudest words, spoken with inspired mouth, reached through a thousand years." . . .

The Hindu Puranas declare that a crocodile swallowed Krishna, and cast him forth unhurt. They also tell of a fish that discoursed with Menu, as the Hebrew books of a serpent that talked with Eve. . . . In the childhood of the world, men understood little and believed much. If a hail-storm dispersed their enemies, Hebrews said Jehovah "cast down great stones from heaven." (Josh. x., 11.) If a man died from exposure to the sun, Greeks verily believed Apollo had shot him with his golden arrow, in punishment for some offence. When any person was struck dead by lightning, Scandinavians believed that Thor, God of Thunder, was angry with him, and had hurled his hammer at his head. . . . Had those men of the olden time witnessed the process of taking a daguerreotype or photograph, they would have believed that it was actually done by the Spirit of the Sun, and that he had illuminated the minds of men, so that they understood how to prepare the plate and concentrate the rays. . . . In order that inspiration from superior powers might flow into their minds, undisturbed by outward obstructions, they retired to the solitude of a cave, as Numa did, or drew nearer to the Divine Presence, as they supposed, by ascending to the summit of mountains, as did Zoroaster and Moses. . . . Ourselves environed by wonders which intellect is helpless to explain, which science carries only a very few steps back toward the Primal Cause, can we marvel that men in the childhood of the world verily believed all things miraculous? . . . Do we in reality know much better than they did what Life *is*? . . . We must away with paintings and poetry, or we are all idolaters. . . .

Sir James Forbes, in his *Oriental Memoirs*, describes a Brahmin

who divined what an English lady, resident in India, was thinking of her son, whom she had left in his native land. He told her what the young man was doing, and predicted what he would do; and, though it was quite different from her own anticipations, it proved as he had said. It is recorded of Egyptian priests that they cured the diseased by passing their hands over them. Balaam is said to have prophesied "in a trance, having his eyes open." Hyrcanus, the Jewish prince and high priest, told of a distant victory gained by his son at the very moment that it occurred. Magicians and wizards were accused of travelling through the air, of being in two places at once, of telling the past, and reading the thoughts of others. The soul of Hermotimus, the Greek philosopher, frequently left his body apparently lifeless, and wandered all over the earth, bringing tidings from remote regions and foretelling futurity. The priestess of the Delphic oracle perceived that Crœsus was boiling flesh in a covered brass vessel, though the secret was known only to himself, and he was hundreds of miles distant. That these phenomena were noticed by the ancients seems to be indicated by their general theory that man was endowed with an intermediate substance between his rational soul and his body. They sometimes called it an aerial body and sometimes a sensuous soul; and they described it as having *all* of sensation in each and every part of it, as "all eye, all ear, and all taste."
— *L. Maria Child* (*Progress of Religious Ideas*, II., 176).

Thus, well illustrated and demonstrated by Mrs. Child, appropriately may the text of Mrs. Cross, prefacing the beginning of our review,—

> We had not walked
> But for Tradition. We walk evermore
> To higher paths, by brightening Reason's lamp,—

become

THE END.

I have gathered a posie of other men's flowers, and nothing but the thread that binds them is mine own.—
Michael de Montaigne.

APPENDIX.

Page 17.

We are eclectics in accepting the teaching of Scripture. We distinguish between its lower and its higher thought; between its teachings which are worthy of all acceptation and those which the rational mind is compelled to reject as unworthy and false. We endeavor to separate the chaff from the wheat, and garner carefully the treasure that remains. We find in the Bible sayings of the sublimest wisdom and of the highest and purest truth; and often, in juxtaposition with these, we have the utterances of human passion, hate, vindictiveness, partiality, and injustice, which it is impossible to accept as of divine warrant or authority. We find deeds recorded, said to be committed some at the express command of God, others with his sanction, which no ingenuity of defence can save from utter condemnation. It is preposterous to say we must accept the whole as of the same character and quality. That would be for our minds to abdicate the function of rational judgment. It would be to silence the divine voice within us, to extinguish the light of the inner eye, and grope in wilful blindness.—*Charles F. Beard (London Inquirer)*.

You will never convince a man of ordinary sense by overbearing his understanding.—*Samuel Maunder*.

Page 19.

They are ill discoverers that think there is no land when they can see nothing but sea. . . . He that will believe only what he can fully comprehend must have a very long head or a very short creed. . . . Because it is silly to believe everything, there are some so wondrous wise as to believe nothing.—*Samuel Maunder*.

Page 76.

When fortune comes smiling, she often designs the most mischief. . . . When fortune caresses a man too much, she is apt to make a fool of him.—*Samuel Maunder*.

> Fear ills, though not yet felt: when fortune smiles,
> Be doubly cautious, lest destruction come.
>
> *Sophocles (Philoctetes)*.

Page 88.

> He still remembered that he once was young,
> His easy presence checked no decent joy.
>
> *John Armstrong.*

It has been questioned whether there be recorded any instance of a sally of humorous pleasantry on the part of Jesus or Paul. It seems hardly safe to predicate much upon the meagre statement in Luke xiii., 32, as to the reply to the Pharisees, calling Antipas a fox. Paul's playful appeal to Philemon's magnanimity (Phil. 19) has been adduced as a model of nice humor. See *The Bible for Learners*, vol. iii., p. 638.

Page 89.

The most glorious exploits do not always furnish us with the clearest discoveries of virtue or vice in men. Sometimes, a matter of less moment, an expression or a jest, informs us better of their characters and inclinations than the most famous sieges, the greatest armaments, or the bloodiest battles whatsoever.— *Plutarch.*

Page 90.

> But midst the crowd, the hum, the shock of men,
> To hear, to see, to feel, and to possess,
> And roam along, the world's tired denizen,
> With none to bless us, none whom we can bless;
> Minions of splendor shrinking from distress!
> None that with kindred consciousness endued,
> If we were not, would seem to smile the less
> Of all that flattered, followed, sought, and sued:
> This is to be alone; this, this is solitude.
>
> *Byron (Childe Harold).*

But if there be "none to bless us, none whom we can bless," we may generally charge the misfortune to our own misspent life. Poor Byron! Alas! few can assume to hurl at him a preachment upon his deferring, until so nigh the Missolonghi scene, to ask himself : —

> Wouldst thou from sorrow find a sweet relief?
> Rouse to some work of high and holy love,
> And thou an angel's happiness shalt prove.
>
> *Carlos Wilcox.*

Page 91.

The greatest of all faults is to believe we have none. . . . We never yet knew a man disposed to scorn the humble, who was not himself a fair object of scorn to the humblest.— *Samuel Maunder.*

Page 119.

The first step to virtue is to love virtue in another.— *Samuel Maunder.*

Page 133.

> Remember me, I pray, but not
>   In Flora's gay and blooming hour,
> When every brake hath found its note,
>   And sunshine smiles in every flower;
> But when the falling leaf is sere,
>   And withers sadly from the tree,
> And o'er the ruins of the year
>   Cold autumn weeps, remember me.
>
> *Edward Everett.*

> ... Inward turn
> Each thought and every sense,
> For sorrow lingers from without,
> Thou canst not charm it thence,
> But all attuned the soul may be
> Unto a deathless melody. — *Elizabeth O. Smith.*

Page 134.
Sophocles being asked what harm he would wish to his enemy, answered, "That he may love where he is not fancied."

The intoxication of anger, like that of the grape, shows us to others, but hides us from ourselves.— *Samuel Maunder.*

Page 136.
If woman lost us Eden, such as she alone restores it.— *John G. Whittier.*

Women are a new race, recreated since the world received Christianity.— *Henry W. Beecher.*

There is a woman at the beginning of all great things.— *Alphonse de Lamartine.*

Woman is the Sunday of man; not his repose only, but his joy, the salt of his life.— *Jules Michelet.*

A beautiful woman is a practical poet; taming her savage mate, planting tenderness, hope, and eloquence in all whom she approaches. — *Ralph W. Emerson.*

Misfortune sprinkles ashes on the head of the man, but falls like dew on the head of the woman, and brings forth germs of strength of which she herself had no conscious possession.— *Anna C. Mowatt.*

True liberty has no enemy so formidable as licentiousness. ... The licentious never love. ... They that marry where they do not love are likely to love where they do not marry. ... He who triumphs over a woman would over a man — if he durst; hence, he is both fool and coward. ... "Throw not a stone into the well from which thou drinkest."— *Samuel Maunder.*

Page 137.
Despise trifling affronts, and they will vanish. A little water will put out a fire, which blown up would burn a city.— *Samuel Maunder.*

Page 138.
Make method your slave, but be not a slave to method. ... Hasty conclusions are the mark of a fool. ... Precipitation is the ruin of the young; delay, the ruin of the old. ... The young are slaves to novelty; the old to custom.— *Samuel Maunder.*

> I am not old, ...
> For in my heart a fountain flows,
> And round it pleasant thoughts repose,
> And sympathies and feelings high
> Spring like the stars on evening sky. — *Park Benjamin.*

> Half of the ills we hoard within our hearts
> Are ills because we hoard them.
>
> *Bryan W. Proctor (Mirandola).*

Page 140.
Every Homer has his Zoilus; and every Zoilus is remembered only to be despised.— *Samuel Maunder.*

Page 141.
As the baggage is to the army, so is riches to virtue: it cannot well be spared nor left behind, but it hinders the march.— *Samuel Maunder.*

Page 142.
Dive not too deep in pleasure; for there is a sediment at the bottom that renders it noxious and impure.— *Samuel Maunder.*

> Nor need we power or splendor,
>   Wide hall or lordly dome:
> The good, the true, the tender,—
>   These form the wealth of home.
>
> *Sarah J. Hale.*

Page 147.
> Let all that now divides us remove and pass away,
> Like shadows of the morning before the blaze of day.
> Let all that now unites us more sweet and lasting prove,
> A closer bond of union in a blest land of love.
>
> *Jane Borthwick.*

Page 157.
> For those who shun the glare of day,
>   There's a composing power,
> That meets them on their lonely way,
>   In the still air, the sober ray,
>   Of this religious hour.
>
> *John Pierpont.*

Page 161.
> The harp at Nature's advent strung
>   Has never ceased to play;
> The song the stars of morning sung
>   Has never died away.
>
> The blue sky is the temple's arch;
>   Its transept, earth and air;
> The music of its starry march,
>   The chorus of a prayer.
>
> So Nature keeps the reverent frame
>   With which her years began;
> And all her signs and voices shame
>   The prayerless heart of man.
>
> *John G. Whittier.*

Page 171.
> The healing of his seamless dress
>   Is by our beds of pain;
> We touch him in life's throng and press,
>   And we are whole again.
>
> *Anon.*

Page 172.

It will be pertinent and instructive to compare two or three cases of death-bed transfiguration, where there was no adequate *physiological* solution; not cases, which are very common, presenting symptoms of cerebral derangement, where some definite object, form, or face appears to be seen. The first, narrated by Frances P. Cobbe, is the case of "a refined, highly educated boy," fourteen years old:—

He was sitting propped up in bed, and had been looking rather sadly at the bright sunshine playing on the trees outside his open window for some time. He had turned away from this scene however, and was facing the end of the room, where there was nothing whatever but a closed door, when all in a moment the whole expression of his face changed to one of the most wondering rapture, which made his half-closed eyes open to their utmost extent, while his lips parted with a smile of perfect ecstasy. It was impossible to doubt that some glorious sight was visible to him; and, from the movement of his eyes, it was plain that it was not one, but many objects on which he gazed; for his look passed slowly away from end to end of what seemed to be vacant wall before him, going back and forward, with ever-increasing delight manifested in his whole aspect. His mother then asked him, if what he saw was some wonderful sight beyond the confines of this world, to give her a token that it was so by pressing her hand. He at once took her hand and pressed it meaningly, giving thereby an intelligent affirmative to her question, though unable to speak. As he did so, a change passed over his face, his eyes closed, and in a few minutes he was gone!— *The Peak in Darien* (*The Riddle of Death*), p. 257.

The second case is that of a lady of middle age:—

Her death, though momentarily expected from cardiac disease, was not announced or preceded by the usual anæsthesia of the dying. During the night, when awake, her mental action was perfect. She conversed a few minutes before dying, as pleasantly and intelligently as ever. There was *no stupor, delirium, strangeness, or moribund symptom indicating cerebral disturbance.* Her cardiac symptoms alone foreshadowed the great change. After saying a few words, she turned her head upon her pillow as if to sleep, then, unexpectedly turning it back, a glow, brilliant and beautiful exceedingly, came into her features; her eyes, opening, sparkled with singular vivacity; at the same moment, with a tone of emphatic surprise and delight, she pronounced the name of the earthly being nearest and dearest to her; and then propping her head upon her pillow, as unexpectedly as she had looked up, her spirit departed to God who gave it. The conviction forced upon my mind, that something departed from her body at that instant rupturing the bonds of flesh, was stronger than language can express.— *Dr. Edward H. Clarke, Visions: A Study of False Sight* (*Pseudopia*), p. 277.

A case occurring at North Danville, Vt., in July, 1838, and published in the *North Star*, Danville. was that of John P. Weeks, who, after lying several minutes without breath or pulsation, opened his eyes, and with glowing features averred that he had been in the other world, had viewed a lovely landscape of grass and flowers, and had been told that he must return to earth and spend more years in religious activity. To the surprise of his physician and friends, he forthwith recovered. He died in 1882.

In cases where the departing person seemed to gaze with interest and delight, and a transfigured countenance, upon something,— whether some strange beauty, as of a radiant glory, or an angelic group, or sainted friends, no one present could tell, and there was no revealing sign,— silence, surprise, wonder, and rapt gazing would be natural. And as the writer last quoted remarks: —

There would be no revival of brain cells, stamped with earthly memories and scenes, but something seen, of which the brain had received no antecedent impression, and of which the Ego had formed no conception. . . . His features would be transfigured, and those around would be amazed, perhaps appalled, at the sight, as some fishermen were, two thousand years ago, upon a mountain in Galilee, by the transcendent glory of a familiar face. In Correggio's "Notte," the light which illuminates the group around the infant Jesus proceeds from the face of the Christ-child, who, reposing on his mother's lap, unconsciously baptizes all with heavenly beauty. Such should, and such must be, the ineffable expression of transfigured humanity upon the features of whoever gets a sight of heaven, before he has left the earth.— *Visions, etc.*, p. 278.

Page 178.
He that can look the other world in the face has nothing to fear.— *Samuel Maunder.*

Page 186.
He that eyes a providence shall always have a providence to eye.— *Samuel Maunder.*

> I have led
> A life too stirring for those vague beliefs
> That superstition builds in solitude.
> *Letitia E. Landon.*

Page 197.
A study of some of the phenomena of pseudopia and pseudotia will render more clear the ideational theory of the record of the resurrection of the body of Jesus. A good illustrative case of false seeing, though without false hearing, is that of Lord Brougham, who, in his autobiography, narrates that (in England), after conversing with Stuart (with whom he had

travelled in Sweden) on immortality, etc., having become severely chilled, he took a bath, which being too hot caused a congestion of the brain approaching apoplexy: —

After I left the High School, I went with G., my most intimate friend, to attend the classes in the University. There was no divinity class; but we frequently in our walks discussed and speculated upon . . a future state. This question and the possibility, I will not say of ghosts walking, but of the dead appearing to the living, were subjects of much speculation; and we actually committed the folly of drawing up an agreement, *written with our blood*, to the effect that whichever of us died the first should appear to the other, and thus solve any doubts we had entertained of the "life after death." After we had finished our classes at the college, G. went to India, having got an appointment there in the civil service. He seldom wrote to me, and after the lapse of a few years I had almost forgotten him. Moreover, his family having little connection with Edinburgh, I seldom saw or heard anything of them, or of him through them, so that all the old school-boy intimacy had died out, and I had nearly forgotten his existence. I had taken, as I have said, a warm bath; and while lying in it, and enjoying the comfort of the heat after the late freezing I had undergone, I turned my head round, looking toward the chair on which I had deposited my clothes, as I was about to get up out of the bath. On the chair sat G., looking calmly at me. How I got out of the bath I know not; but, on recovering my senses, I found myself sprawling on the floor. The apparition, or whatever it was, that had taken the likeness of G. had disappeared. The vision produced such a shock that I had no inclination to talk about it, even to Stuart, but the impression it made upon me was too vivid to be easily forgotten; and so strongly was I affected by it that I have here written down the whole history with the date, December 19. . . . [Sixty years later.] (E. Brougham, Oct. 16, 1862.) I have just been copying from my journal the account of this strange dream: *certissima mortis imago!* And now to finish the story begun about sixty years since. Soon after my return to Edinburgh, there arrived a letter from India announcing G.'s death, and stating that he had died on the 19th of December! — *The Life and Letters of Henry Lord Brougham, written by himself,* New York, 1871, vol. i., p. 146.

Whereupon Dr. Edward H. Clarke comments: —

The cells of young Brougham's brain must have been stamped, more deeply than ever before by any other event with the features of his friend G.'s face, and with the ideas and hopes and resolutions which the compact they had entered into inspired. G. disappeared from the orbit of Brougham's life. The brain-cells which had been thus stamped, sensitized like a photographic plate, were laid away in the recesses of Brougham's brain. There they were deposited, the hieroglyphic representations of G.'s face and form and of the compact and the attendant ideas, like a portrait in a garret, or a manuscript in a drawer, ready to be brought out, whenever anything should occur capable of dragging them into the light. ... A moderate anæmia of the periphery of the brain, and a moderate hyperæmia of the base of the brain, are among the conditions of sleep, and consequently of dreams which occur only in sleep. The congestion produced by the bath naturally intensified these conditions. ... The discussion with Stuart, added to the stimulus of a warm bath, would be sufficient to bring within the sphere of automatic activity the latent cell groups which were the representatives of G. The groups appeared, subjective vision was accomplished, and Lord Brougham saw the friend of his youth apparently projected into space before him.

The connection between the death of G. in India and the vision in Brougham's brain is probably only that of coincidence. At any rate, physiology has no explanation to offer of such a phenomenon. Those who believe that it is more than coincidence must seek for an explanation by means which science cannot employ, and in a region into which physiology cannot enter. And, moreover, such persons must not forget the fact, previously mentioned, that the future life is not conditioned by time or space; so that, when G. died in India, he was as near Brougham in England as if they were in the same room. Hence, looking at the vision from the spiritual side, we can conceive how G., having no limits of space between him and Brougham at the moment of death, should at that moment instantly be near him. But how G. could communicate with Lord Brougham is again a matter about which we are utterly ignorant. In reality, we do not know how we communicate with each other. The lips open, the tongue moves, and the air vibrates; but I do not know how that makes an idea pass from one to the other. Still less can we guess how a disembodied spirit can communicate with flesh and blood.

One other suggestion may be made. God never employs a new method, that is, a supernatural one, when an old method, that is, a natural one, will accomplish the object he has in view. He loves to employ the simplest measures. The same mathematical curve which governs the growth of a violet guides the stars in their courses. Following this law, we should expect that G., if he wished to appear to Brougham, would not reclothe himself with our miserable habiliments of flesh, but would simply act upon Brougham's brain in a way to produce subjective vision. So God may act upon the human brain so as to indicate his presence and become a working force in it, without ever assuming a gross anthropomorphic objective form.— *Visions: A Study of False Sight (Pseudopia)*, p. 310, ff.

A case both of false sight and false hearing is that of C. F. **Nicolai,** of Berlin, in 1791. His narrative and comments **evince a** thinker in advance of that age : —

At ten o'clock in the forenoon, my wife and another person came to console me. I was in a violent pertubation of mind, owing to a series of incidents which had altogether wounded my moral feelings, and from which I saw no possibility of relief, when suddenly I observed, at the distance of ten paces from me, the figure of a deceased person. I pointed at it, and asked my wife whether she did not see it. She saw nothing, but, being much alarmed, endeavored to compose me, and sent for the physician. The figure remained some seven or eight minutes, and at length I became a little more calm; and, as I was extremely exhausted, I soon fell into a troubled slumber, which lasted for half an hour.... In the afternoon, about four o'clock, the figure again appeared, when I was alone. I went to the apartment of my wife, but thither also the figure pursued me. About six o'clock, several stalking figures also appeared; but they had no connection with the standing figure.... I was in general perfectly calm and self-collected on the occasion. I knew extremely well, when it only appeared to me that the door was opened and a phantom entered, and when the door really was opened and any person came in.... Sometimes, the phantasms spoke with one another, but for the most part they addressed themselves to me: these speeches were in general short, and never contained anything disagreeable....

I was alone with the surgeon, but during the operation [of being bled] the room swarmed with human forms of every description, which crowded fast one on another. This continued till half-past four o'clock, exactly the time when the digestion commences. I then observed that the figures began to move more slowly; soon afterward, the colors became gradually paler; every seven minutes they lost more and more of their intensity, without any alteration in the distinct figure of the apparitions. At about half-past six o'clock, all the figures were entirely white, and moved very little, yet the forms appeared perfectly distinct. By degrees, they became visibly less plain, without decreasing in number, as had often formerly been the case. The figures did not move off, neither did they vanish, which also had usually happened on other occasions. In this instance, they dissolved immediately into air; of some, even whole pieces remained for a length of time, which also by degrees were lost to the eye. At about eight o'clock, there did not remain a vestige of any of them, and I have never since experienced any appearance of the same kind.— *A Journal of Natural Philosophy, Chemistry, and the Arts*, by William Nicholson, London, 1803, vol. vi., 166, ff.

A case of false sight, with only slightly deranged hearing, is that of a lady whose account was written out at request of Dr. E. H. Clarke:—

My earliest recollections are of a life made miserable by the daily companionship of a crowd of dreadful beings, visible, I know, only to myself. Like Madame de Staël, I did not believe in ghosts, but feared them mortally. When I was about fifteen, we went to Europe for two years; and the change of scene, and of constant external interest, broke up my invisible world, and I have only entered it since in times of excitement or great fatigue. Of late years, the most distinct visions have appeared only when sharp mental pain or anxiety has been added to bodily exhaustion. My sense of hearing has never deceived me, except that during my girlhood, in frequent nervous states of mind, all sounds would strike my ears discontinuously, that is, with a time-beat as sharp and rhythmical as the movement of the bâton by an orchestral conductor.

Several years ago, one of my sisters was taken ill with typhoid fever. I was not strong enough to be of any assistance in her chamber, so I undertook to finish some work that she had begun, and became daily more and more worn out in my endeavors to carry it on. Anxiety, added to fatigue, finally brought back the old visions, which had not troubled me continuously for some years. Animals of all kinds, men, women, glaring-eyed giants, passed before or around me until I often felt as though I were surrounded by a circle of magic lanterns, and would sometimes place the back of my chair against a wall, that at least my ghosts should not keep me constantly turning, as they passed behind me. One evening, feeling too tired to sit up for the latest report of my sister, which my mother brought me regularly, I went to bed, leaving my door wide open, so that the gas from the adjoining entry sent a stream of light across one-half of my little chamber, leaving the rest somewhat in shadow. Soon, I saw my mother walk slowly into the room, and stop at the foot of the bed. I remember feeling surprised that I had not heard her footstep as she came through the passage. "Well?" I said inquiringly. No answer, but she took two or three steps toward the side of the bed, and stopped again. "What is the matter?" I exclaimed. Still no reply; but again she moved slowly toward me. Thoroughly frightened by this ominous silence, I sprang up in bed, saying, "Why don't you speak to me?" Until then, her back had been turned to the door; but, as I last spoke, she turned, almost touching my arm, and the light falling on her face showed me an entire stranger. She had heavy dark hair; and her face, quite young, was pale, and, though calm, very sad. ... As I stared at her in speechless amazement, she fell to the floor. I instantly stooped over the side of the bed. To my consternation, there was nothing to be seen. Accustomed as I was to ghosts, if there had been anything in the least shadowy about my visitor, I should have suspected her tangibility; but, so well defined was she, so vividly was her reality impressed upon me, that I could not believe that she had vanished. ... — *Visions*, etc., p. 26, ff.

Page 203.

For many are called, but few are chosen. ... We are rather to understand by the chosen those whom God has selected from the number of the invited as worthy to share the blessings of his kingdom. But these can neither be the earthly-minded, who spurned the invitation altogether, nor those who wished indeed to have a share in the kingdom of God, but not to practise [literally, "to actualize in themselves"] the righteousness which belongs to it. They are only the few who by actual possession and practice [literally, "actualization," *Verwirklichung*] of this righteousness have become worthy members of the kingdom.— *Bernhard Weiss* (*Das Matthäusevangelium und seine Lucas-Parallelen erklärt*, Halle, 1876, p. 472). Compare his *Biblical Theology*, § 30, *d*, vol. i., p. 137, English translation.

Page 212.

> Still, near the lake, with weary tread,
>   Lingers a form of human kind;
> And on his lone, unsheltered head
>   Flows the chill night-damp of the wind.
> Why seeks he not a home of rest?
> Why seeks he not a pillowed bed?
> Beasts have their dens, the bird its nest,
>   He hath not where to lay his head.
>   *William Russell.*

> "See how he loved" who never shrank
>   From toil or danger, pain or death;
> Who all the cup of sorrow drank,
>   And meekly yielded up his breath.
>   *Sarah Bache.*

> And learn from self to cease;
> Leave all things to our Father's will;
> And, on his mercy leaning still,
>   Find in each trial peace.
>   *Joseph Anstice.*

> Bonds and stripes, and evil story,
>   Are our honorable crowns;
> Pain is peace and shame is glory,
>   Gloomy dungeons are as thrones.
>   *Ludwig A.* **Gotter.**

> Think what spirit dwells within thee;
>   Think what Father's smiles are thine;
> Think what Jesus did to win thee.
>   Child of heaven, canst thou repine?
>   *Henry F.* **Lyte.**

> And, oh, if thoughts of gloom
>   Should hover o'er the tomb,
> That light of love our guiding star shall be:
>   Our spirits shall not dread
>   The shadowy way to tread,
> Friend, Guardian, Saviour, which doth lead to thee.
>   *Sarah E. Miles.*

Page 215.

A warm heart requires a cool head. ... Think like the wise, but talk like ordinary people. ... Trust not the man who promises with an oath. ... Never expect excellence from a vain-glorious boaster. ... Give not thy **tongue** too great a liberty, lest it take thee prisoner.— *Samuel Maunder.*

One of the advantages of the negative part assigned to women in life is that they are seldom forced to commit themselves. They can, if they choose, remain perfectly passive while a great many things take place in regard to them: they need not account for what they do not do. From time to time, a man must show his hand; but, save for one supreme exchange, a woman **need** never show hers. She moves in mystery **as** long as she likes; and mere reticence in her, if she is young and fair, interprets itself **as** good sense and good taste.— *W. D. Howells* (*The Lady of the Aroostook*, p. 52).

Page 216.
   I give thoughts words, and words truth, and truth boldness. She whose honest freeness makes it her virtue to speak what she thinks will make it her necessity to think what is good.—*John Marston.*

Page 217.
      True courage scorns
To vent her prowess in a storm of words;
And to the valiant action speaks alone.
      Tobias Smollett (The Regicide).

Passion, when deep, is still. . . .
The keen, fixed orbs that burn and flash below
  . are the language it employs.
      James G. Percival.

Far, far beneath, the noise of tempests dieth,
  And silver waves chime ever peacefully;
And no rude storm, how fierce soe'er it flieth,
  Disturbs the sabbath of that deeper sea.
So to the heart that knows thy love, O Purest,
  There is a temple sacred evermore;
And all the Babel of life's angry voices
  Dies in hushed stillness at its peaceful door.
      Harriet B Stowe.

Page 224.
The scourge of earth, the scorn of heaven,
He falls, unwept and unforgiven,
  And all his guilty glories fade.
Like a crushed reptile in the dust he lies,
And Hate's last lightnings quiver from his eyes.
      Charles Sprague.

Page 251.
I love by faith to take a view
  Of brighter scenes in heaven;
The prospect doth my strength renew,
  While here by tempests driven.
      Phœbe H. Brown.

  And we shall see his face;
Then with our Saviour, brother, friend,
  A blest eternity we'll spend
    Triumphant in his grace.
      Samuel Medley.

Page 252.
And while your tears are falling hot
Upon the lips which answer not,
You'll take from these one treasured tress,
And leave the rest to silentness,—
Remember that I used to say,
" You'll think of this again some day,—
    Some day."
      Florence Percy.

Some other world is glad to see
  Our star that's gone away;
The light whose going makes our night
  Makes somewhere else a day.
      Minot J. Savage (Elegy upon Addie R. Coolidge).

QUOTATION INDEX.

Abbott, Abdiel, 217
Abbott, Edwin A., 32.
Abbot, Ezra, 35, 71.
Abdalrahman, 230.
Adams, Nehemiah, 151.
Adams, Robert C., 151.
Addison, Joseph, 238.
Æsop, 182.
Agathon, 189.
Akers (see "Florence Percy").
Alcott, A. Bronson, 91, 246.
Alger, Wm. R., 202.
Allen, E. A. (see "Florence Percy").
Allen, Joseph H., 17.
Ambrose, St., 164.
Ames, Charles G., 14, 80.
Ames, Fisher, 186.
Angelo, Michael, 126.
Anstice, Joseph, 275.
Antoninus, Marcus, 239.
Applebee, James K., 54.
Aristotle, 64, 66, 189, 239, 255.
Arius, 53, 55.
Armstrong, John, 265.
Arnold, Edwin, 205.
Arnold, Matthew, 10, 30, **32**, **58**, **91**, **110**, 128, 183, 218, 223.
Athanasius, St., 55.
Atwater, L. H., 91.
Auerbach, Berthold, 216.
Augustine, St., 72, 91, 92, 253.

Bache, Sarah, 275.
Bacon, Francis, 31.
Bailey, Philip J., **241**.
Baillie, Joanna, 176.
Ballou, Hosea, 19, 216.
Bancroft, George, **12**.
Barbauld, Anna L., 251.
Baring-Gould, Sabine, **21**.
Barrett, B. F., 56.
Barrows, Samuel J., **142**, **143**, **222**, **232**.
Bartol, Cyrus A., 78.
Baxter, Richard, 97.
Beach, Seth C., 200.
Beaconsfield, Ld. (see "Disraeli").
Beard, Charles F., **265**.

Beattie, James, 250.
Beaumont, Francis, 215.
Beecher, Henry W., 76, 88, **100**, **132**, **141**, 231, 266.
Bellows, Henry W., **243**.
Ben Azai, 156.
Benjamin, Park, 267.
Beyschlag, Willibald, 30.
Bias, 219.
Bisbee, Herman, 226, ff.
Blackstone, William, 225.
Blair, Robert, 224.
Boardman, George D., 126.
Bonaparte, Napoleon, 30, 77.
Bonar, Horace, **250**.
Borthwick, Jane, **268**.
Bossuet, Jacques B., 11, 30.
Bowring, John, 174, **241**.
Bremer, Frederika, **139**.
Bristol, Augusta C., 19.
Brontë, Charlotte, 76.
Brooke, Stopford, 216.
Brooke, Ld. (see "Greville").
Brooks, Phillips, 122.
Brougham, Henry, Ld., **271**.
Brown, John, Dr., 168.
Brown, John, Rev., 222.
Brown, Phœbe H., 269.
Browning, Elizabeth B., 236.
Browning, Robert, 74.
Bruyére, John de la, 138.
Bryant, Wm. C., 14, 251, 252, 253
Buckle, Henry T., 100.
Buckminster, Joseph S., 139, 187.
Buddha (Gautama), 162, 239.
Buddha Sakya, 135.
Buffon, Comte de (G. L. le Clerc), 129.
Bulwer, Edward Lytton, 76, 90, 174.
Bunyan, John, 164, 173, 182.
Burke, Edmund, 76, 177.
Burnham, Benjamin, 132.
Burnham, Celeste S., 16, 212.
Burnham, George W., 11.
Burnham, Thomas J., 88.
Burnham, Virtue H., 235.
Burns, Robert, 97, 135, 140.
Bush, George, 56.

Bushnell, Horace, 212.
Butler, Joseph, 9, 183.
Butler, Samuel, 137, 140.
Byron, George Gordon, Ld., 12, 121, 174, 266.

Calhoun, John C., 77.
Calvin, John, 205.
Campbell, Thomas, 63.
Carlyle, Thomas, 13, 76, 80, 123, 184, 209, 229.
Carpenter, Wm. B., 202.
Cary, Alice, 251.
Cary, Phœbe, 158.
Case, Lizzie Y., 20.
Catlin, Hasket D., 155.
Cervantes, Miguel de S., ii.
Chadwick, John W., v, 23, 24, 38, 48, 53, 55, 64, 86, 90, 112, 150, 176, 191, 198, 200, 245.
Chalmers, Thomas, 171.
Channing, Wm. E., iii, 11, 78, 91, 213, 249.
Chapin, Edwin H., 129, 153.
Chateaubriand, Comte de, 130.
Chaucer, Geoffrey, 236.
Cheney, Ednah D., 165.
Chesterfield, Earl of (P. D. Stanhope), 99.
Child, Lydia M., 11, 76, 259, 263.
Cicero, 131, 224.
Clark, Adam, 198.
Clark, Luella, 57.
Clark, Willis G., 171, 252.
Clarke, Edward H., 169, 269, 271, 273.
Clarke, James Freeman, 16, 28, 29, 52, 75, 78, 81, 89, 115, 121, 128, 131, 139, 154, 158, 160, 163, 174, 175, 178, 202, 207, 214, 219, 231, 253.
Cleland, John, 202.
Clemens, Samuel (see "Mark Twain").
Clement of Alexandria, St., 138.
Clement Romanus, St., 189.
Clemmer, Mary, 135.
Cobbe, Frances P., 142, 269.
Coleridge, Samuel T., 153, 197.
Collyer, Robert, 243.
Colton, Caleb C., 235.
Combe, George, 89.
Confucius, 64, 76, 133, 157, 177.
Conway, Moncure D., i, 32, 53, 58, 61, 100, 109, 126, 140, 149, 223.
Cook, Joseph, 13, 22, 53, 225.
Cossitt, Charlotte, 100.
Cousin, Victor, 63, 255, 258.
Cowley, Abraham, 217.
Cowper, William, 13, 78, 137, 229.
Cranch, Christopher P., 217.
Cross, Marian G. Evans (see "George Eliot").
Curtis, George W., iii.
Cuyler, Theodore, 246.

Dana, Richard H., 238.

Dante, Alighieri, 224.
D'Aubigné, Merle, iii.
Davenant, William, 13.
Davidson, Samuel, 17, 22, 182.
Davies, John, 236.
De Finod, J., 13, 130.
De Insulis (see "Insulis").
Disraeli, Benjamin (Earl of Beaconsfield), 126.
Dekker, Thomas, 79.
D'Ossoli, Countess (see "Fuller, Margaret").
De Quincey, Thomas, 225.
Derzhavin, Gabriel R., 241.
De Staël-Holstein, Baronne (Anna L. G. Necker), 77, 148, 268.
Descartes, René, 256.
De Wette, W. M. L., 148.
Dewey, Orville, 208.
Dickens, Charles, 11, 77.
Dillon, Wentworth (see "Roscommon, Earl of").
Diogenes, 137.
Dole, Charles F., 129.
Dorner, Isaac, 206.
Dow, Lorenzo, 213.
Draper, J. W., 183.
Drummond, James, 71.
Drummond, William, 13.
Dryden, John, 20, 99, 140, 216.
Du Moulin, Lewis, 232.
Durbin, John P., 215.
Dutton, J. Frederic, 133, 244.

Eager, John H., 53.
Edwards, Jonathan, 180, 232.
Eliot (see "George Eliot").
Ellicott, Charles J., 21.
Emerson, Ralph W., 30, 41, 43, 57, 92, 160, 209, 215, 216, 236, 240, 267.
Emmons, Nathaniel, 231.
Epictetus, 157.
Erskine, Thomas, 211.
Eusebius, 54.
Everett, Edward, 266.
Ewald, G. H. A. von, 30, 44, 70, 74, 179.

Faber, George S., 235.
Fairbairn, Angus, 250.
Farrar, F. W., 222.
Fay, Caroline, 20.
Feltham, Owen, 91, 136.
Fénelon, Francis de S., 164.
Fichte, John G. T., 96, 145, 256.
Fielding, Henry, 76.
Fields, James T., iii, 135.
Fisher, George P., 22.
Fletcher, Richard, 76, 215.
"Florence Percy" (*Pseud.* of E. A. Allen, formerly Mrs. Akers), 269.
Forbes, James, 262.
Foster, John, 115.

QUOTATION INDEX

Fowle, Thomas W., 10, 106.
Fowler, Orson S., 233.
Fox, George, 109
Franklin, Benjamin, 176.
Frothingham, Octavius B., v.
Froude, Anthony, 13.
Fuller, Margaret (Countess d'Ossoli), 187, 237.
Fuller, Thomas, 160, 237.
Furness, William H., 70, 181, 213.

Galen, 156.
Gannett, Wm. C., 165.
Garfield, James A., ii, 122.
Garth, William, 238.
Gasparin, Countess de, A. E., 133.
Geikie, Cunningham, 48, 103, 114, 175.
"George Eliot" (*Pseud.* of Marian G. Evans Cross), 8, 77, 87, 89, 118, 139, 157, 230, 263.
Gibbon, Edward, 90.
Girardin, Emile de, 230.
Gladstone, William E., 116, 128.
Goethe, John W. von, 14, 61, 80, 91, 115, 120, 130, 168, 188, 215, 219, 238.
Goldsmith, Oliver, v, 78.
Gotter, Ludwig A., 275.
Gould (see "Baring-Gould").
Gracian, Balthasar, 216.
Grange, Olrig, 79.
Gray, Thomas, 115.
Greeley, Horace, 224.
Greenleaf, Simon, 39.
Greenough, Sarah D., 42.
Greville, Fulke (Ld. Brooke), 137.
Griesbach, John J., 21.
Griffin, Richard A., 24.

Hale, Edward E., 42.
Hale, Matthew, 185.
Hale, Sarah J., 99, 268.
Haley, J. W., 17.
Hall, Edward H., 35.
Hall, Elvina M., 205.
Hall, Joseph, 76.
Hall, Robert, 216.
Hall, Ruth P., 236.
Halleck, Fitz G., 136.
Hamilton, William, 12.
Hammond, William A., 167.
Hardenberg, F. von (see "Novalis").
Hare, Francis, 97.
Harris, W. T., 257.
Hase, Carl A., 180.
Hawkesworth, John, 253.
Hawthorne, Nathaniel, 11, 97.
Hayes, John L., 122.
Hayes, Rutherford B., v.
Hazlitt, William, 13, 76, 90.
Hedge, Frederic H., iv, 18, 58, 94, 130, 209.
Hegel, G. W. F., 54, 256.

Heine, Heinrich, 12, 92.
Helps, Arthur, 76.
Hemans, Felicia D., 79.
Henry, Matthew, 76, 198.
Henshaw, J P K., 76.
Heraclitus, 262.
Herbert, George, iii, 13, 90, 119, 133, 216, 224.
Herodotus, 81.
Herrick, Marcellus A., 130.
Higginson, Thomas W., 64, 162.
Hill, Aaron, 176.
Hillel, 133.
Hodge, Charles, 232.
Holland, Josiah G., 75, 131.
Holmes, Oliver W., 90, 99, 137, 152, 217.
Holtzmann, Heinrich J., 71.
Hood, Thomas, 130, 140.
Hooykaas, I., 66, 190, 194.
Hopkins, Samuel, 232.
Hopps, John P., 243.
Horace, 81.
Horne, George, 162.
Houssaye, Arsène, 77.
Howells, W. D., 275.
Howitt, Mary, 19.
Hugo, Victor, 142, 164, 244.
Humboldt, Alexander von, 120.
Hume, David, 11, 181.
Hunt, Leigh, 147.
Huxley, Thomas H., 99.

Ingelow, Jean, 217.
Insulis, Ansalus de, 157.
Irving, Edward, 66.
Irving, Washington, 69, 136.

Jameson, Anna M., 123.
Jefferson, Thomas, vi.
Jeffrey, Francis, Ld., 134.
Jerome, St., 76, 163, 175.
Johnson, Mary E. C., 139.
Johnson, Samuel, iv, 89, 126, 240.
Jones, J. M., 187.
Jones, Wm., 178.
Jonson, Ben, 147.
Josephus, Flavius, 45, 47, 66, 102, 189.
Joubert, Francis, 13, 237.
Justin Martyr, v, 21, 35, 71.

Kant, Immanuel, 234, 255, 258.
Keats, John, 141.
Keim, Theodor, 32.
Kempis, Thomas à, 91, 157.
Kepler, Johann, 185.
Khayyam, Omar, 205.
King, T. Starr, 101.
Kingsley, Charles, 156.
Kirchdorfer, J. S., 71.
Knox, Alexander, 170.
Krauth, Charles P., 232.
Kuenen, Abraham, 22, 23.

Kuntze, Otto, 186

LaFontaine, Jean de, 156.
Lamartine, Alphonse, 267.
Lamb, Charles, 251.
Landon, Letitia E., 270.
Landor, Walter S., 148.
Lanier, Sidney, 136.
Lao-tze, 63.
Larcom, Lucy, 247.
Larrabee, Benjamin F., 246.
Lavater, John G., 216.
Learned, John C., 127.
Lee, Luther, 56.
Leibnitz, Gottfried W., 96.
Leonowens, Anna H., 170.
Lessing, Gotthold E., 12.
Lewes-Cross (see "George Eliot").
Lightfoot, John, 32, 187.
Lincoln, Abraham, vi.
Lippincott, Sara J. C., 80.
Lipsius, Richard A., 71.
Locke, John, 10, 13, 78, 89.
Lockhart, John G., 225.
Long, John D., 194.
Longfellow, Henry W., 77, 82, 92, 124, 157, 237, 238, 247.
Longfellow, Samuel, 221.
Lovelace, Richard, 78.
Lowell, James R., 43, 80, 141, 189, 191.
Lucan, 69.
Luthardt, Christian E., 120.
Luther, Martin, 192.
Lyon, Mary, 178.
Lyte, Henry F., 275.
Lyttelton, George, Ld., 78.

Macaulay, Thomas B., 93, 115, 121, 122.
McCosh, James, iii.
McCrie, George, 210.
MacDonald, George, 224.
Mackay, Charles, 137.
Mackintosh, James, 77.
McLean, John, 11.
Mallet, David, 76.
Manes, 96.
Mann, Horace, 12.
Mansfield, Joseph H., 75.
"Mark Twain" (*Pseud*. of Samuel Clemens), 151.
Marston, John, 76, 276.
Martensen, Hans L., 55, 94, 96.
Martineau, James, 120, 241.
Martyr (see "Justin").
Mary, Queen of Scots, 252.
Maunder, Samuel, 77, 265, 266, 267, 270, 275.
Maurice, F. D., 183.
Maximus, Tyrius, 64.
May, Samuel J., 56.
Mazzini, Giuseppe, 133.
Medley, Samuel, 269.

Merriam, George S., 19.
Merrick, James, 158.
Merivale, Herman, 250.
Metcalf, Richard, 239.
Michelet, Jules, 267.
Miles, Sarah E., 275.
Mill, John S., ii, 182.
Miller, Hugh, 18.
Miller, Joaquin, 97.
Mills, Charles R., 186.
Milton, John, iii, iv, 77, 85, 88, 90, 135, 171, 174, 186, 190, 203, 224, 233, 234.
Mirabeau, Comte de (H. G. Riquetti), 87.
Mitchell, Donald G., 77.
Mohammed, 237.
Montaigne, Michael de, 187, 276.
Montgomery, James, 164, 251.
Moody, Dwight L., 215.
Moore, Edward, 254.
Moore, Thomas, 233, 251.
More, Hannah, 164, 234.
Morell, John D., 62, 100, 101, 258.
Morgan (Lady) Sidney O., 187.
Motley, John L., 100.
Mowatt, Anna Cora, 267.
Moxley, James B., 183.
Müller, Julius, 97.
Müller, Max, 30.
Murray, W. H. H., v, 131.
Musset, Alfred de, 231.

Nairne, Carolina O., 251.
Neander, Michael, 74, 131.
Neff, Felix, 183.
Newton, Reginald H., 14, 194.
Nicholson, Wm., 273.
Nicolai, Christopher F., 272.
"Novalis" (*Pseud*. of Friedrich von Hardenberg), 76.

Omar Khayyam, 205.
Origen, 21.
Orpheus, 63.
Osgood, Frances S., 156.
Otway, Thomas, 138.

Paley, Wm., 124, 233.
Palfrey, Cazneau, 62.
Palmerston, Viscount (H. J. Temple), 132.
Parker, Theodore, 28, 57, 180.
Pascal, Charles, 10.
Paterson, Adoniram J., 225.
Patten, Claudius B, 241.
Paul, St. (see ANALYTICAL INDEX).
Paul, Jean (see "Richter").
Paulus, Heinrich E. G., 191.
Peabody, Andrew P., 145.
Peabody, Francis G., 159.
Penn, Wm., 237.
Percival, James G., 276.
Percy (see "Florence").
Phelps, Elizabeth S., 222, 252.

Pierpont, John, 268.
Phillips, Wendell, 12, 120.
Philo Judæus, 37, 189.
Piatt, John J., 233.
Piatt, Sarah M. B., 79.
Pilate (see "Acts"), 177.
Piper, George F, 23.
Pitman, Isaac, 187.
Plato (see ANALYTICAL INDEX).
Pliny, 189.
Plotinus, 161.
Plutarch, 266.
Pond, Enoch, 232.
Pope, Alexander, iv, 52, 62, 89, 146, 235.
Porter, Jane, 224.
Porter, Noah, 140.
Powell, Wm. S., 76.
Préault, Auguste, 177, 216.
Pressensé, Edmond de, 124.
Price, Robert, 237.
Prime, Samuel I., 149.
Procter, Adelaide A., 138.
Procter, Bryan W., 268.
Punchard, George, 215.
Pythagoras, 52, 64.

Quarles, Francis, 10, 76, 137, 163.
"Queen," 141.

Raleigh, Walter, 217.
Raymond, Henry J., 134.
Realf, Richard, 90.
Reid, Thomas, 255.
Renan, J Ernest, 188.
Réville, Albert, 53.
Richter, Jean Paul F., 77, 139, 156.
Riddle, David, 172
Robertson, Frederick W., 225.
Rochefoucauld, Duc de, 140.
Rogers, Samuel, 79, 136.
Roscommon, Earl of (W. Dillon), 133.
Rousseau, Jean J., 11.
Rowe, Nicholas, 211.
Rush, Benjamin, 167.
Ruskin, John, 90
Russell, Thomas, vi.
Russell, William, 275.
Ryder, Wm. H., 89, 151, 231.
Ryland, John, 149.

Saadi, Moslih-Eddin, 77.
Sabellius, 53.
Sadi Gul, 187.
Saint Augustine, etc. (see "Augustine, St.," etc.).
Sallust, 69.
Saurin, Jacques, 193.
Savage, Minot J., 93, 143, 185, 276.
Savage, Wm. H., 75.
Schelling, W. J., 256, 258.
Schenkel, Daniel, 32.

Schiller, John F. C., 217.
Schleiermacher, Friedrich E. D., 21, 44, 51, 93, 96, 181.
Scholten, John H., 22.
Schumann, I., 11.
Scott, Walter, 18, 26, 88, 225, 241.
Scudder, Eliza, 165.
Sears, Edmund H., 39, 181.
Seeley, John R., 73, 116, 117, 119.
Selden, John, 13, 216.
Seneca, 123.
Shaftesbury, Earl A. A. C., 115.
Shakspere, Wm., i, 9, 11, 114, 152, 156, 186, 216.
Shelley, Percy B., 89, 238.
Sheridan, R. Brinsley, 141, 144.
Shippen, Rush R., 131.
Shute, Henry, 19.
Sidney, Philip, 10.
Sigourney, Lydia H., 137.
Smith, Alexander, 136.
Smith, Elizabeth O., 267.
Smith, Mary R., 246.
Smith, Sydney, 130, 216.
Smollett, Tobias, 276.
Smyth, Newman, 15, 25, 31, 33, 42, 106, 131, 202, 211, 249.
Socinus, 53.
Socrates (see ANALYTICAL INDEX).
Sophocles, 265, 267.
Southey, Robert, iii.
Spencer, Herbert, 201.
Spenser, Edmund, 14, 253.
Spinoza, Benedict, 180.
Sprague, Charles, 276.
Spurgeon, Charles H., 231.
Staniforth, Sampson, 169.
Stanley, Arthur P., 114, 124, 211.
Stebbins, Rufus P., 182.
Steele, Anna, 251.
Sterne, Lawrence, 11.
Stillingfleet, Edward, 164.
Stewart, Dugald, 255.
Storrs, Richard S., 225.
Story, Joseph, 129.
Story, Wm. W., 79, 217.
Stowe, Harriet B., 78, 142, 276.
Strauss, David F., 41, 190.
Strong, James, 38, 105.
Sumner, Charles, 12.
Swedenborg, Emanuel, 88, 213, 249.
Swetchin, Anna S. S., 20, 164.
Swift, Jonathan, 12, 139.
Swing, David, 112, 141.

Tacitus, 45, 189.
Taine, Hippolyte A., 89.
Tappan, Wm. B., 250.
Taylor, Edward, 231.
Taylor, J Bayard, 61.
Taylor, Jeremy, 10, 158, 224.
Temple, Henry J (see "Palmerston").

QUOTATION INDEX

Tennyson, Alfred, vi, 79, 90, 100, 136, 154, 157, 224, 234, 250.
Thackeray, Wm. M., 238.
Thayer, George A., 236.
Tholuck, F. A. G., 148.
Thom, J. H., 160.
Thomson, James, 79.
Thoreau, Henry B., 57, 130, 138.
Tighe, Mary, 78.
Tilton, Theodore, 174.
Tischendorf, Lobegott F. C., 22.
Trench, Richard C., 179, 182, 190.
Trowbridge, J. T., 181.
Tulloch, John, 97.
Tyndall, John, 130, 184.
Tyng, Stephen H., 146.
Tyrwhitt, Thomas, 249.

Ullman, Carl, 206.

Vaughan, Henry, 251, 253.
Venetus, Marcus P., 236.
Vinet, Alexander R., 177.
Virgil, 194.
Voltaire, Francis M. A. de, iv.

Waite, Charles B., 21, 22.
Waller, Edmund, 237.
Walton, Izaak, 88.
Warburton, Wm., v.
Waring, Ann L., 165.
Washington, George, 134.
Wasson, David A., 124.
Watts, Isaac, 251.

Webster, Daniel, 89, 90.
Weiss, Bernhard, 274.
Weiss, John, 63.
Wellington, Duke of, 148.
Wendte, Charles W., 211.
Wesley, Charles, 204.
Wesley, John, 216.
Westcott, Brooke F., 21.
Whately, Richard, 10.
Whedon, Daniel D., 30.
Whipple, Edwin P., 12.
White, Henry K., 79.
Whitney, Adaline D. T., 245.
Whittier, John G., 14, 88, 109, 146, 162, 192, 220, 224, 232, 234, 267, 268.
Wilcox, Carlos, 266.
Williams, H. T., 149.
Willis, Nathaniel P., 69.
Winslow, Edward, 142.
Wirt, Wm., iv.
Withrow, J. L., 167, 232.
Woolsey, Theodore D., 92.
Wordsworth, Wm., 12, 78, 162, 217, 244.
Wotten, Henry, 81.
Wright, Wm. B., 213.

Xenophon, 81.

Young, Edward, 13, 20, 217, 238.
Young, Thomas, 248.

Ziegler, W. C. L., 215.
Zoroaster, 50, 63, 241.
Zschokke, J. H. de, 238.

ANALYTICAL INDEX.

Abandonment of the hierarchy, 109.
Abraham, Sadi's legend of, 187.
Absolute, comprehending the, 258.
Abstract — theory of God, 56; virtues, 130.
Absurdities not mysteries, 9.
Abuses and uses of faculties, 88.
Accretions of tradition, 40 ff; upon the baptism, 71; the temptation, 74; the resurrection, 197.
Action — and thought, 91, 92; in heaven, 253; and being, 256; happiness, 266.
Acts — of the Apostles, 35; of Pilate, 21, 193.
Adam, fall of, 96 ff, 100, 206.
Adaptation to the hearers, 107, 110; and environment, 201.
Adieu, 254.
Adultery, 134.
Adversity beneficent, 76.
Æsthetics in theory of God, 256.
Affectation, 215 ff.
Affection, woman's life, 136; never lost, 238; immortal, 247, 250, 252.
Affronts, parrying, 137, 176, 267.
Age and youth, 267.
Aggression, 175 ff.
Agony and achievement, 78.
Ahaz and Isaiah, 51.
Alexandrian — library, v; school, 35,259.
Allegory in scriptures, 41.
Alleviation of woes, 166 ff, 268.
Allocution, 113 ff.
Amusements, 211.
Analogy and miracles, 183.
Ancestry of Jesus, 44 ff.
Andrew and Peter, 85, 103, 105.
Anger, 134, 267.
Angels at the birth, 46 ff; at the sepulchre, 193, 196, 198; deified persons, 234; future human beings, 249; simile, 253.
Annunciation to Mary, 46 ff.
Answers to prayer, 149 ff.
Anthropomorphism, 58 ff, 64.
Antipas (See "Herod").
Aphorisms — are judgments of sages affirmed, iii; on faith and reason, 9 ff;
on inspiration, 30; on accretion, 43; on God, 63, 64; on sympathy, 69; on trials and character-discipline, 76 ff; on mirth and cheerfulness, 88; on culture, 89 ff; on poetry and parables, 115, on religion, 120; on duty and morals, 130 ff; on chastity and woman, 135, 136; on manners, 137; on kindness, 138; on bigotry, 139; on aspiration, 156, 157, 164; on meekness, 176; on arrogance and humility, 215 ff; on clamor and stillness, 216, 217; on guilt and punishment, 224, 225; on happiness, 230; on immortality, 236 ff; on heaven, 249 ff.
Apocrypha, dates of records, 23.
Apollo — and Jupiter, 261; and Thor, 262.
Apollos, 36, 214.
Apollyon, 182.
Apparitions, 188, 197, 271 ff.
Application of Scripture, 18.
Approximative language, 110.
A priori theories, 180.
Aramaic records, 21, 32, 71.
Araunah and David, 16.
Arbela, 103, 114.
Arbitrary grouping, 39.
Arimanes and Ormuzd, 260.
Aristotelian theory of God, 255.
Arius — at Nicæa, 53 ff; death of 183.
Arms, simile, 119, 246.
Army-baggage, simile, 268.
Arraignment of Jesus, 176.
Arrogance and modesty, 216, 275
Art, progress of, 59; and beauty, 141.
Ascension, 198.
Asceticism, 68, 88, 97, 140, 261, 266.
Aspiration, 156 ff.
Associated charities, 146.
Associations, as affecting the discourses, 102, 103.
Assyrian — period of O. T. records, 23; mythology, 223.
Astrolatry, 58.
Athanasian creed, 55.
Atonement — to pay Satan, 95; intercessional view of, 204 ff; at-one-ment

view, 212 ff; mythological and moral theories of, 219.
Aum and Brahm, 259, 260.
Autumn, simile, 266.

Babbling and repression, 215, 217.
Babe and prayer, 153 ff.
Babylonian ideas, 223, 259 ff.
Bad and good, relative, 97.
Baggage, simile, 268.
Balaam and Hyrcanus, 263.
Banners and ideals, 123.
Baptism of Jesus, 71, 72.
Baptist (see "John").
Bat, simile, 170.
Bathsheba, 134.
Battle — and character, 77; flags, 123.
Beacon, simile, 212.
Beatitudes, 113, 132.
Beauty — comprehended only by its lovers, 16; and truth, 115; and art, 141; transfigured in heaven, 252; female, 254.
Bee, simile, 236.
Begotten and unbegotten, 53 ff.
Being and action, 256.
Belief — depends on disposition, 140, 265; canons of, 182, 184.
Ben Adhem legend, 147.
Bethesda miracle, 179.
Bethlehem not the birth-place, 49.
Bethsaida blind man, 180.
Bible — no unit or fetich, 9; good-will for, 16; distortion of, 17; books of and dates, 23; inspired because true, 27; not book of divinity but of life, 31; from necessities of the times, 34; picture of life struggles, 42; educational method of, 43; growth of, 43; its own corrective, 43.
Bigotry, ii, v, 140, 186 ff.
Birds, simile, 236, 275.
Birth (see "Nativity").
Blinking censors, 140.
Blind — man, miracle, 179; simile, 191; heart is, 215.
Boasting and profession, 215 ff, 275.
Body — and soul, 233; decaying before mind, 237; in heaven, 249.
Bombast, precept against, 215.
Borrowing trouble, 138.
Bowing to straighten, simile, 135.
Boyhood discipline, 82.
Brahm and Aum, 259, 260.
Brahmin divination, 263.
Brotherhood, God's method, 120.
Brougham's pseudopia, 271.
Buddha, birth of, star-heralded, 47; under the bo-tree, 74.
Buddhists' reception of praying men, 156.
Buni, beast mesmerizer, 170.
Burial service, 100.
Busyrane inscriptions, 216.

Cabalistic theory of God, 260 ff.
Callender and Duny, 185.
Calumny, 134, 139, 268.
Calvin on apostasy, 96; on election, 201 ff; on redemption, 205; conversion, 207 ff.
Calyxes, simile, 246.
Cana, 102, 105, 190.
Cannon, simile, 224.
Canon of disbelief, 182, 184.
Capernaum, 102.
Caprice and law, 180.
Carmel, 193.
Carnal and spiritual conditions, 207.
Catechism, Brown's, 222.
Categories of knowledge, 255.
Cathedral, simile, 11.
Censors' blindness, 140.
Census — of Cyrenius, 49; of Joab, 16.
Centurion's servant, 190.
Century plant, simile, 180.
Ceremonial piety, 173.
Chain, simile, 198, 235, 247.
Chaldean period of records, 23.
Character, how to be studied, ii, 266; strength and softness of, 57; growth of, 74 ff; discipline of, 76 ff; not emotional, 77, 131; is size of virtues, 89; is one's collective dispositions, 91; and destiny, 126; Christ's insight into, 139; indicated in trifles, 264.
Charity, 134, 136, 138, 139.
Chastity, 134, 136.
Chattin (or Hattin), 113, 114.
Cheerfulness, duty of, 88; Christ's, 140.
Chest, simile, 90.
Child — estray, simile, 209; hopes of, 244; teaching as to soul, 244; transformed in heaven, 247; germ of man, 249.
Children's Aid Society, 146.
Chillon dungeon, simile, 174.
Chinese — scriptures, 40; superstitions, 186; theories of God, 260.
Chivalry, 134, 136.
Christ (see "Jesus").
Christianity, influence in history, 57; above ethnic and philosophical religions, 120; growth of, 128; establishes the law, 128; not created by revelation, 145.
Christmas, date fixed, 49.
Chronological order — of records, 21 ff; of events, 38.
Church, young as the future, 174.
Cleaving of the sea, 182.
Cleopas, 198.
Climbing toward ideals, 124.
Clouds, simile, 249.
Codex Bezae, 72.
Coin in fish's mouth, 149, 180.
Columbus and inspiration, 28, 29.
Commanding manhood, 66.
Community and fraternity, 120.
Composition of gospels, 32 ff.

ANALYTICAL INDEX 285

Conceit (see "Self").
Conception, immaculate, **48**; not supernatural, 51 ff.
Concord school, 257.
Concreteness of Sermon on Mount, 130.
Condition and conduct, 83, 99, 126, 131.
Confession of faith, **14, 17,** 206.
Congestion and visions, **272.**
Conscience — is not law, **11**; defined, 91; Christ's appeal to, **115**; in Hebraism, **12'**; supreme, eternal, 137; inner light, 145; expelled the traders, 175; makes heaven or hell, 225, 230.
Consciousness of God, 258.
Consecution of N. T. records, 21 ff.
Conservation of forces, **173.**
Constantine at Nicæa, **55.**
Consumptives' Home, prayer supported, 150.
Contagious visions, 188, **197.**
Contemplation generates piety, **91, 157,** 172, 173.
Continence, **134.**
Conventionality, **137,** 140.
Conversion — of Paul and Staniforth, 169; transitional, 207 ff; at-one-ment with God through Christ, 212 ff
Conviction, no greatness without, **15**; and conversion, 210; not by overbearing, **265.**
Co-operation in ministration, 147, **268.**
Corruption blurs perception, 135.
Cottage, simile, 237.
Courage — of the right, 13, 66; **acts,** not talks, 216, **276.**
Courtesy, 137.
Cousinian theory of God, **255.**
Covenant of redemption, **204, 205.**
Covetousness, 219.
Creation, Persian idea **of, 37**; and evolution, **202**; theories of, **259.**
Creative word, 52, 260.
Creeds, imperceptibly dropped, 94; fluctuating currency, 131; learning, 221.
Cremona, simile, 40.
Crime serves order, **235.**
Criminals, 99 ff.
Criticism, precept **on,** 140, **268.**
Cross, only way to **life,** 79; emblem, 122; and crown, **155.**
Crotalus bite, 168.
Crucifixion, 193, 215.
Culture, philosophy of, 89; reduces inflammations, **92**; and anarchy, 127; purity a factor, 136; badges of, 215 ff.
Cumberland's thought-reading, 168.
Curative ministrations, 166 ff.
Currency, simile, 131.
Cynicism, **140.**
Cyrenius, 49.

Daft catechumen, 221.
Damnation, 222 ff, **276.**

Daniel — date of record, 23, 24; and Jonah, **182,** 185.
David — as ancestor, 44; Bathsheba, 134.
Day-star, simile, 234.
Dead raised, 179, 188.
Dead Sea fruit, simile, 254.
Deaf — of heart, 171; man, **miracle,** 179.
Death — sum of misfortunes, 75; **not from** Adam, 100, 206; bed, 139, 174, 213, 269; of P. P. Bliss, 151; landing, **etc.,** new step, 238; mere transition, 247.
Decalogue, date of, 23; regarded by Christ relatively, 108.
Decency, 135.
Deductive method, **258.**
Deeps and shallows, simile, 217.
Defeat, effect of on character, 74 ff.
Deification, 58 ff.
Delphic oracle, 263.
Demas and Gestas, 193.
Demiurge, 33, 52.
Democracy and despotism, 120.
Demonization, 93 ff, 98, 107, 167, 185.
Denial spirit, 95.
Departure from the temple, 109.
Derangement (see "Insanity").
Desert, simile, 233.
Destruction and fortune, 265.
Development of Christ's character, 106 ff.
Devil, 93 ff, 185, 223, 235, 261.
Dewdrop, simile, 100.
Dignity, 176.
Disciples, choosing of the, 165; misapprehended Christ, 111, 176.
Discipline of character, 74 ff.
Discord, simile, 174.
Discrepancies of Scriptures, 17.
Discourses of Jesus, 113 ff
Discretion, **215.**
Distortion of the records, 17.
Ditheism, 53.
Diversions, choice of, 211.
Divinity of Christ, 52 ff, 106.
Divorce, 135.
Doctrinal piety, 173.
Dominion of the higher, **127.**
Dort, Synod of, 233.
Dove, symbol, 72; Noah's, 236.
Dreams, 225, 239, 253, 272.
Dress and ostentation, 215.
Dualism, 93 ff, 260.
Dum vivo, volo, 237.
Dumb man, miracle, 179.
Dunstan's miracles, 188.
Dutch school, 190.
Duty, nearest first, **130, 178, 210.**
Dying to live, **219.**

Earnestness, precepts on, 133.
Earth and **heaven** apart, 97.
Earthquake, 198.
Easter, significance of, 199.
Ebionite document, 47, 51, 71.

Ecclesiastical spirit, 132.
Eclectic interpretation, 265.
Eclipse, simile, 258.
Economy of time **and energy**, 138.
Ecstasy and **repression**, 215.
Eden, simile, 254.
Edinburgh Presbytery's petition, 152.
Educational — method of Bible, 43; life **not** probational, but, 75.
Ego and non-ego, 55, 96.
Egotism falls off, 240.
Egyptian — mythology, 41, 53, 259 ff; plagues, 182.
Ejection of the **traders**, 175.
Election, 201 ff, **274**.
Elijah and Moses, 172.
Elizabeth, Queen, conscience of, 145.
Elsie Venner, 99.
Emmaus, 194.
Emblems and ideals, 41, 122.
Emotion, 101, 131, 173, 215, 217, 255 ff.
Empirical experience, 257.
End **of** the world, 111.
Enthusiasm, badge of faith, 129.
Entry triumphal, 176.
Environment — and adaptation, 201; harmonization with, 225.
Envy, how escaped, 215.
Epigrams, for action and memory, **41**.
Epistles of Paul, dates, 22, 34 (see "Hebrews").
Equanimity, 138, 217.
Error, Paul correcting, 30; Christ, 57, 108; embalmed by a little truth, 137.
Esau and Jacob, 202.
Essenes, 68, **104**.
Eternal **Goodness**, 232.
Eternity, **not** comprehended, 227; negative idea, 233; not length but depth, 240.
Ethics progressive, 145.
Ethnic religion, 119.
Euphemisms, abuses of, 177.
Everlasting Yea, 210.
Evening, simile, 250.
Evidence, rules of, 39.
Evil and good, 97, 208, 228, 235, **260**.
Evolution — of peace on earth, 59; goodwill to men, 60, 125 ff; three factors of, 201; and election, 202; in heaven, 253.
Exaltation, 248 ff.
Example — and **precept**, **116**; **superhuman, of** Jesus, **119, 214, 275**.
Exorcism, **95**.
Expansion **of** character, mission, 106 ff.
Experience — of the race the standard of right, **143**; induction and, 257.
Expiation, origin of the idea, 213; the true, 214.
Expression and silence, 217.
Ezra, redaction by, 17, 33.

Fable, truth in, 115; of father **and sons**, 156; of Dead Sea fruit, 254.

Failure and success, 74.
Fairholme and geology, 18.
Faith, function of, 9 ff, 184; salvation by, a universal law, 15; defined, 16; **temper**, 19; and regeneration, 118 ff; test, 119; indispensable, 121; of youth, 129; **in** woman, 136; and hope, 147, 173; **and** feeling, 153; cures, 166 ff; in man, 213; **not** provable by syllogism, 239; in heaven, 251, 276.
Fall (see "Adam").
Fallibility of records, 27.
Falsehood, 137, 143.
Fame, 217.
Fantasies, 185 ff; **226**.
Fashion-following, **badge of imbecility**, 66, 137.
Fasting, 152.
Fate and free-will, 201 ff, **203**, 205, 207 ff.
Fatherhood of God, 155.
Fatherland of Christian, 124.
Fault, greatest, 266.
Faust, drama of, on God, 61; **death of, 75.**
Feeding multitudes, 179, 190.
Feeling — and God, 61; and motive, 100; and prayer, 160; and utterance, 215 ff.
Felix culpa, 97.
Festivity, 140.
Fetichism, 58.
Fetter, simile, 237.
Fiction, truth in, 115.
Fig-tree, allegory, 190.
Finding God, 165.
Fire, simile, 76; from sky, 182; purification by, 223, 261.
First Cause, 62.
Fish, tradition of, 262.
Fishes, miracle, 179.
Five hundred brethren, appearing to, 195.
Flags and ideals, 122, 123.
Flattery, 264.
Fleeing to the Only, 161.
Flood of years, simile, 253.
Flower, simile, 91, 131, 189, 216, 217, 245, 249, 250, 251, 252, 253, 264; of the Holy Spirit, 167.
Folk-lore, 185.
Fool and Latin, proverb, 13.
Forbearance, 176 ff.
Foreordination, 201 ff.
Forgiveness, 134.
Formal prayer, 159.
Fortune, smiling, means mischief, 265.
Fountain, simile, 97.
Fourth Gospel, authorship of, 32, 35; peculiarities of, 36, 39, 52, 116.
Frankness and truth, 215, 276.
Fraternity and community, 120.
Free-will views (see "Fate").
Freedom and necessity, 55, 56, 209; and fidelity, **147**.

ANALYTICAL INDEX 287

French theory of God, 255.
Friends, sympathy of, 69; meeting of the, 220; reunion of, 253.
Furies, 224.
Future probation and punishment, 222 ff — comprehension of the, 234, 244.

Gabriel, 46.
Gadarene lunatic, 179.
Galilee, 102.
Gargoyles, theological, 139.
Gaulonitis, 102.
Gautama, 93, 205.
Gehenna, 107, 134, 222.
Genealogy of Jesus, 44 ff.
Genesareth, 85, 102.
Genesis, cosmology of, Persian, 37.
Genetic method, 257.
Genius and energy, 90.
Gentiles, dispute on, 38.
Geology and the Bible, 18.
German theory of God, 255.
Gethsemane, 11, 124.
Ghost, "seen," 93; folk-lore, 185; conjuror's, 188; Cock-Lane, 197; fear, 273.
Girard's will, iv.
Glass, simile, 52, 226, 250.
Gnostic belief, 33, 52.
Goats, parable of, 223, 247.
Goblins and folk-lore, 185.
God, Trinitarian and Unitarian views of, 52 ff; anthropomorphic, atheistic, and ideal views of, 58 ff; "who dare express him?" 61; and the universe, 61; love fills our conception of, 62; fatherhood of, 116; "take my hand," 155; "was kinder than my prayer," 164; in Christ, 173; nature "the living garment" of, 209; "omnipotent reigneth," 226; ode to, 241; "knew best," 246; philosophical theories as to the mind's knowledge of, 255 ff.
Golden rule, 133 ff, 138 ff.
Good — and evil (see " Evil "); wrought by " good in thought," 80; men and bad, 97; breeding, 137; "be," "and let who will be clever," 156.
Good-will essential to understand the Bible, 16.
Gospel — of Nicodemus, 21, 199; of the Infancy, 21, 50; of the Hebrews, 71.
Gospels, four (see " Matthew," " Mark," " Luke," and " Fourth Gospel ").
Government and miracle, 180.
Grace to pray, paradox, 158.
Grandiloquence, precept against, 215.
Great and small, relative only, 126.
Greek — period of records, 23; theory of God and mind, 255.
Grief beneficent, 133; solaced in heaven, 253.
Grounds of disbelief, 182, 184.
Grouping of events, 39.

Growth — of Christ's mind, 107; of Christianity, 128.
Guard at the tomb, 198.
Guide in Mammoth Cave, simile, 27.
Guilt and penalty, 224.

Habits — of Jesus, 104; sowing, " reap a character," 126.
Hagiographa records, 24.
Hamiltonian theory of God, 255.
Hampden and Washington, 121.
Hannah, 46.
Happiness and misery, 230.
Harbor, simile, 248, 253.
Harmonization — of four gospels, 38; of human tendencies, 87 ff; of scriptures with nature and reason, 190, 191.
Harrow, simile, 211.
Hatred, 134, 276.
Hattin (or Chattin), 113, 114.
Head and heart, 215.
Healing the sick, 166, 170, 268.
Heart — feels above reason, 11; of woman her world, 136; deafness of, 171; "throbs," 241.
Heaven — near earth, 97; kingdom of, 125 ff; Christ's use of the word, 227; theories of, 248 ff; reunion in, 251 ff; defined, 252.
Hebraism and Hellenism, 127.
Hebrew — ideas, 41, 259 ff; Bible's divisions, 24.
Hebrews, Epistle to the, 22, 34, 36, 214.
Hell — Christ's use of the word, 107, 110; three theories of, 222 ff.
Hellenic and Christian ethics, 131.
Hellenism and Hebraism, 127.
Hen, simile, 103, 109.
Hercules, choice of, 81.
Heredity, 98, 201.
Hermon, 114.
Hermotimus and Hyrcanus, 263.
Hero worship, 123.
Herod Antipas, 67, 102, 177, 266.
Herod the Great, 47, 49, 114.
Herodias, 67, 103.
Heroism and patience, 178.
Heterodoxy, defined, v.
High, the, " the true, the beautiful," 254.
Hillel, precepts of, 17, 130.
Hindu traditions, 72, 259 ff.
History, references to Christ, 45; drama of freedom, 97; and fiction, 115; Christianity, 128.
Holy Ghost, views concerning, 51 ff; sin against, 95.
Home, 124, 136, 141, 147, 266.
Homer and Zoilus, 268.
Homogeneity in evolution, 201.
Homoöusian, 55.
Honor, valor and discretion, 215.
Honover, " word," 260.
Hope and faith, 147, 173; angel, 233.

Hopkins' theory, 232.
Horatius and M'Cook, 122.
Horns of Hattin (see "Chattin").
Hours "are golden links," 138.
Hue and the Buddhists, 156.
Humanity, progress of, 60.
Humility, 132, 215 ff.
Humor, "good," 88; **of** Jesus and Paul, 266.
Hunt's picture of the temple scene, ii.
Husbandman, winnowing, 69.
Hypocrisy and sincerity, 215 ff.
Hypostases of a trinity, 55, 56.
Hysteria, **98**.

Idealism, vulgar notion of, 129.
Ideals — of devotion and greatness, 57, 117, 121 ff; of God, 59, 60; "angels of growth," 124; and realities, 130.
Ideas of Paul (see "Paul").
Ideational theory of resurrection, 194 ff.
Identity in heaven, 242.
Idleness and industry, 156.
Idolatry, emblems and ideals, 41, 121 ff.
Ignatius, silent on miracles, 189.
Ignorance, malady of, 91.
Imagination — and reason, **ii, 9,** 10, 185; essential to goodness, 89.
Immaculate conception, 48.
Immortality — five arguments for, 233 ff; not explained by Jesus, 240.
Imperishable — "something," 239; pleasures, 254.
Imprecatory prayers and psalms, 152.
Imps in folk-lore, 185.
Impulse and action, 219.
Inauguration of disciples and ministry, 104 ff.
Incarnation, 206.
Inception of ministry, 102.
Inchoatal argument, 236.
Indelicacy, 135.
Individuality in heaven, 242.
Indoctrination, manner of, 114 ff; matter of, 130 ff.
Induction and experience, 257.
Industry and idleness, 156.
Infallibility not necessary, 27.
Infant and prayer, 153, 154.
Infectious visions, 188, 196.
Infidel, declamatory word, 139.
Infidelity from literalism, 27.
Infinity, mind's knowledge of, **258**.
Infralapsarian theory, 96.
Ingathering, training and work, 146.
Ingratitude, let punish itself, 138.
Initiation, **71** ff.
Injury, duty **to repel**, **177**.
Inn, simile, 253.
Inner light, 145.
Inoculation, 187.
Insanity — and genius, 66; no distinct empire, 89; Oriental view of, 93; medical view of, 98; and opposite keenness, 169; and visions, 271 ff.
Insect, simile, 33.
Inspiration, two views of, 26 ff.
Instinct, "swift," 20.
Insult, duty to repel, 177.
Insurance in religion, 132.
Intellect, "meddling," misshapes, 14.
Intellection and emotion, 101, 215, 255 ff.
Intemperance, 74.
Intercessional view, 204.
Interpretation — of scriptures, 9 ff, 135, 190, 191, 265; "best," 57.
Introspection, 83 ff, 137.
Intuitional school, 37.
Io victis, 79.
Isaiah, the First, 51, 69; the **Second**, 70, 86.
Israelites, increase in Egypt, 182.

Jacob and Esau, 202.
Jahveh, 66, 69.
Jairus' daughter, 166, 191.
James, Book of, 21; school of, 36; **name** of Disciples, 105.
Javanese superstition, 186.
Jeanie Deans' ethics, 142.
Jedwort's acquisitiveness, 99.
Jehovah, 260.
Jerusalem, entry into, 178; simile, 248.
Jest, 266.
Jesus (compare the Table of Contents with this Index, *passim*).
Jews, credulity of, 187; monotheism of, 203, 259 ff.
Joan d' Arc, 197.
John (see "Fourth Gospel"); the Baptist, 65 ff, 88.
Jonah, 182.
Joseph, father, 44, 51; of Arimathea, 193.
Joshua, 18.
Judas, the Gaulonite, 67; of Karioth, 105; Maccabæus, 175.
Judgment, day of, 110, 248.
Jupiter and Apollo, 261.
Justice and mercy, 118, 213.
Justification by faith, 123, 204.

Kantian theory of God, 255.
Kindness, precepts on, 133 ff, 138 ff.
Kingdom of heaven, 111, 125 ff, 132, 133.
King's evil cured, 167.
Knowledge, not wisdom, 9; depends on purity, 16, 135; multiplies its own power, 89; to be imparted, 143; depends on love, 16, 246.
Krishna and Menu, 262.

Labor — "worship," 156; happiness, 266.
Ladder, simile, 75, 82.
Lamb of Passover, 70.

ANALYTICAL INDEX   289

Lamps of heaven, simile, 247.
Land — of the leal, 251; of Evermore, 253.
Language in morals, 215 ff.
Last supper, 195.
Latin, Saxon proverb on, 13.
Law — of Moses (see "Decalogue"); of right and wrong, 145; breaks the transgressor, 206; of the spirit, 212.
Leadership, 66.
Learning is not wisdom, 13.
Leaven, simile, 115.
Leaves, simile, 249.
Legends of the Bible, 40.
Leiden school, 22.
Lepers, cure of, 190.
Licentiousness, 134, 267.
Lie of nun to Javert, 142.
Life, three aspects of, 9; educational, not probational, 75; victors in, 79; and love, 117; perfect in short measures, 147; Christ lives, "of our life," 221; truest end of, 237; childhood of immortality, 238.
Light to shine, 133: source of, simile, 244; and eclipse, simile, 258.
Lightning, simile, 115.
Lily, simile, 91, 102, 138, 246.
Link to future world, 234.
Litanies unlearned, 221.
Liturgy, 157, 158.
Localizing heaven, 248.
Location of the birthplace, 49, 50.
Logic in Hegel's theory, 257.
Logos, Justin's view of the, v; Persian and Greek origin, 37, 260; Neo-platonic idea, 52; hypostasis of, 55.
Longanimity, 178.
Lord's prayer, 148.
Lourdes water, faith cure, 167.
Love, the principle of progress, 59; fills our conception of absolute being, 62; and life, 117; and reverence, 131; load-stone of love, 134; and wooing, 136; on birth of, "all things rose to men," 139; divining, 155; human is divine, 173; "more of," 174.
Lowestoft witches, 185.
Loyola and Xavier, miracles, 188.
Luck-hillock superstition, 186.
Luke, peculiarities of, 33, 36, 105, 113, 198.
Lust, 134, 135.
Lute, simile, 100.
Luther's devil, 93, 95.
Lyell and geology, 18.
Lying never necessary, 144.

McCook and Horatius, 122.
Machærus castle, 67.
Madness and genius, 66.
Magdala, 114.
Magdalene, Mary, 42, 196.
Magi, 47.

Magnanimity and longanimity, 178.
Malachi, transition from, 24.
Malchus' ear, 179.
Malevolence, 134.
Mammoth cave guide, simile, 27.
Man — a microcosm, 63; the, "who stole a meeting-house," 99; akin to God, 116; one family, 119; "finest fruit," 120; epitome of cosmic forces, 202; of the world, 215; germ of angel, 249.
Manhood development, 81, 82.
Manichean theory, 96.
Manner of Jesus, 83.
Manners, 77, 136, 137, 215 ff.
Marcion's New Testament, 21.
Margaret, the criminal, 99.
Mark, peculiarities of, 36, 39, 198.
Marriage, 135.
Martha and Mary, 141, 191, 239.
Martyrs, life's victors, 79; reverence paid to, 123.
Mary — of the priestly tribe, 44; annunciation to, 46; pondered but wavered, 48; was married before the birth, 51 (see "Magdalene" and "Martha").
Materialist misjudged, 139.
Materiality of bodies in heaven, 248.
Matter — and spirit, 15, 41; and mind, 130, 257; and sin, 261.
Matthew, three divisions of, 32; peculiarities of, 36, 39, 50, 113, 198.
Means and method of Jesus, 83.
Meditation, 12, 157, 172, 173, 268.
Meekness, abuses of, 176.
Meeting kindred spirits, 69; Friends, 220.
Memory and hell, 224, 225.
Memra, "word," 260.
Memento, "some day," 276.
Mephistopheles, 95.
Mercy and justice, 118; atonement, 213.
Mesmerism, 170, 187.
Messiah, premonition of, 66; Jesus believed himself to be, 86; made rites obsolete, 105; claimants, 109; resurrection for office of, 197; a prince, 261.
Metaphysical argument — for a trinity, 55, 56; for immortality, 233.
Meteorology and prayer, 149, 150.
Method and means of Jesus, 83.
Metraton, mediator, 261.
Migratory birds, simile, 236.
Miltiades inspiring Union patriots, 122.
Mimicry and mirth, 88.
Mind — and matter, 130, 257; condemning beyond calibre, 140; reading, 168, 169; outlasting the body, 237.
Ministration, 179 ff.
Minnow, simile, 184.
Minstrel, simile, 236.
Miracles — through prayer, 149 ff; Trench's enumeration, 179; *a-priori* theory, 180; orthodox theory, 180; *quasi*-orthodox

theory, **181**; Hume, 181; Mill, 181; of O. T., **182**; are put aside as experience widens, **183**; Butler, Mozley, and Tyndall, 183; appeal to intellect, not to affections, 184; "minnow" and "Builder," 184; canons of disbelief and folk-lore, 185; modern, 188; doctrine prove, 189; *Zeit-geist*, 189; allegory in, 190; no sign given, **191**.
Mirthfulness, 88.
Miser "a beggar," 92; "a baby," 98.
Misfortune and character, 74, 267
Mistakes of Jesus, 106.
Modesty and arrogance, 215 ff.
Mohammedanism, spread of, 184.
Monotheism — comes by reflection, 5**8**; Jews " elected " to teach, 203.
Moonshine, simile, 245.
Moral and mythological theories, 219.
Morality, vestibule of religion, 129; " aim above," 130; affected by emotion is religion, 131; science, progressive, 145.
Morrow, simile, 246.
Moses and Elijah, 172; creation and evolution, 202; and Numa, 262.
Mother and child, 153, 154, 209, 253.
Motive and feeling, 100.
Multitudes fed, 179, 190.
Music, simile, 90, 174.
Mustard seed, simile, 126.
Mutuality of mankind, 117 ff, 212.
Mystery, not absurdity, 9; "of love and thought," 60; of the fall, 96 ff; of life, 246; of theologies, 252.
Mythologies, 259 ff.

Nain, widow, **179, 191**.
Narcotics, 74, 225.
Narration of the events, 38 ff.
Nathan and David, 134.
Nathaniel, 85, 105.
Nativity, accessories of, 46 ff; **date and place of**, 49.
Natural — religion distinct from revealed, 58; man, 207; methods of God, 272.
Nature and God, 209.
Nazareth, birth-place, 49, 50; and Capernaum, 102.
Nautilus shell, simile, 90.
Nebuchadnezzar, 224.
Necessity and freedom, 55, 56, 209.
Nell Gwynne, 100.
Neo-platonic ideas, 35, 37, 52, 257.
Nero accusing the Christians, 45.
Nettle, simile, 176.
New England, lessons to, 12.
New Testament records, dates of, **22** ff.
Nicene creed, **14**; council, 54.
Nicodemus, 114, 116, 139 (see "Gospel").
Nicolai's case, 272.
Noah, **17**.
Nobleman's son, 179.

Noise and shallowness, **216**.
Non-resistance, 176 ff.
Nova Zembla, simile, **209**.
Numa and Moses, 262.

Oak, simile, 100, 147, 251.
Obedience to law of the spirit, 212.
Object and subject, 255 ff.
Obligation and regeneration, 119.
Ocean, simile, 57, 217, 226.
Odium theologicum, vi.
Odors crushed, simile, 79.
Old Testament records, dates of, **13**; miracles, 182.
Om and Brahm, 260, 261.
Omnipotence, omniscience, of Jesus, 106.
Opinions and fruits, 140, 216.
Oppression, distorting texts for, 17.
Optical illusions, 169, 188.
Optimism, 94, 97, 208.
Order — of New Testament records, 21 ff; of Old Testament records, 23; of incidents, 38 ff, 104, 105; change of in nature not disorder, 180.
Oriental imageries, 41, 51, 70, 73, 189.
Ormuzd and Arimanes, 260.
Orthodoxy defined, v.
Ostentation and repression, 215.

Pain necessary to pleasure, 78, 79, 275.
Pakamaran superstition, 183.
Pantheism, 64.
Papyrus Prisse, 126, 216.
Parable and mnemonics, 41, 114 ff.
Paradox, theological, 158.
Passions, badge of mental vigor, 76, 77; "deep are dumb," 217, 276; and purity, 261.
Passover, 206.
Past "shall vanish," 252.
Paternity of Jesus, 51 ff.
Path, simile, 110.
Patience, badge of Christianity, 120, 127; "beatitude of," 134; "recollect all," 139; "greatest prayer is," 162; "is not passive," 178.
Paul — advocates reasoning, 9; prophetic inspiration of, 29; on the resurrection, 29, 195; mingling error and truth, 30; epigrams of, 41; "all things to all," 112; faith of, in ideal Jesus, 121; "ideas of," 129; on divorce, 135; conversion of, 169; on miracles, 181, 189; the real resurrector of Jesus, 200; on election, 203; on redemption, 205; on salvation, 208; changed his opinions, 218; contrasted impulses, 219; supplementary metaphysics, 255; humor of, 266.
Peace — comes from faith, 16; and love, 163; and feeling, 217, 276.
Pearl, simile, 103, 138.
Pebble, simile, 100, 231.

ANALYTICAL INDEX   291

Pentateuch, date of, 23.
Perception — blurred by impurity, 16, 135; not inspiration, 26.
Perfection — of being, 62; and expansion, 91; "is no trifle," 126.
Periods — of Old Testament records,— Pre-Assyrian, Assyrian, Chaldean, Persian, Greek, Roman,— 23.
Perjury, 137.
Permanence of regeneration, 214.
Perpetuation of soul-life, 233 ff.
Perseverance of the saints, 214.
Persian — idea of creation, 37; Dualism, 93, 259 ff.
Personality, clinging to one's, 241; in heaven, 243.
Perversion of texts, 17, 249.
Peter — and Andrew, 85, 103, 105; and the resurrection, 196.
Pharisaism, 140.
Pharisees and John, 67.
Philosophical religion, 120.
Philosophy and theology, 207.
Phrenology, 87, 187.
Physician and son, simile, 100.
Piccadilly censors, 140.
Piety may be excessive, 89; ceremonial, emotional and doctrinal kinds of 173.
Pilate, 177 (see "Acts").
Pilgrims' music, 142.
Pity from God, 155.
Plain, simile, 251.
Plagues, Egyptian, 182.
Plan of salvation, 204 ff.
Plato — and Christianity, 35, 37; derived bodies from æones, 52; explained immortality, 240; idea of soul, 245; supplementary metaphysics, 255; dialectic method, 257.
Pleasure, pursuit of, 210, 211, 268.
Pleroma in trinity, 56.
Poetry — and inspiration, 26; and parables, 115.
Political economy and higher law, 127.
Polygamy, 17.
Pompeii, sentinel, 123.
Port of rest, simile, 253.
Potter and clay, 202.
Poverty, discipline of, 82; divine, 120; and wealth relative, 228.
Prayer, Lords, 148; supplicational, 149 ff; babe's cry, 153 ff; aspirational, 156 ff; Nature's, 268.
Prayer-books, concession to, 110.
Precipitancy, precept on, 138, 267.
Prejudice, partisan, 139.
Premonition of Messiah, 65.
Present, not "grief-shadowed," 253.
Pretension, badge of imbecility, 215.
Pride and love, 217.
Primordial germ, 202.
Prison, soul has no, 78; simile, 174, 238.

Probation, life not, but education, 75; and damnation, 228, 230.
Problems insoluble, 236.
Procession of the Holy Spirit, 55, 56.
Prodigal son, 214.
Prodigies, 186 ff.
Profanity, 137.
Profession and sincerity, 215.
Progress, law of, 59; of Christianity, 128; and retrogression, 201; perpetual, of the soul, 233.
Prophecy, whole trend of must be observed, 15; old and new view of, 28; of immortality, sense of personality, 243; in mythology, 262.
Prophets, function of, 65.
Prosperity "lets go the bridle," 133.
Protevangelion, the, 21, 50.
Providence, 108, 115, 183, 270.
Prudence and boldness, 216.
Pseudopia, 169, 188, 197, 270 ff.
Pseudopian theory of the resurrection, 194 ff, 270 ff.
Psychical and spiritual man, 207.
Psychological parallel, 185.
Ptolemais (Acre), 102, 103.
Pump, simile, 163.
Punishment certain, 224, 276.
Purana, 64.
Puritans, 141, 142.
Purity essential to insight, 16; sexual, 134.
Pyramids, simile, 27, 81, 82.
Pythoness, 262.

Quaker meeting, 220.
Queen (see "Elizabeth" and "Victoria").
Quirinus (see "Cyrenius").

Rabbinical interpreters, 17.
Rachel, 47.
Raising the dead, 179, 188.
Ransom, Paul's natural naming, 205.
Rarey and Buni, 170.
Rationalism of Jesus, 108.
Rationalistic theory of resurrection, 194.
Realizing the ideal and idealizing the real, 130, 138 ff.
Reaping a destiny, 126.
Reason, function of, 9 ff, 184; "not my tyrant," 14; defined, 16; and love, 59; law within itself, 63; "more of," 174; earthly and heavenly, 254; active and passive, 255; "pure" leads to three irreducible ideas, 256; tradition, 264.
Reasoning urged by Jesus, 9.
Rebuke, Jesus' manner of, 177.
Reconciliation and patience, 134.
Records, dates of, 22, 23.
Recreations, 211.
Red Sea, cleaving of, 182.
Redemption, 204 ff.
Refinement, Christian, 137.

Reforms must be gradual, 110.
Regeneration, 212 ff.
Rejuvenatal argument, 237.
Religion, Christian, triune, 119; defined, 120, 131; has consummation in character, 131.
Remembrance, "wings of," 252, 266.
Renunciation, 68 ff.
Repentance and regeneration, 85.
Repression and babbling, 215, 217.
Resignation, 124, 161
Resisting wrongs, 176 ff.
Rest, "bed of," 210; "port of," 253.
Resurrection — of Jesus' body, 193 ff; of sympathy, 243; "of life," 248; "a mightier," 250.
Reticence, 215 ff; 275.
Reunion in heaven, 253.
Reutterances by Jesus, 115.
Revealed religion and natural, 58.
Revelation, a divine education, 12; of God in the soul, 58.
Reverence, religion depends on, 119; uses and abuses of, 123; and love, matter of Jesus' teaching, 131; deepens with knowledge, 221.
Rhapsody and repression, 215.
Riches, duty to seek, 141; "baggage," 268.
Right and wrong, 143.
Righteousness and creeds, 131.
Rites, uses of, 173.
Ritual and religion, 131, 206.
River, simile, 76, 100, 246, 247, 253.
Rock of ages, simile, 250.
Rocket, simile, 237.
Roman—period of records, 23; festival, 49.

Sabbath, 107, 108, 142.
Sacrifice, Paul's natural naming, 205.
Saints, "perseverance of the," 214.
Salome, step-daughter of Antipas, 103; Zebedee's wife, 196.
Salvation, 204 ff; 218 ff.
Samaritan woman, 106, 116.
Sanctuary "of sorrow," 210.
Sanhedrim, 178.
Santa Claus and folk-lore, 185.
Satan, 223, 262.
Satire — as a pulpit weapon, 88; of dunces, 139.
Savoy; Hester, Lamb's lines to, 251.
Saved and lost, proportion, 231, 232.
Scandal, precept on, 139.
Schellingian theory of God, 255.
Scheme of salvation, 204.
Scholastics, "busily idle," 130.
Schools of apostolic doctrine, four, 36; of philosophy, 255 ff.
Schreckhorn, simile, 209.
Science, from matter to spirit, 15; man of misjudged, 139.
Scorn, 276.

Scotch philosophers, 130, 255.
Sea, cleaving of, 182; simile, 221, 226, 244, 253, 265.
Second sight, 168, 169, 263.
Secret and method of Jesus, 83.
Sectarianism, 10, 139, 187.
Sedgwick and geology, 18.
Segregation of the wicked, 110.
Seed, simile, v, 25, 60, 115, 126, 138, 250.
Self — denial, 76 ff, 81, 116, 215; "chord of," 79; "reverence," "knowledge," "control," 90, 211, 221; conceit, 91, 266; "conquest," "devotion," 117, 212; continence, 134,; assertion, 175 ff; "annihilation," 209; assumption, 216.
Selfishness — "is suicidal," 125; four precepts against, 130 ff; "most inhibited sin," 219.
Sensibility, religious, "easy," 19; "is not saving," 215.
Sensibilities, intellect and will, 255.
Sensuality, 131, 134.
Serenity, precept on, 138.
Sermon on the Mount, not speculative, 33; arbitrarily put together by Matthew, 38; where, when, and how delivered, 113 ff; four precepts of against selfishness, 130 ff; three experiential precepts of, 138 ff.
Serpent, devil tradition, 94, 262; charming, 170.
Sepulchre, real and figurative, 199.
Seventy, sending of the, 105.
Shades, realm of the, 194.
Shadow, "is projecting," 225; "of death," "land," 252.
Sham and sincerity, 137.
Sheep, simile, 137.
Shekinah, simile, 213.
Shell, simile, 90.
Shepherd, simile, 103, 248.
Ship, simile, 14.
Shipwreck, simile, 136, 139, 158, 209.
Shore, simile, 57.
Shu-king, 216.
Sibyls and inspiration, 262.
Sick, healing of the, 166, 170.
Sign, worship of the, 41, 122; prodigies and, 186; from God, 189; none "given," hence no miracles, 191.
Silence — "golden" at the arraignment, 178; "sanctuary of prudence," 216.
Siloam, tower of, 108.
Similes from Capernaum scenery, 102, 103.
Simplicity of manners, 215.
Sin — defined, 87, 91; "mystery of the fall," 96 ff; and death, 206; evil, 226.
Sinai and Hattin, 113.
Sincerity, 132, 215.
Sine and angle, simile, 100.
Sixth sense, 168.
Skeleton, simile, 14.

ANALYTICAL INDEX 293

Sky-prophets, 103.
Slander, precept against, 139, 268.
Slavery, distorting texts for, 17; abolition of prophesied, 28; not odious to Whitfield, 146.
Sleep, simile, **154, 253**; and dreams, 272.
Sliding-scale test, 230.
Small-pox, superstition, 186.
Society "prepares the crime," 100.
Socrates — on God, **64**, 260; on manly virtue, "Arete," 81; on love, 139; on Tartarus, 224; on immortality, 239.
Solace and memento, 251, 276.
Solidarity of mankind, 117 ff, 212.
Solitude, 90, 266, 268.
Somnambulism, 170.
Sorrow, 11, 76, 133, 210, 267.
Soul — "is a universe," 62; "of all beings," 63; uniform, body multiform, 233; does not decay with body, 237.
Sow a habit, reap a character, 126.
Sower, parable, 115.
Space and time, 233, 256.
Sparrow, parable, 115.
Special providence, 108, 183, 270.
Speech and silence, 215 ff; unpremeditated, prophetic, 262.
Spinoza's Christianity, 145; theism, **180**.
Spirit — and substance, 41; guidance, 151; and matter, 261.
Spontaneity of consciousness, 127.
Spread of Christianity, 128.
Spring, simile, 245, 250, 252.
Stairs, simile, 174.
Standard of righteousness, 131.
Staniforth's conversion, 169.
Star — heralding, 46 ff, 50; simile, 19, 77, 78, **234, 250.**
State, **heroes** constitute, 178.
Stenography, bigot attacking, **187.**
Step backward is forward, 74.
Stilling tempest, 179, 190.
Stone at tomb, simile, 200.
Storm, simile, 253.
Stream "of tendency," 60.
Style and culture, 215 ff.
Subject and object, 255.
Sublapsarian theory, 97.
Subtleties not law, 11.
Success, effect on character, 74 ff.
Sufferings, discipline of, 120, 220.
Suffrage, 120, 185.
Summer, simile, 250, **251.**
Sunbeam, simile, iii, **174.**
Sunday, 142, 220.
Sunset, simile, 233, **249.**
Sunshine, simile, 40.
Supernatural, the, as to inspiration, 26; deity of Jesus, 57; omnipotence of Jesus, 106; healing, 166; transfiguration, 172; miracles, 180; God prefers natural methods, **272.**

Supersensible existences, 248.
Superstition — and faith, 14; comparatively harmless, **57**; Jesus not engaged questioning, **107**; profanes worship, **123**; educating out of, 152; Chinese, **Japanese**, 186; Mexican, African, Jewish, **187**; dies out, 208; Oriental, **261** ff; "in solitude," 270.
Supplication, 148 ff.
Supralapsarian **theory**, 96.
Surprise in heaven, 237.
Swaggering, badge of imbecility, **137, 215.**
Swedenborg's second sight, 168.
Sweet reasonableness of Jesus, 83.
Swiss mercenary, simile, 12.
Syllogism in religious science, 13
Symbolism and idolatry, 41.
Sympathy — of Jesus with John Baptist, 69; solacing, 78; as motive, 128; "not lost," 239.
Symphonies, prelude of heaven, 254.
Synoptics, digests of earlier traditions, 32; peculiarity of, 36.
Syro-Phoenician **woman, 179.**

Tabulation of the **records, 23.**
Talmud, date of, 23.
Tartarus, 223, 224.
Telescope, simile, 10, 181.
Teleology — and immortality, **233**; in Hegel's system, **257.**
Temperance, 74.
Tempest, stilling, **179, 190**; simile, **158,** 238, 250, 251, **276.**
Temple, departure from the, 109.
Temptation of Jesus, eight views of, 73 ff; to get body gratification, fame and power, 83 ff, metaphysics of, 94.
Tenderness of Jesus, 64.
Test of character, **81, 82.**
Theanthropism, 58.
Theism, 208.
Theology — **defined, 127**; philosophy, 207.
Thirst for God in prayer, 164.
Thirty-nine articles, 184, 194.
Thor and Apollo, 262.
Thought — and action, 91, 92; reading, 168, 169; and speech, 217; never lost, 238; analysis of, 257.
Threshing floor, 16.
Thundering Legion, miracle, 183.
Tiberias, 102.
Time, precept on economy of, 138; and space, 233, 256.
Tiresias and Hercules, 48.
Tobit, Jonah and Daniel, 182.
Toil and Vigil "guard the gates of Bliss," 81.
Toleration, vi.
Torch, simile, **135.**
Traders, ejection **of, 175.**

Tradition — Triple, 32, 38; and reason, 263.
Trance, prophecy, 262; Weeks' case, 270.
Transcendental and experiential theories of right and wrong, 143.
Transfiguration, 172 ff, 269.
Transformation in heaven, 247.
Transgression (see "Sin").
Transition from the carnal, 207 ff.
Travellers "Faith" and "Reason," allegory, 20.
Treasures taken beyond death, 239, 254.
Tree, rings of, simile, 33.
Triads, Greek and Egyptian, 260.
Triangle, symbol of God, 260.
Trinity — and unity, 52 ff; metaphysical argument for, 55, 56; Hindu, 260; Egyptian, 260.
Triple tradition in Matthew, 32; in the Synoptics, 38.
Triumph of Jesus, 199.
Triumphal entry, 176.
Triunity, 53.
Trouble, precept on borrowing, 138.
Trust and truth, 235.
Truth — perceived by the pure, 16, 135; survives error, 30; seeing, broadens us, 89; and beauty, 115; embalms error, 137; and falsehood, 143; and faith, 147; "more of," 174; great, never leaves us, 238; eternal, 251, 254.
Tübingen school, 41, 190.
Turnus and shade-land, 194.

Ubiquity of spirits, 263.
Ulysses and the Sirens, 77.
Uncle Tom and Jeanie Deans, 142.
Unconscious cerebration, 170.
Understanding — and pure reason, 255; convince, not overbear, 265.
Unity — and trinity, 53 ff; "from devotion," 161.
Universal soul, 64.
Universe — and God, 61, 62; unseen, 248.
Unknown future joys, 234, 244.
Upas tree, 186.
Uriah and Bathsheba, 134.
Uses and abuses of faculties, 88.

Valor and profession, 215 ff.
Vedas, 63.
Veneration, 117 ff.
Vengeance, 231.
Verification of narrations, 189 ff.
Verifying faculty, reason and good will, 16.
Vicarious sacrifice, 204, 213.
Victoria — and the fast-day petition, 152; wreath, flower-miracle, 167.

Victors, life's, 79.
Violet, simile, 245, 252.
Virgin, apparition of the, 188.
Virtue, middle between opposite vices, 89; defined, 91; five constituents of, 133; "is at hand," 157; "first steps to," 266.
Vis a tergo, 98.
Vishnu and Brahma, 261.
Visions, 169, 170, 188, 197, 269 ff.
Volcano, simile, 43.
Volition, intellection, and emotion, 101, 255 ff.
Vulgarity, precept against, 137.

Wagers, fool's arguments, 137.
Waiting wisely, 138.
Waking, simile, 253.
Walking on water, 179.
Washington and Hampden, 121.
Wealth — and poverty, 120; to seek, 141.
Weeks' case, 269.
Wesley — and Johnson, 126; holy mien of, 171.
Whirlpool, simile, 77.
Whitfield and slavery, 146.
Widow's mite, 125; son, 190.
Will, freedom of the, 98 ff (see "Volition").
Wine, miracle, 179, 190.
Winter, simile, 245, 250.
Wisdom, not knowledge, 9 ff; "worldly," 137; learned in heaven, 251.
Witchcraft, 185.
Withered hand, miracle, 179.
Woe necessary to bliss, 78.
Woman, 115, 135 ff, 254, 267.
Wooing "nobler," 136.
Word, creative, 37, 260.
Worship — means mercy, 220; Hindu, 259; Nature's, 268.
Wrath of God, 201.
Wrong and right, 143.

Xavier and Loyola, miracles of, 188.

Yahveh (see "Jahveh").
Yang and Yin, superstition, 186.
Yea, in Jesus, 131; "the everlasting," 210.
Years, flood of, simile, 253.
Youth, enthusiasm and faith, 16, 129, 267.

Zacharias, 46.
Zealots' battles with Herod, 114.
Zeit-geist, 183, 189.
Zeno's morals, 145.
Zoilus and Homer, 268.
Zoroaster and Moses, 262.

SUPPLEMENTAL NOTE.

The comment upon the precepts of the Sermon on the Mount, enjoining economy, simplicity, etc., and the animadversion at page 186 upon our present outrageous alphabet and "orthography,"— cacography, rather,— may here be supplemented by an illustration of the proposed "International Alphabet" of the Spelling Reform Association, for an electrotype duplicate of which the author is indebted to the courtesy of T. R. Vickroy, Ph.D., editor and publisher of the *Phonetic Teacher*, St. Louis, Mo., official organ thereof. This alphabet of thirty-six letters is at least a good approximate ideal goal for future achievement under the battle-cry, *One symbol for each sound, one sound for each symbol.* Its general adoption can hardly be expected, until after some gradual reforms (already initiated by several newspapers) as to certain anomalies or "literal depravities," whose amendment requires no new type; thus, "tho," "enuf," "program," "shal," "hav," "givn," "hed," "alfabet," "sum" (some), "dum," "tung," "catalog," "dipt," "drest," etc.

[SEE NEXT PAGE]

INTERNAŞUNAL ALFABET.

Aa Aa Ɐɑ Bb Cc Ꞓꞓ Dd Ee
Ėė Ff Gg Hh Ii Jj ᴊ Ll
Mm Nn Ŋŋ Oo Ɵɵ Ɔɔ Pp Rr
Ss Ʃʃ Tt đđ ŧŧ Uu ɯ Ʊʊ
Vv Ww Yy Zz

Blesed ar ði pur in spirit: for ðarz iz ði kiŋdum ³
ov hevn. ⁵ Blesed ar ða ðat morn: for ða ʃal bė cumferted. ⁴
Blesed ar ði mėk: for ða ʃal inherit ði erŧ. ⁵
Blesed ar ða ðat huŋger and ŧerst after raiʃius- ⁶
nes: for ða ʃal bė fild.
Blesed ar ði mersiful: for ða ʃal ɵbtɑn mersi. ⁷
Blesed ar ði piur in hart: for ða ʃal sė God. ⁸
Blesed ar ði pėsmakerz: for ða ʃal bė cɔld ⁹
sunz ov God.
Blesed ar ða ðat hav bin perseciuted for raiʃius- ¹⁰
nes' sak: for ðarz iz ði kiŋdum ov hevn. ' Blesed ¹¹
ar yė hwen men ʃal reproʃ yɯ, and perseciut yɯ,
and sa ɔl maner ov ėvl agenst yɯ fɔlsli, for Įmai
sak. ' Rejɵis, and bė ecsėdiŋ glad: for grat iz yur ¹²
rewɵrd in hevn: for so perseciuted ða ði prɵfets
hwiʃ wer befor yɯ.

www.ingramcontent.com/pod-product-compliance
Lightning Source LLC
Chambersburg PA
CBHW022104230426
43672CB00008B/1276